# The
# Dynamic
# Environment

# The Dynamic Environment

## Water, Transportation, and Energy

RAMAPO COLLEGE **Edwin H. Marston**

XEROX COLLEGE PUBLISHING

*Lexington, Massachusetts / Toronto*

*This book is dedicated to*
**Betsy Pilat Marston**

ISBN: 0-536-01071-4

Library of Congress Catalog Card Number: 74-82346

Printed in the United States of America.

# Foreword

This book is based on a course I have taught five consecutive years, two years at a large institution and three years at a small four-year state college. My judgment is that the course has been successful: I enjoyed teaching the classes, and the students, judging from their written evaluations, their attitudes in class, and their enrollments, appreciated the course.

The course originally was conceived as an alternative to the traditional physical science course taken by non-science students. The idea was to illustrate basic physical principles with selected environmental problems, an approach that ran into trouble the first few weeks of the first term it was offered. The students simply expected more than a series of disconnected urban and environmental examples (auto accidents, traffic flow, thermal pollution, and so on) tacked on to the usual physics. From the first few weeks of that first term the course began to evolve into a descriptive, systems look at the way in which technology functions. It has also evolved from a course that had all the answers (mainly technical fixes to pollution problems) to one that has many more questions than answers.

The present text is the result of those ten terms of evolution. It examines three physical systems—water, transportation, and energy—qualitatively and quantitatively. How these systems operate, how they came to operate that way, and the possibilities and impossibilities of change are the main themes.

It might seem that a book which considers such different systems as water, transportation, and energy would be forced to cover many physical topics. That would be true if it looked at water in terms of pressure, viscosity, and molecular structure; or at transportation in terms of the thermodynamic efficiency of different engines; or at electric energy in terms of electron flow or Maxwell's equations. Instead, the book examines the systems in terms of a few common physical models: the flow of water through aqueducts and pipes; the flow of people and vehicles on roads, tracks, and sidewalks; and the flow of energy as fuel through pipelines and as electricity over power grids. Work and power are relevant to all the systems considered, whether it is water being pumped over or through mountains to Los Angeles or Denver, coal being carried by train or oil flowing through pipelines, or autos or bicycles moving along highways and streets. The book, then, is guided more by what is seen as the logic of our technological systems than by the subject matter usually presented in a course at this level.

My desire to build a foundation of understanding and appreciation of our technological systems determined that the text begin with water systems. Although our society takes water systems for granted, they are probably our most important life support systems. Water provides a dramatic way to illustrate both the dependence of cities and suburbs on rural areas and the profound effects technological systems have on the environment. Water also interacts very strongly with energy (hydroelectric power, coolant for steam electric plants, processing of oil shale) and is therefore a useful introduction to the last half of the text, which deals with energy.

The next system discussed in the text is transportation. Transportation systems bind the nation together and determine the physical form of urban areas. Suburbia, for example, was built for the auto and could not exist without it. Cities could not exist without mass transit, which has determined their generally radial pattern of development. The text, therefore, develops the physical characteristics of transportation systems, including land use, energy use, noise and air pollution, and safety. These boundaries help explain the performance, or lack of performance, of existing transportation systems and indicate what future changes are possible and impossible.

The last half of the text examines our use and production of energy. Although present and potential sources of energy and related environmental problems are covered in detail, the emphasis is on the way in which we use energy in transportation and in the home, office, and factory. It is the continuous and rapid growth of energy use that has helped create fuel shortages and environmental problems. The source of this demand, and the possibility of moderating or reducing it, must be understood before methods of producing energy are investigated.

The scientific reasoning and mathematical content of this text are on the same level as the usual physics or physical science course taken by freshmen nonscience students. The emphasis in the mathematical treatment is on "exact enough" rather than on exact, and the reader is encouraged to make order-of-magnitude estimates and do simple back-of-the-envelope calculations to derive new information. This gives the text an additional unity since only a few parameters are used to derive important facts about the system being considered. For example, knowledge of a region's population and precipitation yields watershed, reservoir, and aqueduct sizes; knowledge of the number of people to be moved from one place to another and of a few characteristics of transport systems yield the land and energy needs of different transport modes.

The text also quantifies the ways in which components of physical systems interact with each other. There must be enough fuel pipeline capacity into an area to keep its autos and planes running and homes heated; enough electric power available to pump drinking water through aqueducts and water mains. The hope is to give a sense of the scale of the technological world and to encourage students to make their own estimates and calculations. To make this easier, the British system of units is used. Introduction of the metric system—however desirable from other points of view—would hinder the central purpose of this book.

Some comments here on other aspects of the book may be useful to the reader. Two types of references are provided in the text at the end of the chapters. A "Further Reading" list is given which includes articles, studies, collections of essays, and novels which are meant to provide a broad, usually nonphysical, view of the material covered in the chapter. The "Source Notes" list refers to specialized material directly pertinent to the chapter's physical approach. Specific facts within the chapter have numbered source notes corresponding to this list.

The end of each chapter contains questions and numerical problems that should be seen as an integral part of the book. Many of the questions have no single answer but are intended as starting points for discussion. Several of the numerical problems require that students assume magnitudes for different physical quantities before the problems can be done. Instructors who feel this is too difficult or otherwise undesirable can supply the students with data. Answers are provided for problems that do not require assumptions.

I wish to thank first and foremost the several hundred students who have used this book in its various forms. Their encouragement and criticisms have been invaluable. Clifford Swartz and Robert Karplus early encouraged me to pursue the initial idea that eventually led to this book. Bill Bowman, Mike Marmor, Bob Shine, Jerry Sturman, and Jerry Wheeler were good enough to read various chapters in manuscript form. Mistakes that remain are, of course, the author's responsibility.

Peter Flack was most helpful in the area of energy use in high-rise buildings. Thanks are due to Lowell Bridwell and Chris Glaister for many useful discussions of urban transportation. Especially deserving of thanks are the New York Scientists' Committee for Public Information and its executive director, Ms. Carolyn Konheim, for providing support and expertise in the area of New York City's transportation problems.

I am most grateful to Warren Blaker for his involvement with this book from beginning to end, and to editors Arthur Evans and Carol Beal for an enormous amount of help. The late Tony Jensen was vital to the writing of this book in many ways. I am indebted to Ms. Cathy Pullis for the questions she asked and mistakes she caught while typing the manuscript.

# Contents

*Our civilization has decided, and very justly decided, that determining the guilt or innocence of men is a thing too important to be trusted to trained men. If it wishes for light upon that awful matter, it asks men who know no more law than I know, but who can feel the things I felt in a jury box. When it wants a library catalogued, or the solar system discovered, or any trifle of that kind, it uses up its specialists. But when it wishes anything done that is really serious, it collects 12 of the ordinary men standing about. The same thing was done, if I remember right, by the founder of Christianity.*

G. K. CHESTERTON*

# Scope and method

Our technological systems provide us with food, water, and energy. They also help determine the work we do, the pace at which we live, and the education we require. They set the sight, the smell, and the sound of society. Nevertheless, these systems are designed by experts on narrow, technical grounds. The public uses the products of the technology but has little say in determining how the technology works. It is the thesis of this book that technology is too important to be left to experts alone. If technology is to work properly, the experts must do their work under the broad direction of the public.

To achieve this goal it is necessary that the public have a better understanding of technology. Nonexperts must have the skills and information to understand the existing system and to see how it can be changed. It is the object of this book to provide these needed skills and information to nonscientists.

Until recently, society viewed technology as a kind of magic that could satisfy whatever wishes we made. We now realize that often our wishes were answered in unforeseen and even diabolical ways. Autos and airplanes

---

*From Chesterton's essay "The Twelve Men" in *Tremendous Trifles* (New York: Dodd, Mead and Company, 1909).

The ancient Egyptian pyramids are among man's oldest and most impressive technology. The pyramids of Giza shown here honor three Pharaohs of the Fourth Dynasty (about 2600 BC). The pyramid to the rear, called Cheops' Great Pyramid, is still the largest stone structure in the world. *Photo courtesy Museum of Fine Arts, Boston.*

give us mobility and freedom—and air pollution, noise, and 1000 deaths a week. Appliances and power machinery free us from physical labor and inconvenience—and produce strip mining, oil spills, and noise. And beyond these direct effects, our technologies often set in motion cycles which create the need for more technology and produce more destruction.

Transportation systems provide the clearest example of these cycles. We build jetports in or near urban centers to provide convenient and efficient travel. But the noise from the planes landing and taking off at the jetports affects millions of Americans. Noise from New York's John F. Kennedy Jetport alone affects about 750,000 people. One obvious response of residents and businesses in jetport areas is to install air-conditioning so that windows can be kept shut in warm months to reduce noise. But air-conditioning uses large amounts of electric energy, and generating this electricity requires the burning of coal and oil, which can lead to strip mining and oil spills. Electric power plants themselves dump heated water into rivers, lakes, and bays, and this heated water degrades their quality. In addition, the noise from the planes discourages use of backyards or local parks for recreation so a jetport increases the travel, or escape, needs of those near it. The jetport creates a need for travel, which, for a price, it then satisfies.

Whether the "cycles" described above are long-term trends or temporary difficulties that we shall solve in the near future is not yet clear. But it is clear that the problems are more difficult and complex than just cleaning up auto or electric-power-plant pollution or devising a technique to quiet jet engines. As we shall see later, such problems as highway and air travel, and electric-energy production and use, are entangled in a web of difficulties which cannot be solved with a single, brilliant, technological stroke. They will yield only, if at all, to a slow, painful, expensive unraveling based on understanding of the human, physical, political, and economic boundaries of the problem.

Increasingly the narrow technological solution is losing favor with both the public and with the experts. We are gradually learning, for example, that building a bigger and better highway to relieve traffic congestion often generates bigger and better traffic jams; that the development of a wonder drug or wonder pesticide can lead to a supergerm or superbug. Nor do we have as much faith in applying technology to solve social problems as we had formerly. Areas that fight crime with better lighting often find that crime rates and electric bills continue to climb. Cities that install exact-fare strong boxes on buses to stop robberies of bus drivers learn that criminals turn to cab drivers and other victims; medical programs in poor countries that reduce diseases may cause population to increase to the point where starvation becomes a serious threat.

The complexity of these problems has produced more sophisticated approaches. Environmental and technological problems are now often studied by multidisciplinary teams of experts. But this approach is no guarantee of success. Experts usually defer to each other in their specialties, and they have a common interest in seeing expertise in charge. More important, it is in the very act of defining the problem that expertise is of least help. Often the very act of assembling the experts, that is, defining who is to be on the committee, determines the solution. If an auto-safety panel consists of specialists on the drinking driver, air-bags, and highway design, then one gets an auto-centered solution. If the panel includes urban planners and specialists on mass transit, a broader solution may be obtained.

Ideally the experts should be sources of information and technique. But it is society that must formulate the questions to be answered and determine which experts are relevant. Ultimately each technological problem is a human problem and must be seen and presented as such. Once this is done, the needed technical tools can be brought into play.

There are those who argue that the general public can never become knowledgeable enough to guide the technology. Modern physical systems, it is said, are so sophisticated they can be understood only by specialists. It is undoubtedly true that we cannot all become experts on DDT, nuclear energy, thermal pollution, and catalytic converters. But most of us can learn enough to interpret and act on technical information in terms of our own values, needs, and perceptions.

Moreover we have already tried the alternative of leaving technology to the technologists. At present, the majority are ignorant of the "machine" which surrounds and sustains (or destroys) them. Out of this ignorance,

An unreclaimed strip mine is one of the unpleasant results of modern technology. However, strip mining is safer, easier, and more economical than tunnel, or underground, mining. The United States has about forty million acres of coal deposits which could be strip mined, creating a potentially vast problem for the future. *Photo courtesy U.S. Department of the Interior, Geological Survey.*

they strain and abuse the machine (demand too many autos, too much electricity, too much food, too much water). And when the machine begins to break down (emit pollution, destroy open space, produce noise), the natural reaction is to accuse the machine and its high priests (our various leaders and their technicians).

Proposed highways, dams, power plants, offshore oil wells, and strip-mining sites have become the battlegrounds on which the environmental-technological problem is currently being fought. It is probably one of the most fateful and interesting battles of the century, involving technological, social, political, and economic factors. In the rest of this chapter and in the ones to follow, we shall try to present the information and skills needed to at least understand the physical aspects of the problems. Assuming, of course, that the "machine" we have built is not already so complex as to be beyond us.

In this book we will attempt to give nonscientists a physical picture of how the three basic urban technologies — water, transportation, and energy — work. Our method is to outline the systems in terms of a few basic physical principles and models and then to develop those models using some basic mathematics.

The workings and misworkings of the system will be developed on two levels. First, it will be developed verbally, or qualitatively, without the use of numbers. For example, we will discuss urban water systems in terms of pipes that stretch unbroken from mountain snowfields and streams to the centers of distant cities. Once the physical model for each technological system is developed, we will apply numbers. For example, we will calculate the acres of rural land it takes to supply a city with water and the acres of land a city must devote to its transportation system. This verbal and numerical development of some selected technologies is not meant as empty exercise. It is hoped that the understanding and skills gained will eventually influence the development of our physical machine.

## The Physical Framework

The Flow Model.   Water, transportation, and energy can be looked at in terms of a flow model: flow of water through aqueducts and pipes; flow of vehicles and people along roads, sidewalks, and tracks; flow of energy through oil and gas pipelines, electric power lines, and in railroad coal cars along tracks. The following chapters will emphasize the marked similarities between the different systems. The development will be progressive: after you have learned to think about and calculate water flow through aqueducts, it is easier to visualize and calculate flow on transportation arteries.

Peak-hour Demand.   The three physical systems are conceptually unified by the necessity to meet peak-hour demands. Rush-hour traffic congestion; household water-pressure drops at supper time due to high demand; and electric power blackouts and brownouts during hot summer days are all examples of peak-hour demands stressing the systems. We shall see that the peak-hour problems and solutions are often similar although the systems are very different.

Technological Cycles.   As we mentioned earlier, technological systems all too often interact with each other to form destructive cycles. Destructive cycles don't automatically happen. But they are likely to occur if we look at the technology in a narrow way. The different parts of our technology do not stand alone. Technology is a system — a web of interacting parts — and we must be sensitive to the way changes in one part of the system affect other parts. Often the side effects turn out to be bigger than the desired effects.

Quantitative Methods.   Much of the information about our technology can be presented qualitatively. We are all familiar with certain aspects of it—we routinely use water faucets, toilets, highways, and electric appliances. This will make the descriptions easier. However, some difficulty may arise when we use physical models and mathematics to describe the systems. But use of the models and math is absolutely essential if the systems are to be understood. In addition, the skills learned are likely to be generally useful since the emphasis is on estimating the magnitude of physical quantities and then using the estimates to make rough-and-ready, back-of-the-envelope calculations. As samples of this approach, let us look at the following problems.

## Some Physical Examples

Example 1.   Assume you are the architect in charge of designing a ten-story office building. The first floor will be lobby and shops, and the next nine floors will be offices; an average of 250 people are employed per floor. How many elevators should the building have?

At first glance, the problem may seem impossible, and it is—unless the correct questions are asked and the correct assumptions made. The key question is this: What maximum demand will be made on the elevators? Clearly, one elevator could handle the 8:00 P.M. to 8:00 A.M. traffic. But it is the demand occurring when people arrive for work in the morning, go out for lunch at noon, and leave for home in the evening that determines the number of elevators.

Once this is seen, some assumptions and estimates can be made. We shall assume that peak demand occurs in the morning and that all 2500 people arrive for work between 8:30 and 9:00 A.M. We shall also assume that each elevator carries 20 people and can take on a full load in the lobby, discharge all passengers, and return to the lobby in 3 minutes. This assumption means that in the 30-minute rush period each elevator can make 10 round trips carrying a total of 200 people. Since 2250 people are to be carried in this 30-minute period, the building will need

$$\frac{2250 \text{ people}}{200 \text{ people/elevator}} = 11.25 \text{ elevators}.$$

We round the answer to 11 elevators. Notice that this fairly sophisticated problem required only simple arithmetic. The difficulty was in formulating it conceptually so that numbers could be applied. Some will argue that the model used was too idealized: that everyone will not arrive within a half hour; that the elevators may take different times to make a round trip; that we should calculate the effect of having a few express elevators; and so on. This is true, and an architect would be foolish to design the elevators on the basis of this calculation alone. But the calculation gives us an *order-of-magnitude answer* (tells us we need about 10 elevators rather than 1 or 100 elevators) and also shows the kind of research that should be done to refine the answer. The architect could now go to an existing office building and see when traffic peaks, how long a round trip takes under full load conditions, and what kind of traffic is created by visitors to a building.

This example illustrates the general need mentioned earlier for a physical system to meet peak-hour demand. If the 2500-employee arrivals and departures were spread throughout the day, fewer elevators would be required. But as with all physical systems, demand peaks strongly and a large amount of people-moving capacity must be provided, even though that capacity will be fully used only a short period each day. This is typical of many of our physical systems, including highways, subways, water mains, electric power plants, and telephone lines. Physical systems must be able to meet peak demands, and often these peaks occur only once or twice a day and sometimes, as with roads to ski areas or summer resorts, only a few times a year.

Elevators interact strongly with other physical systems. They are part of a total transportation system that includes sidewalks, highways, bus terminals, and subways. People feed from roads, buses, and subways to sidewalks and then to elevators. Elevators also make large electric power demands and so have an effect on the area's energy system. Elevators even

## Elevators and Office Buildings

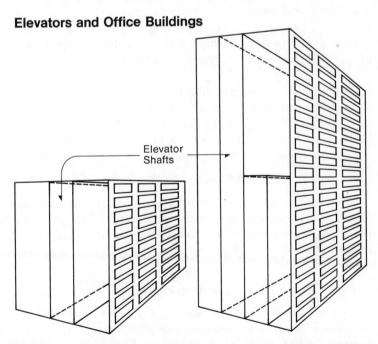

Elevator
Shafts

**Figure 1.** The left figure represents a 10-story office building and the right figure a 20-story office building. The lower 10 stories of the 20-story building devote twice as much space to elevator shafts as does the 10-story building.

influence the form of cities. Before elevators were perfected in the 1880s, buildings were limited to five or six stories. Today buildings routinely rise one hundred stories or more. In theory, although not in practice, it is elevators that limit a building's height. If the height of our ten-story building were doubled, the number of elevators needed would also double (see Figure 1). Elevators for the twenty-story building would take up twice as much space in the lower ten floors as at present. If the building were doubled to forty stories, still more elevators would fill the lower stories. Eventually there would be no room in the first ten stories for additional elevators to serve the upper floors, and the building could grow no more.

Notice that a large amount of information and some provocative questions can be gained from a simple calculation without the need to learn about the motor or braking systems elevators use or their rates of acceleration and deceleration. We do not wish, after all, to build an elevator bank but only to understand the way in which they help determine the shape and functioning of cities. That is not to imply that it is always easy to know how much information and detail is needed to understand a system. Throughout, that will be a very difficult problem. But we will not try to solve it by simply piling on every available fact.

We do not wish to pretend that elevators are the key element in urban technology. But they are as "key" as any other element. Everything fits together and depends on everything else. A city cannot function without electricity, or water, or roads, or elevators. And as a result you cannot change anything without changing many other things. That is why a study of technology is both fascinating and frustrating.

**Example 2.**   Newsprint, like most paper, is made from trees. We want to calculate the number of trees it takes to produce the 1,500,000 copies printed each Sunday of the *New York Times*. For those who have never hefted the *Times*, we note that the average Sunday edition weighs 5 pounds.

First we calculate the total weight of newsprint the *Times* consumes.

$$(1,500,000 \text{ copies}) (5 \text{ lb/copy}) = 7,500,000 \text{ lb}$$

Now we must estimate how many pounds of paper a typical tree yields. We shall assume that the average tree weighs 250 pounds and that after processing in a paper mill it yields 125 pounds of paper. This means the edition of the Sunday *Times* requires

$$\frac{7,500,000 \text{ lb}}{125 \text{ lb/tree}} = 60,000 \text{ trees}.$$

A lot of trees. To find out how large a forest must be chopped down, we calculate what area 60,000 standing trees occupy. Let us assume that the trees stand 10 feet apart, as in Figure 2. Since area is equal to length times width, this means each tree occupies an area of

$$(10 \text{ ft}) (10 \text{ ft}) = 100 \text{ ft}^2.$$

Notice that the dimensions of area are length squared ($L^2$). In this case we are using a foot as the unit of length so the unit of area is a square foot.

If each tree requires a space of 100 square feet, then 60,000 trees occupy 6,000,000 square feet. A more useful unit of area is the acre. An acre is equal to 43,560 square feet, but to simplify calculations we will assume 1 acre is 44,000 square feet. (We shall make such simplifications throughout the text, losing in precision but gaining in speed and understanding.) The total acreage needed is

$$\frac{6,000,000 \text{ ft}^2}{44,000 \text{ ft}^2/\text{acre}} = 136 \text{ acres.}$$

Our answer may be off because a typical tree may yield more or less than our guess of 125 pounds of paper, and trees may be spaced closer or further than 10 feet. But this calculation has very quickly given us an *order-of-magnitude answer* – about 100 acres rather than 10 or 1000 acres – and told us what information to look up if we need a more precise result.

## Paper and Trees

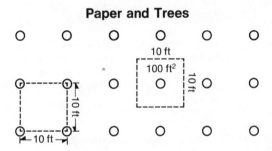

**Figure 2.** The circles represent trees spaced on 10-foot centers. Each tree occupies a plot 10 feet by 10 feet, for an area of 100 square feet.

In the following chapters, we shall do many similar resource calculations to find out how much land auto use requires; how much land is needed to supply and store a city's drinking water; how many gallons of water and pounds of coal it takes to run a color TV for an evening; how much fuel is used to make an aluminum soda can. The questions raised by these calculations will often be much more difficult than the calculations themselves. The preceding calculation, for example, leads to technical questions about forest management and paper-making techniques. But even if we answered these questions, we would still face the difficult social question of whether the publication of the *Times,* which carries information about environmental problems and in theory enables its readers to act to preserve the environment, outweighs the destruction of trees and the water and air pollution emitted by paper plants. The question is larger than we have stated it, but this formulation should indicate how very complex and inter-

Modern technology has created some impressive structures; the best of these blend the technology with the environment, as does this highway bridge spanning Bixby Creek in the Big Sur region of California. *Photo courtesy George Strauch, California Department of Transportation.*

acting the social-environmental-resource problems are. Clearly, the problem of trees versus newspapers goes beyond the disciplines of forestry and journalism.

Example 3.   A family has just had built a swimming pool 15 feet wide, 30 feet long, with an average depth of 4 feet (see Figure 3). Estimate how long it will take to fill the pool using a faucet and garden hose.

The key question here is how much water flows out of a faucet per unit time. This can be measured, for example, by timing how long it takes to fill a quart bottle. Or a person might remember that it takes, let's say, about 10 minutes to fill a bath. Since a bath is roughly 5 feet long, 2 feet wide, and is filled, let's say, 1 foot deep, then it would hold a volume of water equal to

$$\text{(length) (width) (height)} = (5 \text{ ft}) (2 \text{ ft}) (1 \text{ ft}) = 10 \text{ ft}^3.$$

Here ft³ means cubic feet. This unit has the dimensions of length cubed $(L \times L \times L = L^3)$ and describes three-dimensional space, or volume, just as area (length squared) describes flat, or two-dimensional, space.

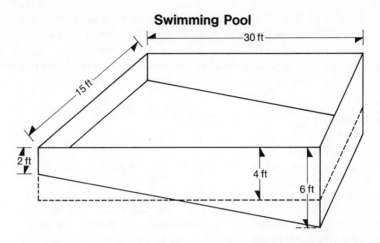

**Figure 3.** The drawing of the swimming pool shows the actual shape in solid lines and the average depth in dotted lines. Both shapes have the same volume.

To return to the problem, we have assumed the bath fills in 10 minutes. This means the water flows at a rate of 10 cubic feet per 10 minutes or 1 cubic foot per minute. The volume of the pool is

$$V_{\text{pool}} = (\text{length})\,(\text{width})\,(\text{depth}) = (30\ \text{ft})\,(15\ \text{ft})\,(4\ \text{ft}) = 1800\ \text{ft}^3.$$

So the pool will take 1800 minutes to fill. 1800 minutes is

$$\frac{1800\ \text{min}}{60\ \text{min/hr}} = 30\ \text{hours}.$$

A precise answer, of course, would require a measurement of the water flow of the garden hose and the dimensions of the pool. But this very rough method again gives us an order-of-magnitude answer.

Many of the facts and statistics concerning modern technology are so large as to be beyond our ability to visualize. In order to better portray their size, we often use physical analogies of the following type.

**Example 4.** If all the cars in the United States were arranged in a straight line, bumper to bumper, how far would they stretch?
There are roughly 100,000,000 (100 million) autos in the United States. Assuming they are 15 feet long on the average, their total length is

$$(100{,}000{,}000\ \text{autos})\,(15\ \text{ft/auto}) = 1{,}500{,}000{,}000\ \text{ft}.$$

To convert 1 billion, 500 million feet into miles, we divide by 5280 feet/ mile, the number of feet in 1 mile.

$$\frac{1{,}500{,}000{,}000\ \text{ft}}{5280\ \text{ft/mile}} = 284{,}000\ \text{miles}$$

This is roughly the distance to the moon, so we can triumphantly state that if all the cars in the United States were lined up bumper to bumper, they would reach to the moon. If we prefer a more earthly image, we can point out that it would take 95 highway lanes stretching from New York to Los Angeles to park all the cars bumper to bumper.

## Bibliography

*Further Reading*

GILBERT K. CHESTERTON. *Tremendous Trifles*. New York: Dodd, Mead and Company, 1909.
  Many of the essays by this British journalist have surprising relevance to the human-technological problems we face today. See especially "In Topsy Turvy Land" and "The Dragon's Grandmother," as well as the essay "Twelve Men" from which this chapter's opening quotation is taken.

JACQUES ELLUL. *The Technological Society*. New York: A. A. Knopf, 1970.
  A pessimistic book by this great French social theorist on what he sees as a remorseless invasion of technique, expertise, and super-organization into every aspect of human life.

LEWIS MUMFORD. *Technics and Civilization*. New York: Harcourt, Brace, Jovanovich, Inc., 1934.
  A survey of the development of man's technics, which includes both social organization and machinery, is given in this book.

CHARLES SINGER; E. J. HOLMYARD; A. R. HALL; and TREVOR I. WILLIAMS, eds. *A History of Technology*. London: Oxford University Press, 1958.
  This series is a monumental five-volume study of the development of technology and technique. It is profusely illustrated and well written.

## Problems and Questions

1. A building is being constructed on a 75,000-square-foot plot. Making some estimate about the area needed for a 20-person elevator, calculate the maximum height of a building constructed on this plot. Assume 250 workers per floor and use the results of Example 1.

2. As discussed earlier, elevators take up a large amount of space in high-rise buildings. Do you have any ideas on how the number of elevator shafts could be reduced without reducing passenger capacity? It might help to compare the way an elevator shaft operates with the way a railroad track or even a highway lane operates.

3. Calculate the approximate weight of rubber dust given off by auto tires in the United States in a year. Assume the average tire is 27 inches in diameter, has a 5-inch-wide tread, and wears off one-half inch of tread during its lifetime. A cubic inch of rubber weighs 0.04 pounds. Estimate any other information needed.

4. Do a rough, order-of-magnitude calculation of the amount of household garbage produced by the U.S. population (assume 200 million people) in a year. Each of us generates about 4 pounds of garbage daily.

5. A home has a basement which is 40 feet by 30 feet by 10 feet high. A large pipe breaks in the basement and water pours out at 15 gallons per minute. How long will it take to fill the basement, assuming it is watertight?

6. The text describes the way in which jetports set up a cycle which leads to a need for more technology. Are you aware of any other such cycles?

7. A large portion of the American public is very knowledgeable about a complex technological device—the auto. Does this indicate that the public has the capability to learn about various technological systems, or is the comparison inappropriate?

8. The chapter discusses the roles the expert and the public should play in making technological decisions. The question may seem more concrete if you think about your own relationship to experts. When you consult a doctor or teacher or lawyer, do you go to them for advice and information and then make your own decision, or do you go to them for a decision? If you go to them for a decision, on what basis do you judge the validity of that decision?

9. Let us assume for the moment that the world is so complex that the public is unable to make policy decisions about its physical form. What consequences do you see resulting from such a situation?

*The society which scorns excellence in plumbing because plumbing is a humble activity and tolerates shoddiness in philosophy because it is an exalted activity will have neither good plumbing nor good philosophy. Neither its pipes nor its theories will hold water.*

JOHN W. GARDNER*

# 2 Urban water systems

A city or suburb is not self-sufficient. It must reach out into the surrounding countryside for water, food, clean air, energy, and raw materials. The physical systems which help an urban population drink, eat, breathe, and work are quite literally lifelines; without them millions of us would perish. Let us start by examining the life-support system we take most for granted — urban water supply.

## History of Urban Water Use

Man's earliest sources of water were those most obvious to him — lakes or rivers. But often good pasture or an ideal site for a village or fortress did not have nearby surface water. Or the local streams and lakes were undependable — they froze, dried up, or were polluted. So at some point in prehistory the first wells were dug. No more than holes in the ground, they reached down to the water table, that depth at which the top of the underground water lies. Then by steps leading into the well or by a bucket on the end of a rope, water that was

---

*From Gardner's book *Excellence* (New York: Harper and Row, 1961).

ten or twenty or more feet below ground could be reached. In general, ground water was more dependable, was cooler to drink, and seemed purer than surface water.

**Inadequacy of Well Water.**   In America, wells served as a major source of urban water through the eighteenth and into the nineteenth centuries. But dependence on well water had serious weaknesses which became apparent as American cities expanded in size and population. The most dramatic failure was the inability of well water and surface sources to cope with urban fires. American cities of the time were constructed mainly of wood and were congested. A fire in one building spread easily to others. The bucket brigades and hand-powered pumpers of the day could not put enough water on a serious blaze to put it out or even control its spread. In 1828 New York City suffered a total fire loss of about $600,000 – a large sum for the time. In 1835 a huge fire destroyed twenty square blocks of the city, causing about $20 million in damage. Even that was dwarfed by Chicago's fire of 1871 (supposedly started when Mrs. O'Leary's cow kicked over a kerosene lantern) which killed several hundred people and caused about $200 million in damage.

**Water and Disease.**   Disease was as serious a threat to the continued existence of these cities as was fire. Most of the surface sources of water were obviously polluted. Water drawn from underground only seemed pure: the wells drew up water from deposits located a few feet below the town's houses, garbage dumps, sewage collects, and graveyards. Rain and discharged waste water seeped through the earth, carrying contaminants into the underground water. Although the soil somewhat filtered and cleaned the water, we know now that diseases such as cholera and typhoid fever – which plagued American cities during the eighteenth and nineteenth centuries – were spread in large part by contaminated water.

Americans were made sensitive to impure water and general uncleanliness by yellow fever epidemics in the 1790s. The major cities of Philadelphia, Boston, New York, Baltimore, and New Haven lost large numbers of citizens to summer epidemics. In 1793, 4000 Philadelphians – about ten percent of the population – died. In 1798 another 3000 died. New York City in the same year saw 2000 die from the disease. It was not then realized that yellow fever was spread by the bite of a mosquito. The two theories of the day blamed the disease on crowded living conditions, poor ventilation, and filth, or on ships coming from disease-ridden foreign ports. Those who held to the theory of congestion and filth urged the use of large amounts of pure water to clean the city, its people, and their homes. There was no hard evidence at the time linking yellow fever or other diseases to dirty water (in the cases of typhoid fever and cholera the connection would be made later and for yellow fever it would never be made). Nevertheless, the cities of the time set about obtaining pure water to fight disease and fire.

In some ways our current environmental problems present us with a similar situation. For example, it is difficult to establish definite connections between air pollution or noise levels and ill health. Nevertheless the nation has haltingly begun work to reduce air, water, noise, and visual pollution without waiting for precise, definite proof of ill effects.

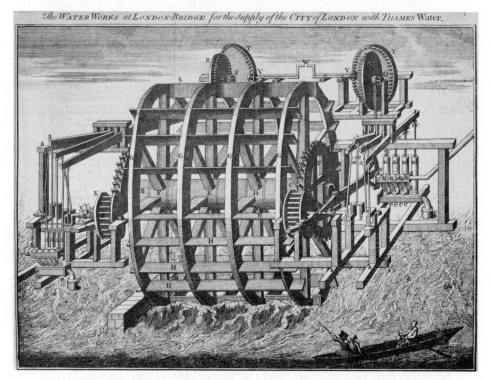

This sketch shows part of an early (1749) urban water system. The flow of the Thames River turned this gigantic wooden waterwheel located under the arches of London Bridge. It operated the machinery at left to pump the water to London. This water system was used until 1822, when it and the original London Bridge were demolished. *Photo courtesy Metropolitan Water Board of London.*

**First Water Systems.**   In 1801 Philadelphia became the first American city to have a waterworks. Two steam engines lifted water 100 feet from the Schuylkill River to a distribution reservoir. From there the water flowed by gravity throughout the city. At first it was used mainly to wash streets and fight fires. Few Philadelphians were willing to pay to hook their homes into the new water system. People were used to free water—just as we are used to free air—and as late as 1810 Philadelphia's water system had only 2000 customers out of a population of 90,000.

By the mid-nineteenth century the twin arguments of health and fire protection had convinced most cities and their inhabitants that ample, pure water was a necessity. By 1860 the country's sixteen largest cities (all with populations over 50,000) had some kind of water system, and water use by individual homes was increasing rapidly. In the nineteenth century, urban water demand was about 25 gallons/person/day. Today our consumption is 150 gallons/person/day and by 2020 is expected to rise to 185 gallons/person/day.[1]

In addition to considerations of health, a major push for increased use of running water was economic—the desire to eliminate labor. A hotel with running water no longer had to employ people to bring water to guests, and a family with running water did not have to spend a great deal of time at the backyard or kitchen pump. Because the motive was to eliminate labor, the introduction of the flush toilet lagged behind the use of running water for other purposes: the indoor toilet had no great time-saving or labor-saving advantage over the waterless privy or the woods. But by the end of the nineteenth century, the spread of urban sewage systems and an increasing awareness of the dangers of disease from fecal matter led to widespread adoption of the flush toilet. Since toilets use six gallons of water per flush, they became and still are major water consumers. They were followed in this century by washing machines, water-cooled air-conditioners, dish washers, swimming pools, and other labor-saving, convenience, and luxury devices.

Water systems, then, evolved in response to the changing physical and social nature of cities. Today, indoor running water is so built into our lives that we could not live as we do without it. Backyard privies just barely served nineteenth-century cities with their five-story walk-ups. Today's high-rise apartment and office buildings, immense shopping centers, sports arenas, and restaurants could not function without running water. If we had to pump all the water we use, a good part of our lives would be spent at the pump. One hundred years ago we used less water and our lives had a different pace. Devoting several hours a day to pumping water, chopping wood, and emptying ashes was perfectly natural. Today our lives are more structured; we have no time for such activities. Running water—originally a labor-saving device and convenience—is now an absolute necessity. Its labor-saving aspects are as important as its health and fire-control functions.

**Technological Cycle.** Water systems interact strongly with other aspects of technology. For example, Philadelphia's first water system used a then-modern example of technology—the steam engine—to draw water from the Schuylkill River into the city. In the mid-nineteenth century, water use in many cities peaked during cold weather because people left their taps open to prevent the pipes from freezing: the introduction of central heating eliminated this waste and the fact that it did must have been an additional factor in convincing a family to install central heating. Today, modern high-rise buildings would not be habitable without water-cooled air-conditioning systems. And water could not enter a city without electric and diesel pumps lifting it from underground or shipping it from one area to another.

The net effect of this water use is seen in Table 1, which shows overall growth of water use and separates water use into four categories: irrigation; municipal (urban) and rural domestic; industrial; and steam electric-power generation. Urban use is further broken down in Tables 2 and 3. Almost half of the daily per-capita need of 150 gallons is used directly in the home. The rest leaks away, or is used by stores and offices, or is used to wash streets and fight fires. Table 4 shows the indirect ways in which we use water. One pound of newsprint requires 20 gallons of processing water while a kilowatt-hour of electricity (a 100-watt light bulb burning for 10 hours) requires 60 gallons of cooling water. When direct and indirect uses of water are added together, it turns out that each of us consumes about 1600 gallons per day.[2]

**United States Water Use**

| | Total | | Irrigation | | | | Industrial & Misc. | | Steam Electric Generating Plants | | |
|---|---|---|---|---|---|---|---|---|---|---|---|
| | bgd | per capita (g/d) | Total (bgd) | per capita (g/d) | Munici-pal Water (bgd) | Rural Domestic (bgd) | Total (bgd) | per capita (g/d) | Total (bgd) | per capita (g/d) | U.S. Popula-tion (millions) |
| 1900 | 40 | 526 | 20 | 263 | 3.0 | 2.0 | 10 | 132 | 5 | 66 | 76 |
| 1910 | 66 | 717 | 39 | 424 | 4.7 | 2.2 | 14 | 152 | 7 | 76 | 92 |
| 1930 | 110 | 900 | 60 | 488 | 8.0 | 2.9 | 21 | 171 | 18 | 146 | 123 |
| 1950 | 203 | 1353 | 100 | 666 | 14.1 | 4.6 | 38 | 253 | 46 | 306 | 150 |
| 1970 | 327 | 1610 | 119 | 586 | 27.0 | 4.3 | 56 | 275 | 121 | 596 | 203 |

SOURCE: *Statistical Abstract of the United States, 1971*, U.S. Government Printing Office.

**Table 1.** U.S. water use in various categories is shown in bgd (billion gallons per day) and in g/d (gallons per day) for per-capita use.

**Per-Capita Urban Water Use**

| | |
|---|---|
| Household Use (drinking, washing, lawns) | 65 g/d |
| Municipal Use (street washing, fire fighting) | 15 g/d |
| Commercial Use (stores, offices, and industry) | 55 g/d |
| Leaks | 15 g/d |
| Total | 150 g/d |

**Table 2.** These figures will vary from area to area depending on lawn size, cost of water, and so on. Industrial use is low because most factories get their water directly from rivers or lakes rather than from municipal supply systems.

**Household Water Use**

| | |
|---|---|
| Toilet | 6 g/flush |
| Clothes Washer (12 lb) | 45 g/load |
| Dishwasher | 15 g/load |
| Drinking and Cooking | 1 g/person/d |
| Bath | 30 g/bath |

**Table 3.** Some direct uses of water in the home are shown here. In addition, we consume water indirectly in food, industrial products, electric power, and so on.

**Water in Manufactured Goods**

| | |
|---|---|
| Daily Newspaper (1 lb) | 20 gallons |
| Iron and Steel in One Auto (3000 lb) | 52,500 gallons |
| Gallon of Gasoline | 18 gallons |
| Can of Lima Beans | 250 gallons |
| Can of Apricots | 80 gallons |

SOURCE: *Water Resource Engineering,* Ray K. Linsley and J. B. Franzini (New York: McGraw-Hill, 1964).

**Table 4.** The quantity of water required to produce some common products is shown in this table.

## How an Urban Water System Works

The story is told of a group of desert dwellers who visited Chicago as part of a trade delegation. As they were about to board a plane at O'Hare Field at the end of their visit, airport personnel discovered the suitcases of the delegates were filled with water faucets. The visitors had been so impressed with the running water found everywhere in Chicago that they were returning home with faucets to transform their own dry nation.

Modern city dwellers are a bit more knowledgeable about the massive network needed to supply faucets with water. But so quietly and so well do urban water systems function, it is easy to forget their size, complexity, and impact on the environment.

Watersheds and Reservoirs.   The heart of a water system is its watershed—the land drained by a stream, river, or reservoir. Usually a metropolitan area reaches out into the countryside, to undeveloped rural areas, for its water since water which drains over urban land is polluted. Rain or melted snow meets one of four fates: it may seep into the ground and become part of the underground, or ground, water; it may stay in the upper soil and eventually be evaporated by the vegetation; it may evaporate directly back to the atmosphere; or it may flow along the ground in sheets or rivulets. It is this last category—the runoff water—that we are concerned with.

Runoff water flows downhill along the ground until it reaches a small brook or stream. This brook or stream picks up the water and may carry it to a larger stream which eventually merges into a river. In a typical water supply system, that river will end in a reservoir whose purpose is to store the water until it is needed by the distant urban area. Reservoirs are large artificial lakes made by constructing a dam across the low end of a valley (see Figure 1). Water flowing into the valley piles up behind the dam, flooding the valley and forming the artificial lake. The existence of the reservoir allows a region to draw on water that was collected months earlier. If there had been no reservoir, that water would have flowed via the river to the ocean and would be unavailable for use when needed.

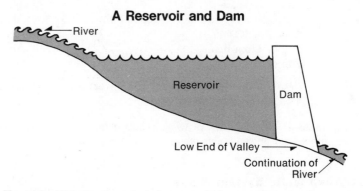

**A Reservoir and Dam**

**Figure 1.** The diagram shows a reservoir formed by damming the low end of a valley. The river which supplies the reservoir flows in from the left. Water released from the reservoir flows away to the right.

The role of the streams and rivers as collectors and of the reservoirs as storage areas should be emphasized. Only a small amount of the rain or snow falls directly into rivers and streams. Most of their water comes from rain falling on the land they drain, perhaps hundreds of square miles of land. A reservoir of a few thousand acres may store the water generated from a thousand square miles of upland watershed.

Every bit of land in a region is part of the local watershed. Rain falling on a field, farmhouse roof, or road eventually flows into the stream or river that drains the area. The contours of the land determine where one watershed ends and another begins. A typical boundary is a mountain ridge. Rain falling on one side of the ridge flows into one river and rain falling on the other side flows into a different river. If no dams block the rivers, they may eventually merge — one is said to be the other's tributary — and flow together to the ocean.

The amount of water an urban water system collects yearly depends on the size of its watershed, the quantity of rain and snow the watershed receives, the percentage of that precipitation that runs off, and the storage capacity of its reservoirs. In a wet region, ten or twenty square miles of watershed can produce as much water as several hundred square miles in

A large water distribution tunnel being carved through rock 700 feet below Manhattan is shown in this photo. The tracks are used in moving the drilling machinery. City water tunnels such as this one in some places reach 2500 feet below the surface. *Photo courtesy New York City Department of Water Supply.*

a dry region. The minimum amount of water a watershed is expected to produce in a year is called its safe yield. In average and wet years, this minimum is exceeded. To be effective, the annual safe yield of the system must equal or exceed the metropolitan area's yearly demand for water.

The water system must also have adequate reservoirs to store the water until it is needed. The reservoir capacity required depends on the seasonal patterns of water runoff and use. If the monthly quantities of runoff and use are equal, then only a very small storage capacity is needed since the water is used as it is produced. But if very heavy water use occurs in the summer and most runoff occurs in the fall, then the system's reservoirs must be able to hold almost a year's supply of water. Any runoff that occurs in the winter and spring will reduce the needed reservoir capacity.

Aqueducts, Water Mains, and Sewers.    Once the water is in the storage reservoir, it must be transported to the user when it is wanted. To accomplish this, the water is carried to the outskirts of the metropolitan area by an aqueduct, which is a large, man-made, underground river. Aqueducts are made of masonry, concrete, or steel pipe, or are tunnels drilled through solid rock. They are up to several hundred miles long, as much as twenty feet high by twenty feet wide, and able to carry hundreds of millions of gallons daily. If the storage reservoirs are at a higher elevation than the water users, the water will flow by gravity, just as water in a river flows downhill. If the reservoir is at the same or at a lower elevation than the users, pumps will be needed to move the water.

At the outskirts of the urban area, the aqueduct feeds into a series of water mains or distribution tunnels, much as a tree trunk splits into a series of branches. The water mains—which are pipes up to five feet or so in diameter—run beneath streets to different sections of the city, where they divide into smaller pipes which distribute the water to individual streets. Finally, pipes branch off these street mains to serve each home or business (see Figure 2).

**Water Distribution**

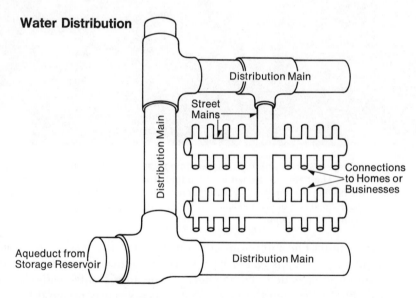

**Figure 2.** The aqueduct feeds into several smaller distribution mains which in turn feed into street mains. The street mains supply the homes and businesses.

Thus the pipe system stretches from the storage reservoir through the aqueduct to water mains and then to every faucet in the city. If you were small enough (and a strong enough swimmer) you could make your way from a faucet in your home to the reservoir. The only hint we get of this underground system is an occasional glimpse of water mains when a street is torn up or when a main breaks and floods the streets. The sight of a city street under two or three feet of water during a major water-main break brings home to us that rivers run beneath the streets.

**Peak-hour Demand.**   Water distribution is complicated by the need to respond to the population's fluctuating demand for water. Water use is usually high during the day and low at night. Seasonally it peaks in the summer and is low in the winter, as shown in Figure 3. If the aqueduct— which is the bottleneck in the system—is built to meet only average year-round demand, the system will run dry during peak hours. Even if the storage reservoir has plenty of water the system will run dry because the aqueduct will not be able to deliver that water at a sufficient rate. So the situation is similar to the elevator problem considered in Chapter 1.

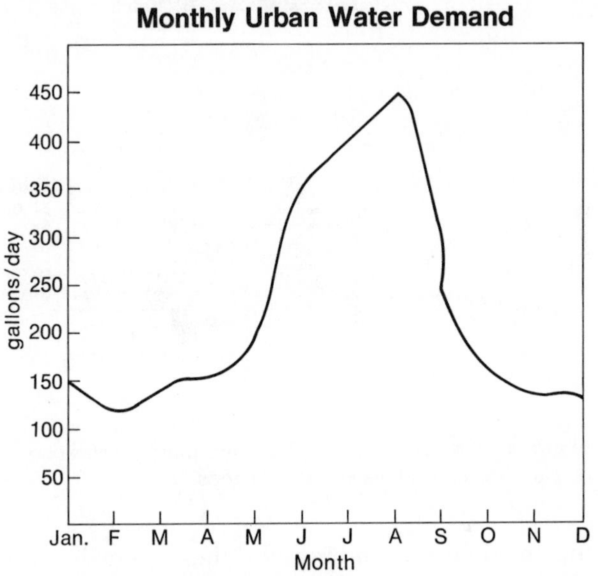

**Monthly Urban Water Demand**

**Figure 3.** Daily per-capita consumption is shown here for Seattle, Washington, by month.

**Aqueduct Capacity and Distribution Reservoirs.**   The amount of water an aqueduct can carry hourly depends on the speed with which the water flows through it and its cross-sectional area. The higher the speed and the fatter the aqueduct, the greater the capacity. If the maximum speed is taken as fixed, the only way to increase an aqueduct's capacity is to enlarge its cross section for the entire length. If the aqueduct is long, this increase can be very expensive.

An alternative way to meet peak demand is to construct distribution reservoirs or large storage tanks close to the city. This allows an aqueduct capable of meeting average 24-hour demand to supply the system. At night, when demand is low, the aqueduct flows at full capacity, with most of its flow going to fill the distribution reservoirs or tanks. During the day, when demand is high, both the aqueduct and the distribution reservoir are used to meet demand (see Figure 4 on the next page).

## Meeting Peak-hour Demand

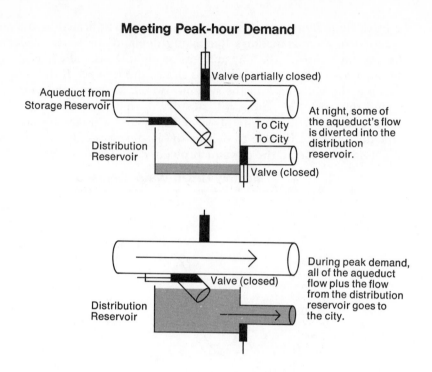

Valve (partially closed)

Aqueduct from
Storage Reservoir

At night, some of
the aqueduct's flow
is diverted into the
distribution
reservoir.

To City

To City

Distribution
Reservoir

Valve (closed)

Valve (closed)

During peak demand,
all of the aqueduct
flow plus the flow
from the distribution
reservoir goes to
the city.

Distribution
Reservoir

**Figure 4.** An average-sized aqueduct plus a distribution reservoir enable an area to meet peak-hour demands.

Another method of handling peak-hour demand is simply not to meet it. When a large amount of water is demanded (people "demand" water by turning on faucets and flushing toilets), water pressure in an inadequate system drops. This means water flows out of taps at a slower rate since the volume of flow depends on the water pressure and on the size of the faucet. So baths take longer to fill, lawns longer to water, and so on. The demand is spread over a greater period of time, just as traffic congestion or a busy telephone circuit spreads use of these facilities. But water pressure must not be allowed to drop too low or pressure-operated flush toilets won't work, water won't reach the upper floors of high-rises, and fire fighting may be hampered.

Removing the Water.   Any water that flows into an urban area must be removed. This is done by a sewage system that is a twin to the distribution system just described. Water coming out of faucets empties into sink drains or is flushed down toilets. These are connected to a home drainage system which empties into street sewers. The sewers run together and empty into a large sewer main which leads, in areas that have them, to a sewage treatment plant. The sewage is subjected to a cleansing treatment and is then dumped into a local river, lake, or ocean. The semisolid sludge which is a by-product of sewage treatment is either incinerated, used as land fill, or dumped into the ocean. Areas without sewage treatment plants dump the waste water directly into a local body of water. Figure 5 shows the portion of the U.S. population for which there are sewage treatment facilities of some kind.[3]

Sewage systems also have peak-hour problems. In many urban areas, the sewers carry sewage from homes and businesses as well as rainwater collected from the streets. When it rains, the extra water entering the system can overwhelm the sewage treatment plant, usually built to handle only the day's flow of waste water. Because the plants lack the capacity to treat the mix of rainwater and sewage, a large amount of it will have to be dumped into the river, lake, or ocean without treatment. This discharge is quite dirty because the heavy flow of water through the sewers flushes out material that has settled to the bottom of the pipes and because the rain washes pollutants off the land and into the sewage system.

## Growth of Public Waste-handling Services

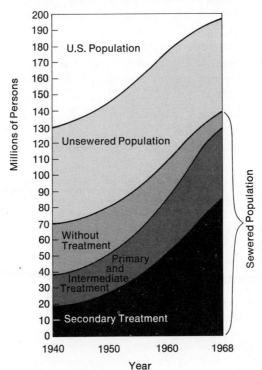

**Figure 5.** The growth in sewage treatment facilities since 1940 has more than kept pace with the population.

Drought Protection. A community may allow itself the "luxury" of not treating sewage, but protection against a severe water shortage is a must. Providing such protection is complex because both water supply and demand vary from year to year. Precipitation and runoff are not constant: they fluctuate from wet years in which runoff is very high to drought years in which runoff is a fraction of the average.

Protecting a metropolitan area against drought involves both physical and economic considerations. Theoretically, there are two ways to obtain drought protection: a larger watershed or an enlarged reservoir capacity. If a watershed is twice as large as is needed in periods of normal runoff, then the city can get by in years when runoff is fifty percent of normal. Larger reservoir capacity gives protection because years of below-average water runoff are interleaved with years of above-average runoff. If the reservoirs are built to hold only the average yearly runoff, then in wet years water will escape from the 100-percent full reservoirs. But additional storage capacity would hold the extra water, making it available during the dry years.

However, there are problems which complicate our solution of additional reservoir capacity. Water sitting in a reservoir, lake, or pond evaporates. Water collected but not used during wet years may evaporate by the time a dry year occurs. The amount of evaporation from a reservoir or lake can be appreciable, as Table 5 shows: in the dry Southwest a lake will lose six to seven feet of water yearly and gain back no more than a foot from direct precipitation. Lake Mead, near Las Vegas, Nevada, supplies part of Los Angeles' water needs. But it also loses through evaporation an amount of water almost equal to the total yearly water needs of that city.

Work has been under way for many years to perfect evaporation suppressants such as hexadecanol to be spread over lake and reservoir surfaces in order to limit evaporation. Such compounds would increase the effective capacity of existing reservoirs and make long-term water storage possible.

**Runoff and Lake Evaporation for Selected States**

| State | Runoff (inches) | Lake Evaporation (inches) |
|-------|-----------------|---------------------------|
| Arizona | 0.4 | 72 |
| California | 13.2 | 50 |
| Colorado | 4.7 | 45 |
| Georgia | 15.1 | 44 |
| Kansas | 3.2 | 55 |
| New Jersey | 20.6 | 32 |
| New Mexico | 0.7 | 56 |
| Oregon | 19.6 | 30 |
| Washington | 30.2 | 32 |

**Table 5.** Lake evaporation and runoff for selected states is shown here.

At present, the damming of a river actually decreases the amount of water available for use because evaporation is higher from a reservoir than from a freely flowing river.

However, there are problems with evaporant suppressants. First, winds tend to disperse the suppressant, so that it does not cover the entire surface. Second, storage reservoirs and lakes are not dead bodies of water; they contain fish and plant life and they are often used for fishing, boating, and swimming. Evaporation from the surface costs water, but it cools the reservoir just as cooling occurs when water evaporates from your hand. The temperature regulation of the lake or reservoir resulting from this evaporation is important to the health of the fish and plant life and also helps cool the surrounding region.

The Natural System.   The man-made system described here functions within a more complex natural system called the hydrologic cycle. The sewage or treated water discharged by the city into a local river eventually reaches the ocean (if it does not evaporate en route). There the sun evaporates some water from the ocean surface which re-enters the atmosphere. Winds may carry the moisture back over the land where it falls as rain or snow, available to be used again during its new journey to the ocean. Because of this cycle, it is possible that the water you drank yesterday was used earlier by yourself or perhaps by a Caesar. It is the pattern of rain or melted snow flowing by river or stream to the ocean where it is evaporated to fall again as precipitation that we call the hydrologic cycle. A more-or-less fixed amount of water passes again and again through the system (see Figure 6).

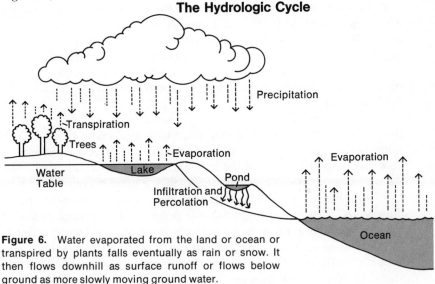

**The Hydrologic Cycle**

**Figure 6.** Water evaporated from the land or ocean or transpired by plants falls eventually as rain or snow. It then flows downhill as surface runoff or flows below ground as more slowly moving ground water.

The hydrologic cycle also purifies water. The moisture evaporated from a polluted lake is quite pure. Unless water falls through dirty air, it is still pure when it hits the ground as rain or snow. Whether it remains pure depends on the ground it flows over and the quality of the water it mixes with. Most urbanized areas pollute their runoff. Rain flowing over lawns picks up fertilizer and dog droppings; driveways yield oil and grease; roads contribute oil, grease, and deicing salts; and home septic tanks leak sewage into local streams. If an area has factories, they may add an additional burden of pollution.

**Water Systems and Land Use.**   Because developed areas inevitably degrade water quality, cities and suburbs must go to rural areas for their water. To prevent contamination of their watersheds by development, some metropolitan regions own and maintain in a rural state the land from which they collect water. So water supply systems are one of the few forces in society working to maintain open spaces.

Water systems also illustrate the dependence of densely settled areas on open land. Since cities and many suburbs cannot use their local water, they must reach out into the countryside. They also depend on open spaces for food, raw materials, recreation space, and even cleansed air. The city dweller occupying a few thousand square feet, or the suburbanite on an acre, draws on many times that land area to stay alive. A rule of thumb is that it takes one acre of land to supply each person with a year's worth of grain, vegetables, and fruit, and another acre of pasture to supply meat and dairy products.[4] Recreation, oil, metal, paper, and other items add to the required amount of land.

Many metropolitan areas do not own their watersheds. They merely own the water produced by the land, and in many cases this water-producing land is in danger. The story of metropolitan areas is sprawl—the continuing spread of homes, stores, and industry into the once-rural areas around cities. Since the 1920s the suburbs surrounding our cities have spread great distances until today we talk of megalopolis, spread city, Bosnywash, and Sanfrangelodiego.

Towns, suburbs, and cities whose watersheds are under attack have three choices: do nothing; install purification plants to treat the collected water before use; or go further afield to find still undeveloped watersheds. In many cases, they have done nothing. A U.S. Environmental Protection Administration study[5] found that, in 1973, 23 million people—10% of the U.S. population—were getting substandard water, 8 million "potentially dangerous" water, and over 500,000 people water so impure the federal government banned it from interstate commerce (see Table 6). One reason for this problem is the small amount of money spent to safeguard water supplies. Although the federal government recommends that each state spend 20 cents per person per year protecting water supplies, the national average in 1970 was 6.3 cents. This ranged from New Hampshire's high of 18 cents to Connecticut's low of 1.7 cents (see Table 7).

**Banned Drinking-Water Systems**

| Place | Date of Ban | Reason | Population Served |
|---|---|---|---|
| Asheville, N.C. | 1/71 | B, CC | 123,000 |
| Haverhill, Mass. | 5/72 | E, C | 46,120 |
| Miami Beach, Fla. | 3/73 | B | 90,000 |
| Pascagoula, Miss. | 1/71 | B, S, E | 27,000 |
| Quincy, Mass. | 4/72 | B, S | 87,000 |
| West Palm Beach, Fla. International Airport | 3/73 | B | 2,100 |

KEY: B = high bacteria count; C = inadequate chlorination; CC = possible cross connections with pollution sources; E = equipment deficiencies; S = inadequate sampling.

**Table 6.** A few of the areas in which the water systems were banned by the federal government as of May 1973 are shown in this table.

**Water-Supply-Protection Expenditures Per Capita, 1970**

| | |
|---|---|
| Federal Recommendation | 20.0¢ |
| National Average | 6.3¢ |
| New Hampshire (nation's highest) | 18.0¢ |
| New York | 8.9¢ |
| Florida | 2.5¢ |
| New Jersey | 2.2¢ |
| Connecticut | 1.7¢ |

**Table 7.** Shown here is the amount of money spent by some representative states on water regulatory and protection programs per person per year.

**Cost-Benefit Analysis.** Construction of urban water systems and expenditure of money to maintain purity does not just happen. Decisions must somehow be reached. Once it is determined that a city or suburb needs an expanded water system or new sewage treatment plant, the best way to accomplish these ends must also be determined. Should the new system be adequate for the next twenty or the next forty years? Should it use local ground-water sources or go to a rural region for its water?

To help answer these questions, public agencies generally make a cost-benefit analysis. In such an analysis, the total dollar value of the benefits and the costs of the proposed project are calculated. If the ratio of benefits to costs is greater than 1, then the project is considered feasible. The greater the value of the ratio, the more attractive the project. This corresponds to private industry's criterion of future profitability for any new venture it considers.

To see how a cost-benefit analysis might be used, suppose an evaporation suppressant were under consideration. The dollar value of the water saved by using the suppressant would be the benefit. The cost would be the price of making and applying the suppressant, the loss of tourist trade due to lack of fish or to warming of the local climate, and any other dollar value that could be put on the changed ecology.

Cost-benefit analysis is widely used and widely criticized. The major criticism is that it considers only factors to which dollar values can be applied. In the example just discussed, if the suppressant destroys species of plants or fish which have no commercial or tourist value, the analysis would not take their destruction into account. Another criticism is that the government agencies which do these analyses can always justify a favored project by making the proper assumptions. It is said that the U.S. Bureau of Reclamation will invariably arrive at a satisfactory ratio for a dam having strong political backing in the Congress and that state highway departments can always prove that a proposed road will pay its way. With the rise of environmental concern, the cost-benefit approach is less used as the sole justification for a project, and the analyses done are more sophisticated and inclusive.

## Cities and Nature

Many important decisions are made without a cost-benefit analysis or even an awareness that a major decision is being made. An example is the urban water system we have described. It is a substitute for use of local wells, streams, and ponds. High population densities make such sources inadequate, and even if they were large enough, pollution would rule them out. Population pressures also encourage intensive use of every bit of land. Both of these factors, water supply and land use, result in the draining of lakes, ponds, and marshes, and the burying of brooks, streams, and even small rivers in concrete culverts and steel pipes. So little by little the face of the urban area changes as the city's needs and demands grow.

Urban Flooding.   In most urban areas watertight concrete and asphalt surfaces and buildings cover the land. Trees and vegetation which would slow and help the ground absorb rainwater are long since gone. Because the absorbing, braking effect of trees and vegetation is gone, rainwater rushes quickly downhill or collects in depressions. If the city or suburb does not have sufficient street gutters and unblocked storm sewers to collect the water, then streets and homes will be flooded.

Even with a good storm-sewer system, the water must empty into something. Usually all storm sewers for an area discharge into a local stream or river that had drained the area before it was urbanized. Therefore the stream should have the capacity to carry off the rainwater. But in an urban area more water will reach the stream or river in a shorter period than when the area was undeveloped. In fact, peak urban runoff volumes are increased by up to five times[6] as a result of land development. The quick, large influx of water may overwhelm the stream or river, with the water flooding over the banks. If homes or businesses are in this flood plain, they will be damaged. People may be killed.

This flooding situation creates a demand for the local government to do something. One possible step the government might take is to increase the water-carrying capacity of the stream or river. It can be dredged or deepened; it can be bulldozed (so-called channelization) to eliminate flow-reducing curves; its sides can be raised; its bottom can be covered with concrete to reduce friction and increase the speed of water flow. If this is not enough, dams can be built at critical points on the river to hold back flood waters until they can safely be released. The reservoirs thus formed may also be used for electric power generation, water supply, and recreation, thereby increasing the benefit-cost ratio.

Of course, the local municipalities can also forbid the development of the flood plain, leaving it as open space. In such a case there is no need to channelize the stream or build dams. But most areas are unable to practice such discipline, and flood plains are usually developed. Those living on the flood plain then succeed in obtaining some flood protection through alteration of the river; and this encourages further development which creates a further need for flood protection.

**Technological Cycles.** The elimination of streams and ponds within cities and the harnessing of rivers have progressed without any overall design, although each individual detail of the progression has been planned and discussed. One action inevitably leads to another. The progression is an almost unnoticed side effect of the way our cities developed, an example of the technological cycles discussed in Chapter 1. Many see the side effect as another example of our rapid movement toward an artificial environment. To some it is a sign of progress, of man gaining increasing control over his life and destiny. To others it is an indication of impending disaster, of urban man's alienation from nature.

**The Urban Environment.** One side effect of urbanization is increased temperatures. Cities and their suburbs are thermal islands, warmer by as much as ten degrees Fahrenheit[7] than surrounding rural regions. In part this is due to heat released by the great concentrations of autos and other urban equipment: lights, air-conditioners, stoves, power plants, and people all release heat. The high temperatures are also due to the lack of vegetation and surface water. Grass, bushes, and trees transpire large amounts of water in hot weather, maintaining a healthful temperature for themselves. Ponds, lakes, and streams also evaporate water. Both processes work to keep surrounding areas cool. This natural temperature regulation does not exist in a city. The lack is aggravated by the heat-holding ability, or heat capacity, of buildings and streets. They sop up heat all day and then give it off long after sundown, preventing the nighttime cooling that occurs in the countryside.

In part as a result of often intolerable urban summer temperatures, there has been a great increase in air-conditioning for offices, stores, homes, and schools over the past twenty years. Since air-conditioners function best in sealed buildings, the result has been a trend toward windowless and sealed-window buildings. The need for energy to run the air-conditioning has caused more fuel consumption, more air pollution, and more power lines both above and below ground. So the removal of vegetation, surface streams, and lakes has led to even more environmental artificiality. We begin by sealing water in pipes underground and end by sealing ourselves in buildings.

**Congestion.**   It was said earlier that water systems are a successful technology which alleviate urban disease and fire without causing noise, air pollution, or other side effects. But from the perspective of 150 years, we see that these systems have both solved and created problems. When a region had to get along on local water supplies, its size and density were limited by natural forces. With the introduction of water, electric power, and communications systems, restraints on density were eliminated. Today in some downtown business districts there is no room on the streets and sidewalks for all the office occupants.

Water, energy, and communications utilities have helped create the congestion in some of our metropolitan areas. A rural existence requires that a person have enough room for a well, an outhouse, an energy supply (wood from a forest), and land to grow food. But when utilities bring in water and energy, and trucks and trains bring in food from distant farms, then great population concentrations can be achieved. Urban residential populations can exceed 70,000 persons per square mile, with office-worker populations approaching one million persons per square mile.

Such concentrations require extremely dependable utilities. Even a short cessation of the flow of water, energy, or food into an urban area can spell disaster. One result of that need is the engineering applied to the rural areas that supply cities with water. Valleys are dammed to form reservoirs; streams and rivers are used as open pipes to move water between a system's storage reservoirs; and aqueducts are built to carry the water to the users. As a result there can be important changes in the biological communities. For example, when a stream is used to transfer water between reservoirs, its water flow will fluctuate wildly. For a few hours it may run brimful; then a water-system employee will turn a few valves and the stream will dry up. These changes prevent the fish and plant communities from developing normally. At a time of vanishing open space, many reservoirs and often entire watersheds are kept closed to public use in order to safeguard the purity of the water. So the urban or suburban dweller, who lives on a small plot of land sustained by a distant water system, does not even have access to the land that generates the water.

In many cases the sheer size of the population defeats well-planned technological systems. For example, construction of a sewage-collecting system solves the problem of waste water accumulating on the land. But if too much waste water is generated, even a large river may be polluted.

The next step is to construct sewage treatment plants. If the population continues to grow, disposing of the inert sludge which is the end product of sewage treatment becomes a problem. This kind of problem is now confronting the communities in the New York-New Jersey area, which have created a huge "dead sea" off the Atlantic coast by their ocean dumping of sludge.

## Three Case Studies

As we have seen, a large metropolitan area cannot exist unless it reaches into surrounding areas for water. This reaching out is a mix of technology, politics, economics, and even violence. In this section we look briefly at the development of water systems in three very different metropolitan areas — New York, southern California, and Denver — to see what is involved in securing water for cities.

New York.   Today, New York City's water supply system can deliver about 2 billion gallons per day[8] to its almost 8 million users — a flow equivalent to a river about seventy-five feet wide and eight feet deep moving at five feet per second. But until the first third of the nineteenth century, New York got its water from local wells and streams. The high death rates due to disease and costly fires led to the construction in 1842 of the Croton Aqueduct, a forty-five-mile tunnel capable of carrying 90 million gallons per day into the city. Fifty years later this was supplemented with a second Croton Aqueduct, which brings in an additional 300 million gallons a day. Population growth and annexation of surrounding regions overwhelmed this new supply, and in 1917 the city completed the Catskill Aqueduct, 120 miles long and the largest yet with a capacity of 555 million gallons per day.

By now recognizing the treadmill it was on due to population growth and increasing per-capita water use, the city almost immediately began to reach out to the east branch of the Delaware River, thereby moving into an entirely new water basin drained by a separate river system. However, New York first had to fight legal battles against Pennsylvania and New Jersey since both states also claimed the water. The depression and World War II caused additional delays, and it was not until 1955 that the eighty-five-mile Delaware Aqueduct was completed. It has a capacity of 400 million gallons per day and increased the city's supply to about 1400 million gallons a day.

Even before this first Delaware tap was completed, New York obtained a ruling from the U.S. Supreme Court permitting it to withdraw an additional 400 million gallons per day from the Delaware. Philadelphia opposed the additional diversion. It feared a decrease in the flow of fresh water down the Delaware would allow salt water to creep upriver from Chesapeake Bay, endangering its own supply of drinking water. It also

This photograph from about 1890 shows construction of the enlarged Croton Aqueduct. The pipes visible below the new tunnel are part of the Old Croton Aqueduct. The Harlem River is visible in the foreground; then-rural Bronx is the area in the background. This aqueduct was constructed to meet additional water requirements of New York City. Nearly the entire line was tunneled beneath the island. *Photo courtesy The New-York Historical Society, New York City.*

feared that the water level of the Delaware would drop, interfering with navigation. This threat by New York to the drinking and navigation water of a city ninety miles away illustrates the city's scale of consumption and the distance it goes for water.

New York also met internal opposition to its water plans from critics who claimed there was no need to go to the Delaware. Support for this position came in a 1951 report by a panel of water-supply experts.[9] The report said there were cheaper ways for New York to meet its water needs and made three major suggestions. First, they estimated that an intensive program of searching for and repairing water-main leaks could save 150 million gallons per day. Second, they recommended the metering of all water users. They estimated that full metering instead of flat-rate payments would encourage people to conserve 320 million gallons a day, a reduction of per-person household use from 80 to 40 gallons per day. Their estimate was based on experience with cities that have full water metering. Their last recommendation was that New York meet future water needs by tapping the Hudson River. Since the Hudson could be tapped near the city, collection and distribution costs would be low. However, Hudson water is not as pure or as sweet tasting as the mountain water New York gets from its distant reservoirs, so in this case a filtration plant would have to be built. Although estimated savings from repairing leaks and metering would have amounted to more water than the additional Delaware tap would produce, the decision was made to build the new aqueduct and the Cannonsville Reservoir to store water the aqueduct would carry.

At present, there is strong pressure from the surrounding, mainly suburban, communities for New York City to share its 2000 square miles of watershed and its transmission aqueducts and storage reservoirs. New York took control of these watersheds when it was the only urban area — and therefore the only unified political and economic force — in the region. But for the past several decades, the city's population has remained steady at 8 million people while the surrounding suburbs have grown rapidly. In many cases, land in these suburban counties is part of New York's watershed or contains its reservoirs and aqueducts. While the city, by law, must supply such counties with water, it does so by a formula based solely on population. This limits the water the counties have and discourages industrial development to New York City's advantage.

**Southern California.**   The water-gathering efforts of the populous but well-watered East are dwarfed by those of Los Angeles. In 1913 Los Angeles built an aqueduct 233 miles long to the Owens River in southern California. To reach the river, which is on the eastern slope of the Sierra Nevada mountain range, the 284-million-gallon-per-day aqueduct had to pierce the mountains. Even after Los Angeles had solved the formidable technological problems and had bought the water rights (they owned the water produced by the land but not the land) from the Owens Valley owners, Los Angeles had trouble obtaining the water. During a drought in 1923, Owens Valley farmers filled their irrigation ditches, causing the Owens River and thus the Los Angeles Aqueduct to run dry. This marked the beginning of a four-year feud during which Los Angeles bought most of the farms in Owens Valley. Today the city owns 300,000 acres in the Valley, which it maintains in a rural state so that Los Angeles may survive as a city.

The Los Angeles Aqueduct was extended to Mono Basin in 1940, for a total length of 338 miles, tapping new sources of water. But the original section of the aqueduct, with only a 284-million-gallon-per-day capacity, could not carry all the water the high, snowcovered Sierra mountains produced. So in 1963 construction began on a second Los Angeles Aqueduct. Completed in 1970, the new aqueduct has a capacity of 136 million gallons per day, for a total capacity of 420 million gallons a day.

Before this second Los Angeles Aqueduct was built, both Los Angeles and the rest of southern California were forced to reach out further for water. Their new source became the Colorado, the 1400-mile river that carved the Grand Canyon and whose watershed is eight percent of the continental United States. Like the Delaware, the Colorado is an interstate river, and before California could tap it, the states laying claim to the water had to reach some agreement on its division. In 1923 six states (California, Colorado, Nevada, New Mexico, Utah, and Wyoming) ratified the Colorado River Compact. Unfortunately this compact was based on faulty estimates of water flow and distributed more water than the Colorado – on the average – produces. This mistake is causing serious problems today as the states find they cannot get the water the law guarantees them.

To take advantage of the compact, 13 southern California political entities formed, in 1928, the Metropolitan Water District. Today the District includes 10 million people, 122 cities, and 6 counties (Los Angeles, Orange, Riverside, San Bernadino, San Diego, and Ventura). In 1941 the District completed the 242-mile Colorado River Aqueduct, which now brings about one billion gallons a day to southern California. To reach the Pacific coast, the water must be pumped 1600 feet above the river's elevation. From this height it flows by gravity to the coastal region. The immense amount of electric power needed to pump this water is generated by other Colorado River water as it flows over the Hoover Dam at Lake Mead. The federal government's construction of Hoover Dam in 1936 was a vital part of California's tapping the Colorado, since without cheap electricity the water could not be shipped to California. In 1971 the Metropolitan Water District completed its second major project – the California Aqueduct. This 450-mile system reaches into northern California to bring south 1.8 billion gallons per day from the Sacramento and Feather rivers. Like Colorado River water, the California Aqueduct's flow requires pumping energy. Only the Owens Valley water flows completely by gravity.

Although New York and the Metropolitan Water District have comparable populations, New York gets by on 1.8 billion gallons per day while the District requires several times that amount. The reason is agriculture. Southern California is near-desert, but thanks to irrigation it produces a large part of America's citrus fruits and vegetables. In the Northeast, agriculture requires little or no irrigation since rainfall is about 3½ feet annually.

The irrigation of southern California by these huge water systems affects society in several ways. First, the California farms take the place of the local vegetable and truck farms that once surrounded all urban areas. These small local farms are gradually converted to subdivisions, shopping centers, and roads, while rail and truck transportation are used to distribute canned or frozen California produce around the nation. Irrigated, intensive, mechanized agriculture – using large amounts of energy, packaging materials, and transportation – takes the place of small,

Irrigation water to support year-round agriculture flows southward through the 152-mile-long, concrete Friant-Kern Canal toward San Joaquin Valley and Bakersfield in California. Notice that the canal is raised above the level of the surrounding land. Part of the Sierra Nevada range is visible in the background. This canal is part of the Central Valley Project, an undertaking of the U.S. Bureau of Reclamation. *Photo courtesy U.S. Bureau of Reclamation.*

less efficient, dispersed farms. The abandoned farms then become a suburb or a city dweller's second home.

By now, California has fully developed its own water resources and those to the west and has begun looking north to Oregon, Washington, and Idaho. Those states fear California's great political and economic power and have banded together to block attempts at future interbasin transfer projects. The northwestern states say that long-distance water transfers are wasteful and economically inefficient. They are also afraid that if Congress allows California to tap their water, they will be reduced to the status of Owens Valley or New York's suburbs.

**Denver.**   Although a very different kind of city in a very different location, Denver, Colorado, faces many of the same problems as New York and Los Angeles. Denver is beautifully situated on the eastern slope of the Rocky Mountains at an altitude of one mile. But the eastern slope is dry because the high mountains intercept whatever moisture is in the air moving in from the west, causing it to fall mostly as snow on the western slope. As a result, Denver has built reservoirs on the western slope and aqueducts through the Continental Divide to bring the water east.

There is great pressure for additional trans-mountain diversions because of the rapid rate of growth of Denver, Boulder, and other eastern-slope communities. But the western-slope population is well aware of the dangers posed by water diversion and they fight proposed projects at every step. In addition, the suburban towns around Denver fear that Denver wants to use its water-gathering ability to take them over, so the eastern-slope communities are not united. The situation is complicated by the fact that the water diverted to the eastern slope is taken from the Colorado River. Denver and Los Angeles—although 1000 miles apart—are competing for the same water.

## Bibliography

*Source Notes*

1. "Environmental Protection in the City of New York." Merrill Eisenbud. *Science,* vol. 170 (November 1970), pp. 706–712.

2. *Statistical Abstract of the United States, 1971.* Washington, D.C.: U.S. Government Printing Office.

3. *The Economics of Clean Water.* U.S. Department of the Interior. Washington, D.C., 1970.

4. "Food from the Land." Sterling B. Hendricks. In *Resources and Man,* Committee on Resources and Man. San Francisco: W. H. Freeman and Co., 1969.

5. "Impure Tap Water a Growing Hazard." *The New York Times,* 13 May 1973.

6. *Water Resources and the National Welfare.* Walter U. Garstka. Walter U. Garstka (Route 1, Pine, Colorado 80470), 1974.

7. "Man-Made Climatic Changes," Helmut E. Landsberg. *Science,* vol. 170 (December 1970), pp. 1265–1274.

8. *Water for Tomorrow.* Temporary State Commission on the Water Supply Needs of Southeastern New York. New York, 1973.

9. *Water Supply.* Jack Hirschleifer. Chicago: University of Chicago Press, 1969.

*Further Reading*

## Water Use

NELSON M. BLAKE.  *Water for the Cities.* New York: Syracuse University Press, 1956.
A good history of water supplies for American cities from colonial times to the present is given in this book.

LYNN W. GELHAR.  "The Aqueous Underground." *Technology Review,* March/April 1972, pp. 45–53.
This article presents an overview of ground water.

D. L. INMAN and B. M. BRUSH.  "The Coastal Challenge." *Science,* vol. 181 (6 July 1973), pp. 20–32.
An excellent review of coastal problems is given in this article.

WESLEY MARX.  *The Frail Ocean.* New York: Ballantine Books, 1969 (paper).
This book presents a survey of several man-ocean environmental problems. It contains a very good description of the current state of our beaches.

NATIONAL WATER COMMISSION.  *Water Policies for the Future.* Washington, D.C.: U.S. Government Printing Office, 1973.
This government publication is a monumental survey of the U.S. water situation (supply, demand, quality, and relevant laws) and presents recommendations for future policies.

PETER K. WEYL.  *Oceanography.* New York: John Wiley and Sons, Inc., 1970.
This oceanography text has a strong physical orientation. Those wishing to know more about water-related processes will find it useful.

## General

DANIEL J. BOORSTIN.  *The Americans: The Democratic Experience.* New York: Random House, 1973.
In this third volume of *The Americans,* Boorstin looks at how the development of America's technology affected and was affected by the way we live. It has some interesting sections on water.

JOHN HARTE and ROBERT H. SOCOLOW, eds.  *The Patient Earth.* New York: Holt, Rinehart and Winston, 1971 (paper).
This book contains a collection of essays, edited by two physicists, on several urban and environmental topics. It contains a good deal of information on water problems.

FRANK HERBERT.  *Dune.* Philadelphia: Chilton Books, 1965.
This book is a science-fiction novel about a planet with very little water.

SEARS, ROEBUCK & CO.  *The Great Price Maker.* Northfield, Ill.: Gun Digest Books, 1969.
This 1908 Sears, Roebuck & Co. Catalogue—or any of the other old catalogues that have been reprinted—gives a good picture of how Americans lived at the turn of the century. Especially relevant for Chapters 2 and 3 are the plumbing items.

## Questions

1. If you live in a private home, go through it and diagram or otherwise describe the water system. Show where the water enters and leaves the home, where it is metered, how it is heated, the valving, and so on. If you live in an apartment house or dormitory and the water system is inaccessible, consult a reference book and describe a system for a one-family home. (If the system is accessible, then describe it.) Where does your household water come from?

2. If you can obtain a water bill, calculate your household's daily water use and try to relate this to the different water-using activities in your home. As part of this determination, try to discover how much water is used in such everyday activities as washing dishes, washing hands, showering, bathing, and cooking. Compare your answers with average in-home consumption of 60 gallons/person/day.

3. Describe a tank toilet by sketching the way in which the tank itself empties and fills. What is the point of putting a solid object, such as a plastic bottle filled with water or a brick, in the toilet tank? Could the same effect be realized in some other way? Sketch the interior of the bowl. What maintains the water in the bowl?

4. In many areas water flows out of faucets faster late at night than it does earlier in the evening. Why?

5. One disastrous effect of the 1906 San Francisco earthquake was a fire that burned down what the quake had failed to knock down. Today beneath many San Francisco street intersections there are reservoirs of water to be used to fight fires in case of another quake. Since the city has a network of fire hydrants fed by water mains, what is the purpose of these pools?

6. Should a reservoir be built at the high or low elevation section of a watershed? Why?

7. This chapter cited at least one case where an act of changing the environment created a demand for another such act — with both acts tending to increase the extent of the man-made world at the expense of the "natural" world. Describe any similar cycle you are familiar with from your own experience.

8. TV and newspaper photos of drought-lowered reservoirs are important tools in keeping water use low during droughts.
   a. Is it a fortunate accident that the needs of a sophisticated water system are met by an equally sophisticated communications system? Or is there more of a connection than just happenstance?
   b. Usually, people will attempt to conserve water or electric power during a shortage. Does the same helpful reaction occur during a shortage of meat, canned goods, gasoline, heating oil? Why or why not?

9. It was stated earlier that to increase an aqueduct's capacity, its cross-sectional area must be increased along its entire length. Describe qualitatively why capacity won't increase if the aqueduct is widened along just part of its length. (We are assuming the water speed in the aqueduct is held to a maximum of

5 feet/second throughout.) It may help to understand the question if you use a highway as a rough physical analogy, where extra lanes correspond to extra cross-sectional area.

10. Assume a water-system planner has available two distribution-reservoir sites of the same potential capacity. One site will result in a shallow reservoir covering a large area. The other will yield a deep reservoir over a smaller area. Which site should be chosen? Why?

11. Assume a farm valley is to be dammed to create a reservoir to store drinking water. Make up a list of factors which would go into a cost-benefit analysis. Are there factors which you consider important but to which a dollar value cannot be assigned? Can you suggest alternative methods of determining whether or not to go ahead with a technological project such as this one? Should the reversibility or irreversibility of a project be a factor?

12. Why do you think the bathroom—which performs an important function in the modern home—is usually a small, cell-like area? In most apartments and houses it is not even counted as a room.

13. Until the turn of the century, most urban and rural residents used privies, that is, outdoor bathrooms. They consisted of a seat placed above a pit in the ground. Privies were often "two holers"—two seats placed side by side over the same pit so that people could keep each other company. Today, of course, privacy is the rule in such matters. Speculate on the reasons for the change.

14. The text discusses the impact of urbanization on streams, lakes, and marshes. Are you aware of the present status of natural bodies of water in your area? Are they under pressure from development? Is there a local or regional flood problem? Is the flood problem a recent one or has it existed for years? What solutions are under discussion?

15. For almost all states, lake evaporation is greater than rainfall or runoff. Why, then, aren't most lakes dry?

16. The text states that today we do not have the time to pump water, chop wood, and haul ashes. If such conveniences (necessities) as running water and gas or electric ranges disappeared, we would have to do a great deal more work of this sort. Is it possible, however, that elimination of these systems or devices might save us time in other ways? How?

17. Which shape pan would you use to measure precipitation? In a pinch, could they all be used? What shape pan would you use to measure a light rainfall?

a.            b.            c.            d.

18. Assume 0.1 inch of rain falls. To what depth will water accumulate in the collecting pan shown below?

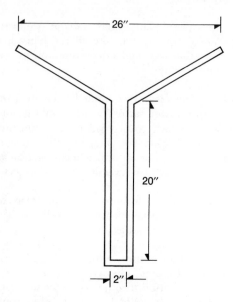

19. Discuss the effect snow has on the reservoir capacity needed to store drinking water for an urban area. Make some assumption about seasonal demand and precipitation patterns and discuss whether the falling of precipitation as snow rather than rain increases, decreases, or leaves unchanged the need for reservoir capacity.

20. What information in Table 1 indicates that the rural population has been decreasing while farming activity has been increasing?

*But today he only saw one of the river's secrets, one that gripped his soul. He saw that the river continually flowed and flowed and yet it was always there; it was always the same and yet every moment it was new. Who could understand, conceive this?*

HERMANN HESSE*

# 3 Quantifying urban water systems

The preceding chapter provided a qualitative view of urban water systems. In this chapter we shall do a series of calculations to obtain some idea of the sizes involved in watersheds, reservoirs, and aqueducts for an urban water system. In our calculations we will be "exact enough" rather than exact; our emphasis will be on the flow of reasoning and on order-of-magnitude answers rather than exact results. To speed the calculations we will use power of ten notation.† In this notation, 200,000,000 (200 million) becomes $2 \times 10^8$, and 5000 multiplied by 23,000 becomes $(5 \times 10^3)(2.3 \times 10^4)$.

In the course of the many calculations throughout the book, we will routinely convert from one physical unit to another.‡ In this chapter we will go back and forth between gallons, cubic feet, and acre-feet for volume, and square feet, acres, and square miles for area in order to express our answers in the units easiest to visualize.

To further speed and simplify calculations—so that the arithmetic does not obscure the logic—we will usually work with only two significant figures. For example, 6830 will be written as 6800, or $6.8 \times 10^3$ in power of ten notation; 10,004 will be $10^4$, and 1870 will be $1.9 \times 10^3$. As a corollary, we will also simplify the relations between physical units. An acre will be $4.4 \times 10^4$

---

* From Hesse's book *Siddhartha* (New York: New Directions, 1951).
† Those unfamiliar with power of ten notation should consult Appendix A.
‡ Those unfamiliar with unit conversion should consult Appendix B.

square feet instead of 43,560 square feet; a square mile will be $2.8 \times 10^7$ square feet instead of 27,878,400 square feet; and a cubic foot will be 7.5 gallons instead of 7.481 gallons.*

**A National Water Budget.** Before calculating the parameters of an urban water system, we wish to establish the national context within which that system must operate. We will begin, then, by calculating the average water supply and use for the United States as a whole. The United States has a total land area of 3.6 million square miles ($3.6 \times 10^6$ mi²).[1] If the rain and snow that fell on this area in a year were distributed uniformly, it would average out to 30 inches, or 2.5 feet, per year.[2] (Ten inches of newly fallen snow is assumed to melt down to one inch of water.) Of the 2.5 feet of rain and melted snow, 21 inches will evaporate or be transpired by plants.[3] The remaining 9 inches flow downhill into collecting streams, rivers, and lakes. It is the 9 inches of runoff which supply our annual water needs.

To obtain the total available water, we would multiply U.S. land area by the 9 inches (0.75 feet) of runoff. However, this would give such enormous and difficult-to-grasp numbers, we prefer to look at water supply and demand on a per-acre basis. The runoff produced by an average acre is

$$\text{volume of runoff/yr} = (\text{area}) (\text{runoff/yr})$$

$$= (1 \text{ acre}) (0.75 \text{ ft/yr}) = 0.75 \text{ acre-ft/yr}.$$

An acre-foot of water is the amount of water it takes to cover an acre of land to a depth of one foot (see Figure 1). The acre-foot is widely used to describe large quantities of water and is especially useful to farmers cal-

**An Acre-Foot of Water**

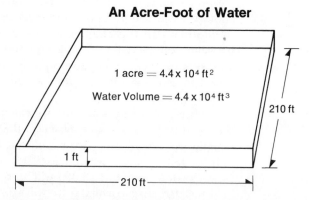

1 acre $= 4.4 \times 10^4$ ft²

Water Volume $= 4.4 \times 10^4$ ft³

210 ft

1 ft

210 ft

**Figure 1.** An acre-foot of water is the amount of water which covers one acre of land to a depth of one foot. Since an acre is 44,000 square feet, an acre-foot of water is 44,000 cubic feet. The acre-foot is a useful measure to farmers and other large water users.

---

* The exact and approximate conversion relations are listed in Appendix C.

culating irrigation needs. We will find it more convenient to work with cubic feet and gallons so we perform the following unit conversions.

$$(0.75 \text{ acre-ft/yr}) (4.4 \times 10^4 \text{ ft}^2/\text{acre}) = 3.3 \times 10^4 \text{ ft}^3/\text{yr}$$
$$= (3.3 \times 10^4 \text{ ft}^3/\text{yr}) (7.5 \text{ gal/ft}^3)$$
$$= 2.5 \times 10^5 \text{ gal/yr}$$

An average acre produces $2.5 \times 10^5$ gallons of runoff annually. To see if this is adequate, inadequate, or marginal, we must calculate how much water is consumed yearly by the people living on an average U.S. acre. In 1970, the United States' population density was 57.4 persons/square mile,[4] which is less than 1 person per 10 acres, or 0.1 persons/acre. (There are 640 acres in a square mile.) Average total water use (municipal, irrigation, and industrial) was very close to 1600 gallons/person/day. In a year, this totals

$$\text{water/person/year} = (1.6 \times 10^3 \text{ gal/person/day}) (3.7 \times 10^2 \text{ days/yr})$$
$$= 5.9 \times 10^5 \text{ gal/person.}$$

The runoff from 10 acres is $25 \times 10^5$ gallons/year, so the United States can easily support its 1970 population density of less than 1 person per 10 acres. The $25 \times 10^5$ gallons/year produced by 10 acres of land is four times the $5.9 \times 10^5$ gallons each person uses yearly. In theory then the population density could quadruple before water supply became a problem. However, increased population density would mean more urbanization, more watershed destruction, and more water pollution, all of which would work to reduce the quantity of usable water. Conversely, increased use of recycled water or large-scale desalting of ocean water would increase the maximum possible population density.

Local population densities are in part determined by available water. The Los Angeles region was only able to achieve its present urbanized state because it tapped distant water supplies. Population densities vary widely. Nevada, for example, has less than 5 persons/square mile, or about 0.008 persons/acre, while Manhattan has 68,000 persons/square mile,[5] which is more than 100 persons/acre. This is a typical central-city density; suburban densities are from 3 to 20 people per acre. If all our land was populated to the average density of our least built-up suburbs (3 persons/ acre), we would not have sufficient water.

## An Urban Water System

Water Planning. Having established a national water context, we narrow our view and turn to a typical urban water system. Figure 2 shows the flow of water through an urban system and the way in which the different natural and man-made components of a system affect each other. For our specific example, we look at a developing metropolitan area. We assume it is still sparsely populated but that planners predict an eventual

## An Urban Water System

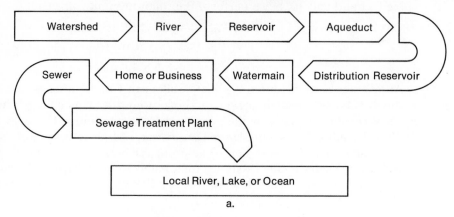

a.

## Water System Interactions

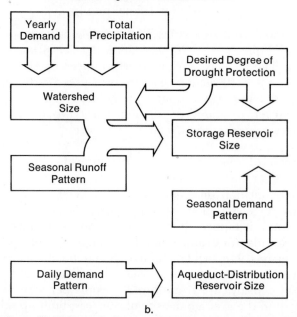

b.

**Figure 2.** a. The schematic diagram traces the course of rainfall through an urban water system from the time it falls on the watershed until it is discharged as treated sewage into a river, lake, or ocean. b. The schematic diagram shows the way in which the population's demand for water and other factors influence the size of a water system's components.

population of one million people using 150 gallons/person/day, or $5.6 \times 10^4$ gallons/person/year. The local government wishes to construct the water system before the area develops further, causing costs to soar. The watershed under consideration is 100 miles from the urban center, has an annual precipitation of 3.5 feet, and a runoff of 2.5 feet.

Most urban areas pollute their runoff and degrade their local water sources. Rain flowing over lawns, driveways, and streets picks up fertilizers, oil, grease, and deicing salts; septic systems leak sewage into ground-water sources and local streams. In addition, high population densities mean intensive use of available land so that local lakes, ponds, and marshes are covered over for housing, factories, and roads. Thus cities and their suburbs are forced to go to rural areas for their water supply. *Photo courtesy Office of Economic Opportunity.*

To determine how many square miles of watershed must be purchased to supply the projected population, we calculate the annual water needs of the $10^6$ people. Each person is assumed to use 150 gallons/day, or 20 cubic feet/day.

$$\text{water/yr} = (20 \text{ ft}^3/\text{person/day}) \ (10^6 \text{ persons}) \ (3.7 \times 10^2 \text{ days/yr})$$
$$= 7.4 \times 10^9 \text{ ft}^3/\text{yr}$$

Each square foot of the prospective watershed will produce 2.5 cubic feet of water annually. To find the total area, $A$, needed to supply $7.4 \times 10^9$ cubic feet of water per year, we use the equation

$$(\text{area}) \ (\text{runoff/yr}) = \text{water needed/yr}.$$

Since we know both the runoff/year and the water needed/year, we have

$$\text{area} = \frac{\text{water needed/yr}}{\text{runoff/yr}}$$

$$A = \frac{7.4 \times 10^9 \text{ ft}^3/\text{yr}}{2.5 \text{ ft/yr}} = 3.0 \times 10^9 \text{ ft}^2.$$

We now convert 3 billion square feet to more easily grasped units of acres and square miles.

$$A = (3.0 \times 10^9 \text{ ft}^2) \left( \frac{1 \text{ acre}}{4.4 \times 10^4 \text{ ft}^2} \right) = 6.8 \times 10^4 \text{ acres}$$

$$A = (3.0 \times 10^9 \text{ ft}^2) \left( \frac{1 \text{ mi}^2}{2.8 \times 10^7 \text{ ft}^2} \right) = 110 \text{ mi}^2$$

Then the watershed's area should be about 100 square miles. A block of land 10 miles long by 10 miles wide would have an area of 100 square miles.

**Reservoir Size.**   Having determined the watershed size as about 100 square miles, we must now calculate the necessary reservoir capacity. At first thought, it might seem that the area's reservoirs should hold a year's supply of water. While some reservoir systems do hold a year's supply, others will vary from a few months' to two years' supply. The major factors determining reservoir capacity are monthly runoff and use patterns.

Figure 3 illustrates some runoff and demand possibilities. In Figure 3a the runoff is always greater than demand and the reservoir need hold no more than a month's supply of water. In Figure 3b demand exceeds runoff in the summer months so the reservoirs must hold several months' supply to carry the region through the summer. In Figure 3c most of the runoff occurs in the spring, with water use again peaking in the summer.

**Runoff vs. Demand**

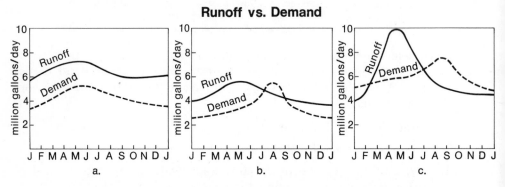

**Figure 3.**   In each diagram, the solid line is runoff and the dotted line demand, in million gallons per day. a. Runoff is always greater than demand and a small storage reservoir is needed. b. Summer demand is greater than summer runoff and a reservoir that holds a few months' water is required. c. The bulk of the runoff occurs in the spring and a reservoir holding almost a year's supply of water is needed.

This last situation is qualitatively similar to the runoff-demand relation assumed for our metropolitan area. As shown in Table 1, the watershed is assumed to produce all its runoff from March through June. Monthly

**Runoff-Demand**

| Month | Runoff | Demand | Amount in Reservoirs (at end of month) |
|-------|--------|--------|-----------------------------------------|
| January | 0 | $\frac{1}{24}$ | $\frac{1}{24}$ |
| February | 0 | $\frac{1}{24}$ | 0 |
| March | $\frac{1}{3}$ | $\frac{1}{12}$ | $\frac{3}{12} = \frac{1}{4}$ |
| April | $\frac{1}{3}$ | $\frac{1}{12}$ | $\frac{6}{12} = \frac{1}{2}$ |
| May | $\frac{1}{6}$ | $\frac{1}{12}$ | $\frac{7}{12}$ |
| June | $\frac{1}{6}$ | $\frac{1}{12}$ | $\frac{8}{12} = \frac{2}{3}$ |
| July | 0 | $\frac{1}{6}$ | $\frac{6}{12} = \frac{1}{2}$ |
| August | 0 | $\frac{1}{6}$ | $\frac{4}{12} = \frac{1}{3}$ |
| September | 0 | $\frac{1}{12}$ | $\frac{3}{12} = \frac{1}{4}$ |
| October | 0 | $\frac{1}{12}$ | $\frac{2}{12} = \frac{1}{6}$ |
| November | 0 | $\frac{1}{24}$ | $\frac{3}{24} = \frac{1}{8}$ |
| December | 0 | $\frac{1}{24}$ | $\frac{2}{24} = \frac{1}{12}$ |

**Table 1.** The above chart shows on a monthly basis the relation between runoff, demand, and water in the reservoir. All numbers are fractions of annual demand. Reservoir water peaks in June, when it contains two-thirds of the year's use of water. So the reservoir—at a minimum—must be able to hold two-thirds of a year's supply of water.

water use is assumed to vary from one twenty-fourth of annual demand for November through February to one-sixth of annual demand for July and August. The right column in Table 1 is the amount of water that would be in the storage reservoirs under these conditions. As can be seen, the total reservoir capacity would have to be two-thirds of annual demand. In the idealized model shown in Table 1, it is assumed that on February 28 the reservoirs are completely empty, with runoff beginning again on March 1. Runoff would supply more water than needed through March, April, May, and June, filling the reservoirs by the end of June. From then on, demand would draw the reservoirs down, leaving them empty by the end of February.

Of course, no system would be built with so slim a safety margin. Nor would runoff begin like clockwork on March 1 and end on June 30. Demand would also vary from year to year, with an unusually cool July or hot September causing changes in consumption. Nevertheless, this simplified model provides an example of some of the factors, runoff and demand, determining reservoir capacity.

Another factor contributing to reservoir size is the quantity of drought protection the city planners wish to build into the system. There are several ways of achieving drought protection. The most obvious approach is to have an over-sized watershed. In years of normal runoff the watershed produces more water than necessary. But in dry years, the reduced runoff may still be adequate. For example, to protect against a twenty percent drop in runoff, the 110-square-mile watershed calculated earlier would have to be twenty-five percent larger, or about 138 square miles. A second approach is to have over-sized reservoirs which can accumulate water from years of above-average runoff.

In an urban area, water use usually will drop during a drought, giving an extra margin of safety. Through coverage by newspapers and TV, many people would be moved to conserve water – in effect turning the shortage into a large urban game. This is another example of two seemingly un-related systems – water and communications – strongly interacting.

**Aqueducts.**   We now calculate the size of the next link in the water system, the aqueduct's cross-sectional area. We assume water flows through the 100-mile aqueduct at a maximum speed of 5 feet/second. To find out what the aqueduct's cross-sectional area must be, we first calculate the number of gallons the city demands per unit time. As emphasized earlier, it is not enough for the aqueduct to meet average yearly demand, as with the watershed. An aqueduct and the water-main system it feeds must satisfy the population's momentary water needs. We therefore calculate the gallons needed per second rather than per year. We start by making the unreasonable but simplifying assumption that demand is rock steady day and night, and adds up to 150 gallons/person/day. This gives a total demand of

$$\text{volume/day} = (1.5 \times 10^2 \text{ gal/person/day}) \ (10^6 \text{ persons})$$

$$= (1.5 \times 10^8 \text{ gal/day}) \left(\frac{1 \text{ ft}^3}{7.5 \text{ gal}}\right)$$

$$= 2 \times 10^7 \text{ ft}^3/\text{day}.$$

Now we will convert this answer to cubic feet/second (there are $8.6 \times 10^4$ seconds in a day).

$$\text{volume/second} = (2 \times 10^7 \text{ ft}^3/\text{day}) \left(\frac{1 \text{ day}}{8.6 \times 10^4 \text{ sec}}\right)$$

$$= 230 \text{ ft}^3/\text{sec}$$

To supply the $10^6$ people, 230 cubic feet of water must pour out of the aqueduct into the distribution mains each second. To visualize the aque-duct, think of a long square tunnel containing a solid (that is, no air spaces) tube of water. This 100-mile square tube moves along as a unit at 5 feet/second. Each second a 5-foot section of water exits from the city end of the aqueduct. The aqueduct stays full because the exiting water's place is taken at the storage-reservoir end by a similar 5-foot section. It is important to realize that once the aqueduct is filled with water, its length is irrelevant – what counts is how fast the water flows and what its cross-sectional area is. Whether the aqueduct is a mile long or a thousand miles long does not directly affect its capacity, its ability to deliver water per unit of time. The length only determines how long it takes a drop of water to get from the reservoir to the city.

This mole, or tunnel borer, is being used to bore a four-mile-long, ten-foot-diameter, concrete-lined tunnel to carry water through a mountain to Las Vegas Valley. The head of this mole turns at nine revolutions per minute and can tunnel at a rate of 600 feet a week (compared to previous human-labor output of about 125 feet a week). The two curved pads, visible behind the head, grip the tunnel walls and push the machine forward. *Photo courtesy U.S. Bureau of Reclamation.*

Let us now calculate what the aqueduct's cross-sectional area must be. Since the water is flowing at 5 feet/second, a 5-foot section will emerge from the end of the aqueduct each second:

distance = (velocity) (time) = (5 ft/sec) (1 second) = 5 feet.

This 5-foot section must have a volume of 230 cubic feet in order to supply the city. The volume, $V$, of a section of uniform cross-sectional area, $A$, is

$$V = A \times L$$

so

$$A = \frac{V}{L} = \frac{230 \text{ ft}^3}{5 \text{ ft}} = 46 \text{ ft}^2.$$

If the aqueduct is assumed to be a square of side $a$, the dimensions can be found from the formula $A = a \times a = a^2$.

$$a = \sqrt{A}$$

$$a = \sqrt{46 \text{ ft}^2} = \sqrt{46} \text{ ft} = 6.8 \text{ ft}$$

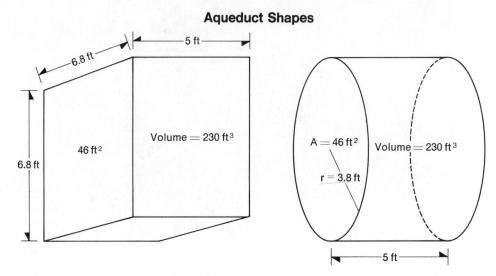

**Aqueduct Shapes**

**Figure 4.** Two "tubes" of water having different geometries but the same volume are shown here. The cross-sectional area of the cylinder is $\pi r^2$, where $\pi = 3.14$ and $r$ is the radius of 3.8 feet.

If the aqueduct is round, we must use the formula for the area of a circle, $A = \pi r^2$, to find the radius ($\pi = 3.14$).

$$r = \sqrt{\frac{A}{\pi}}$$

$$r = \sqrt{\frac{46 \text{ ft}^2}{3.14}} = \sqrt{14.6} \text{ ft} = 3.8 \text{ ft}$$

A round aqueduct, then, would have a radius of 3.8 feet, or a diameter of 7.6 feet, large enough for a man to walk through upright. Figure 4 shows the two cross-sectional shapes.

Later in this book we will apply this same kind of reasoning to solve flow problems for roads, sidewalks, oil pipelines, and so on. It can clearly be applied to a river, which can be thought of as an open aqueduct (unless you wish to think of an aqueduct as an enclosed river).

If demand fluctuates, the aqueduct problem becomes more complicated. Here we assume that the area's water mains are large enough to handle almost any demand fluctuation so we will look only at the aqueduct. Instead of the steady demand of 230 cubic feet/second assumed earlier, demand is now assumed to be 440 cubic feet/second during the peak 5 P.M. to 8 P.M. period and 200 cubic feet/second from 8 P.M. to 5 P.M. (see Figure 5). This demand situation averages out to the original 230 cubic feet/second over 24 hours.

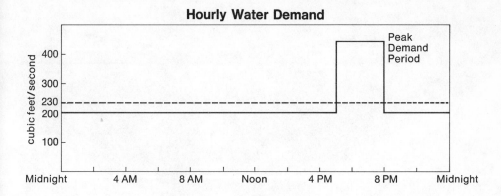

**Figure 5.** The solid line represents the hourly demand. The dotted line is the average demand. The areas under the solid line and the dotted line are the same.

If we are to meet the peak demand of 440 cubic feet/second by means of the aqueduct alone, its cross-sectional area must be almost doubled, assuming the rate of flow of the water is to remain at 5 feet/second. The expanded area, $A_e$, can be calculated using a proportion. We know that the 46-square-foot aqueduct delivers 230 cubic feet/second of water. Thus

$$\frac{230 \text{ ft}^3/\text{sec}}{440 \text{ ft}^3/\text{sec}} = \frac{46 \text{ ft}^2}{A_e}$$

so that

$$A_e = \left(\frac{440}{230}\right) (46 \text{ ft}^2) = 88 \text{ ft}^2.$$

Rather than build a much bigger aqueduct (88 square feet), the water-system engineers may stay with the 46-square-foot aqueduct and build instead an in-city distribution reservoir. To calculate the capacity needed for a distribution reservoir, we note that from 8 P.M. to 5 P.M. (21 hours) the demand is only 200 cubic feet/second and the aqueduct can deliver 230 cubic feet/second. The extra 30 cubic feet/second can be stored in the distribution reservoir until needed during the peak hours. To store this water the reservoir capacity must be

capacity $= (30 \text{ ft}^3/\text{sec}) \ (21 \text{ hr}) \ (3600 \text{ sec/hr}) = 2.3 \times 10^6 \text{ ft}^3.$

During the three-hour peak period this accumulated water must be fed out at a rate of 210 cubic feet/second so that, added to the aqueduct's 230 cubic feet/second, the 440-cubic-feet-per-second peak demand will be met. At the end of the three-hour period the reservoir will be empty since

$V = (210 \text{ ft}^3/\text{sec}) \ (3 \text{ hr}) \ (3600 \text{ sec/hr}) = 2.3 \times 10^6 \text{ ft}^3.$

This 1893 photograph shows a central-city distribution reservoir. It stood at Fifth Avenue and 42nd Street in Manhattan, a site now occupied by the New York Public Library. *Photo courtesy The New-York Historical Society.*

But at 8 P.M. – in our model – demand drops back to 200 cubic feet/second and the aqueduct overflow begins to refill the empty distribution reservoir.

The 2.3-million-cubic-foot reservoir is a large one to fit into a city. One way to visualize it is to think of a swimming pool about an acre in area (200 feet by 200 feet) and 60 feet deep. Accordingly, economic considerations may require it to be placed somewhere between the main storage reservoir and the city, with a 88-square-foot aqueduct leading from the distribution reservoir to the city.

An additional complication to our simplified model for building an aqueduct is caused by seasonal variation in demand. Our 150-gallons/person/day figure is the average of the entire year's use of water. But average daily summer use may be two or three times higher than average daily winter use. Since now we are talking about a month or more of above-average use, the problem cannot be solved by building a small distribution reservoir holding one or two days' supply of water. Instead, a large aqueduct capable of at least meeting average, daily, hot-weather demand must be constructed. The distribution reservoir can then be used to average out the hot-weather flow, keeping the aqueduct from having to be even larger than average summer demand dictates.

An obvious question is this: Why not move the water through the aqueduct at, let's say, 10 feet/second? The same size aqueduct could then deliver twice as much water per second as at 5 feet/second because a 10-foot length of water would flow out of the aqueduct each second instead of a 5-foot length. Once more we are faced with the problem of balancing benefits and costs. A higher speed would permit a smaller cross section or elimination of a distribution reservoir and thus achieve savings. But the higher speed would mean more wear on the tunnel walls by the rushing water. So the smaller tunnel might require tougher walls, or a friction-reducing coating, and both would cost money. More rapid flow might also require more powerful pumps and therefore consume more electricity per unit of water delivered. The higher speeds would also need larger, stronger valving to control the water. We are accustomed to seeing water placidly flowing out of a faucet or past us in a stream. But in the aqueduct, a 100-mile length of water moves along at 5 to 10 feet per second. Slowing or stopping this mass of water is a difficult job. If the operators tried to stop the flow by slamming a valve closed somewhere in the aqueduct, the valve and possibly the aqueduct itself would be ripped apart by the resulting shock wave (what is called a water hammer[6]). The higher the speed, the more difficult the control problem becomes.

Water hammers occur on a reduced scale in some homes. The sharp knock heard when a faucet is abruptly closed results from the shock wave sent through the pipe by the rapid stopping of the water flow. If the plumbing has been put in properly, however, it will have an air cushion (see Figure 6) and water hammers will not occur. A different problem results if the home builder skimped and installed water pipe whose diameter is too small. In that case, the water will move at a high speed through the pipes, causing a great deal of noise. If larger diameter pipe had been installed, the same volume/minute flow of water would be achieved at lower – and quieter – speeds.

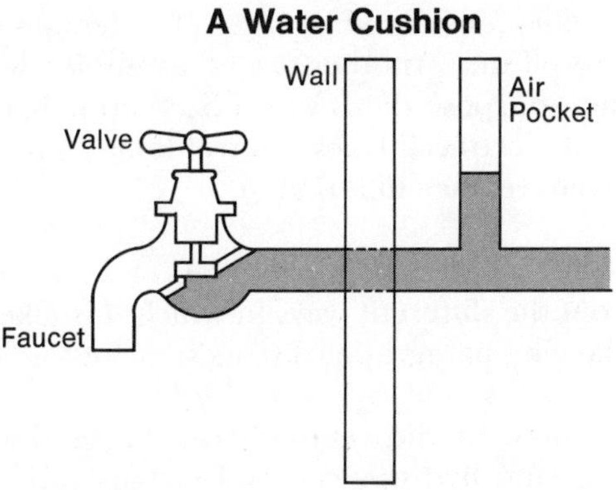

**A Water Cushion**

**Figure 6.** The vertical pipe with its pocket of air prevents water hammers because air is more compressible than water. Like most of our plumbing, this water cushion is hidden behind a wall.

In the above discussion we have outlined the relation between aqueduct size and patterns of daily demand. This is primarily an economic problem; there is no physical reason the aqueducts cannot be made as large or as small as wanted. Economics – which is a vital consideration in all physical systems – can create some interesting problems and solutions. If, for example, the storage reservoirs are close to the city, an in-city distribution reservoir or tank may be more expensive than a fat aqueduct. This is because urban land for the distribution reservoir will be expensive while the extra cost of the larger aqueduct depends on both the extra cross-sectional area and the length. For a short aqueduct, the extra cost will therefore be low.

If the aqueduct is long, then a distribution reservoir will probably make economic sense. But even here, high, in-city land costs may dictate placing the distribution reservoir outside the city. Let's assume we are dealing with a 200-mile aqueduct. If land increases in cost as you approach the city, it may turn out that the cheapest solution is to build the distribution reservoir 50 miles from the city, which would require the aqueduct to be average-sized for 150 miles and then large enough to meet peak demand for the 50 miles from the distribution reservoir to the city. If the reservoir were built closer to the city, the extra land costs would outweigh the savings in aqueduct construction. If the reservoir were moved further out, the savings in land costs would be less than the cost of the longer, large aqueduct. Physical considerations, such as an available site for the reservoir or an already existing lake which could be used to store the water, could also enter the picture.

## Dams: Their Effects and Side Effects

To this point, we have looked primarily at the direct effect of a water system: the collecting, storing, and distribution of water. But it is almost an axiom of modern technology that the desired effects of a physical system are often smaller than the undesired effects. The interaction of urbanization with water systems considered in Chapter 2 demonstrates several instances of these side effects. Another set of examples is provided by dams. The giant, multipurpose dams which back up millions of acre-feet of water create immense artificial lakes, control floods, and alter the ecology, landscape, and even weather in a region.

Planned Uses.   The prime effect of a dam is to back up a lake behind it. The multi-purposes result from the different ways in which this lake and its water can be used. The following paragraphs discuss some of the many ways a dam is used.

*Water Storage.*   The water stored in the reservoir can be used when needed for irrigation, drinking, and hydropower, and not just when the river is flowing.

*Hydropower.*   The dam creates a height difference between the top of the reservoir and the continuation of the river below the dam. In effect, the gradual drop of the river is concentrated at the dam (see Figure 7). This makes possible the large-scale use of the falling water at the dam to spin turbines and generate electricity. The alternative is to put hundreds of waterwheels into the river to tap the energy of the flowing water along the river's length.

The electric power generated by a dam is proportional to the product of

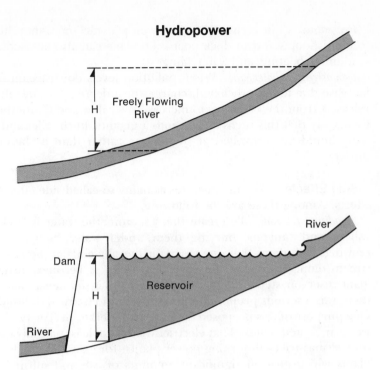

**Figure 7.** The freely flowing river in the top diagram is shown again in the lower diagram after it has been backed up behind a dam. The slope, or steepness, of the river is greatly exaggerated in the illustrations. But the principle is valid: dams concentrate at the dam itself the height drop (*H*) that originally occurred over the river's entire length. The height drop provides the energy to generate electricity.

the weight, *w*, of water flowing through the turbines per second and the height, *H*, through which this water falls.

$$\text{Power} \propto (w)\,(H)$$

Later we will derive an equation which lets us calculate the horsepower or kilowatt rating of a dam. But for now we note that a 200-foot-high dam generates twice the power a 100-foot-high dam generates, assuming the same flow of water. Of course, dams cannot be made arbitrarily high. Their height is constrained by the drop of the river and the existence of a suitable valley for flooding. A river flowing through a broad flat region cannot be dammed without flooding a huge area.

*Flood Control.*   A dam can prevent the downstream portion of the river from overflowing its banks by holding flood waters in its reservoir. The water is released only as fast as the river can carry it away without flooding. The reservoir, of course, must have sufficient capacity to store the flood waters.

*Recreation.*   The creation of a reservoir provides more shoreline on which to build homes and to dock boats. The lake can also be used for fishing, swimming, boating, and waterskiing.

*Downstream Abatement.*   When pollution levels downstream from a dam increase due to extra-heavy discharges or a decreased water flow, water is released from the reservoir to increase river flow and dilute the pollution. Critics say that this turns a river into a gigantic flush toilet and that pollution should be controlled at the source rather than by building a dam upriver.

**Side Effects.**   A dam generates as many so-called side effects as desired effects. Among these are the following.

*Flooding of Land.*   To create the reservoir, the water is backed up into valleys and canyons, burying them under water. Some rivers are so crowded with dams that one reservoir literally ends at the base of the up-stream dam, destroying the river as a river. It becomes instead a set of giant reservoir steps. The drive to dam rivers is so intense that at one time there was a serious proposal to flood the Grand Canyon by building a dam. One purpose of this proposed dam was to generate electricity for the south-western United States. That electricity is now at least partially generated by several massive coal-burning power plants (for example, the Four Corners Plant) which give off significant amounts of ash and sulfur dioxide.[7] So one environmental and esthetic problem was avoided and another resulted.

*Increased Water Temperatures.*   Reservoirs have a much greater surface area than do freely flowing rivers. A large amount of solar energy is therefore absorbed and causes the water temperature to rise. This increased water temperature can destroy fish and plant species that once lived in the river.

*Increased Evaporation.*   In a reservoir, the larger surface areas and higher temperatures increase the amount of evaporation, causing greater water loss than when the river ran free. However, what water remains is available when wanted, not just when the river is running heavy.

*Alteration of the Ecology.*   The transformation of a section of a river into a lake changes the existing ecological balance. One of the most spectacular effects is the explosive growth in some reservoirs of aquatic weeds (for example, the water hyacinth). Especially in warm regions, these weeds can grow so thick that they block navigation and increase water evaporation by almost a factor of four[8] over what would occur from the uninfested reservoir. In the United States it is estimated that aquatic weeds in reservoirs and irrigation ditches evaporate enough water to irrigate 750,000 acres[9] of farmland. Often the weeds are fought by spraying them with chemical herbicides, which causes the additional problem of pollution.

The river's fish population is also affected by construction of the dam. The dams present physical barriers to the migration of fish such as salmon,

The concrete arch Yellowtail Dam backs up 1.3 million acre-feet of irrigation water into 71 miles of Bighorn River Canyon in south central Montana. The 525-foot-high dam can generate 250,000 kilowatts from the powerhouse visible at the base of the dam. *Photo courtesy U.S. Bureau of Reclamation.*

although this can be partially compensated for by construction of fish ladders. An additional threat to fish occurs because water flowing over dams can become supersaturated with nitrogen. This causes fish downstream to get the bends (too much nitrogen in the bloodstream), which kills them.

*Lost Recreation.* The damming of a river destroys fishing for those who like river fishing and destroys canoeing and raft trips. At the same time, the dam creates recreation opportunities for those who like lake fishing, motor boating, and water skiing. It is impossible to be quantitative and scientific about this change in recreation opportunity. It is a matter of values, with some preferring lakes and others preferring rivers. We shall see that many — perhaps all — of the environmental-technological problems we face involve these questions of personal value, as when we are faced with a choice between energy and clean air, or mobility and low noise levels, or electricity and the Grand Canyon.

Silting. The most serious threat to reservoirs is silt, or sediment. Rivers carry large quantities of sand, pebbles, and organic matter. A portion of the material is scoured out of the river channel, but most is washed off the land by runoff. Some rivers receive thousands of tons of sediment annually from each square mile of watershed.

The fine material is carried along in suspension while heavier matter, such as pebbles, is pushed along the riverbed as bottom load. The greater the river's speed, the more sediment it can carry. When the river moves swiftly, as in steep mountain valleys, the sediment stays in suspension. But when the river descends to the less steep lowlands, its speed decreases and some sediment drops out of suspension and settles to the river bottom. The settling is especially large where the river enters the ocean: here the marked slowing and a chemical reaction with the salt water result in deposition of whatever sediment and bottom load the river still carries. Some of this material goes into building a river delta. The rest is carried away by currents which move parallel to the ocean coast.

But if the river is dammed, the sediment never reaches the delta or ocean coast. The drastic slowing in speed that occurs when the river reaches the reservoir causes the sediment to drop out of the water. As sediment accumulates in the reservoir, its ability to store water is reduced. Eventually—in a period varying from a few years to many centuries—the reservoir becomes completely filled with sediment. It is transformed into an alluvial plain, with its volume occupied by sand, gravel, and decaying organic matter. The river still flows through the reservoir, but since the reservoir has lost its storage volume, that flow cannot be stored. The alluvial plain will contain a large amount of ground water, but this water can only be obtained by pumping.

The rate at which a reservoir loses storage volume depends on the amount of sediment carried by the river flowing into it. This in turn depends on the type of land drained by the river. In general, forests yield very little sediment while farmland and urban areas yield a great deal. In terms of volume, sedimentary yield varies from less than an acre-foot to eighty acre-feet per year per square mile of watershed. At one extreme is the Columbia River in the Northwest, which carries so little silt it will take centuries before its reservoirs begin to lose storage volume. At the other extreme is the Bennington Reservoir in Rago, Kansas. It loses five percent[10] of its storage capacity yearly, giving it a twenty-year lifetime.

In between are Norris Reservoir in Tennessee, which loses 0.05 percent[11] of its capacity yearly, and Lake Mead on the Colorado River, which until 1964 lost about 0.3 percent[12] of its capacity each year. In 1964 Glen Canyon Dam was completed upriver of Lake Mead, and it now traps the sediment which formerly entered Lake Mead. To get some idea of the amount of sediment involved, note that the Grand Canyon (from 4 to 18 miles wide, 1 mile deep, and 217 miles long) was cut away by the Colorado River and carried to the ocean as sediment. In addition, of course, the Colorado also carried material washed off the land by runoff.

**Downstream Effects.** Although sediment is invariably fatal to reservoirs, its downstream effects are more mixed. On some rivers, the upstream trapping of sediment reduces flooding. This occurs because sediment deposition can raise the level of a riverbed, making the channel shallower, thereby increasing the likelihood of flooding and of a river abruptly changing course to cut a new channel. The Mississippi, a very muddy river, is famous for its massive wanderings and its shifting channel. When sediment is trapped behind an upriver dam, the problem is reduced.

The trapping of sediment can also cause problems downstream of the reservoir. In the United States, the most noticeable effect has been on the California coast. Inland dams have reduced the flow of sand to this coast. But ocean, or littoral, currents still move along the coast, continually rearranging sand deposits. Before the dams were built, the currents brought sand from the river mouths to replace the sand carried away into offshore submarine canyons; now they only carry sand away from the beaches. To preserve the beaches, government agencies often dredge sand from offshore and deposit it on denuded areas. Or the coast may be fortified by building rock or concrete walls out into the ocean. This, however, usually increases erosion on some other section of the beach, forcing construction of still more fortifications. So building dams can lead to intervention with natural processes on beaches hundreds of miles from the dams.

The construction of Egypt's Aswan Dam on the Nile River has caused very serious problems. Lack of the 134 million tons[13] of sediment the Nile formerly carried to the Mediterranean Sea each year has resulted in widespread coastal erosion. The sediment trapped behind the Aswan Dam also contains a large amount of organic matter which formerly nourished large numbers of Mediterranean fish. Before construction of the dam, fishermen caught 18,000 tons of fish each year. After the dam was completed the catch dropped to 500 tons[14] per year. Downstream of the Aswan Dam the Nile moves quickly because it no longer carries a burden of sediment. As a result of this high speed, it is eroding the river channel and endangering the existence of hundreds of bridges and other riverside structures. About $250 million will be required to protect the bridges and riverbed against this erosion.

**River and Reservoir Flow Speed.**   The cause of these many problems is the drastic loss of the water's sediment-carrying ability due to the slowing of the river when it reaches the reservoir. The following example provides a quantitative illustration of this slowing. In Figure 8, a 100-foot-wide river is shown flowing into a reservoir 2000 feet wide, 10,000 feet long, and 40 feet deep. The river has an average depth of 10 feet and a speed of 6 feet/second. Its flow is therefore

$$\text{volume/second} = (100 \text{ ft})(10 \text{ ft})(6 \text{ ft/sec}) = 6000 \text{ ft}^3/\text{sec}.$$

On the average, water flows out of the reservoir through the dam at the same rate. The reservoir can therefore be thought of as a broad, deep,

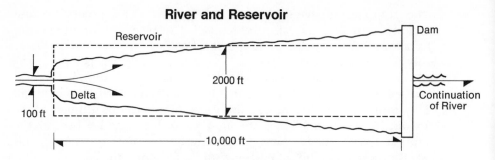

**Figure 8.** The river flows at 6 feet/second and is 10-feet deep. It flows into a reservoir which is 40-feet deep. A delta forms in the reservoir at the point the sediment-laden river meets the reservoir. The water flowing out of the reservoir is largely free of sediment.

slowly moving river. To calculate the speed at which the water flows through it, we note that its cross-sectional area is

$$A = (2000 \text{ ft}) \ (40 \text{ ft}) = 80{,}000 \text{ ft}^2.$$

To achieve a flow of 6000 cubic feet/second requires a reservoir speed, $v$, of

$$v = \frac{\text{volume/second}}{\text{cross-sectional area}} = \frac{(6 \times 10^3 \text{ ft}^3/\text{sec})}{(8 \times 10^4 \text{ ft}^2)}$$
$$= 7.5 \times 10^{-2} \text{ ft/sec} = 0.075 \text{ ft/sec}.$$

At this slow speed the sediment-carrying capacity of the water is reduced to zero. Most of the material will be dumped where the river meets the reservoir, forming a delta in the reservoir. It is possible, however, to design the reservoir and dam so that there are swifter moving channels that distribute the sediment throughout the reservoir and even move some of it through openings in the dam.

**Sedimentation and Lake Mead.** Before construction of Glen Canyon Dam, Lake Mead received the sediment from 170,000 square miles of watershed. On the average, each square mile yielded 880 tons[15] of sediment annually. Almost all of this material remained in the 31-million-acre-foot reservoir (see Figure 9[16]). The annual weight, $w$, of sediment carried annually into Lake Mead was

$$w = (8.8 \times 10^2 \text{ tons/mi}^2) \ (2 \times 10^3 \text{ lb/ton}) \ (1.7 \times 10^5 \text{ mi}^2)$$
$$= 3.1 \times 10^{11} \text{ lb}.$$

The important factor is not the weight but the volume the material takes up in the reservoir. This is a tricky question because the sediment contains organic matter which gradually decays. In addition, the bottom sediment is compressed as new sediment accumulates on top of it, so the occupied volume changes with time. On the average, it can be assumed that each

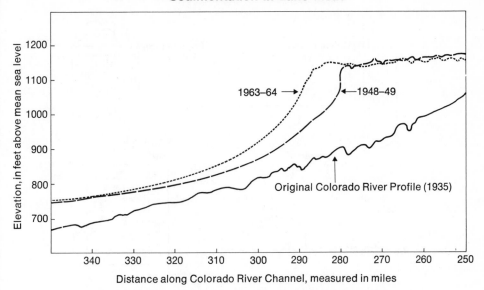

**Figure 9.** A cross section of Lake Mead is shown in this graph. The solid line is the original profile of the Colorado River prior to its flooding. The two dotted lines show the profiles in 1948–1949 and 1963–1964 due to the accumulation of sediment. Note the delta that has formed on the right, where the Colorado first enters the lake.

70 pounds of sediment occupies 1 cubic foot (70 pounds/cubic foot). The volume, $V$, occupied by a year's supply of sediment is

$$V = \frac{(3.1 \times 10^{11} \text{ lb})}{(70 \text{ lb/ft}^3)} = 4.4 \times 10^9 \text{ ft}^3$$

$$= \frac{(4.4 \times 10^9 \text{ ft}^3)}{(4.4 \times 10^4 \text{ ft}^3/\text{acre-ft})} = 10^5 \text{ acre-feet.}$$

The total volume of Lake Mead is $31 \times 10^6$ acre-feet, so the percent of volume lost to sediment annually is

$$\frac{(10^5 \text{ acre-feet})}{(3.1 \times 10^7 \text{ acre-feet})} = 0.32 \times 10^{-2} = 0.32\%.$$

This means Lake Mead originally lost about 1 percent of its volume every 3 years, giving it a lifetime of 3 centuries. Construction of Glen Canyon Dam extended this lifetime by approximately 500 years.

## Ground Water

Until now we have ignored ground water and concentrated on the more visible and more easily quantified surface water. But ground water is both important and abundant, as Figure 10[17] shows. In fact, 98 percent of the

## An Annual Water Budget for the World

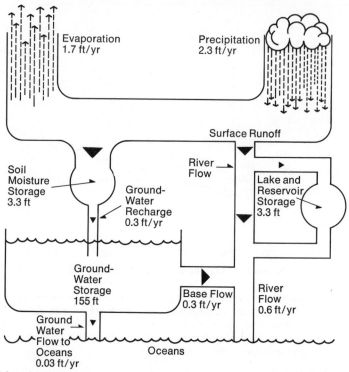

Adapted by permission of *Technology Review.* Copyright 1972, Alumni Association of Massachusetts Institute of Technology.

**Figure 10.** The numbers above apply to average worldwide conditions on land. For example, the equivalent of 0.6 feet spread over the world's surface area flows via rivers to the oceans each year. If all of the world's ground water were spread over the surface, it would cover the land to a depth of 155 feet, but the water stored in lakes and reservoirs would only accumulate to a depth of 3.3 feet. Base flow refers to the flow of ground water into surface streams and rivers.

world's fresh water is found underground. In the United States 20 percent[18] of all water used is pumped from underground, and indications are that this percentage will grow. U.S. man-made reservoirs have a capacity of 1 billion acre-feet and natural lakes hold another 13 billion acre-feet,[19] but recoverable ground-water reserves are thought to be about 75 billion acre-feet.[20]

While there is a large amount of ground water, it is by no means limitless. Many communities have pumped ground water out at too high a rate, exhausting their supply and sometimes causing other problems. In Mexico City, ground-water removal has caused the ground to sink, endangering many buildings. In San Jose, California, land has subsided up to four feet due to ground-water removal. In Brooklyn, New York, which borders the Atlantic Ocean, excessive ground-water removal resulted in salt water from the ocean seeping inland, destroying the well water.

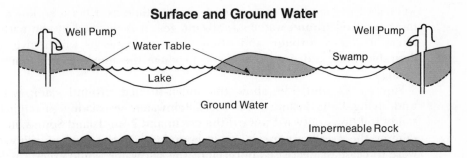

**Figure 11.** The ground water shows itself at the surface as a lake and swamp. The two pumps shown have lowered the water table in their vicinity. If enough ground water is pumped out, the water table would drop, causing the swamp to dry up and lowering the water level of the lake.

Ground water can be thought of as an extension of surface water. If you dig a hole near a lake or ocean, you will, sooner or later, hit water. The top of the water in the hole will be on about the same level as the ocean or lake surface. The top of the ground water is called the water table. Most lakes, swamps, and springs are places where the water table intersects the earth's surface (see Figure 11).

Ground water originates as rainwater filtering down through the soil (a process called percolation) until it reaches the water table. The ground water mixes with underground material, occupying the pores, or empty spaces, in sand, gravel, limestone, and other matter: a loose material like sand may be as much as twenty-five percent water;[21] compact substances contain less water.

In some cases, ground and surface water are indistinguishable. It is ground water that keeps some rivers and lakes from drying up during periods of no rainfall and therefore no runoff. These rivers and lakes are maintained by so-called base flow, which is the flow of ground water into stream and lake beds. If a drought is long lasting, however, the water table will drop and the base flow diminish or cease. This will cause the lakes, rivers, and streams to dry up.

**Ground-Water Movement.** The ground water does not just sit underground. It is a dynamic system: water seeps underground through a mountainous region, eventually flowing to the surface, or moves totally underground to the salt water underlying coastal regions. The rate of flow is leisurely, varying from a few feet a day to a few feet a year, depending on the steepness of the underground water "bed" and the resistance of the material through which the water is moving. It takes ground water an average of 400 years[22] to make a land-to-ocean trip. By contrast, surface water flowing in rivers will make the same trip in a matter of weeks. Even surface water which passes through a series of lakes will make the land-ocean trip in as short a time as a decade. The slow movement of ground water has advantages. It is purified by the natural filters it passes through and often picks up minerals which give it a desirable taste and, in a few cases, produce the much-desired mineral springs.

Figures 12 and 13[23] show the much-studied ground-water system underlying Long Island, New York. Rainwater percolating through the sandy soil flows outward toward the ocean and Long Island Sound, maintaining the fresh water-salt water boundary. If the flow of rainwater were to cease or decrease appreciably, the salt water would creep further inland. Because salt water is 2.5 percent denser than fresh water, the fresh water floats on the salt water. Ground water supplies the eastern Long Island counties of Suffolk and Nassau with all of their water. But the western Long Island counties of Brooklyn and Queens overpumped their wells around the turn of the century. As a result, the water table dropped and salt water moved in, ruining the underground reservoir, or aquifer, in that region.

## Ground Water in Long Island

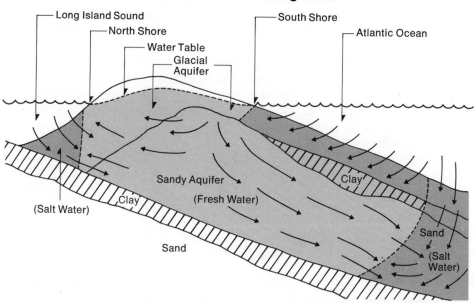

Adapted by permission of *Technology Review*. Copyright 1972, Alumni Association of MIT.

**Figure 12.**   A cross section of Long Island's underground water system is shown here. Especially important is the boundary between the salt water and the fresh water. If the salt water moves inland, ground water supplies will be destroyed. Keeping the salt water out depends on there being a continuing flow of fresh ground water outward. The dashed lines show the progress of the salt water if the ground water is overpumped or there is insufficient flow of fresh water.

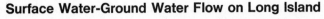

## Surface Water-Ground Water Flow on Long Island

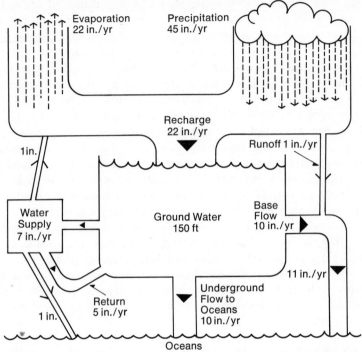

Adapted by permission of *Technology Review.* Copyright 1972, Alumni Association of MIT.

**Figure 13.**  This diagram shows annual water flow on Long Island. On the average, 45 inches of precipitation fall each year, 22 inches evaporate, 22 inches sink underground, and 1 inch runs off aboveground. The underground water supply would cover the island to a depth of 150 feet if it were all brought to the surface.

**Tapping Ground Water.**  Ground water is removed by drilling a well to a depth below the water table. Water seeps into the well hole through its walls and sits there until it is pumped out. If a great deal of water is removed in a short time, the water table near the well may drop because the water cannot flow through the soil quickly enough to keep the well supplied. A larger diameter, deeper well, or slower pumping will solve that problem. A more serious difficulty occurs when so much water is removed from underground that the entire water table drops. If it is in a coastal region, salt water may invade. In any case, deeper wells will have to be drilled into new, water-bearing underground regions, or surface sources will have to be found.

If ground water is removed no faster than rainwater percolates into the soil, the water supply will last indefinitely. However, anyone who owns land can drill a well, and many areas find it difficult to keep use on a self-sustaining basis. In addition, as an area becomes developed, water demand increases, and less and less surface is available for the water to seep into. Instead of soaking into soil, the rain and melted snow flow quickly over streets and sidewalks into gutters and storm sewers which lead to a local lake or stream. To solve this problem, some communities dig recharge basins, or recharge ditches, in which the water is allowed to stand until it penetrates the soil. Another solution is to simply pump the used water back into the ground through deep recharge wells.

Many communities do not recharge their underground aquifers because even treated sewage may contaminate the ground water. There are also other sources of contamination. Rainwater seeping underground may carry lawn and farm fertilizers, pesticides, and other chemicals picked up on the surface. Buried garbage may leach into the ground water. Significant amounts of road deicing salts have been found in some water deposits. In certain areas, highly toxic chemical waste is disposed of by deep-well injection. Efforts are made to ensure that the strata into which the materials are discharged do not connect with strata used as sources of drinking water, but such mixing is possible since underground maps are far from complete or accurate. Strip mining, in which the land is dug up by huge bulldozers to obtain the underlying coal, often disrupts the water table and may cause wells to run dry or become muddy and useless. Strip mining also greatly increases the amount of sediment produced by the land.

**Flooded Basements.**   Ground water can threaten as well as be threatened. In periods of heavy rain, the water table may rise. If it reaches to within ten feet of the surface, it will seep into homes with basements. An unfortunately typical example is presented by Suffolk County, Long Island, which has thousands of chronically flooded basements. The trouble resulted because a drought during the 1960s caused water tables throughout the county to drop. Rainfall, which had previously averaged 45 inches a year, was 37, 37, 27, and 35 inches from 1963 to 1966, respectively. Some assumed the resulting 6-foot drop in the water table was permanent and the building codes in many towns in the county permitted basement floors in new homes to come within two feet of this lower water table.

The towns were implicitly assuming that rainfall would remain at 1963–1966 levels and that increased use of ground water by the growing population would cause the water table to drop even more. Residents and town officials at the time were more worried about a ground-water shortage and a resulting invasion of fresh water by salt water than about a rising water table. But from 1967 to 1971, rainfall was between 36 and 50 inches. When it was topped off in 1972 by a record 55 inches, the resultant rise in the water table flooded the basements of thousands of homes. Areas that had a more conservative building code — requiring basement floors to be at least 18 inches above the highest recorded water table — had comparatively little trouble. Figure 13 shows the average flow of ground water and surface water on Long Island.

## Bibliography

*Source Notes*

1. *Statistical Abstract of the United States, 1971.* Washington, D.C.: U.S. Government Printing Office.

2. *Water Resources and the National Welfare.* Walter U. Garstka. Walter U. Garstka (Route 1, Pine, Colorado 80470), 1974.

3. Ibid.

4. *Statistical Abstract, 1971.*

5. *Plan for New York City,* vol. iv. New York City Planning Commission. New York Department of City Planning, 1969.

6. *McGraw-Hill Encyclopedia of Science and Technology,* vol. 14. New York: McGraw-Hill, 1971.

7. *Problems of Electric Power Production in the Southwest.* Hearings Before the Committee on Interior and Insular Affairs, U.S. Senate. Washington, D.C.: U.S. Government Printing Office, 1971.

8. "Aquatic Weeds." L. G. Holm; L. W. Weldon; R. D. Blackburn. *Science,* vol. 166 (November 1969), pp. 699–709.

9. Ibid.

10. *The Water Encyclopedia.* David K. Todd, ed. Port Washington, New York: Water Information Center, 1970.

11. Ibid.

12. Ibid.

13. *Water Resources and the National Welfare.*

14. Ibid.

15. *Handbook of Applied Hydrology.* Van Te Chow, ed. New York: McGraw-Hill, 1964.

16. *The 1963–64 Lake Mead Survey.* J. M. Lara and J. I. Sanders. Denver, Colorado: U.S. Department of Interior, Bureau of Reclamation, 1970.

17. "The Aqueous Underground." Lynn W. Gelhar. *Technology Review,* March/April 1972, pp. 45–53.

18. Ibid.     20. Ibid.     22. Ibid.

19. Ibid.     21. Ibid.     23. Ibid.

*Further Reading*

MARION CLAWSON; HANS H. LANDSBERG; LYLE T. ALEXANDER.   "Desalted Seawater for Agriculture: Is It Economic?" *Science,* vol. 164 (January 1969), pp. 1141–1148. This article presents a hard-nosed look at the technology, economics, and environmental impact of desalted seawater.

JERRY H. HUBSCHMAN. "Lake Erie: Pollution Abatement, Then What?" *Science,* vol. 171 (February 1971), pp. 536–540.

This article discusses the possibility of putting the pollution of Lake Erie to good account by harvesting the intense biological activity resulting from the large inputs of sewage and other pollutants.

ROY MANN. *Rivers in the City.* New York: Praeger Publishers, 1973.

Mann's book is a well-illustrated survey of several urban rivers and how they affect and are affected by their surroundings.

M. GORDON WOLMAN. "The Nation's Rivers." *Science,* vol. 174 (November 1971), pp. 905–918.

This article presents a comprehensive survey of the factors (for example, dissolved solids, sediment, urban trash, pesticides, waste heat) that affect the quality of the nation's rivers.

GALE YOUNG. "Dry Lands and Desalted Water." *Science,* vol. 167 (January 1970), pp. 339–343.

Young takes an optimistic look at the economics, technology, and environmental impact of using desalted water for agriculture in dry lands.

## Problems and Questions

1. Toledo, Ohio, has 400,000 residents spread over 86 square miles.
   a. What is the population density per square mile and per acre?
   b. Assume Toledo's sewage treatment plants are just capable of handling the water produced by the city's residents, who use 150 gallons/person/day. If $\frac{1}{4}$ inch of rain falls on the city in a day, and the city's sewers mix rainwater with sewage, how much additional water would that dump into the sewage system? By what factor would the city's sewage treatment plants have to be expanded if they were to handle the mix of sewage and rainwater produced during such a day?
   c. Can you think of solutions other than construction of larger treatment plants?

2. The Wanaque Reservoir in New Jersey has a capacity of $2.8 \times 10^{10}$ gallons and occupies an area of 2300 acres.
   a. Calculate its average depth.
   b. Using the data on evaporation (see Chapter 2, Table 5) for New Jersey, calculate the number of gallons the reservoir would gain or lose in an average year due to the combined effect of evaporation and direct precipitation. Assume precipitation is 44 inches/year.
   c. Explain qualitatively how the answer to part b would change if the reservoir's depth was doubled and area halved. Does that mean the reservoir should be as broad and shallow as possible?

3. The text states that if a city with a 110-square-mile watershed wishes to protect itself against a 20% drop in runoff, it needs a watershed 25% larger, or 138 square miles. Show that this is true.

4. Assume a suburban area has an average density of 10 people per acre and 2 feet of runoff yearly. Can the area get enough water from its own land if consumption is 195 gallons/person/day?

5. Why must we work with gallons per year when watershed size is being calculated but gallons per second when aqueduct size is being calculated?

6. The text states that a demand of 440 cubic feet/second from 5 P.M. to 8 P.M. and of 200 cubic feet/second from 8 P.M. to 5 P.M. averages out to 230 cubic feet/second. Show that this is so. (See Figure 5.)

7. What is the diameter of a round pipe having an 88-square-foot cross-sectional area?

8. What is the diameter of a round pipe having a 44-square-foot cross-sectional area?

9. Assume the soil in an area is such that water seeps into it at a rate of 1 foot per day. This means that if the ground were covered with water to a depth of 1 foot and the water did not flow off, it would completely infiltrate the ground after 24 hours.
   a. What is the maximum rainfall in inches per hour that can fall on the area without water accumulating?
   b. Assume the area is urbanized so that 75% of it is covered with roads, parking lots, homes, and so on. What is the maximum rainfall that can now occur without flooding or accumulation?

10. How large a river would it take to supply the 17 million people in the New York metropolitan area with their per-person needs of 150 gallons/day? Assume the river flows at 8 feet/second and has an average depth of 20 feet.

11. Average U.S. runoff is 0.75 feet and total U.S. area is 3.6 million square miles.
    a. Calculate the average number of gallons available to each U.S. resident daily, assuming a population of 200 million persons.
    b. Assuming use stays at its present figure of 1600 gallons/person/day, what is the nation's maximum population?

12. It takes about 33 gallons of cooling water to make 1 kilowatt-hour of electricity (enough to run a color TV for 2 hours). Three-fourths of a gallon of this water evaporates; the rest is returned in a heated state to the river or lake. It is predicted that electric power use will double every 10 years for the foreseeable future.
    a. If in 1970 steam electric plants produced 1300 billion kilowatt-hours of electricity, what percentage of 1970 runoff water was used to make electricity?
    b. What percentage of runoff will be used as coolant in the year 2000?

13. Because its well water is contaminated, a farm commune of 10 persons wishes to use rain barrels to collect and store drinking and cooking water. They plan to collect the water running off their farmhouse and barn roofs. Total precipitation in their region is 3 feet, and they estimate almost all of the water that hits the roofs will be collected. The roofs are flat with a total area of 1000 square feet.

a. How much water will they have per person per day? Will this be sufficient?
b. Would they collect more water if the buildings were covered with slanted rather than flat roofs? (A slanted roof covering the same building has a greater area than a flat roof.)

14. Three families in a rural area get household water from a spring which runs steadily at 2 gallons/minute. If each family uses 200 gallons/day, what capacity collecting tank, or reservoir, should they install to ensure an adequate supply? To minimize expense, they want to put in the smallest tank that will do the job. You must make some assumptions about use patterns.

15. Calculate the watershed area required by the metropolitan region of Denver (1.2 million people) if runoff from its watershed averages 2.5 feet annually. Assume per-person use is 150 gallons/day.

16. New York City gets its 1.8 billion gallons/day from three sources: the Croton system, the Catskill system, and the Delaware system. The Catskill system contributes about 555 million gallons/day and drains a 570-square-mile watershed.
a. Calculate how much water the Catskill system delivers in a year.
b. If the amount of water found in part a is equal to the annual runoff from the Catskill watershed, how many feet of runoff does it generate?
c. Assume all runoff occurs in March, April, and May. Making some reasonable assumptions, calculate what the capacity of the Catskill-system reservoirs should be.
d. What cross-sectional area aqueduct is needed to carry 555 million gallons/day if the water moves at 4 feet/second?

17. The average annual flow of the Colorado River is 14 million acre-feet.
a. How many people would that provide with municipal water?
b. Lake Mead was formed when the Hoover Dam, constructed in 1935, blocked the Colorado River. The lake is 115 miles long, has an average width of 4 miles, and contains 31 million acre-feet of water. Calculate its average depth.

18. Assume that in the years after completion of the Hoover Dam, the Colorado flowed at 14 million acre-feet per year. If 10 million acre-feet were used for irrigation water each year and the rest was allowed to remain in the lake, how long did it take to fill Lake Mead?

19. Assuming yearly evaporation from Lake Mead is 6 feet, estimate its yearly water loss.

20. Assume Lake Mead gets about 6 inches of rain annually. What percentage of its stored water (31 million acre-feet) is lost annually?

21. How would taking evaporation into account change your answer to question 18? Do you have enough information or can you make reasonable estimates so that you can do the question more accurately? If yes, do so.

22. It had been suggested, before construction of Glen Canyon Dam, that sediment be removed from Lake Mead as it accumulated and hauled to the ocean by train. A typical railroad freight car carries 50 tons.

    a. How many fully loaded freight cars would it have taken to remove a day's accumulation of sediment from the lake?

    b. If it costs 1.5 cents to move a ton of freight 1 mile (1,5 cents/ton/mile), what would have been the daily and yearly cost of hauling the sediment some 400 miles to the Pacific Ocean?

23. Earlier we discussed some of the harmful effects of the Aswan Dam. On the positive side, however, it has added 1,000,000 acres to Egypt's agricultural land and a potential 10 million kilowatts of electric power. However, only 3 million kilowatts (1972) are being utilized because Egypt does not have sufficient industry or home appliances (air-conditioners, televisions, and so on) to consume the available electricity.

    To some the dam is a prime illustration of technological mismatch. Egypt, a developing country which needed Russian technical and economic help to build the dam, has—the critics say—mortgaged itself and wasted much effort on an inappropriate piece of technology. Opponents of this view say that the dam will stimulate Egypt's industrial development and that soon its power output will be fully utilized.

    Does this discussion of technological pros and cons perhaps miss the point? Is the dam possibly more important to Egypt as a symbol of industrialization and advanced, mammoth technology than as a useful "machine?" Is it a modern pyramid? This is a question we shall ask repeatedly about our own technological behemoths, such as the interstate highway system, our jetports, the space program, and so on. Basically, it is a question of whether technology means what it appears to mean on the surface.

24. Could a silted-up reservoir still be used to generate hydroelectric power? If your answer is yes, then what difference does it make—in relation to hydropower—whether the reservoir is silted or not?

25. The Trans-Alaska Pipeline will carry 2 million barrels/day of crude oil 800 miles from Prudhoe Bay, Alaska, to the port town of Valdez, Alaska. Calculate the diameter of the circular pipe needed if the oil is to flow at 10 feet/second. (One barrel is equivalent to 42 gallons, and 7.5 gallons has a volume of 1 cubic foot.)

26. In one example we assumed peak-hour demand was 440 cubic feet/second and off-hour demand 200 cubic feet/second. Assume the peak-hour demand goes to 500 cubic feet/second with off-hour demand remaining the same. What parts of the water system will have to change? Be qualitative in your answer.

27. As a general rule, a small watershed delivers more sediment per square mile to the local river than a large watershed. Speculate on the reason for this.

28. The Norris Reservoir in Norris, Tennessee, collects sediment from an area of 2800 square miles which produces an average of 450 tons/square mile. If the Norris Reservoir has a volume of 2 million acre-feet, what percentage of storage capacity does it lose yearly? The reservoir was completed in 1936. In what year will it be 80 percent filled with silt? (Assume a density of 60 pounds/cubic foot. The low density is due to voids in the material.)

# 4 Transportation safety

We begin the examination of transportation by looking at transportation safety. Unlike the broader area of transportation, there is a wealth of accurate and up-to-date statistical and physical information concerning transportation safety. It is therefore possible to develop transportation safety more accurately and factually than transportation generally, making it a good introduction to that complex subject.

Even in transportation safety there are few straight-forward technical answers to problems. Instead we find ourselves faced with the need to make trade-offs between desired and undesired effects, to proceed on the basis of inadequate information, and to recognize that beyond the technical and statistical problems lie difficult questions of human values. So transportation safety will both ease us into the general area of transportation and raise fundamental and recurring questions about the meaning and purpose of the man-made world.

**Auto Safety.** Each year in America more than 50,000 people are killed, 150,000 permanently maimed,

---

*From Cabell's novel *The Silver Stallion* (New York: Robert M. McBride and Co., 1926).

and over 2,000,000 injured by motor vehicles. In the last decade, the auto and truck have produced a half million deaths and 1,500,000 permanently injured people. These are huge numbers, and in addition to the suffering, pain, and anxiety caused the victims and their kin, it has cost the nation upwards of $20 billion a year. It is as if there were a quiet, dispersed, unpublicized war going on across the nation. Anyone who crosses a street or drives to work or to shop becomes a participant.

Although the problem affects and threatens everyone, it stirs little interest or concern. By comparison with the Vietnam War (40,000 American dead in ten years), our highways are bloodbaths. Yet Vietnam caused profound upheavals while highway fatalities are ignored. There appears to be an unspoken agreement between the people who use cars and those who manufacture them to ignore highway danger.

Shea Stadium in New York holds roughly 55,000 people—the number of annual U.S. highway deaths.

When we do focus on highway deaths and injuries, we delude ourselves by speaking of "accidents," although there is nothing accidental about a yearly total of 50,000-plus deaths. Those deaths are a statistical certainty given the existing mix of drivers, vehicles, roads, and law enforcement. Statisticians know to the hundreds how many deaths will emerge annually from the trillions of interactions that occur each year on our roads—deaths which are the inevitable result of the man-machine system we have built. What is more or less accidental is which of us gets killed. If someone leaves home 10 minutes late, he may reach an icy highway just after it has been sanded, avoiding a collision. Or the same 10-minute delay may bring him to an intersection the very moment a drunk or heart-attack victim roars through a red light.

**Causes of Deaths and Injuries.**   Before progress can be made toward reducing transportation deaths and injuries, it is necessary to understand that they have been designed into the roads and vehicles. That does not mean highway and auto engineers figured out how to produce 50,000 deaths: the accidents were predesigned in the same inadvertent way floods and high summer temperatures were built into the design of urban areas. Accidents are a result of the interaction of certain fundamental physical laws (which shall be considered in the following chapter), human frailties such as inattention, anger, and recklessness, and a desire for comfortable, stylish vehicles and fast, point-to-point transportation.

It will not be an easy task to reduce accidents. They may have been built into the system inadvertently, but they have been built in strongly. To eliminate the 10,000 annual pedestrian deaths alone would require that highways and streets be totally rebuilt to separate vehicles from pedestrians. There is no way to "package" pedestrians to survive collisions with autos or trucks. It should be simpler to reduce driver and passenger deaths by packaging, but here, too, there are problems. Stronger cars are heavier and therefore cost more. Drivers resist use of such simple but effective devices as safety belts. Even these devices become less effective at high speeds, and our traffic continues to flow at about 55 miles/hour. In addition, we mingle small and large cars, trucks and buses, presenting the same kind of problem the auto-pedestrian mix presents.

The situation is aggravated by the large amount of catching up we have to do. Even in areas where danger could easily have been eliminated long ago, we lag behind because until recently the auto was totally ignored as a safety factor. The auto manufacturers' position was that if they built a safer car, the "nut behind the wheel" would merely drive it faster and more recklessly. As a result of Detroit's attitude and general lack of public concern, safety was a minor influence on auto engineering. When auto companies had to choose from among safety, styling, and cost, safety came last.

**Dangers in Auto Equipment.**   Until the federal government intervened, many obvious safety measures were not built into cars to save auto makers money. As a result, motorists received concussions from unpadded dashboards and were ripped and gouged by protruding window cranks and door handles. In front-impact collisions, some drivers were stabbed by the steering-wheel column or crushed when the engine moved back into the passenger compartment. If the car turned over, the occupants were likely to be crushed when the roof collapsed. The laminated glass used in cars until the mid-1960s was such that a head would penetrate if it struck the windshield above 12.5 miles/hour.[1] If, instead of sailing completely through the windshield, the victim fell back into the car, the glass would snap together, causing severe or fatal neck cuts.

Dangers were also designed into cars for reasons of style. To make compact models look larger, they would be equipped with tires too small to safely support the car. The wrap-around windshield gave a car a modern look but distorted vision. Tinted windshields made cars look luxurious and helped the air-conditioning function more efficiently, but reduced night vision. Manufacturers achieved a jet plane look with floor-mounted gearshifts and an array of instruments. But in an accident these sticks, panels, and knobs were there to poke and probe as auto occupants slammed about the interior.

The exterior of the car was subject to the same design criteria. Economics and styling dictated that bumpers become ornaments which did little to cushion impacts or protect the car body. Bumpers on different model cars—including those made by the same company—were at different heights; even in a very low speed accident they would penetrate each other's guard to crush grills and break headlights. More seriously, cars sprouted all sorts of fins, headlight shields, and grillwork which stabbed and punctured pedestrians struck by cars or children who ran into parked vehicles. In some cases, bumpers were so shaped that a struck pedestrian was pushed under the car instead of out of the way.

Few of the designed-in dangers were due to technical ignorance. The bumpers which tended to shove struck pedestrians under cars were built 140 years after the use of the train cowcatcher—an item which efficiently pushed objects off the tracks. The fins and grillwork ignored the fundamental physical principle—known to all engineers—that a flat surface will do less damage when it strikes something than will a sharp surface. The flimsy but decorative bumpers were in use 50 years after the Model T Ford, which had bumpers that protected the auto's chassis and vital parts. The problem was not in engineering know-how but in engineering priorities.

**Ralph Nader and the Traffic Safety Act.**   The neglect of motor vehicles as a safety factor began to change in 1965 with the publication of the book *Unsafe at Any Speed,* written by a then-unknown lawyer named Ralph Nader.[2] Nader's book is best known for its attack on the Corvair— a rear-engine car manufactured from 1959 to 1969 by the Chevrolet Division of General Motors—but it also widely publicized for the first time many of the dangers we have mentioned above.

Included in the book is an analysis of the politics and economics that Nader thought created the highway safety situation. He says that the auto industry believed styling and performance sold cars; they therefore sacrificed everything to looks and power. Immense sums, he writes, were spent on market research to discover what turned on customers and then on engineering to translate consumer desires into chrome, sheet metal, and plush interiors. To be competitive and increase profits, he charges, manufacturers skimped on safety research, door lock and body strength, tire and brake size, and quality.

Nader also devotes a chapter of his book to "The Traffic Safety Establishment," in which he focuses on the National Safety Council (NSC), an organization devoted mainly to highway safety. He says the NSC slanted its entire safety campaign to make it seem that only drivers and pedestrians could prevent accidents. Their publicity efforts centered on such slogans as "Be Wise, Use Your Eyes," and "Cross at the Green, Not in Between." Before holiday weekends the NSC would predict the number of traffic deaths expected; then during the holiday, radio and television stations would broadcast the prediction and the current running total of highway deaths. In a sense, this was a way of not thinking about the accident problem. It turned death into a lottery or sports event—a number to be striven for. Safety did not depend on preventing all or even a significant number of deaths—just on not having more deaths than predicted. Presumably, the holiday was "safe" if the NSC predicted 450 deaths and only 410 people died.

#### Injury Analysis of Automobiles by Year and Make

| Index | Automobile | Index | Automobile |
|---|---|---|---|
| >200 | VW Bus (all years to '68) | 108 | Corvette (all years to '68) |
| 200 | MG (all years to '68) | 100 | '65 Belvedere; '61 Pontiac |
| 197 | '62 Corvair | 95 | '66 Buick |
| 189 | '65 Chevy II | 93 | Mustang (all years to '68) |
| 167 | '65 Valiant | 80 | '68 Buick Special |
| 143 | '60–'67 VW Beetle | 78 | Cougar (all years to '68) |
| 128 | '68 VW Beetle | 69 | '68 Pontiac Tempest |
| 124 | '68 Oldsmobile | 64 | '68 Fairlane |
| 116 | '66–'68 Falcon | <50 | '67 Buick |

SOURCE: "Driver Injury in Automobile Accidents Involving Certain Car Models," B. J. Campbell (Chapel Hill, N.C.: University of North Carolina Highway Safety Research Center, 1970).

**Table 1.** The index next to each car indicates the relative likelihood of an unbelted driver suffering a severe or fatal injury. If an MG (index 200) and a '65 Belvedere (index 100) are involved in the same kind of accident, the MG driver is twice as likely to suffer a serious or fatal injury as the Belvedere driver. The average index for all cars investigated is 100. In computing the index, injuries suffered in similar accidents were compared. In general, the lighter the car, the greater the danger. Station wagons and hardtops seemed significantly safer than the average. The above list was selected from a total of 175 auto models covered by the study, which investigated 270,000 vehicles involved in collisions in North Carolina from 1966 to 1968. (> means greater than; < means less than.)

Nader points out that although they had the capability, the NSC never collected data such as that listed in Table 1, showing which model cars have the lowest accident and death rates. He says that if safety differences among cars became known, it would focus attention on the auto as a safety factor. Competition among auto makers on the safety issue would bring the danger of auto travel to people's attention. The car would become identified with risk, injury, and death – the opposite of the carefree, fun, adventurous image assumed to sell cars and encourage their use. Nader says the NSC served the auto industry's interests because it was in large part controlled by the auto, tire, and gasoline companies through their contributions and their membership on its Board of Directors.

The book and its claims were vigorously denied by the auto industry, but in large part as a result of *Unsafe at Any Speed* and the publicity sur-

This car has been ripped in half by a rigid, unyielding sign support. The sign support emerged unscathed; the occupants of the car were killed. Such signposts are still commonly used, even though designs for signposts which would yield on impact or break away have been available for years. *Photo courtesy Insurance Institute for Highway Safety.*

rounding Nader's battles with General Motors, Congress in 1966 passed the National Traffic and Motor Vehicle Safety Act. This law gave the federal government the power to set safety standards for all new cars and to order the manufacturer to recall for repair any cars found to have safety defects.

The first cars affected by the Traffic Safety Act were 1968 models, which had to have lap-shoulder harnesses, residual braking, interior padding, and tires that met certain minimum standards. In following years more safety measures were specified, including flame-resistant interiors, impact-resistant door latches, head restraints, strong bumpers at a uniform height, double-latched hoods, and fail-safe operation of headlight concealment devices.

Passage of the Traffic Safety Act marked a fundamental change in the way the country thought about auto accidents. Much of the debate on the law had centered on whether the driver or the auto was responsible for accidents. Nader's position was that the auto was at fault. His opponents argued that driver error or drunkenness caused most accidents and it was therefore silly to pass a law requiring safer cars. Today the view is that highway dangers result from the interaction between drivers, vehicles, and roads. It is also felt that even when the driver is clearly at fault, he or she should not be punished with injury or death. The transportation system should be "forgiving." Cars should be built to help even inattentive or reckless drivers avoid accidents and to offer protection once accidents occur. Proponents of building protection into cars believe it is easier to protect people than to change their behavior to the point where accidents no longer occur.

## Measuring Safety

We now shift from a description of transportation safety to a quantitative, statistical study. Statistics describe the number of transportation deaths and can be interpreted to indicate the success of past safety efforts. They can also be used as a guide to such future efforts as improved roads, intensified driver education, auto safety equipment, and reduced speed limits. But the statistics do not provide a direct path to the truth. Depending on how they are presented and interpreted, statistics say different things. It is in the presentation and interpretation that figures are made to "lie." In transportation safety, the "lying" is done by choosing a statistical approach that supports a point of view that other presentations would oppose. In this chapter we shall present the same information in several ways to show how this works and how differing interpretations are possible.

The most direct approach to transportation safety is in terms of total yearly deaths. In Figure 1, motor-vehicle deaths for 1972 are divided into several categories.[3] In addition to the 56,600 people killed in 1972, another 170,000 persons were left permanently impaired by motor-vehicle accidents, and 2 million were disabled for at least a day. The permanent impairments ranged from an amputated finger to complete crippling. Table 2 presents the deaths caused by all motor vehicles, by buses, and by trains and airplanes from 1955 to 1972. The number of motor-vehicle deaths includes not only occupants of autos, trucks, and buses but also pedestrians, motorcyclists, bicyclists struck by motor vehicles, and so on.

### Motor Vehicle Deaths, 1972

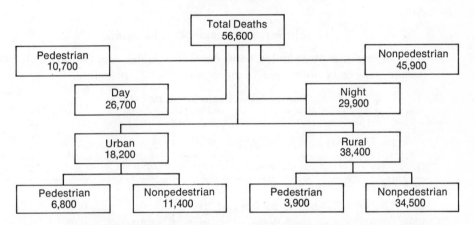

**Figure 1.** The total number of motor vehicle deaths occurring in 1972 are divided into day-night, pedestrian-nonpedestrian, and rural-urban categories. A disproportionately large number of deaths occur at night and in rural areas. Most pedestrian deaths, however, occur in urban areas.

### Transportation Deaths, 1955–1972

| Year | Motor-Vehicle Deaths | Motor-Vehicle-Caused Pedestrian Deaths | Bus Occupants | Train Occupants | Scheduled Domestic Airline Occupants |
|------|------|------|------|------|------|
| 1955 | 38,426 | 8,200 | 100 | 19 | 156 |
| 1960 | 38,173 | 7,850 | 70 | 33 | 297 |
| 1965 | 49,163 | 8,900 | 100 | 12 | 205 |
| 1968 | 54,862 | 9,900 | 140 | 13 | 258 |
| 1969 | 55,791 | 10,100 | 130 | 9 | 132 |
| 1970 | 54,800 | 10,400 | 130 | 10 | 0 |
| 1971 | 54,700 | 10,600 | 130 | 17 | 174 |
| 1972 | 56,600 | 10,700 | 130 | 48 | 160 |

SOURCE: "Accident Facts, 1973," National Safety Council, Chicago.

**Table 2.** The motor-vehicle-deaths figure includes auto and truck occupants, cyclists, pedestrians, and bus passengers.

**Passenger-mile Death Rates.** A comparison of the total number of people killed by different transportation modes does not take into account different rates of use. To make such a presentation it is necessary to introduce two units of travel: the passenger-mile and the vehicle-mile. A passenger-mile is generated when one person travels one mile by auto, bus, or whatever. A vehicle-mile is generated when a vehicle travels one mile. For example, a car carrying three people (the driver is counted as a passenger) for twenty miles generates

$$(3 \text{ passengers})(20 \text{ miles}) = 60 \text{ passenger-miles}$$

and

$$(1 \text{ vehicle})(20 \text{ miles}) = 20 \text{ vehicle-miles}.$$

A jet flying the 3000 miles between Los Angeles and Miami with 200 people generates 3000 vehicle-miles and 600,000 passenger-miles.

**Transportation Death Rates, 1955–1972**

| Year | Motor-Vehicle Deaths per | | | | Bus Deaths per $10^8$ p-m | Train Deaths per $10^8$ p-m | Scheduled Domestic Airline Deaths per $10^8$ p-m |
|------|------------|------------|--------------|--------------|------------|------------|------------|
|      | $10^8$ v-m | $10^8$ p-m | $10^4$ vehicles | $10^5$ persons | | | |
| 1955 | 6.34 | 2.70 | 6.12 | 23.4 | 0.18 | 0.07 | 0.76 |
| 1960 | 5.31 | 2.20 | 5.12 | 21.3 | 0.13 | 0.16 | 0.93 |
| 1965 | 5.54 | 2.40 | 5.36 | 25.4 | 0.16 | 0.07 | 0.38 |
| 1968 | 5.40 | 2.40 | 5.32 | 27.5 | 0.21 | 0.10 | 0.28 |
| 1969 | 5.21 | 2.30 | 5.19 | 27.7 | 0.19 | 0.07 | 0.13 |
| 1970 | 4.89 | 2.10 | 4.93 | 26.8 | 0.19 | 0.09 | 0.00 |
| 1971 | 4.61 | 1.90 | 4.70 | 26.5 | 0.19 | 0.24 | 0.15 |
| 1972 | 4.53 | 1.90 | 4.66 | 27.2 | 0.19 | 0.53 | 0.13 |

SOURCE: "Accident Facts, 1973."

**Table 3.** Listed above are transportation death rates in terms of deaths per 100 million passenger-miles (p-m), per 100 million vehicle-miles (v-m), per 10 thousand motor vehicles, and per 100,000 persons. The deaths per $10^8$ passenger-miles refer only to deaths of auto and taxi occupants and thus is not consistent with the vehicle-mile rates, which include private auto, taxi, bus, motorcycle, and truck occupants as well as pedestrians.

Table 3 expresses transportation deaths in terms of these and other units. Note that the passenger-mile rates refer only to vehicle occupants killed — not to pedestrians or other victims. In 1972, on a passenger-mile basis, travel by auto was ten times more dangerous than travel by bus and about fourteen times more dangerous than travel by plane. A person who drove from Boston to San Francisco that year ran fourteen times more risk than the person who made the trip by scheduled aircraft. In other words, if auto travel was completely replaced by bus, plane, or train travel, the approximately 56,000 annual traffic deaths would drop by a factor of fourteen to 4000 deaths. The comparison is even more stark for 1970, when not a single person died in a scheduled, domestic flight. Ironically, air travel is feared by many people although the most dangerous part of a trip by air is often the drive to and from the airport.

Comparisons between auto and air travel should not be made glibly. The two modes serve different purposes, have different costs, and in most cases cannot be substituted for each other. In addition, most airplane accidents occur on takeoff or landing. This means a flight from San Francisco to Alaska may be little more dangerous than one from San Francisco to Los Angeles. It also means that a growth in the number of shuttle flights to substitute for auto travel between neighboring cities would probably raise the passenger-mile death rate because there will be more takeoffs and landings per miles traveled. The same effect exists with highway travel. The most dangerous part of a long trip is the drive to and from and on and off the limited-access road.

Vehicle-mile Death Rates.   The vehicle-mile death rate is the statistic used by newspapers and safety organizations in evaluating motor-vehicle safety. In Figure 2 the deaths per $10^8$ vehicle-miles are plotted yearly

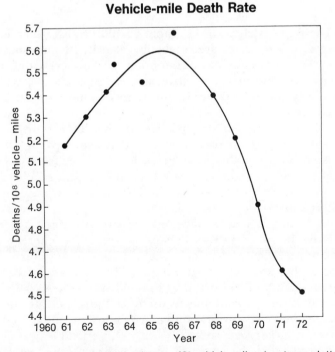

**Figure 2.** Motor vehicle deaths per $10^8$ vehicle-miles (v-m) are plotted from 1960 to 1972. The vehicle-mile death rate began to decline in 1966, the year the Traffic Safety Act was passed.

from 1960 to 1972.[4] This rate includes both occupant and nonoccupant deaths. An abrupt decline began in 1966 and continued through 1972. This decline has been interpreted as meaning motor-vehicle travel has grown safer, perhaps as a result of increased public awareness and of vehicle improvements such as safety belts, head restraints, and padded dashboards ordered in accord with the Traffic Safety Act. Before discussing the implications of the vehicle-mile statistics, let us see how they translate into yearly number of deaths.

We can calculate the number of deaths predicted for 1969 from the rate of 5.2 deaths per $10^8$ vehicle-miles. The number of vehicle-miles logged that year can be determined from gasoline-tax records; these show that in 1969 the nation consumed about 88 billion gallons of fuel.[5] It is estimated that the average motor vehicle that year got 12.2 miles/gallon,[6] yielding

$$\text{(vehicle-miles/gal)(gal)} = (12.2 \text{ vehicle-miles/gal})(88 \times 10^9 \text{ gal})$$
$$= 1.1 \times 10^{12} \text{ vehicle-miles.}$$

The product of death rate and vehicle-miles gives total fatalities.

$$\text{(death rate)(vehicle-miles)} = (5.2 \text{ deaths}/10^8 \text{ vehicle-miles})$$
$$\times (1.1 \times 10^{12} \text{ vehicle-miles})$$
$$= 57,200 \text{ deaths}$$

The result is close to the actual 56,400 deaths, which is not surprising since the death rates are originally calculated from estimates of vehicle-miles based on gasoline consumption. So we merely did the original calculation backwards. The government keeps tax records of all motor-vehicle fuel sold so the only uncertainty comes from translating the fuel into vehicle-miles.

The death rate per $10^8$ passenger-miles is less certain for motor vehicles because there is no precise way to determine average auto occupancy. Presumably, then, the passenger-mile death rate for autos is less accurate than the vehicle-mile data. However, the passenger-mile data for busses, trains, and planes are very dependable since the precise number of tickets sold is known.

Both the passenger-mile and vehicle-mile rates can conceivably be affected by other factors besides the vehicle's inherent safety. To see this, assume there has been a slight decline in auto occupancy from one year to the next. As a result, there will be a larger percentage decline in the occupancy of the seat next to the driver—the so-called death seat. So even if accidents continue to occur at the same rate, fewer people are likely to be killed because fewer people are in an exposed situation. The person who last year rode to work with a friend is now in a more secure position behind the wheel of his or her own car. The cars may be just as dangerous (or safe) but the passenger-mile death rate will decline.

Auto occupancy can also influence vehicle-mile death rates. To take an extreme example, assume that average auto occupancy declines in one year from two persons to one. Further assume that each person travels the same number of miles as previously, so the total passenger-miles generated remain the same but the vehicle-miles generated double. It seems reasonable to further assume that drivers would get into accidents at the same rate. But the deaths per $10^8$ vehicle-miles would be halved because the average accident now kills half as many people (we are disregarding the effect of "death-seat" occupancy here). For example, a two-car, high-speed, head-on collision that formerly would have killed four people (two in each car) would kill two people when average occupancy is one person per car.

**Population Death Rates.** Figure 3 shows motor-vehicle deaths on a population and motor vehicle basis.[7] As can be seen, motor-vehicle-caused deaths have held steady at around 25 deaths per $10^5$ people. That is, 25 out of 100,000 people die each year from motor vehicles. Despite declines in the passenger-mile and vehicle-mile death rates, people continue to die from motor vehicles at a constant rate because society's motor-vehicle use increases each year. This increase outweighs any gains from safer vehicles or roads. The fact that the death rate per 100,000 people has held constant in the face of increasing travel is interpreted by some as a good sign. Others see it as evidence that despite all effort, motor vehicles are as dangerous as ever. In this case, the statistics are exact and agreed on, but the interpretation varies according to one's values. A person who prizes the mobility afforded by the auto will probably be forgiving of its dangers and will point out the decline in passenger-mile and vehicle-mile death rates. Those who already object to the auto's pollution or noise will see its danger, as demonstrated by the total death figures, as another argument against it.

**Deaths per 100,000 Persons and per 10,000 Motor Vehicles**

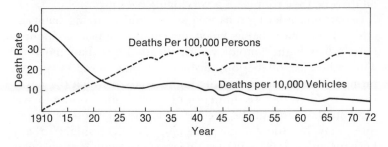

**Figure 3.** The graph is a plot of deaths per 100,000 persons and per 10,000 registered motor vehicles. There has been a long-term decline in the deaths per 10,000 motor vehicles but the rate per 100,000 people has more or less held steady since 1945.

**Another Look at Fatalities.** Table 4 refines our view of motor-vehicle fatalities by classifying fatalities according to age-group. It shows that the 15–24 age-group has the highest motor-vehicle death rate: they are 2½ times more likely to die in a one-vehicle, off-the-road accident than those between 25 and 44. For this reason, young drivers pay very high insurance premiums.

**Motor-Vehicle Deaths per 100,000 Persons by Age-Group, 1969**

| Type Accident | All Ages | 0–4 | 5–14 | 15– 24 | 25– 44 | 45– 64 | 65– 74 | 75– |
|---|---|---|---|---|---|---|---|---|
| All Motor Vehicle Victims | 28.8 | 11.7 | 9.9 | 51.7 | 29.2 | 27.3 | 34.3 | 42.6 |
| Pedestrian Victims | N.A. | 5.5 | 4.5 | 3.0 | 3.0 | 5.0 | 10.0 | 16.0 |
| One-vehicle, Non-collision Victims | N.A. | 2.0 | 1.8 | 20.5 | 8.0 | 6.5 | 6.5 | 5.3 |
| Two-vehicle Collisions | N.A. | 3.8 | 2.2 | 21.0 | 13.5 | 13.3 | 15.5 | 17.8 |
| Other | N.A. | 0.4 | 1.4 | 7.2 | 4.7 | 2.5 | 2.3 | 3.5 |

Source: "Accident Facts, 1973."

**Table 4.** Here several categories of motor-vehicle deaths are arranged by age-group. The numbers are deaths per 100,000 members of that age-group. The very young and very old suffer a disproportionate number of pedestrian deaths while those in the 15–24 age-group are most likely to be killed while motor-vehicle occupants.

Another special group is the drinking driver. As Figure 4 shows, half of all motor-vehicle fatalities are attributed to alcohol.[8] Chronic drinkers cause two-thirds of alcohol-related deaths, which is one-third of all highway deaths. Since chronic drinkers comprise only 7 percent (1 out of 14) of all drivers, they represent a very dangerous group.

Geographical location as well as age and drinking habits can affect the odds of a person being killed in a motor-vehicle accident. Rural states have much higher motor-vehicle death rates than more urban states.[9] This is because of the long distances to be covered in sparsely populated farm and ranch areas and the high speeds at which the narrow, two-lane roads are driven. The influence of urbanization on motor-vehicle deaths suggests that some of the decline in vehicle-mile and passenger-mile death rates may be due to our becoming an increasingly urbanized nation. Perhaps an effective way to cut deaths is through land-use planning which minimizes the need for high-speed auto travel. But the relatively large number of urban pedestrian deaths shown in Figure 1 suggests this solution may be self-defeating.

## Alcohol and Death

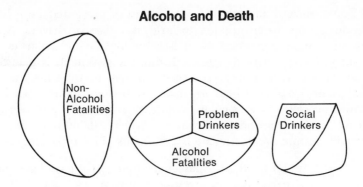

**Figure 4.** The diagram shows the percentage (about half) of motor-vehicle deaths attributed to alcohol. Problem drinkers — representing 7% of all drivers — cause about ⅔ of all alcohol involved deaths.

Another influence on accident risk is the road a traveler uses. Table 5 shows that the vehicle-mile death rate on rural interstate highways is half that on regular rural roads. The low rate occurs because interstate roads have dividing median strips, limited access, relatively long entrance and exit lanes, 12-foot-wide lanes, and broad shoulders. They also exclude pedestrians, cutting deaths immediately by 20 percent.

**Highways and Accidents**

|  | *Noninterstate* | *Interstate* |
|---|---|---|
| Rural Roads |  |  |
| Deaths/$10^8$ vehicle-miles | 7.41 | 3.52 |
| Injuries/$10^8$ vehicle-miles | 194.00 | 71.00 |
| $10^6$ vehicle-miles/road-mile/year | 1.55 | 3.22 |
| Urban Roads |  |  |
| Deaths/$10^8$ vehicle-miles | 3.66 | 2.30 |
| Injuries/$10^8$ vehicle-miles | 364.00 | 111.00 |
| $10^6$ vehicle-miles/road-mile/year | 0.89 | 13.50 |

SOURCE: *Cumulative Regulatory Effects on the Cost of Automobile Transportation (RECAT)*, RECAT Ad Hoc Committee (prepared for the White House Office of Science and Technology, Washington, D.C., 1970).

**Table 5.** The data show the difference in death and injury rates between interstate and noninterstate roads. On rural noninterstate roads, 7.41 deaths occur for each $10^8$ vehicle-miles traveled. On rural interstate roads, 3.52 deaths occur for each $10^8$ vehicle-miles traveled. The $10^6$ vehicle-miles/road-mile/year figure specifies the number of vehicle-miles traveled on each type of road per year. For example, urban interstate roads generate $13.5 \times 10^6$ vehicle-miles traveled per mile of road per year.

Some Risk Calculations.   The statistics presented here have precise meaning only when applied to large numbers of drivers. Applying the statistics to a single individual is a bit like saying a particular football team will win half of its games during the season. It is true that, on the average, teams in any given league win half their games (ties aside), but that is no basis on which to make predictions about a particular team. With that caveat, we calculate the death risk run by an "average" motorist who travels (not necessarily as the driver) 10,000 miles in a year. Here we will assume the death rate is 2.5 deaths per $10^8$ passenger-miles.

$$\text{risk} = (2.5 \text{ deaths}/10^8 \text{ passenger-miles}) \, (10^4 \text{ passenger-miles})$$
$$= 2.5 \text{ deaths}/10^4 = 2.5 \times 10^{-4} \text{ deaths}$$

No one suffers 0.00025 deaths. We interpret the number to mean that the odds against the average 10,000-mile-per-year traveler being killed are 10,000 to 2.5, or 4000 to 1. Alternatively, it means 1 out of 4000 average auto users is killed yearly. Notice that if the person drove 20,000 miles in a year, the odds against being killed would drop to 2000 to 1.

If the traveler had flown the 10,000 miles, at 0.1 deaths/$10^8$ passenger-miles, the risk would be

$$\text{risk} = (0.1 \text{ deaths}/10^8 \text{ passenger-miles}) \, (10^4 \text{ passenger-miles})$$
$$= \left(\frac{1}{10^5}\right) \text{deaths}$$

or a 100,000 to 1 shot. Traveling by bus or train would produce about the same odds.

Odds can also be computed from the death rates per 100,000 persons. A rate of 25 deaths/$10^5$ people is equivalent to 1 death/4000 people, or 4000 to 1. The agreement between this calculation and the above passenger-mile calculation is fortuitous since they measure different things. The passenger-mile rate is the risk to an auto occupant while the population rate includes nonoccupant deaths as well.

Although statistics do not give any one person an accurate picture of the risks he or she runs when traveling, they are precise and valuable for society as a whole. Statistical information—whether it is about transportation safety, divorces, or the average time children spend watching television—is one way in which society takes its pulse and measures its collective health. Statistics and the trends they indicate allow plans to be made for the future. If motor-vehicle transportation, for example, becomes significantly safer in the future, fewer auto body shops, auto wreckers, bone surgeons, and plastic surgeons will be needed than if the accident rate stays as it is now. Accurate interpretation of statistical trends allows society to allocate its resources properly and to direct itself in a desired direction.

Flipping Pennies. The higher risk run by the 20,000-mile-per-year traveler should not be misinterpreted. It does not mean the death *rate* increases with distance traveled, but that the *chance* of death occurring does increase. This can be seen if fatality odds are compared to flipping a coin. When a penny is tossed in the air, the odds are 50-50 it will come up a head. Even if a penny comes up heads ten times in a row, the odds are still 50-50 that on the eleventh flip it will come up a head. The previous history of the coin cannot influence the odds on future flips. In the same way, the theoretical odds of the average person being killed while traveling a mile is constant no matter how many miles have been previously traveled. (For a death rate of 2.5 deaths/$10^8$ passenger-miles, the odds of being killed while traveling 1 mile are 40 million to 1.)

But while the per-mile odds stay constant for the average traveler, the overall chances of a fatality increase with additional travel. This can again be compared with flipping pennies. The odds of a head coming up are always 50-50 for any one flip, but the more flips, the greater the chance of a head occurring. For example, the chance of a head coming up is doubled if a coin is flipped ten times instead of five times.

## Cost-Benefit Analysis

Once statistical data have been collected, the difficult job of interpretation begins. What is the significance of the numbers presented? What do they tell us about the future? How can we act to influence the future in a desired direction? Interpretations of the statistical data range between two extremes: those who say the present number of auto deaths and injuries is a small price to pay for our great mobility, and those who say the number of deaths and injuries is intolerable and must be immediately and drastically reduced. Even among those who hold the latter view, there is wide disagreement over what is an "acceptable" number of deaths and injuries and how that number can be determined.

Seemingly the most objective way to approach auto safety is through the kind of cost-benefit analysis discussed in connection with water projects. No overall cost-benefit analysis has been done for auto travel, although such analyses are done for individual highway projects. Auto use has grown without any demonstration that, on balance, benefits outweigh costs. If such an analysis has been done at all, it has been done indirectly as the sum of the billions of individual, uncoordinated decisions and actions that have brought us our present transportation system. That large decision — as shall be seen in following chapters — involves much more than safety considerations. For now, let us look just at safety costs and benefits.

The Cost of Safety. We begin with the value judgment that deaths and injuries are bad and should be minimized. Ideally, the goal is zero deaths and injuries. This goal is routinely reached with elevator and subway transportation and in 1970 even with domestic air travel. But our information and experience indicate that this goal would be immensely expensive and perhaps physically impossible to achieve for auto travel. At a minimum, a new road-sidewalk system would be needed throughout the nation to separate pedestrians and motor vehicles. The roads themselves would have to be better engineered—at least to interstate standards—and cars would need many changes. The cost to effect such improvements for our almost 4 million miles of road would be in the trillions. For comparison, the 42,500-mile interstate system will have cost, when completed, about $80 billion, while the gross national product (GNP) is only about $1000 billion ($1 trillion) per year.

This guard rail has speared the car and emerged through the rear window. Such "guard" rails create rather than reduce highway dangers. Guard rails could have flared and buried ends, making it more likely that cars crashing into them would be guided to safe stops. *Photo courtesy Insurance Institute for Highway Safety.*

The Cost of Lives.  Some argue the money would be well spent if one life were saved. But the expenditure of a large amount of money, resources, and talent on auto safety would mean that less money would be available for reduction of auto-caused noise and air pollution, hospital construction, education, and so on. The net result of spending huge sums on auto safety might be an even greater loss of life due to other causes. For example, large auto-safety expenditures might cause neglect of auto-caused air pollution, resulting in increased deaths from respiratory problems. In a finite world, human and physical resources must be allocated in the most effective way. In many cases, a difficult choice must be made between several desirable goals.

### Cost of Accidents, 1970

| | | |
|---|---:|---|
| Income Loss/Motor-Vehicle Death | $140,000.00 | |
| Loss/Motor-Vehicle Injury | $ 2,750.00 | |
| Total Cost of Deaths | | $7.7 billion |
| Total Cost of Injuries | | $6.1 billion |
| Property Damage Cost/Accident | $ 178.00 | |
| Total Cost of Property Damage | | $4.9 billion |
| Total Accident Cost | | $18.7 billion |
| Accident Cost per Capita | $ 91.00 | |
| Accident Cost/Vehicle-mile | 1.7 cents | |
| Death Cost/Vehicle/Year | $ 69.80 | |
| Injury Cost/Vehicle/Year | $ 55.10 | |
| Property Damage Cost/Vehicle/Year | $ 44.90 | |
| Total Accident Cost/Vehicle/Year | $ 169.80 | |
| Total Death Cost/Passenger-Car Lifetime | $ 657.60 | |
| Total Accident Cost/Passenger-Car Lifetime | $ 1,599.00 | |

SOURCE: RECAT.

**Table 6.**  Shown here are some costs associated with motor-vehicle accidents. Note that of the roughly 15 cents per mile it costs to operate a car, 1.7 cents goes for accidents. This is roughly the cost of auto insurance. Each of us — on the average — pays $91 per year for auto accidents. On a per-vehicle basis, it costs $69.80 yearly to pay for motor-vehicle deaths. Accidents increase the cost of operating a car through its lifetime by $1599.

An Analysis.  One way to attempt an allocation is through cost-benefit analyses of proposed safety measures. If a safety device can save more money through accident prevention than it costs, then it is "cost effective." It removes sand from society's gears, leaving more resources available for other activities. Tables 6 and 7 contain the first items of information needed in making any such analysis. They show the cost of auto accidents in the year 1970 and the number of accidents per car.

The total cost of the 54,800 deaths is estimated at $7.7 billion, or $140,000

**Statistics on Autos and Accidents, 1970**

| | |
|---|---|
| Number of Passenger Cars | 89 million |
| Passenger-Car Miles/Year | 900 billion |
| Passenger-Car Life Expectancy | 9.42 years |
| Accidents/Car Lifetime | 2.37 |
| Time Between Accidents (years) | 3.97 |
| Accidents/Vehicle/Year | 0.25 |
| Total Number of Accidents | 28 million |

Source: RECAT.

**Table 7.**  Assorted statistics are shown here for automobiles and accidents in 1970. The average car is in an accident every 3.97 years.

per death. The $140,000 is based on the estimated, average future earnings of those killed in motor-vehicle accidents. Needless to say, it is a narrow measure of the value of human life. The total injury cost is $6.1 billion. When averaged over all autos, this figure becomes about $170 per car per year, or 1.7 cents/vehicle-mile. Accidents add $1599 to the lifetime cost of operating the average car. Unlike other accident statistics, accident cost averaging is partly achieved in practice through insurance premiums. The average driver pays about 1.7 cents per mile for auto insurance, and the premiums collected by the insurance companies — less operating costs — go to accident victims.

Once the cost figures are in hand, the data of Table 8 can be used. Table 8 shows the percentage of accidents and deaths caused by different types of collisions. Because front-impact collisions cause 45% of all deaths, this is an obvious accident type to protect against. Table 8 shows that the steering wheel is a major cause of death, which indicates the need for a collapsible steering column or some other defense. The large percentage of people killed in side-impact accidents due to ejection shows a need for stronger door locks and reinforced side structures. Figure 5[10] is a supplement to the information in Table 8. It shows the percentage of time a particular seat position is occupied. It is useful information because there is no sense spending a great deal of money to protect, for example, the rear middle seat, which is occupied only 3.7% of the time. The money could be better spent on the right front seat, occupied 29% of the time.

Once the above information has indicated areas of need, experimental safety devices are developed and tested in the laboratory by mathematical modeling and by experimental collisions using dummies equipped with sensors. The readings registered by these sensors are interpreted to indicate the amount of protection a particular device would afford.

From this data and from the cost of a safety device and knowledge of its effectiveness, we can calculate the cost and benefit of the device. For

**Causes of Fatal Injuries**

| Accident Type | Percent of all Accidents | Percent of Deaths | Steering Wheel | Instrument Panel | Windshield | Ejection |
|---|---|---|---|---|---|---|
| Front Impact | 49 | 45 | 37% (16.65%) | 17% (7.65%) | 17% (7.65%) | 0 |
| Side Impact | 17 | 26 | 0 | 0 | 0 | 42% (10.92%) |
| Rear Impact | 29 | 2 | 0 | 25% (0.5%) | 0 | 25% (0.4%) |
| Roll- over | 4 | 27 | 11% (2.97%) | 0 | 0 | 59% (15.93%) |
| Other | 1 | — | — | — | — | — |

SOURCE: RECAT.

**Table 8.**   The above data show the frequency of occurrence of various accidents and the particular instrument of death (steering wheel, windshield, ejection). In the last four columns the numbers without parentheses are the percentages of deaths in that impact class and the numbers in parentheses are percentages of total deaths. Not all causes of death are listed (for example, fire, door-structure impact) so the percentages do not necessarily add up to 100.

## Auto Seat Occupancy

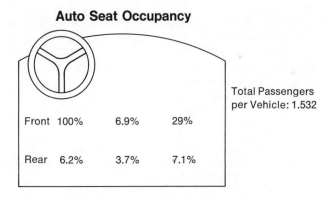

Total Passengers per Vehicle: 1.532

Front  100%    6.9%    29%

Rear   6.2%    3.7%    7.1%

**Figure 5.**   The numbers show the percentage of the time a particular seat position is occupied.

example, if it is known that a particular collapsible steering column can prevent 80% of the fatalities now caused by steering columns, then the money saved in the course of a year can be calculated. This is the benefit. The price of the collapsible column is the cost. If the benefit outweighs the cost, the collapsible steering column is "cost effective."

In Table 9, the results of this kind of analysis are presented for several different devices. As shown, lap and shoulder harnesses could save large amounts of money—which means they could prevent a large number of deaths and injuries—if they were used 100% of the time. It is estimated that lap belts alone could prevent about 40% of auto-occupant deaths yearly, and use of lap and shoulder harnesses could prevent 52% of all occupant deaths.[11] That would have cut 1972's total from 35,100 auto-occupant deaths to between 18,000 and 21,000 deaths. In 1970, only 25% of all auto occupants used lap belts and a tiny 4% used shoulder harnesses.[12] But even at that use rate they prevented enough deaths and injuries to be cost effective. Although seat belts are cheap, they benefit only users, and there is great resistance to "buckling up." As a result, the ignition-safety belt interlock system was introduced on 1974 cars. Should that approach fail, a passive device like the air-bag will be introduced. Unfortunately, air-bags are more expensive than safety belts and may even give less protection since they are not very effective in side-impact collisions. It is estimated that air-bags would reduce auto-occupant deaths by only 30%.

**Safety Device Costs and Benefits**

| Safety Device | Benefit | Cost |
|---|---|---|
| Interior Padding | $11.00 | $10.00 |
| Head Restraints | $ 9.50 | $10.00 |
| Collapsible Steering Column | $82.75 | $22.00 |
| Dual-Braking System | $15.00 | $12.50 |
| Lap Belts—25% use | $64.75 | $25.00 |
| Lap (25% use) and Torso (4% use) Belts | $74.00 | $35.00 |
| Lap and Torso Belts with 100% Use due to Interlocks | $486.00 | $55.00–$75.00 |
| Front and Rear Air-bags | $370.00 | $161.00–$384.00 |

SOURCE: RECAT.

**Table 9.** Estimated benefits and costs for several safety devices over the car's lifetime are given here.

## A Question of Values

Whether applied to dams, highways, or auto safety, the cost-benefit analysis has come under increasing criticism. It is said that such analyses include only things that can be measured in dollars, although so-called intangibles may be as important or even more important. For example, the cost of an auto death is set at $140,000—which is the average victim's estimated future income if he or she had lived. Critics of the cost-benefit approach say such a narrow measure of death is meaningless.

Juries judging auto-accident cases often award hundreds of thousands or even upwards of a million dollars to accident victims, disregarding the lower guidelines established by compensation experts. Some say that such "irresponsible" awards endanger the entire motor-vehicle transportation system by creating impossibly high insurance costs. The high awards are attributed to the naïveté of the jurors, whose sympathies are caught by the one case presented to them — not realizing that tens of thousands suffer the same fate each year but that few victims have the resources and tenacity to bring their case to trial.

But it is also possible to view the generous jurors as the realistic ones. They see the human suffering caused by accidents with a fresh eye instead of with the dulled, necessarily hardened eye of a trial judge, insurance lawyer, or state trooper. In this light, the high awards are not seen as naïve; they are seen as a statement that the nation cannot afford its auto accidents.

**Technology Assessment.**   These and other speculative considerations are outside the scope of the narrowly defined cost-benefit analysis, which takes the present system as given and merely tries to fine tune it. In response to the deficiencies of such analyses, the new discipline — or art — of technology assessment has been developing.[13] Technology assessment attempts to consider the impact of all aspects of a technology. In addition to the usual economic considerations, it tries to evaluate the intangibles to which dollar values cannot be assigned as well as the second and third order effects of a technology. For example, in the area of water power, technology assessment would not only evaluate the dollar value of the electricity to be produced by a dam and the cost of the dam, but also the effect of the use of the electricity, the pollution that would be caused if the same electricity were generated using coal or oil as a fuel, and so on.

A technology assessment of auto safety includes but goes well beyond an economic analysis to consider many of the assumptions underlying the cost-benefit analysis. Instead of accepting the safety savings of interstate highways, a technology assessment asks by how much the existence of the interstate highway increased auto travel. It is known that good roads generate additional travel and so may increase the number of deaths and injuries even as they lower the accident rate. A complete analysis takes this travel increase into account when calculating safety savings. It also compares the accident rate on interstate roads not just to old highways but to other possible transportation means such as trains and buses.

**Secondary Impacts of Accidents.**   A pure dollar analysis of traffic deaths does not consider the secondary impact of accidents. For example, the statistics on pedestrian deaths in Table 4 show that children below age 4 and people over 65 are more likely to be killed by autos. Parents know this and try to restrict their children to backyards and to train them to be careful. But it is not in a child's nature to be careful and to look both

Motor vehicles on urban streets represent a serious barrier to the young and the old, as accident statistics indicate. In 1969, 5.5 out of 100,000 youngsters under age 5 were pedestrian victims. This is a far higher death rate for this age-group than from other auto-related fatalities. For those over 65 there were 13 pedestrian deaths per 100,000. *Photo courtesy Office of Economic Opportunity.*

ways before running across a street. We try to force children to stop being children in order to adapt to a machine.

Old people are also well aware of the dangers to them from the auto. Even if they have not seen the statistics cited in Table 4, they know they do not see or hear well enough or move quickly enough to dodge a careless or aggressive driver at a street crossing. They also know they are less likely than a younger person to recover from an accident. The pedestrian death statistics show that some old people continue to venture outside, but many must react by just not going places.[14] Since they generally cannot afford to own a car or are physically unable to drive, this severely limits their mobility. For them, the streets of cities and suburbs become the walls of a jail. Overall, in building a transportation system, society has been insensitive to the well-being of the very young and the very old.

Social Problems. Technology assessment would also raise questions about a possible deeper meaning to the strong resistance many people have to using seat belts. It has been proven that the belts save lives and prevent injuries, yet only 4% of the motoring public willingly use shoulder harnesses. Possibly people are careless or forgetful or don't like the discomfort, but a technology assessment must consider the possibility that part of the auto's attraction is its danger; that people use the auto to experience risk and release aggression and hostility. If this is true, then it just might be a mistake to make cars safer, since people would then presumably find new ways to take risks and be aggressive. Or perhaps a program to make cars safer should be combined with substitute outlets for aggression. The point is not that auto safety is necessarily self-defeating, just that we must look for complications lest our solutions make matters worse.

The interaction of alcohol and the auto is clearly an area for technology assessment. Probably a majority of Americans drink, many drink heavily, and a surprisingly large percentage are alcoholics. The nation's one attempt to ban alcohol was a disaster, and in 1933 the Prohibition Amendment was repealed, having proved unenforceable. Despite this experience, we have built a transportation system that cannot be operated safely by intoxicated drivers (see Table 10). As a result we have at least 25,000 alcohol-related traffic deaths yearly. It is almost as if the auto is a mechanical enforcer of prohibition. The nation repealed prohibition but failed to repeal the auto.

Attempts to deal with the alcohol-auto problem have tended toward changing the driver to adapt to the machine rather than changing the machine to adapt to man. Judges are often reluctant to punish the drinking driver because the penalty of removing a person's license may cause him

### A Guide to Drinking and Driving

| Body Weight | Number of Drinks Consumed | | | | | |
|---|---|---|---|---|---|---|
| | 1 | 2 | 3 | 4 | 5 | 6 |
| | Hours to Wait After Start of Drinking and Before Driving | | | | | |
| 100 lb | 0 | 3 | 6 | $9\frac{1}{2}$ | $12\frac{1}{2}$ | $15\frac{1}{2}$ |
| 120 lb | 0 | 2 | $4\frac{1}{2}$ | $7\frac{1}{2}$ | $9\frac{1}{2}$ | 12 |
| 140 lb | 0 | $1\frac{1}{2}$ | $3\frac{1}{2}$ | $5\frac{1}{2}$ | 8 | 10 |
| 160 lb | 0 | $\frac{1}{2}$ | $2\frac{1}{2}$ | $4\frac{1}{2}$ | $6\frac{1}{2}$ | $8\frac{1}{2}$ |
| 180 lb | 0 | 0 | 2 | $3\frac{1}{2}$ | $5\frac{1}{2}$ | 7 |
| 200 lb | 0 | 0 | $1\frac{1}{2}$ | 3 | $4\frac{1}{2}$ | 6 |
| 220 lb | 0 | 0 | 1 | $2\frac{1}{2}$ | $3\frac{1}{2}$ | $5\frac{1}{2}$ |

Source: New Jersey Division of Motor Vehicles.

**Table 10.** A drink is a 12-ounce bottle of beer, 5 ounces of wine (12 percent alcohol), or 1½ ounces of 86-proof whiskey, gin, vodka. Adhering to the above chart ensures that a person's blood-alcohol content stays below 0.05 percent. It has been found that a driver's probability of causing a crash doubles at slightly above 0.05 percent blood-alcohol content.

or her to lose a job, be unable to go shopping or get medical care, and so on. As a result, many communities have turned to rehabilitation. One U.S. city has a program in which people convicted of drunken driving must report daily to a drugstore, where they swallow a drug which causes extreme nausea if they should then drink alcohol. Technology assessment would ask whether it is healthy or constructive for a society to bend people in this way, and whether it would not make more sense to think about a transportation system that could be used by the drunk and the sober, the very young and the very old, the careful and the careless.

The question of bending people to fit machines is an old one. Certainly in many ways we are bound to the modern technological machine—to its pace and demands. That pace and rhythm pervades all of our society but is especially striking on a superhighway, where thousands of vehicles per hour roar past. Those in the vehicles—often blending the surrounding roar with loud music—must pay constant aggressive attention as they move along with the traffic. One of the costs of the pace and scale of this movement was pointed up in late 1973, when gasoline shortages forced reductions in the speed and volume of highway travel. As a result, traffic deaths and accidents declined, showing the direct cost our pace extracts from society. Undoubtedly there are indirect costs. It may well be, for example, that a long-term decline in motor-vehicle speed will show up eventually as a decline in heart attacks or ulcers, two tension-related diseases. Again speculating, the extra years of life due to fewer accidents and less illness might more than make up for "lost" time due to lowered highway speeds.

The point is not to analyze all of society's ills in terms of auto travel. But to understand autos or any other technology we must stop thinking of them as simple, rationally constructed machines. Transportation systems are actually a major manifestation of our culture—the dominant folk art. Archaeologists deduce all sorts of things from the pottery and axes of long-dead civilizations, but the autos, phones, and tunnels of our own time are taken for granted. It is not until we notice that one of our technologies is killing a thousand persons a week that we begin to scratch the surface a bit. Technology assessment is the name of that first tentative scratching.

## Bibliography

*Source Notes*

1. *Unsafe at Any Speed.* Ralph Nader. New York: Grossman Publishers, 1965.

2. Ibid.

3. "Accident Facts, 1973." National Safety Council. Chicago, Illinois.

4. Ibid.

5. *Statistical Abstract of the United States, 1971.* Washington, D.C.: U.S. Government Printing Office.

6. Ibid.

7. "Accident Facts, 1973"

8. *Cumulative Regulatory Effects on the Cost of Automobile Transportation (RECAT).* RECAT Ad Hoc Committee. Prepared for the White House Office of Science and Technology. Washington, D.C., 1972.

9. "Accident Facts, 1973"

10. *RECAT.*

11. Ibid.

12. Ibid.

13. *Technology Assessment.* Committee Hearings before the Committee on Science and Astronautics, U.S. House of Representatives, 91st Congress. Washington, D.C.: U.S. Government Printing Office, 1970.

14. *The Coming of Age.* Simone de Beauvoir. New York: Warner Paperback Library, 1973.

## Further Reading

W. J. CURRAN and NEIL L. CHAYET, eds. *Trauma and the Automobile.* Cincinnati: The W. H. Anderson Co.
  This book is a collection of technical papers on auto accidents by doctors, lawyers, and engineers.

Hearings before the Committee on Commerce, U.S. Senate, 92nd Congress. *Auto Safety Oversight.* Washington, D.C.: U.S. Government Printing Office, 1972.
  This document gives the hearings on the need for revision of the National Traffic and Motor Vehicle Safety Act of 1966. See especially the testimony on the Corvair controversy by Ralph Nader and others.

ROBERT N. HOFFMAN. *Murder on the Highway.* New York: A. S. Barnes and Co., 1966.

PAUL W. KEARNEY. *How to Drive Better and Avoid Accidents.* New York: Thomas Y. Crowell Co., 1963.
  Unlike Nader, these two authors emphasize driver skill as a means to preventing accidents.

RALPH NADER. *Unsafe at Any Speed.* New York: Grossman Publishers, 1965.
  Nader looks at what he sees as the physical, institutional, and economic forces which combine to produce highway deaths.

RALPH NADER STUDY GROUP. *Small-on Safety.* New York: Grossman Publishers, 1972.
  The Nader Study Group presents here an examination of the handling and crash-worthiness of the Volkswagen Beetle.

## Questions and Problems

1. Tractors, because of their work, must sit high off the ground on short axles. This makes them relatively unstable and they often turn over while working hills or inclines, injuring or killing the operator. Tractor manufacturers have developed more stable tractors which will not tip on inclines that would have tumbled older models. It is found, however, that farmers now use the newer tractors to work still steeper areas and suffer about as many accidents. Does this support the old auto-industry argument that if cars are made safer the "nut behind the wheel" will drive faster and more recklessly? Are other interpretations possible?

2. At one time a bill was proposed to Congress requiring that there be a shield overhanging the rear of each truck to prevent cars from running under them in rear-end collisions. When a car runs under a truck, the windshield and the front-seat occupant hit the truck first, so the cushioning effect of a collapsing hood section is lost. This can turn even a low-speed accident into a fatal one. The bill was defeated in part by the trucking industry, which argued that the cars which ran into the trucks were at fault so it was not fair to require the truckers to spend money for shields. What is your view of this argument?

*3. Safety belt-ignition interlocks have been ordered by the government because only 4% of all auto occupants willingly use lap and shoulder harnesses.
   a. As you see it, should the 96% who choose not to protect themselves be left to take the consequences or does society have a responsibility to protect them despite themselves? Alternatively, does the introduction of interlocks or airbags represent an unwarranted intrusion into people's lives? Should people be free to run risks?
   b. The interlocks and – if adopted – the air-bag increase the cost of cars. Is that fair to the 4% of the population who voluntarily use safety belts? How would you resolve the overall question?
   c. Why do you think most people refuse to use shoulder harnesses?

4. In many parts of the nation a person cannot get to work, to shops, or to medical care without an auto.
   a. Because of the auto's importance, should obtaining a driver's license be a right instead of the privilege it now is?
   b. If you feel it should remain a privilege in order to protect people against those unable to drive "safely," would you be in favor of tightening up license requirements by excluding groups of drivers who are statistically highly likely to have accidents? For example, should persons 24 or younger be banned from driving in order to safeguard the safer age-groups over 24?
   c. Table 4 shows that the 15–24 age-group is 2.5 times more likely to die in a one-car, noncollision accident than the 25–44 age-group but only 1.5 times more likely to die in a two-vehicle collision. Do you have any theories as to the reason for this?

5. In 1972, the death rate on interstate highways was 2.5 deaths/$10^8$ vehicle-miles and on noninterstate roads 4.5 deaths/$10^8$ vehicle-miles. Assume there were $2 \times 10^{11}$ vehicle-miles of travel on interstate roads in 1972.
   a. How many deaths occurred on interstate roads that year?

b. How many deaths would have occurred if that travel had taken place on non-interstate roads? What were the dollar benefits due to the saved lives?

c. Does the calculation in part b demonstrate that interstate roads saved an appreciable number of lives or is interpretation necessary?

6. A politician flies 200,000 miles on scheduled, domestic airlines during 1972.
a. What were the chances of the politician being killed?
b. What would the chances have been if the same distance had been flown in only 9 months?
c. What would the chances have been if the politician had driven that distance during 1972?

7. The death rate for motorcyclists in 1969 was about 22 deaths per $10^8$ vehicle-miles. Assume there were 2000 motorcycle fatalities.
a. What were the number of vehicle-miles traveled by motorcycles in 1969?
b. How many miles was the average motorcycle driven? (Assume 2,300,000 motorcycles were registered that year.)

8. After the Boeing 747 airplane, which can hold about 400 passengers, had been in commercial service for several months, a U.S. government official announced that the plane was proven safe because it had traveled one billion passenger-miles without a fatality. Was this statement statistically sound?

9. What premium should an insurance company charge to insure a traveler against death for $100,000 on (a) a 10,000-mile auto trip? (b) a 10,000-mile plane trip? Use 1972 data and disregard the insurance company's operating expenses and profits. Remember that the idea of insurance is that the premiums paid by all the insured people go to those few who get in an accident.

10. It is believed by some safety experts that a significant number of auto deaths are suicides or homicides. Assume you wished to investigate this possibility by looking at available statistical evidence rather than by going into the field and checking into actual accidents. What kind of statistical information would you want? What correlations (relations) would you look for among the statistics you gathered?

11. A survey indicated that about 15% of driver fatalities in one-vehicle, non-collision accidents (for example, car runs off the road) had died of a heart attack or stroke before the accident. If these results are used to reinterpret Table 4, would they affect the judgment that under-25 drivers are, as a group, reckless?

12. Assume a survey shows that 20% of all auto occupants wear safety belts and that 10% of all auto occupants who were fatally injured in an accident had on safety belts at the time of the accident. Does this show that in an accident safety belts protect the wearer, or is some other interpretation possible? Is more information needed to make an analysis?

13. It is estimated that fires feeding on auto seats, trim, and so on, cause $80 million in damage annually. Fireproofing interior materials so that this loss would be cut to zero would cost $7.50 per car built. Would this be cost effective in the first year; second year; ever? Assume 100 million cars on the road with an average lifetime of 10 years (10 million cars manufactured each year).

14. Refer to Table 8.
    a. If you had to get into an accident, which type would you pick?
    b. Which would you avoid? Explain.

15. According to Table 8, does the steering wheel, instrument panel, windshield, or ejection cause the largest number of deaths?

16. In Figure 5, how is the total passengers-per-vehicle figure of 1.532 derived? (Your answer should be 0.003 people too low. What would you guess is the source of the discrepancy?)

17. In Table 4, the total death rate for all ages is 28.8. However, the rates for the given age-groups do not add up to or average 28.8.
    a. What additional information must you have to translate the death rates by age-groups into 28.8?
    b. Make a rough estimate and try to calculate the 28.8 figure from information in the table. Assume U.S. life expectancy is 70 years.

18. In 1960, the U.S. birth rate was 23.7 annual births per 1000 people. Since then it has dropped, hovering around 17 births per 1000 people in the early 1970s. What implication does this have for motor-vehicle fatality rates starting in the 1980s?

19. The nationwide reduction of highway speed limits to 55 miles/hour caused by the motor-vehicle fuel shortage in the winter of 1973–1974 had several side effects. The trucking industry, for example, said that the speed reduction should be balanced by an increase in the legal limits for truck sizes and weights.
    a. What was the basis for their argument?
    b. What side effects might an increase in truck size and weight have?

20. A highway engineer in the May, 1971, issue of *Highway User* writes:

    In 1909 about 26 million horses traveled some 13 billion miles and 3850 people were killed in accidents involving horse-drawn vehicles. This gives a mileage death rate of over 30 per 100 million vehicle-miles, more than 10 times as high as the rate on California's freeways, and further improvements are on the way.

    Is the above argument valid? Defend or attack it.

*Thou shalt not unnecessarily cultivate high power, for error, destruction, noise, and excess vigilance are its evil wastes.*

HOWARD T. ODUM*

# 5 Accident dynamics

The statistics in the previous chapter give a good overview of motor-vehicle accidents, injuries, and deaths. But statistics give a dry, bloodless approach to a problem. In this chapter we will look at the dynamics of accidents: the forces generated and energy released in motor-vehicle collisions.

A car moving at 60 miles/hour has a large amount of kinetic energy, or energy of motion. This energy of motion comes from the gasoline burned in the engine to accelerate the car to 60 miles/hour. In a collision the energy is released explosively, almost as if the gasoline were vaporized in the car and then ignited. A person driving at 60 miles/hour can be compared to someone tossing a lighted Molotov cocktail from hand to hand. In both cases, one slip can release a large amount of energy in an explosive manner.

An auto accident releases its energy differently from exploding gasoline. In place of the heat and shock wave generated by burning gasoline, tremendous mechanical forces are produced as several thousand pounds of metal rip into a tree, wall, or other barrier.

---

*From Odum's book *Environment, Power, and Society* (New York: Wiley-Interscience, 1971).

**103**

The enormous amount of energy inherent in highway travel is indicated by this accident in the fall of 1973 on the New Jersey Turnpike. It resulted primarily from reduced visibility caused by a fire in a nearby dump. At least nine persons were killed and forty injured in a series of chain-reaction accidents involving sixty-five vehicles. *Photo courtesy U.S. National Transportation Safety Board.*

These forces bring the vehicle to rest in about one-tenth of a second. A stationary car struck from behind would be propelled into motion in the same tenth of a second. The rapid changes in motion generate tremendous forces experienced by both the auto and its occupants, causing property damage, injuries, and deaths.

Inertia.   The forces generated in a collision result from inertia, a property of matter which resists changes in direction and in rate of motion. We experience the inertial property when a car or plane speeds up (accelerates) or slows down (decelerates). During acceleration, we feel ourselves being pushed back into our seat. What we are experiencing is the seat pushing on our back. In effect, the seat is pushing us to give us the same acceleration as the car — the push tries to overcome the body's inertia or resistance to being accelerated. When a car decelerates, we continue moving forward with the car's original speed, again due to inertia. To decelerate with the car we push on the floor with our feet, or depend on the seat belt or the friction between our body and the auto seat to provide the decelerating force.

The auto is subject to the same inertial forces as our bodies. If it were not for the existence of friction and air resistance, a moving car would continue to move forever in a straight line at a constant speed due to its inertia. Thus to stop a car faster than friction and air resistance would, we use brakes. The brakes exert a force on the wheels and the tires then exert a force on the pavement, which in turn acts back on the tires, slowing and eventually stopping the car. Similarly, if it were not for the force exerted by a stationary auto's tires on the pavement and the pavement's reaction force on the tires, a car at rest would remain at rest forever. There can be motion without forces. But whenever there is change in rate or change in direction of motion, there must be forces.

Seat Belts and Air-bags. In contrast to the controlled stop produced by braking, a car striking a wall comes to an abrupt, violent halt. But the car's unbelted occupants continue to move at the vehicle's original speed until they are stopped by a collision with the interior of the car, the windshield, or the pavement. (See Figure 1.) The collision of the occupants with the car interior or the pavement is called the "second collision." It is this second collision which causes injuries and deaths; the first collision damages only the auto.

### First and Second Collision

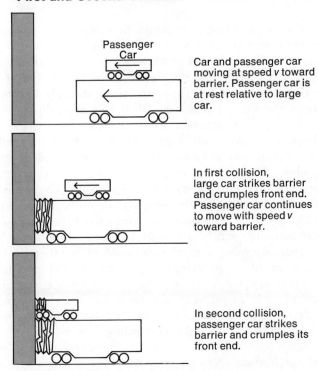

Passenger
Car

Car and passenger car moving at speed *v* toward barrier. Passenger car is at rest relative to large car.

In first collision, large car strikes barrier and crumples front end. Passenger car continues to move with speed *v* toward barrier.

In second collision, passenger car strikes barrier and crumples its front end.

**Figure 1.** Shown here is a collision between a barrier and a flat car carrying a second, smaller car. After the first collision halts the large car, the smaller car continues moving until it strikes the barrier in the second collision. If the small car had been tied to the first car, there would have been no second collision.

The purpose of seat belts and air-bags is to eliminate the collision between auto occupants and the car interior or pavement. Seat belts and air-bags cannot eliminate the forces generated in a collision. If a car crashes into a barrier at 30 miles/hour, large forces (about 2000 pounds) must be exerted by the belt to restrain the passenger. But the flexible, yielding seat belt distributes the generated forces over a larger and less vulnerable part of the body than would a steering column or windshield.

A properly designed seat belt will do more than just restrain a person. It will have enough stretch so that in a crash the restraining force it exerts is minimized. But it will not stretch so much that the occupant smashes into the steering column or dashboard. Nor will it act like a large rubber band and snap the belted person back into the seat. This means that as the seat belt is stretched, it must dissipate energy. Otherwise all the energy that went into stretching the belt would be used to smash the seat occupant back into the seat. A good seat belt should also be self-adjusting so that it fits snugly but does not restrict movement. Nonadjusting belts are likely to be worn loosely for comfort. In a crash, the loosely belted person will move forward until the slack is taken up with a jerk. This will increase the forces the person will experience but is still better than wearing no belt at all.

Like seat belts, air-bags function by distributing forces generated in an accident over a larger part of the body. In an accident, sensors respond to abnormally high rates of acceleration or deceleration and cause a porous bag placed under the dashboard to be rapidly inflated with gas. As the auto occupants move forward within the rapidly decelerating car, they strike the soft, yielding, gas-filled bag, spreading the forces generated by the rapid deceleration over a relatively large area.

Air-bags are more complicated and more likely to malfunction than seat belts. They can inflate when there is no accident or perhaps not inflate when there is an accident. Even when triggering properly, air-bags present problems. They must expand quickly to cushion the auto occupants before they hit the steering wheel, dashboard, or windshield. But in a closed car, the explosive expansion of the bag can cause a rapid pressure increase, with the risk of bursting an occupant's eardrum. A slower expansion solves the pressure problem, but then the auto occupants —traveling at 30 or 40 miles/hour relative to the car—may hit a solid object before the bag inflates. Other problems are that air-bags do not position properly to protect small children, and they provide little protection against side-impact accidents. But the air-bag is a new technology and work on these problems is continuing.

**Head Restraints.**  Neither seat belts nor air-bags are useful in protecting against rear-impact crashes, in which a moving car smashes into the back of a stationary or slowly moving car. Because of inertia, the occupants of the struck car tend to remain at rest as their vehicle is jolted into motion. However, the seat backs—assuming they do not collapse—exert a large force on the occupants, moving them forward. But the passenger's head is not being pushed on by any part of the accelerating car and the neck is not strong enough to accelerate the head at the same rate that the seat is accelerating the body. (See Figure 2.) As a result, the head snaps back. In extreme cases an accident victim can end up looking out the rear window before the head is snapped back in place by the over-extended neck. It is this sequence which causes whiplash injuries. To prevent whiplash, federal safety standards require that the front seats of autos be equipped with head restraints designed to prevent the head from snapping back.

### A Collision

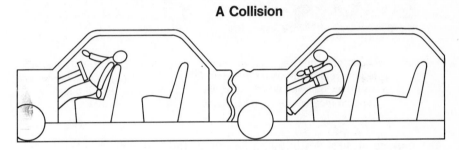

**Figure 2.** The car on the left has been propelled into motion after being struck by the car on the right. The head of the driver of the struck car has snapped back. The driver of the car on the right has pitched forward.

## A Quantitative Look

The Crush Constant. We now look more precisely at what happens in an accident by applying physical laws and numbers to collisions. When a car strikes an immovable barrier, the front end of the car is compressed, or crushed. For each mile per hour of speed, the average auto is crushed an inch. A car that hits a brick wall at 12 miles/hour will be shortened 12 inches. If the car was originally 15 feet long, it would be 14 feet long after the crash, with all the compression taking place in the very front.

To visualize a collision, it may help to think of the car as having a large spring mounted on its front. In a collision, the spring is compressed as the auto's energy of motion goes into squeezing it. The same thing happens with an auto body in a collision; but unfortunately the auto body does not spring back. It remains crushed and rent by the energy of motion that poured into it during the collision. It is the absorption of the energy of motion by the metal that brings the car to rest. The spring analogy helps illustrate the difference between a car-brick wall collision and a car-car collision. When a car going 30 miles/hour smashes into a brick wall, all of the energy of motion is dissipated by the car since the wall does not yield and therefore does not absorb energy. But if a car

Crush constant has a clean, clinical sound to it. The reality is very different. This front-impact collision with an unyielding physical barrier on an urban highway was fatal to the car's occupants. *Photo courtesy Insurance Institute for Highway Safety.*

moving at 30 miles/hour plows into a stationary car, both cars will "share" the energy of motion. So here the moving car's damage will in theory be less than it would be in a collision with a brick wall. We cannot, however, say that a 30-mile/hour crash into a stationary car is equivalent to a 15-mile/hour crash into a brick wall. Energy of motion increases as the square of the speed, and doubling the speed therefore quadruples the energy that must be dissipated in a collision.

To quantify damage done in collisions, we define the crush constant, $k$, as

$$k = \frac{\text{speed}}{\text{length crushed}} = \frac{1 \text{ mi/hr}}{1 \text{ in.}}$$

for a car of average stiffness. In a 30-mile/hour barrier crash, the crush experienced is

$$\text{length crushed} = \frac{\text{speed}}{k} = \frac{30 \text{ mi/hr}}{1 \text{ mi/hr/in.}}$$
$$= 30 \text{ in.} = 2.5 \text{ ft.}$$

To express $k$ in different units, we note that 30 miles/hour = 44 feet/second.

$$k = \frac{\text{speed}}{\text{length crushed}} = \frac{44 \text{ ft/sec}}{2.5 \text{ ft}} = 17.6/\text{sec}$$

Although $k = 17.6$/second describes the average car, there are variations among cars. A light auto generally has a larger crush constant, which means it collapses less in a collision. For example, if a car's crush constant is 2 miles/hour/inch (or 35.2/second), in a 30-mile/hour collision

$$\text{length crushed} = \frac{\text{speed}}{k} = \frac{30 \text{ mi/hr}}{2 \text{ mi/hr/in.}} = 15 \text{ in.}$$

or

$$\text{length crushed} = \frac{44 \text{ ft/sec}}{35.2/\text{sec}} = 1.25 \text{ ft} = 15 \text{ in.}$$

A heavy car generally has a smaller crush constant and in a collision suffers a larger-than-normal collapse.

**Impact Duration and Average Speed.** It is the crush constant that determines the duration of the collision. The collision period starts when the auto first strikes the barrier and ends when the car comes to rest. To calculate the collision period—which we need in order to obtain the forces generated during the collision—we recall from Chapter 3 that the relation between distance ($d$), speed ($V$), and time ($t$), is

$$d = (V)(t).$$

A car traveling at 60 miles/hour for 3 hours goes

$$d = (V)(t) = (60 \text{ mi/hr})(3 \text{ hr}) = 180 \text{ mi.}$$

Since 60 miles/hour is 88 feet/second, the same car in 20 seconds goes

$$d = (V)(t) = (88 \text{ ft/sec})(20 \text{ sec}) = 1760 \text{ ft.}$$

This situation is represented by the graph in Figure 3a.

**Speed Versus Time**

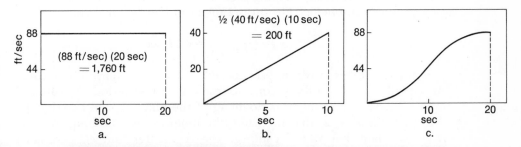

**Figure 3.** The distance traveled can be obtained from these speed-time plots by calculating the areas under the curve. a. The speed is constant at 88 feet/second for 20 seconds. The region under the curve is a rectangle whose area is the product of the base (20 seconds) and the height (88 feet/second). b. The region under the curve is a triangle whose area is one-half the base (10 seconds) times the height (40 feet/second). This plot is an example of uniform acceleration. C. This plot shows a case of irregular acceleration. Because of the irregular shape, the distance traveled—which is still the area under the curve—cannot be exactly calculated from a simple geometric formula. Note that the "area" under the curves has the dimensions of distance.

The above calculation applies only if the speed stays constant, as in Figure 3a. But the essence of collisions is that speeds change drastically. As an example of a relatively gentle change in speed, assume a car starts from rest, accelerating to 40 feet/second during 10 seconds, as represented by the graph in Figure 3b. To calculate how far the auto went while accelerating, we need a speed. Clearly, the speed is not 40 feet/second, for the car went that fast only at the very end, and the car did not travel 400 feet (40 feet/second × 10 seconds) during its acceleration. Nor is 0 feet/second the appropriate speed. But because the change in speed during acceleration was uniform, we can introduce the idea of average speed. We note that the "middle" speed is 20 feet/second – halfway between the initial and final speeds. For the first 5 seconds the car was going slower and for the last 5 seconds faster than 20 feet/second. Therefore, we call 20 feet/second the average speed.

$$V_{av} = \tfrac{1}{2}(V_{initial} + V_{final}) = \tfrac{1}{2}(0 \text{ ft/sec} + 40 \text{ ft/sec}) = 20 \text{ ft/sec}$$
$$\text{distance} = (V_{av})\,(\text{time}) = (20 \text{ ft/sec})\,(10 \text{ sec}) = 200 \text{ ft}$$

As can be seen from Figure 3b, this is also the "area" under the speed curve. In reality, autos accelerate nonuniformly, as shown in Figure 3c, but throughout this chapter we will assume speed change (acceleration or deceleration) is uniform.

With the concepts of crush distance and average speed in hand, impact times can be calculated. As an example, we consider a 30-mile/hour (44-foot/second) collision in which a car is crushed 2.5 feet. The average speed during the impact, assuming uniform deceleration, is

$$V_{av} = \tfrac{1}{2}(V_i + V_f) = \tfrac{1}{2}[(44 \text{ ft/sec}) + (0 \text{ ft/sec})] = 22 \text{ ft/sec}.$$

Here the car is initially moving and finally at rest, but the concept of average speed still holds. The impact time can now be obtained.

$$t = \frac{d}{V_{av}} = \frac{2.5 \text{ ft}}{22 \text{ ft/sec}} = 0.11 \text{ sec}$$

So the car comes to rest in 0.11 seconds, a bit over a tenth of a second. All cars of the same stiffness come to rest in the same period regardless of impact speed. For example, a doubling of the impact speed also doubles the crush distance so that the ratio (the time) in the above equation remains constant. For an extra stiff car, the impact duration will be smaller since the crush distance in the above equation will be less, but the average speed, which depends only on initial and final speeds, will be the same.

**Acceleration and Deceleration.** We now will quantify the concept of acceleration. This further complicates matters, but this information is necessary to calculate the forces generated in collisions. Acceleration is the time rate at which velocity changes, just as velocity is the time rate at which distance changes. For example, if a car goes uniformly from rest to 40 feet/second in 5 seconds, the car's speed increases by 8 feet/second every second (see Figure 4). So the acceleration, *a*, is (8 feet/second)/second, or 8 feet/second/second, or 8 feet/second².

$$a = \frac{(V_f - V_i)}{t} = \frac{(40 \text{ ft/sec}) - (0 \text{ ft/sec})}{5 \text{ sec}} = 8 \text{ ft/sec}^2$$

If a car goes from 40 feet/second to rest (0 feet/second) in 5 seconds, it is decelerating at a rate of

$$a = \frac{(V_f - V_i)}{t} = \frac{(0 \text{ ft/sec}) - (40 \text{ ft/sec})}{5 \text{ sec}} = -8 \text{ ft/sec}^2.$$

Here the minus sign shows that the auto is decelerating.

**Figure 4.** Acceleration is the change in speed divided by the change in time, or $a = (V_2 - V_1)/(t_2 - t_1)$. Because the acceleration is constant, we can calculate it from any point on the curve. We have taken a time interval of 2.5 seconds which corresponds, as shown by the dotted lines, to a speed change of 20 feet/second. Therefore, $a = (V_2 - V_1)/(t_2 - t_1) = $ (20 feet/second)/(2.5 seconds) = 8 feet/second². The same acceleration is obtained if the entire 5-second interval is used. Because $V_{av}$ is 20 feet/second during the 5 seconds, the distance covered is 100 feet.

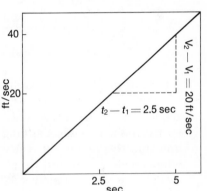

**Acceleration**

If the acceleration, time, and initial speed are known, the final speed and distance covered can be found using the following relations.

$$V_f = V_i + at$$
$$\begin{aligned} d &= V_{av}t \\ &= \tfrac{1}{2}(V_i + V_f)t \qquad\qquad [\text{since } V_{av} = \tfrac{1}{2}(V_i + V_f)] \\ &= \tfrac{1}{2}[V_i + (V_i + at)]t \qquad [\text{since } V_f = V_i + at] \\ &= V_i t + \tfrac{1}{2}at^2 \end{aligned}$$

If an auto starts from rest and accelerates at 6 feet/second² for 15 seconds, its speed after 15 seconds is

$$V_f = V_i + at = (0 \text{ ft/sec}) + [(6 \text{ ft/sec}^2)(15 \text{ sec})] = 90 \text{ ft/sec}.$$

This situation is represented by the graph in Figure 5. To find the distance traveled during the 15 seconds, we can use the average speed of 45 feet/second.

## Acceleration

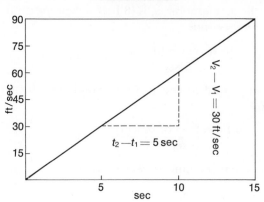

**Figure 5.** Here the acceleration is $a = (V_2 - V_1)/(t_2 - t_1) = (30$ ft/sec)/(5 sec) $= 6$ ft/sec². From the area, the distance traveled during the 15 seconds is $d = \frac{1}{2}$(base)(height) $= \frac{1}{2}$(15 sec)(90 ft/sec) $= 675$ ft.

$$d = V_{av}t = (45 \text{ ft/sec}) \ (15 \text{ sec}) = 675 \text{ ft}$$

Or we can use the relation $d = V_it + \frac{1}{2}at^2$.

$$d = V_it + \tfrac{1}{2}at^2 = 0 + \tfrac{1}{2}[(6 \text{ ft/sec}^2) \ (15 \text{ sec})^2] = 675 \text{ ft}$$

**A Rule of Thumb for Collision Forces.** The most common example of acceleration is a freely falling body. When an object falls freely, it accelerates at 32 feet/second². This acceleration holds for all bodies — whatever their weight — as long as air resistance is neglected. The acceleration due to gravity, 32 feet/second², is called *g*, and we can express all other accelerations and decelerations in terms of *g*. If a person is decelerated in an auto collision at 320 feet/second², we say he experienced 10 *g*'s. Associated with 10 *g* is a force equal to 10 times the person's body weight.

$$\text{force} = (\text{number of } g) \ (\text{weight})$$

Therefore, a 160-pound person would experience a force of 1600 pounds. The force might be exerted by a seat belt pushing on the person's body and decelerating him as the car decelerates. Or the force might be exerted much more destructively by the steering wheel or windshield, also producing deceleration.

**Catching Our Breath.** We have been through a fair amount of technical material and should pause a moment to take our bearings and sum up. In a collision with a barrier or another auto, tremendous forces are generated. These forces cause a deceleration which brings the auto to rest. The auto's occupants, however, tend to continue moving forward. If they are belted, they may avoid a second collision and be decelerated to rest along with the car to which the belts are anchored. This deceleration is produced by the belts, which exert a force on the auto occupant equal to the occupant's weight times the number of *g*'s of deceleration experienced.

The unbelted person continues forward with the car's original speed until striking the dashboard, steering wheel, or windshield. The struck object then exerts decelerating forces on the person, bringing him to rest.

**Example 1.**  As an example, let us calculate the forces experienced by a belted, 120-pound passenger in a 60-mile/hour (88-foot/second) collision into a barrier. The average speed is

$$V_{av} = \tfrac{1}{2}[(0 \text{ ft/sec}) + (88 \text{ ft/sec})] = 44 \text{ ft/sec}.$$

The distance traveled during impact (the crush distance) is

$$\text{crush distance} = (k)\,(V) = \left(\frac{1}{17.6 \text{ sec}}\right)(88 \text{ ft/sec}) = 5 \text{ ft}.$$

The duration of the collision is

$$t = \frac{d}{V_{av}} = \frac{5 \text{ ft}}{44 \text{ ft/sec}} = 0.11 \text{ sec}.$$

The deceleration is

$$a = \frac{(V_f - V_i)}{t} = \frac{(0 \text{ ft/sec}) - (88 \text{ ft/sec})}{0.11 \text{ sec}} = -800 \text{ ft/sec}^2.$$

This deceleration corresponds to 25 $g$ [(800 ft/sec²) ÷ (32 ft/sec²) = 25], so the 120-pound person will experience a force of

$$(25)\,(120 \text{ lb}) = 3000 \text{ lb}.$$

## Newton's Laws of Motion

The information above is sufficient to permit us to calculate the forces generated in collisions. We now wish to make the chain of physical reasoning more coherent by introducing Sir Isaac Newton's three laws of motion. These laws—formulated in 1686 by the English mathematician-physicist-Biblical scholar—are general laws and apply to all motion not approaching the speed of light (186,000 miles/second).

**The First Law.**  Every body persists in its state of rest or in its state of uniform motion in a straight line unless compelled to change that state by forces impressed on it.

This is the law of inertia, which describes why an unbelted person in a collision continues to move forward. It also describes why a person in an accelerating car must be pushed on by the seat back. Although the law of inertia may seem obvious, people before Newton thought that to keep an object in motion it must be continually pushed. This view resulted from the fact that air resistance and friction are everywhere, causing all everyday moving objects to eventually come to rest.

**The Second Law.** The acceleration of a body is directly proportional to the force applied to it and inversely proportional to its mass. (This law is written

$$a = \frac{F}{m}$$

where $F$ is the applied force and $m$ the mass.)

The second law quantifies the relation between the force, acceleration or deceleration, and an object's mass. Mass quantifies the inertia of matter — its resistance to acceleration or deceleration. The more massive an object (the larger $m$), the more difficult (the more force it takes) to set it in motion or to stop it once in motion. The second law allows us to calculate the forces generated during collisions.

**The Third Law.** To every action there is always opposed an equal reaction. (This is the action-reaction law.)

The third law describes what happens when an object exerts a force on another object. For example, during acceleration of a car, the rear wheels push on the pavement. According to the third law, the pavement pushes back with an equal and opposite force, which, in effect, pushes the car forward.

**Slugs and Kilograms.** The unit of mass in the British system is the slug; in the metric system the unit of mass is the kilogram. An object of mass 1 slug weighs 32 pounds on the earth; a 2-slug object weighs 64 pounds; and so on. To convert from mass to weight we use

$$\text{weight} = (\text{mass}) \, (\text{acceleration due to gravity})$$
$$= (m) \, (g) = (m) \, (32 \text{ ft/sec}^2).$$

For conversion purposes, a slug has units of pounds/feet/second$^2$. Thus a 5-slug mass weighs

$$\text{weight} = (m) \, (g) = (5 \text{ slugs}) \, (32 \text{ ft/sec}^2)$$
$$= (5 \text{ lb/ft/sec}^2)(32 \text{ ft/sec}^2) = 160 \text{ lb}.$$

These units will take some getting used to. The mass of a 200-pound object is

$$m = \frac{\text{weight}}{g} = \frac{200 \text{ lb}}{32 \text{ ft/sec}^2} = 6.3 \text{ lb/ft/sec}^2 = 6.3 \text{ slugs}.$$

**Applying the Second Law.** We can now use Newton's second law to calculate the forces occurring during collisions and in other instances of acceleration and deceleration.

**Example 2.** A car traveling at 15 miles/hour (22 feet/second) strikes a wall head-on. Calculate the deceleration experienced and the strength required of a seat belt used to restrain a 192-pound person.

A car of typical stiffness will collapse 15 inches, or $1\frac{1}{4}$ feet, before stopping. Assuming the car decelerated uniformly, its average velocity will be

$$V_{av} = \tfrac{1}{2}(V_i + V_f) = \tfrac{1}{2}[(22 \text{ ft/sec}) + (0 \text{ ft/sec})] = 11 \text{ ft/sec}.$$

All the deceleration occurs while the car is traveling that last, crushing $1\frac{1}{4}$ feet. The time it takes to travel this distance at an average speed of 11 feet/second is

$$t = \frac{d}{V_{av}} = \frac{1.25 \text{ ft}}{11 \text{ ft/sec}} = 0.11 \text{ sec}.$$

The deceleration is the change in velocity divided by the time.

$$a = \frac{(V_f - V_i)}{t} = \frac{-22 \text{ ft/sec}}{0.11 \text{ sec}} = -200 \text{ ft/sec}^2.$$

The mass of a 192-pound person is

$$m = \frac{\text{weight}}{g} = \frac{192 \text{ lb}}{32 \text{ ft/sec}^2} = 6 \text{ slugs}.$$

The force experienced by the 192-pound (6-slug) person will therefore be

$$F = (m)(a) = (6 \text{ slugs})(200 \text{ ft/sec}^2) = 1200 \text{ lb}.$$

The seat belt or belts must be strong enough to take a force of 1200 pounds without breaking.

**Example 3.** Assume a car is struck from behind so that in one-tenth of a second it accelerates from rest to 6 miles/hour (8.8 feet/second).
    a. What is the acceleration?

$$a = \frac{V_f - V_i}{t} = \frac{8.8 \text{ ft/sec}}{0.1 \text{ sec}} = 88 \text{ ft/sec}^2$$

    b. What force will the seat have to exert on a 160-pound man so that he accelerates with the car?

$$m = \frac{\text{weight}}{g} = \frac{160 \text{ lb}}{32 \text{ ft/sec}^2} = 5 \text{ slugs}$$

$$F = (m)(a) = (5 \text{ slugs})(88 \text{ ft/sec}^2) = 440 \text{ lb}$$

If there were two people in the front seat, the seat would have to exert a force of 880 pounds. Seats often give way under this kind of stress.
    c. If the person's head weighs 20 pounds, what force must the neck exert on the head to accelerate it along with the rest of the body? Assume no head restraint.

$$m = \frac{\text{weight}}{g} = \frac{20 \text{ lb}}{32 \text{ ft/sec}^2} = 0.63 \text{ slugs}$$

$$F = (m)(a) = (0.63 \text{ slugs})(88 \text{ feet/sec}^2) = 54 \text{ lb}$$

This is an appreciable force and without a restraint the head will tend to snap backwards.

**Air-bag Expansions.**  It was mentioned earlier that an expanding air-bag in a closed auto can possibly cause ear damage to the occupants. One way to reduce this possibility is to expand the bag slowly so that the pressure increase is less abrupt. But the bag must be fully expanded in time to intercept the auto occupant who is hurtling forward. Let us therefore calculate how fast the bag must inflate in a 30-mile/hour (44-foot/second) collision with a barrier if we allow $\frac{1}{2}$ foot of forward motion before the bag is to intercept the occupant.

Auto occupants are especially vulnerable to injury in side-impact collisions since the car offers only slight cushioning protection on the sides. Seventeen percent of all motor vehicle accidents are side-impact collisions, but twenty-six percent of all traffic fatalities result from such collisions. *Photo courtesy Federal Highway Administration.*

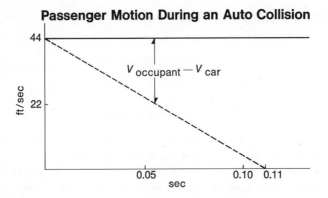

**Passenger Motion During an Auto Collision**

**Figure 6.** The solid horizontal line is the speed of the auto occupant; the sloping dotted line is the speed of the auto during the crash. The difference between the two speeds – shown by $V_{occupant} - V_{car}$ at 0.05 seconds – is the speed of the auto occupant relative to the auto. At 0.11 seconds, the auto has come completely to rest and the unbelted occupant is moving forward at 44 feet/second toward the front of the auto. For the diagram above, the motion is idealized. Actual deceleration of the auto and motion of the passenger would be highly irregular.

   Initially, both occupant and auto are moving at 44 feet/second. As the car crushes into the barrier, its speed decreases while the occupant continues to move at 44 feet/second. As a result, the occupant moves forward relative to the car. Figure 6 gives a plot of the speed of the car and of the occupant. The difference between the two speeds at any instant is the speed of the occupant relative to the auto. We know from previous calculations that it takes a car of ordinary stiffness 0.11 seconds to stop during a collision, whatever the initial speed. The acceleration is therefore

$$a = \frac{-44 \text{ ft/sec}}{0.11 \text{ sec}} = -400 \text{ ft/sec}^2.$$

At time $t'$ after the crash begins, the speed, $V'$, of the occupant relative to the car interior will be

$$V' = (400 \text{ ft/sec}^2)t'$$

which is also the amount by which the car has slowed. The average speed of the occupant relative to the auto interior during the crash is

$$V'_{av} = \tfrac{1}{2}(V_i + V_f) = \tfrac{1}{2}(0 + at')$$
$$= \tfrac{1}{2}(400 \text{ ft/sec}^2)t' = (200 \text{ ft/sec}^2)t'.$$

The distance traveled by the auto occupant relative to the auto interior during the crash is

$$d = V'_{av}t' = (200 \text{ ft/sec}^2)t'^2.$$

We want to know how long it will take the auto occupant to travel $\frac{1}{2}$ foot.

$$d = V'_{av}\, t'$$

$$\tfrac{1}{2} \text{ ft} = (200 \text{ ft/sec}^2)\, t'^2$$

$$t'^2 = \left(\frac{1}{400}\right) \text{ sec}^2$$

$$t' = 0.05 \text{ sec}$$

So the air-bag must expand 0.05 seconds after the crash. We should point out that although the answer of 0.05 seconds is correct, the actual deceleration in a crash and the motion of the passenger relative to the auto is far more complicated and irregular than assumed here.

**Force and Pressure.** As discussed earlier, it is the first collision that damages the car and the second collision, in which the auto occupants collide with the car interior or the pavement, that causes injury and death. Federal safety standards require that dashboards be padded, control knobs and window cranks be recessed, and sharp edges and corners be eliminated. In other words, eventually it is expected that equipment that can stab and puncture occupants or pedestrians will be eliminated in favor of flat surfaces.

As the previous section showed, the total forces generated in a collision cannot be changed because they are due to the accelerations or decelerations involved. Newton's laws of motion cannot be repealed. The object of flat dashboards, seat belts, and air-bags is not to eliminate forces but to distribute them in a less damaging way. A classic example of distributing or concentrating forces is illustrated by an ordinary straight pin. A one-pound force can drive the point of a pin into a piece of wood. But if the head of the pin is placed against the wood, the same one-pound force will not cause the pin to even penetrate the wood.

Steering columns, dashboard knobs, windshields, door columns, and exterior "ornaments" all can be viewed as the point of a pin. The object of seat belts, padded interiors, and air-bags is to eliminate the point, to bring the careening auto occupant into contact with a flat, yielding surface. In more technical terms, the goal is to reduce the *pressure* exerted on the body. Pressure is defined as

$$P = \frac{F}{A}$$

where $P$ is the pressure, $F$ the force, and $A$ the area over which the force is exerted. As the formula shows, for the same force, the smaller the area the greater the pressure.

As an example, let us calculate the pressure exerted by the point and by the head of a pin. Assume the area of the head is $10^{-2}$ square inches and the area of the point is $10^{-7}$ square inches. If a one-pound force is applied to the pin, the pressure exerted by the head will be

$$P = \frac{F}{A} = \frac{1 \text{ lb}}{10^{-2}\text{in.}^2} = 100 \text{ lb/in.}^2$$

But if the same force drives the point, its pressure will be

$$P = \frac{F}{A} = \frac{1 \text{ lb}}{10^{-7}\text{in.}^2} = 10^7 \text{ lb/in.}^2$$

10 million pounds per square inch!

**Example 4.** Let us now look at an auto situation. Assume that in an accident a 160-pound person is decelerated at 200 feet/second². Assume that in one case the occupant is decelerated when her face hits the windshield and in the second case the occupant is decelerated by a 2-inch-wide lap and torso belt, with 3 feet of the belt's length actually in contact with the person's body. Find the pressure on the occupant in each case.

a.  In the first case we assume that initially 10 square inches of the victim's face come in contact with the windshield. This is a very rough approximation to a complicated problem since both the windshield and the face will "give," but it illustrates the point. The force needed to decelerate the 160-pound (5-slug) person is

$$F = (m)(a) = (5 \text{ slugs})(200 \text{ ft/sec}^2) = 1000 \text{ lb.}$$

The pressure on the victim's face will be

$$P = \frac{F}{A} = \frac{1000 \text{ lb}}{10 \text{ in.}^2} = 100 \text{ lb/in.}^2$$

b.  In the case of the belt, the area in contact with the person will be

$$A = (\text{width})(\text{length}) = (2 \text{ in.})(3 \text{ ft})$$
$$= (2 \text{ in.})(36 \text{ in.}) = 72 \text{ in.}^2$$

The pressure on the occupant will be

$$P = \frac{F}{A} = \frac{1000 \text{ lb}}{72 \text{ in.}^2} = 14 \text{ lb/in.}^2$$

**Tires, Road Surfaces, and Safety.**  Much of the preceding discussion has centered on ways of minimizing the damage done by accidents. But there are steps that can be taken to make accidents less likely to occur. Tires and road surfaces are major areas of accident prevention. Acceleration, braking, and turning all require that the tire and road push on each other. When the road-tire adherence, or traction, is reduced by wet or icy roads or by worn tires, skids and accidents happen. From the all-too-familiar loss of traction has come the metaphor "spinning your wheels," which refers to any situation in which a large amount of effort is repaid with little or no effect.

The problem of road-tire traction is a complex one, without the kind of clean, precise laws that govern the relation between acceleration, mass, and force; or pressure, area, and force. What rules exist are empirical — developed from experiment and observation. In addition, there is no "best" solution to the traction problem — only compromises between the differing needs of driving on dry, wet, and snowcovered roads.

In dry weather, the best traction is obtained with slick tires — tires with no tread at all — because they put the most surface area into contact with the road. But on wet roads, slick tires hydroplane, or float, on a thin film of water, leading to skids. Tires with tread, however, do not hydroplane as readily because the water is squeezed between the treads, allowing them to contact the road (see Figure 7). Snow tires, with their exaggerated tread, do a good job of pushing through snow to reach the ground or of getting a grip on the packed snow itself.

Treaded tires wear more quickly than slick tires because there is less surface area in contact with the ground. A tire that is 50% tread will wear twice as fast as a slick tire under the same driving conditions. In addition, treaded tires must be designed to behave the same on wet or dry roads. Otherwise, the change in the way the car handles under different conditions may contribute to accidents.

## Slicks and Treads

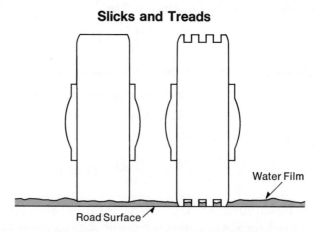

**Figue 7.** The slick tire on the left floats on the film of water covering the roadway while the treaded tire on the right makes contact with the road.

There is some evidence that a handling change does occur with changing weather conditions and that this change causes accidents. It is known that the first half-hour of rain produces a high rate of accidents. After the first half-hour the accident rate falls. One theory holds that this is caused by the oil slick on roads combining with the rain to produce a very slippery road. Within a half-hour or so, according to the theory, the rain has washed away the oil and the road become less slippery. Recent measurements show that the road's slipperiness does not change during rain, which seems to eliminate the oil-water explanation as a cause of the accidents. Rain does, however, change a car's handling characteristics and the new theory is that when the rain first starts, people drive as if the roads were still dry. After a while, however, they adapt to the new conditions and the number of skids and accidents drops.

Roads as well as tires can cause skids. If the roads are not properly crowned, water may accumulate, increasing the danger of hydroplaning. Roads should also be rough for the same reason tires have tread. But tires gradually polish a road, again increasing the likelihood of skids when the road is wet. To reduce skidding some state highway departments have put grooves in the roads at locations where accidents are judged likely to occur. Usually, the grooves are $\frac{1}{8}$ inch wide, $\frac{1}{8}$ inch deep, and 1 inch apart. The rain runs off in the grooves allowing the tires to make contact with the road.

A recent and controversial development in the traction problem is studded tires. Studs are cylindrical pieces of metal with tungsten carbide cores which are placed in blind holes in the tires. The theory is that the studs provide a better grip in ice and snow. However, several state highway departments, including those of Minnesota and New York, claim that the studs very quickly wear ruts into the highways. These ruts reduce a car's maneuverability since the tires tend to follow them. More seriously, in rain they fill with water and increase the likelihood of hydroplaning. Some tests show that studded tires are useful only on glare, or shiny, ice. In snow, slush, or on dry pavement, standard or snow tires stop a car more effectively. (See Tables 1 and 2.) Since glare-ice conditions are comparatively rare, some highway officials say studded tires actually increase accidents by damaging the roads.

### Tires and Braking Performance

| Road Condition | Tire Type | Braking Distance (from 50 mi/hr) |
|---|---|---|
| | Studded Tires | 665 ft |
| Glare Ice | Snow Tires | 780 ft |
| | Regular Tires | 787 ft |
| | Studded Tires | 177 ft |
| Wet Concrete | Snow Tires | 166 ft |
| | Regular Tires | 154 ft |

SOURCE: Hearings before the Subcommittee on Investigation and Oversight of the Committee on Public Works, U.S. House of Representatives (Washington, D.C.: U.S. Government Printing Office, 1971).

**Table 1.** Stopping distances obtained in controlled tests on glare ice and wet concrete are given in this table.

**Tire Performance**

| Road Condition | Percent of Year Condition Exists | Tires Giving Best Performance |
|---|---|---|
| Bare (wet and dry) | 64.3 | Regular Tires |
| Snow and Slush | 34.6 | Snow Tires |
| Icy | 1.1 | Studded Tires |

SOURCE: Hearings before the Subcommittee . . . Public Works.

**Table 2.** The above data for Ontario, Canada, show that 98.9% of the time regular or snow tires provide superior performance to snow tires with studs.

## Bibliography

*Further Reading*

PATRICK M. MILLER. "The Crashworthiness of Automobiles." *Scientific American,* February 1973, p. 78.

In this article Miller discusses various approaches to decreasing the damage suffered by those involved in automobile accidents.

## Questions and Problems

1. Does the inertial property of matter increase or decrease the force a driver can apply to the brakes while decelerating? Is this an example of positive or negative feedback?

2. A car with a crush constant of 30/second crashes into a brick wall while traveling 60 miles/hour (88 feet/second). How much will the front end collapse?

3. Sketch a device you think could be used as a sensor to detect when an accident is occurring. Such a device might be used to trigger air-bags.

4. Cars are being designed with energy-absorbing front ends to reduce the stress on occupants during accidents. Will these cars have greater or smaller crush constants than an average car? Will they be more, or less, crushed in an accident?

5. A car accelerates uniformly from 0 to 80 feet/second in 10 seconds, travels for one minute at 80 feet/second, and then decelerates uniformly to rest in 15 seconds.
   a. Draw a speed-time plot of the motion.
   b. Find the distance traveled during the 85 seconds by calculating the area under the speed-time curve.

6. A plane preparing for takeoff accelerates at 10 feet/second/second for 25 seconds.
   a. How fast is the plane going at the end of 25 seconds?
   b. How far has it gone during that time?

7. A car initially traveling at 10 feet/second accelerates at 5 feet/second/second for 8 seconds.
   a. How fast is it going after 8 seconds?
   b. How far has it gone during the 8 seconds?

8. A car decelerates from 60 miles/hour (88 feet/second) to rest in 22 seconds.
   a. If the car weighs 4480 pounds, what is its mass?
   b. What braking force must be exerted to decelerate the car at that rate?

9. In a parking-lot accident, a car of average crush constant runs into a concrete barrier at 12 miles/hour.
   a. How much will the front end collapse?
   b. What deceleration will the car experience?
   c. What force will a 128-pound driver experience during the collision?

10. A car of average crush constant carrying a 160-pound driver crashes at 40 miles/hour into a tree.
    a. Calculate the deceleration.
    b. Calculate the force the driver's seat belt must exert to restrain him.

11. A steel plate 1 foot by 1 foot by 4 inches in thickness weighs 160 pounds.
    a. If laid flat on the ground, what pressure does it exert?
    b. If stood on an edge, what pressure does it exert?

12. In a testing procedure, a 128-pound dummy—equipped with devices to measure acceleration and force—is run into by two different cars, each moving at 15 miles/hour. In both cases the dummy is accelerated from rest to 15 miles/hour in one twenty-fifth of a second.
    a. What force is exerted on the dummy, assuming uniform acceleration?
    b. One car has a flat front surface and during the collision the dummy is in contact with one-half square foot (72 square inches) of car surface area. What pressure is experienced?
    c. The second car has fancy grillwork and during the collision the dummy is in contact with only 3 square inches of auto surface. What pressure is experienced in this collision?

13. The best known investigator of high rates of deceleration is a U.S. Air Force colonel named John Paul Stapp. In one run on a tracked, rocket-powered sled, he decelerated from 937 feet/second to rest in 1.4 seconds.
    a. What was his rate of deceleration?
    b. What force did he experience if he weighed 160 pounds? Interestingly enough, the main dangers in these experiments are such things as detached retinas or a blood vessel breaking away from the heart or lungs. The subjects are so well restrained and cushioned that they do not suffer puncture wounds or broken bones due to a second collision.

14. Safety advertisements occasionally show a car being pushed off the roof of a tall building. The narrator then announces in ominous tones that the resulting crash was the equivalent of a car hitting a brick wall at some speed or other. Calculate from what height building a car must fall to equal a 60-mile/hour barrier crash. Then explain the significance, if any, this calculation has for

safety. Does it show that one shouldn't drive cars off tall buildings or cliffs, or is there a more subtle point?

15. If an air-bag is designed to intercept people in crashes at 60 miles/hour, how fast must it inflate? Assume one-half foot of forward motion is allowed and that the car is of average stiffness.

16. In a front-end collision, would you expect a person restrained by a seat belt to experience greater, lesser, or the same pressures as a person restrained by an air-bag? Assume the accidents are exactly the same and the auto occupants weigh the same.

17. Information on the performance of studded tires comes either from tire manufacturers or state highway officials. Are the state highway officials likely to be completely impartial or do they also have a vested interest?

*In short, the American has sacrificed his life as a whole to the motorcar, like someone who, demented with passion, wrecks his home in order to lavish his income on a capricious mistress who promises delights he can only occasionally enjoy.*

LEWIS MUMFORD*

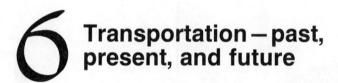

# Transportation – past, present, and future

The construction, maintenance, and use of transportation systems consume a large part of America's time, ingenuity, and resources. The auto, which is the most important means of transportation, carries 81 percent of workers to and from their jobs, takes up more than 25 percent of urban and suburban land, and causes about 55,000 deaths and 2 million injuries annually. All together, the nation spends about $150 billion[1] on highway transportation. Transportation of people and goods by auto, truck, bus, train, and plane consumes about 25 percent[2] of our yearly supply of energy, emits more than 60 percent[3] of all air pollution, and generates a large portion of urban and suburban noise.

Function of Modern Transportation.  The function of transportation is to move people and goods. The deaths, injuries, pollution, and noise are the costs that accompany this movement. Until now, at least, we have been willing to accept these undesired effects because of the great need transportation fills. Good transportation and communications allow industry to concentrate

---

* From Mumford's essay "The Highway and the City," in his book *The Highway and The City* (New York: Harcourt Brace Jovanovich, 1963).

production in large, central, efficient factories. Without good transportation, factories would be forced to become small, individual, local plants, and consequently goods would be produced less efficiently. Fast transportation and communications also allow a company or government to concentrate management functions in a central location and from that point manage far-flung enterprises. This contributes to the making of an efficient, productive, profitable system, benefiting both business and the general public.

This photo of the Third Avenue Line in Manhattan about 1948 shows how an urban mass transit system intrudes into a city. The tall office building in the center is the Chrysler Building. *Photo courtesy Museum of the City of New York.*

Local and national transportation systems introduce flexibility as well as concentration into business affairs. A person in an urban area having good mass transit and adequate roads may be within commuting distance of thousands or even millions of jobs. At the same time, a company can draw on a large labor pool. If the job is so highly specialized that no one in the commuting area can fill it, communications and air transportation make a nationwide search routine. As a consequence, roughly ten percent of Americans move each year, which means almost one percent of the population, or two million persons, move monthly. Even those who are not relocating from one house or apartment to another are on the move. In the summer, urban traffic jams are transferred to the seashore or countryside. National parks are jammed throughout July and August by vacationers pulling campers or "mobile homes" behind their cars. Mobility is also an end in itself since people go for a ride just for the sake of the ride. Driving or riding in a car is our most popular form of recreation, with the average American spending twenty-one activity-days (a unit of leisure time) a year riding in a car for pleasure.

**Resistance to Change.**   The immense national investment in transportation means that our transportation systems have a large, built-in resistance to change. This is especially so because the "system" includes not only transportation facilities such as roads and tracks but also the cities, suburbs, and industry that have adapted to and depend on particular forms of transportation. The nation could not abandon auto transportation without also abandoning Los Angeles, San Diego, Houston, and most suburbs. It could not abandon bus and subway transportation without abandoning Boston, Chicago, New York, and San Francisco.

As a result of this inertia, transportation systems cannot be changed overnight. If the nation were to decide tomorrow to replace the auto with mass transit and the jet plane with high-speed ground transportation, it would still be decades before such a transformation could be achieved. Time would be needed to build the new systems and the new urban forms which would go with them. The staying power of transportation systems is indicated by the age of existing modes. The railroad industry is over 100 years old; highway transportation more than 60 years old; and even air travel has been big business for 30 years. Canals, whose heyday was the 1830s, still carry large amounts of freight today. Despite the slow pace, however, transportation systems do change, and it is possible that we live in a time of especially rapid change.

**Effects on Society.**   If our existing transportation systems do change radically, they will force changes on the rest of society. Housing, work, and recreation patterns will shift to adapt to the new systems. This interaction between transportation and society makes any examination of transportation very complex. We live within a web of transport systems which are used not only to move people and goods from place to place but also as a means of expression—as a kind of street or folk culture.

By comparison, the urban water systems examined earlier are objective. We do not express ourselves through our plumbing; our water needs—unlike our transportation needs—change only gradually in response to a rising standard of living; and water systems take up only a small portion of our attention and resources. If a radically different system were proposed to bring water to or sewage from our homes, we would be concerned only with its cost and dependability. But proposals to introduce even minor changes into transportation systems (for example, lower horsepower engines, matched-height bumpers, seat belts) generate passionate debate that usually has nothing to do with the objective functioning of the system.

We got a hint of the kinds of issues transportation raises in the discussion of transportation safety. The human cost of highway travel is so high it calls into question the logic of the entire highway system. These larger questions arose implicitly within Chapters 4 and 5 as we concentrated on the technical questions. In general we took the overall system as given and looked for ways to optimize it by reducing deaths and injuries without making the system too expensive or unwieldy.

It is also possible to take such an optimization approach to the broad question of transportation. Highway and air-transport systems are bedeviled with air, noise, and water pollution, and extravagant energy use. By looking at alternative auto-power systems, such as the Wankel engine or the external combustion (steam) engine, or at noise-control technology for jet engines, we could get some idea of the room for improvement in the present systems.

But we live at a time when larger issues than the best type of auto engine are being raised. One such issue is the relative strengths and weaknesses of auto and mass-transit systems. Some believe that we need more balance in the kinds of transportation systems available; others question whether autos have any place at all in urban areas. Some who are discouraged with the capabilities of both autos and mass transit say the answer is to gradually rebuild urban areas so as to minimize the need for transportation. Such rebuilding could be supplemented with increased use of communications such as television-phones, cable television, and better mail service. These communication aids would replace some physical movement, just as televised Sunday football games now replace trips to the stadiums.

This larger view raises the question of how to approach transportation without taking on the entire world. One way would be to look only at such "hardware" problems as road design, pollution-control devices, and futuristic mass-transit systems in the hope that this would bring us to grips with the fundamental problems. The other extreme would be to look primarily at the social context in which the transportation systems function. In this chapter, and the next, we will try to take a middle road, looking at the physical systems within their social context. We begin this investigation with a description of past and present urban and rural transportation in America.

## A Chronology of Urban Transportation

The first, urban, public transportation in the United States was begun in New York City in 1827[4] by Abraham Brower, a local businessman. The

Horse-drawn street railways were widely used in New York and other major cities in the 1880s. Yet by the turn of the century, they had virtually vanished, replaced mainly by electric trolleys. The electric and telephone wires which blacken the sky in this photo are today underground. *Photo courtesy American Telephone and Telegraph.*

service consisted of a horse-drawn carriage which traveled up and down the dirt or cobblestone streets, picking up and discharging passengers every block or so. This was a primitive form of mass transit but an advance for the times. In 1827 the only other public transportation consisted of a few long-distance stage coaches and a ferry running from the island of Manhattan to Brooklyn—then a village of 15,000. However, public transportation was not behind other urban services: in 1827 New York did not have a fire or police department, running water, or gas lights.

Street Railroads.   At about the time Brower started his transportation system, railroads were being experimented with in this country. However, the locomotives that were needed to pull the trains were too large, noisy, and dirty to run on city streets. But in 1832 railroads were adapted to city service when tracks were laid along several New York streets. In this new street-railroad system, horses were used to pull iron-wheeled carriages along the tracks. The low friction of iron wheels rolling on iron tracks allowed the horses to pull large loads quickly (two horses could pull a car carrying seventy people at six miles/hour). This meant more people could be moved along a street with less effort and less expense than with horse-drawn carriages moving on dirt or stone streets. At first, street railways spread slowly, but as America became more urbanized, their use grew. By the 1850s most large cities and many small cities had adopted them.

Street railways had a major impact on the form of American cities. Because they gave comparatively speedy service, the street railway extended the effective boundaries of the city. A person had only to live within walking distance of a street-railway line rather than within walking distance of the job. Typically, street-railway lines developed in a spoke-like, or radial, pattern. All lines converged on a hub, which was the city's central business district, because the major transportation demand came from workers who wanted to reach their downtown jobs. There was rarely enough demand to support lines running between points on the outskirts of the city. The effect of this pattern was to confine most businesses to the central city; only in the central city were they accessible to workers and customers from all areas of the city and its suburbs. Some businesses serving local areas did grow up along street-railway lines. But the regions between the lines remained relatively undeveloped.

It is hard for us to imagine, but the seemingly quaint cars pulled by teams of horses were as important to those times as cars and buses are to ours. It is estimated that in the 1880s there were 100,000 horses and mules pulling 18,000 cars along 3000 miles of track.[5] Just as we have our gas stations, body shops, and auto-supply stores, a large support technology grew up to keep the street railways running. The tracks, carriages, and harnesses all required care. The horses had to be properly bred, shod, fed, and stabled. The importance of good equine health practices was dramatized in the fall of 1872 when a horse flu epidemic paralyzed the transportation systems of Philadelphia, Baltimore, New York, and other cities. The situation was so serious that in some cases the street-railway employees were reduced to pulling the carriages themselves.

Some of the less obvious problems facing street railways were manure storage and snow removal. Manure was usually stored in or near the street-railway company's horse and mule stables before being hauled to the countryside for use as fertilizer. This interim storage generated odors which local residents objected to. The problem was "solved" only when the street railways went out of business. Snow caused still other difficulties. The horse-drawn cars were derailed by snowcovered tracks and so the companies desired to plow them clear. But other residents—accustomed to substituting horse-drawn sleighs for carriages in the winter—objected to the plowing. Boston, for example, passed a law requiring the street-railway companies to leave snow on the tracks until it melted naturally. The companies were, however, allowed to operate their own sleighs for hire in place of the inoperable wheeled vehicles.

Cable Cars.   Although the street railways were modern in their use of the newly developing metal technology, they were still tied to animal power. But the newer technology of steam power was soon to be adapted to urban transportation in two ways. About the time of the Civil War, elevated railroad tracks, called els, were built in several cities and steam-powered locomotives were used to pull passenger cars along them. In 1873 steam power was introduced in a more interesting way with the construction of a cable-car line in San Francisco. This system consisted of a large, stationary steam engine which pulled several miles of underground copper cable. The cable ran in a slot beneath the street and was mounted on large, freely turning wheels situated at regular intervals. (See Figure 1.) The cable car itself rode on iron tracks, like the street railway, and had a long arm, called a grip, which reached through a slot in the street to grab the constantly moving cable. To move, the operator used the grip to grab the cable, which pulled the car along. To stop, the gripman released the grip's hold on the cable and applied the brakes.

## Cable Cars

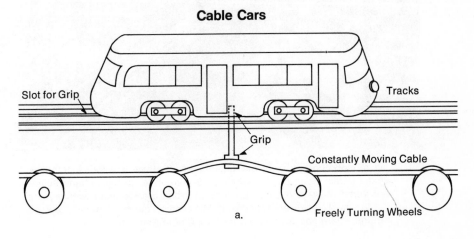

a.

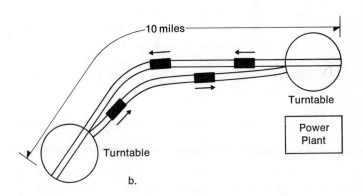

b.

**Figure 1.**  a. This diagram of a cable car shows the grip grabbing the moving cable and the car being pulled along with it. The cable rides on the freely turning wheels. To stop, the grip releases the cable and brakes are applied. Should the grip become stuck to the cable, the entire cable must be stopped to halt the car. b. The power plant sits at one end of the cable-car system. The turntables at either end are used to turn the cable cars around and put them on the proper track for the return trip.

In this photograph from the 1880s, a small steam-powered locomotive pulls a train along an el in Chatham Square in lower Manhattan. Steam-powered railways did not last long in urban areas—about twenty years at the most; they were replaced by the cleaner, quieter, electric-powered trains. *Photo courtesy Museum of the City of New York.*

The advantages of the cable car were its power, speed, cleanliness, and relative quiet. The distant steam engine generated lots of smoke and noise and took up a large amount of space, but the cable car was nowhere near it. The disadvantages were the large investment needed to build a cable-car line, the need for a great deal of maintenance, and the inflexibility of the system. From San Francisco, the cable car spread to Chicago in 1882,[6] which eventually had eighty-six miles of route, and then to Denver, Kansas City, and other cities.

**The Electric Streetcar and Subway.** However, at this time the still-thriving street railways and the budding cable-car systems were already doomed by a new invention. In 1886[7] the city of Montgomery, Alabama, installed an electric-powered trolley, or streetcar, and this innovation spread rapidly across the country. In one way the trolley was similar to the cable car: the electric power was generated at a central plant and transmitted over copper wire to the trolley car. But this different method of power transmission was very important. The cable car's power was transmitted mechanically by the moving cable. This caused great wear on the cable and occasionally resulted in the car being caught tight by the cable.

It would then race through the streets until the entire cable was stopped or the car smashed into something. The ponderous machinery required by this mechanical system meant that the cable had to be laid underground at great expense. But the electric streetcar, or trolley, received its energy from a relatively light and stationary copper wire strung above ground. Instead of the wire itself moving, the wire's electric charges moved within it to transmit the energy. The only wear came from the streetcar's electric conductor—called a trolley—brushing against the overhead wire.

After their introduction in Montgomery, streetcar lines grew rapidly— from 1260 miles of track in 1890, to 22,000 in 1902, to 45,000 miles of track and 80,000 cars in 1917. It was possible in that year to travel from Boston to New York by trolley, if you were willing to change many times and had 20 hours to spare. Such a trip was made only as a stunt, however, for the railroads provided fast, regular service between American cities.

When first introduced, the trolleys caused a great deal of excitement. Their high speeds and use of the then-new electric power made them the jet planes of the day. They panicked most of the horses they passed in the street and inspired Oliver Wendell Holmes to write in *Over the Teacups:*

> Look here! There are crowds of people whirled through our streets on these new-fashioned cars, with their witch-broomsticks overhead—if they don't come from Salem they ought to!—and not more than one in a dozen of these fish-eyed bipeds thinks or cares a nickel's worth about the miracle which is wrought for their convenience. We ought to go down on our knees when one of these mighty caravans, car after car, spins by us, under the mystic impulse which seems to know not whether its train is loaded or empty.*

At the turn of the century, the obvious happened and the trolley went underground to become the subway. The evolving of the trolley into the subway can still be seen in several cities, including Philadelphia and Boston, where trolleys move along streets in suburban areas, then travel underground within the central city. The first subway built in the United States was Boston's Tremont Street line, completed in 1897. In 1904, New York completed its first subway. That city now has a 240-route-mile system which carries over one billion passengers yearly.

## A Chronology of Rural Transportation

Nineteenth-century American cities had to solve the problem of moving large numbers of people short distances through densely populated areas. Outside the cities, the nation faced a very different problem—to make accessible to settlers the huge land areas of the far west (Kentucky, Ohio, Illinois, Indiana, and so on) and to funnel into the cities the grain, flour, salted meat, coal, and lumber these regions would generate. The major

---

* The Works of Oliver Wendell Holmes, vol. iv (St. Clair Shores, Michigan: Scholarly Press, 1972).

problem, then, was not moving people short distances but moving large quantities of bulk goods long distances.

### Overland and River Transportation.

The establishment of good transportation was necessary not only to settle excess population and establish trade but to bind the new and vast country together. George Washington was as concerned with the physical linking of the country as with the legal and political framework within which it operated. Soon after the Revolutionary War, Washington turned down invitations to make state visits to European capitals in order to travel through the Great Lakes region exploring potential trade routes. The region was bounded on the north by British Canada and on the south by the Spanish-owned Louisiana region, which prompted Washington to write:

> No well-informed mind need be told that the flanks and rear of the United territory are possessed by other powers, and formidable ones too—nor how necessary it is to apply the cement of interest to bind all parts of it together by one indissoluble bond—particularly the Middle States with the country immediately back of them—for what ties let me ask should we have upon those people; and how entirely unconnected should we be with them if the Spaniards on their right or Great Britain on their left, instead of throwing stumbling blocks in their way as they do now, should invite their trade and seek alliances with them?ψ

Washington, then, did not expect the nation to be unified through allegiance to a political doctrine or legal charter alone; he expected the westerners' loyalty to follow trade. But the natural trade routes were the then-western rivers, the Mississippi, Ohio, and Tennessee, which flowed mainly south to Louisiana, and the Great Lakes, which gave water access to British-controlled Canada. The eastward route to the original thirteen colonies was primarily overland through hilly or mountainous country: the rivers in these regions were swift and interrupted by falls and rapids as they descended from the mountains to the Atlantic. The presence of these falls and rapids meant that cargo had to be unloaded from one boat, portaged (or carried) past the barrier, and then loaded onto another boat to continue the trip downstream. This made river transportation to the East too expensive to be practical.

So trade goods from the West—mainly animal skins and later whiskey—could only be carried on packhorses or mules following Indian trails. Many of these trails were so well chosen that eventually railroads or highways were constructed along them: the New York Central follows the Mohawk Trail; the Boston and Albany Railroad follows the Bay Path; U.S. Highway 25 follows the Wilderness Road blazed by Daniel Boone through the Cumberland Gap into Kentucky. Packhorses, however, could only carry

ψ Archer B. Hulbert, *The Paths of Inland Commerce* (New York: U.S. Publishers Association, 1920).

comparatively light, valuable cargo such as skins and whiskey. But the wealth of the West was grain, meat, lumber, coal, and other bulk materials. Packhorses, treading their way down muddy or snowcovered ridge trails, could not carry the huge tonnages such trade would require. So, for the meantime, these resources of the West were unavailable to the large populations settled along the eastern seaboard.

In comparison with the eastern rivers, the rivers of the Ohio and Mississippi valleys were widely used by barges and flatboats to float goods downstream. Unlike the Potomac and other eastern rivers, which flowed through narrow mountain valleys in the Appalachian chain, the western rivers flowed through the broad central plains. Although these rivers were relatively free of falls and rapids, sandbars and shifting riverbeds made navigation difficult. Riverboats floated downstream to New Orleans or to one of the numerous towns further upstream (Vicksburg, Mississippi; Memphis, Tennessee; St. Louis, Missouri; Louisville, Kentucky) carrying cider, flour, iron, salt, and brandy. Since travel upstream against the current was very difficult, the boatmen generally sold their craft as firewood and returned home overland.

But in 1807 the problem of the return trip upstream was overcome when Robert Fulton's steam-powered boat, the *Clermont,* chugged from New York City to Albany, New York, against the Hudson River current. In 1811 the steamboat *Orleans* navigated the southern end of the Mississippi, where the currents are comparatively weak, and in 1816 the *Washington* moved against the swifter, headwater currents, traveling from Louisville, Kentucky, on the Ohio River to New Orleans on the Mississippi and back again in forty-one days. The era of the steam-powered riverboat, celebrated by Mark Twain in *Life on the Mississippi,* had begun.

**Turnpikes and Canals.**   Around the end of the eighteenth century, then, water was the preferred—and often only—means of transportation. The eastern population was concentrated on the Atlantic coast or on the bays and rivers accessible to that coast and there was a thriving sea trade up and down the coast and with Europe. In the West the rivers served as highways south toward New Orleans. The development of the steam-powered riverboat improved water transport but did not change the inland situation.

In the East—away from the coast and navigable rivers—the country was crisscrossed with a network of country roads. These country roads were little better than trails, becoming impassable mudholes in wet weather. New England roads were best in the winter, when they were covered with hard, packed snow and negotiable by sled. As a result of this poor overland transportation, trade was difficult and only the most valuable cargoes could be carried out of and into the inland regions.

The first successful effort to improve inland transportation was the sixty-two-mile Lancaster Turnpike, which connected Philadelphia with

This experimental elevated cable car was given a trial run in 1867 by Charles Harvey in Manhattan. Eventually elevated cable cars were put into regular use. The cars were propelled by an enormous cable which passed around pulleys enclosed in a wooden cover directly under the tracks. *Photo courtesy Museum of the City of New York.*

Lancaster, Pennsylvania. Completed in 1794 by a private company chartered by the Pennsylvania legislature, it was thirty-seven feet wide, stone paved, and cost $465,000 to build. The company got its initial investment back and made a good profit by collecting tolls at nine tollgates along the road. This and other turnpikes made hauling goods by large freight wagons much easier.

The success of the Lancaster Pike began a road-building boom that lasted until about 1825. During this period, Maryland built the Baltimore-Reisterstown Pike at a cost of $10,000 per mile and the Baltimore-Frederick Pike at $8000 per mile. Combined with her access to the sea via Chesapeake Bay, these and other roads made Baltimore a major trade connection with the West. New York State, in the first seven years of the century, constructed 3000 miles of road and 20 major bridges. The nation's new roads made possible for the first time the large-scale movement of people and goods between different towns and states and played a part in creating the "era of good feeling" which some historians call this period.

But for the most part, paved roads met with relatively little success in

The most famous freight wagon was the Conestoga, which, like the turn-pike, originated in Pennsylvania. At its largest, the wagon and its six-horse-team were sixty feet long. Able to carry eight tons of freight, the Conestoga was the equivalent of today's long-distance trucks, which are still driven by "teamsters." *Photo courtesy Smithsonian Institution.*

the early 1800s. They were expensive to build and maintain, and tolls were difficult to collect. More important, there were fundamental forces working against turnpike travel. Even a road which had been cut and filled, or leveled, and was well paved and drained to provide easy passage, required a large amount of human and animal labor to move a compara-tively small quantity of goods. The technology of roads and freight wagons simply could not move goods quickly or cheaply enough to pay. As a result, most of the turnpikes lost money. Starting in 1844 there was a brief enthusiasm for plank roads—made of thick wooden planks laid on the ground—but although these were cheap and easy to build, they rotted quickly and proved to be no answer to overland transportation.

The interim solution to overland transportation was the artificial water-way, or canal. In 1817 the first dirt was turned in the digging of the Erie Canal across New York State. By 1825 the 364-mile pioneering canal[8] was completed and a fleet sailed from Lake Erie to Albany by canal and then down the Hudson River to New York City. This huge engineering task connected the Great Lakes with the Atlantic Ocean, giving New York City a direct water connection with the West. Grain, flour, lumber, coal, iron, meat, and other western products which had previously moved overland to Baltimore and other cities now went by horse-towed barge to New York. The 40-foot-wide, 4-foot-deep canal was such an immediate success that in 1835 it was enlarged to an overall width of 70 feet and depth of 7 feet. Its success ended the turnpike-building boom and started a canal boom which lasted until about 1850.

**Railroads.**   Just as canals, by virtue of their low labor needs and large load-carrying ability, had great advantages over the turnpikes, so railroads had great advantages over the canals. In northern regions canals went dry in drought and froze in winter while railroads functioned in all but the most severe snowstorms. While a few canals used steam-powered boats, most used horses or mules to tow the heavy barges. This, plus the need for locks to raise and lower the barges (see Figure 2), made for a slow average speed. By contrast, steam-powered locomotives could move along at 20 or 30 miles/hour. Also, railroad tracks could be laid almost anywhere, while canals required favorable terrain. It was the impossibility of building a canal to Baltimore that lead her to build the first railroad. Because of the superiority of railroads, the canal-building boom started by the Erie Canal lasted only about 20 years. In 1830 there were 1200 miles of canal, in 1840, 3300, and today about 1000 miles.

At first railroads were built as local feeder lines, connecting mines, lumber mills, or farming areas with nearby towns. There were hundreds of these very short lines but no regional or national rail networks. People were not thinking on that scale. But starting about 1840, the railroads were built on a larger scale, connecting not only rural areas with neighboring cities, but also linking the cities to each other. People began to see the railroads as state, regional, and national systems that could connect the country.

From the 1850s on, the railroad became the major means of transportation in America. The country had limited resources to put into transportation and these were channeled into railroads rather than canals, roads, or river improvements. The railroad trackage went from 9000 miles in 1850 to over 200,000 miles in 1900. In 1869, when the Union Pacific was completed, the United States was spanned coast to coast by rail, and by 1890 the national rail network was in place. At that point, the United States— physically at least—became a united nation.

**Understanding a New Technology.**   The spanning of the nation by rail required the solution of many difficult technological problems. These involved not only the problems of spanning rivers and gorges and laying durable, straight tracks but also the problems in the closely related iron and steel industry. The railroads—with their demand for advanced technological products and techniques—interacted more strongly with the rest of industry than did turnpikes and canals.

## A Canal Lock

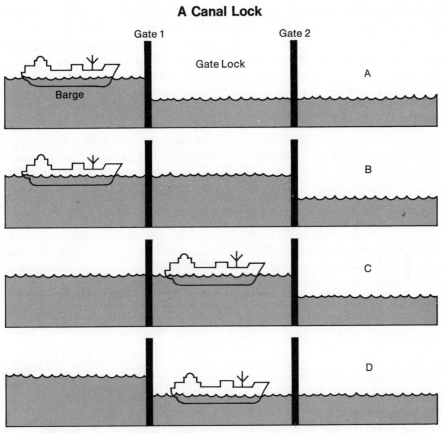

**Figure 2.** In A, Gate 2 is sealed and water flows from the upper section of the canal, raising the water level in the lock. Once the level has risen to the proper height (B), Gate 1 is swung out of the way and the barge enters the lock. In C, Gate 1 has been sealed and water has begun flowing out of the lock. Once the level in the lock has dropped to the water level on the right, Gate 2 is swung open and the barge can continue its trip. Of the world's two major canals, the Panama Canal has several sets of locks, but the Suez Canal is at a single level and has no locks.

The problems faced by the new railroad industry were conceptual as well as technological. Railroads were a unique technology, but at first they were thought of in terms of turnpikes and canals. A trivial illustration is provided by the fact that early locomotives were built like stagecoaches, with the engineer located on an outside, elevated seat. More seriously, it was at first assumed that the railroad companies would supply the tracks, with those shipping the goods supplying the trains. This was analogous to turnpikes and canals, where the shippers supplied the wagons and the barges and the turnpike and canal companies collected tolls for the use of the facility. It soon became clear that railroads would have to provide a more comprehensive service.

Standardization.   The early view of railroads as local systems bringing ore out of a mine, logs to a sawmill, or coal to the local iron mill was another conceptual difficulty. But it resulted in a serious physical problem: railroad lines were built with a variety of gauges because the builders were not thinking in terms of a system. The track separation ranged from 3 feet or so for narrow gauge lines to 5 feet in the southern United States to 6 feet on the Erie Railroad. As a result cargo often had to be unloaded and loaded several times during a single trip. It meant that locomotives and trains built for one line could not be used on another line, and merger and consolidation of adjoining systems was often impossible. Because of the difficulties and economic losses, there was great pressure to settle on a standard gauge. In the mid-1880s, 4 feet $8\frac{1}{2}$ inches was chosen as the standard. It is thought that this peculiar width, which is still used, can be traced back to the wheel separation of horse-drawn freight wagons.

Railroad travel also created the need for uniform time zones. Before 1885 every locality had its own time standard. Two towns only a few miles apart might be on time systems differing by an hour, a half-hour, or $13\frac{1}{2}$ minutes. Such a situation caused little difficulty in prerailroad days, but it made for confusing railroad timetables and created dangerous conditions because it was never clear just where a train was at a given time. In 1885 an international conference in Washington, D.C., decided on the present, uniform, worldwide system of time zones.

Some Implications.   To return to rural transportation, hand-dug canals, horse-drawn barges, street railways, and cable cars today seem primitive and quaint. But canals, turnpikes, railroads, and street railways are associated with periods of tremendous change in the nation. Today, many of the canals are silted up or filled in, and thousands of miles of railroad track have been torn up or lie rusting and neglected. Nevertheless, these now neglected or abandoned systems were the bootstraps by which the nation pulled itself into the modern age. They were the dominant and seemingly indestructible structures of their time. The fact that new systems came on the scene and overshadowed them — often in a matter of decades — may be a guide to the permanence of our own highways and jetports.

Especially striking is the effect of transportation systems on the industrial and social nature of the nation. Without the canals, turnpikes, and railroads, the United States would have remained a rural nation with a few small cities. The countryside would have been self-sufficient, raising and processing its own food and manufacturing most of its own goods. The cities — dependent for food and raw materials on nearby rural areas — would have remained small. But efficient, economical transportation broke down barriers and allowed the nation to come together as a single unit. The standard gauge, uniform time zones, and interchangeable machine parts were the technological manifestations of this unity. Other manifestations were the transition from household to factory manufacturing, increasing specialization in work, and the growth of urban areas. Today the issue of metrication shows that the push towards unification, which allows the physical and social machine to function smoothly and on a larger scale, is still continuing. Also familiar from the past is our present dissatisfaction with the existing transportation systems. If the now-vanished transportation systems had continued to meet the country's needs, they might still be in existence.

How much help is the past as a guide to the present? The historian, from the perspective of a century, can paint with broad strokes the era of the turnpike, canal, and household manufactories: knowing the technology to come and the way it will be used, it is possible to explain why turnpikes lost out to canals, and canals to railroads. But the men who went broke building roads at the end of the so-called Turnpike Era, or building canals when the railroads were already on the horizon, had no such perspective. They were in the midst of their time and had to make decisions based on the immediate past and guesses about an unknowable future.

Similarly, we are moving in the midst of our own time. We will be confronted with statistics and confusion, and, like our predecessors, we will have to make our own decisions based on guesses about an unknowable future. It is not clear if cities are dying or being renewed, if money and attention should flow to the new suburbs and their highways or back to the cities with their subways and railroads, or if none of the old forms are any longer suitable and new forms must be developed. It may be that the next act of this play has been written by the things already done, in which case we need only the wit to read the words from existing evidence. But if the next act is not yet inevitable, then we must now choose a future and stir ourselves.

## Twentieth-Century Transportation

Because twentieth-century transportation is so familiar to us, it should be much easier to study than nineteenth-century transportation. To visualize the transportation systems of the nineteenth century requires imagination. The plank roads, canals, street railways, and steam-powered locomotives are long vanished, leaving only such clues as truck drivers who belong to the "teamsters" union, an off-beat railroad gauge, and San Francisco's cable car. But as inhabitants of the twentieth century, we are all intimately acquainted with the operation of autos, the flow of traffic on highways and streets, the use of trucks to move goods, and the look and sound of a modern jetport. We may be less familiar with railroads, buses, and subways, but these also are part of our time and most of us have some understanding of them.

However, familiarity with present-day systems can also hinder understanding. We can see canals, turnpikes, and Mississippi river boats with a fresh and objective, although sometimes overly romantic, eye; we are so immersed in modern systems that it can be hard to look at them critically or to note trends and currents of change. On the time scale of our personal experience, everything seems permanent and unchanging; we are so habituated to what is, that asking questions about autos and planes often seems like empty exercise. This questioning is especially difficult for those who grew up in suburbs where there is only one transportation system — the auto. Lacking experience with mass transit and life in a city, it is hard to imagine an existence in which the auto plays a small or nonexistent role. The difficult task, then, will be to use our intimate knowledge of twentieth-century transportation systems and still stand back and view them from a distance.

**Transportation Problems.** By the late nineteenth century, rural areas were tied to cities and cities to each other by a network of railroads. The cities had internal transportation systems consisting of electric-powered trolleys, subways, and elevated trains. But neither rural areas nor cities had satisfactory transportation. In the countryside, the railroads were accessible only to rural communities and farms close to the stations and even these people had problems. Generally crops were stored on the farm until the dirt roads dried sufficiently for wagons to move over them. Then everyone's grain and produce arrived in market at once, forcing down prices and creating a shortage of railroad freight cars.

Even many large villages and small cities had no railroad line and were therefore effectively cut off from trade and industry. The railroads, not forced by any laws to consider the general public good, were uninterested in building lines through regions which generated comparatively little freight or which were unwilling or unable to offer the railroad builders large tracts of land or money as an inducement to build. Often the bidding for a new railroad line by competing cities or regions was intense. Seattle, Washington, around 1871, offered the Northern Pacific Railroad half of its dock area, valuable land, and $250,000[9] in cash and bonds if that line would make Seattle its western terminus. With the railroad terminus, Seattle could prosper by shipping food, lumber, and minerals west to the Orient. But the railroad instead chose the smaller — and more easily dominated — town of Tacoma. In response, the citizens of Seattle volunteered their labor and began building their own line east to the farms, mines, and forests — a manifestation of civic spirit one does not often see today.

The weaknesses of urban transportation of the time were less dramatic but in many ways as serious. The major problem was its essentially radial form. Only the central district was accessible to all, and the land between the transportation "spokes" was left undeveloped. This made for great crowding both within the central city and in the residential areas near the transportation lines.

The Auto.   The shortcomings of existing urban and rural transportation created a demand for something better. One temporarily popular transportation means was the bicycle, manufactured in the United States in quantity starting about 1877. In 1880 cyclists banded together as the League of American Wheelmen to campaign for better roads. And while cycling did create some improvement in roads, the major step in America's transportation evolution occurred in 1908 when Henry Ford began producing the Model T Ford. During the next 19 years, Ford produced 15 million Model T's, which at times sold for as little as $250. Strictly utilitarian, they generated 20 horsepower and got 30 miles to the gallon. The Model T's cheapness, simplicity, and serviceability changed the auto and motoring from a rich man's plaything to a transportation device available to large numbers of people.

The Model T created an irresistible demand for better roads, and in 1916 the Federal Bureau of Public Roads was organized. It marked the first federal involvement in road building since the Cumberland Road of 1817 was built into the far west of Kentucky and Ohio. The government now undertook highway building and improvement and made cash grants to the states to organize highway departments and build roads.

Henry Ford is shown here at the wheel of a Model T Ford in 1921. The Model T was the original "Tin Lizzie." First appearing in 1908, fifteen million Model T's were eventually manufactured. *Photo courtesy Ford Motor Company.*

The Internal Combustion Engine.   The automobile itself was a blend of several technologies. The first auto builders borrowed heavily from carriage and bicycle makers: early horseless carriages even had a bracket to hold a horsewhip. The auto also required use of the still-developing electrical technology for the lighting and ignition system. Ford himself had begun his career working for the first Detroit electric utility. But the heart of the auto was the gasoline-powered internal combustion engine. (See Figure 3.)

The internal combustion engine succeeded where the steam engine had failed—it was small enough, simple enough, safe enough, powerful enough, and quiet enough to propel a personal-sized transportation vehicle along urban streets and country lanes. The steam engine—although it had been used in the United States since 1800—was unable to compete with the internal combustion engine. The only extensive use of steam to power urban vehicles was in cable cars, subways, and trolleys, where the power could be generated in a central plant and transmitted to the vehicle.

The auto powered by an internal combustion engine had a major impact on American industry. Its construction required huge amounts of iron and steel for the engine and body (sixteen percent of all iron and steel produced today goes to the auto), glass for the windows and windshields, and rubber for the tires. Once built, the autos depended on the petroleum

## The Four-Stroke Internal Combustion Engine

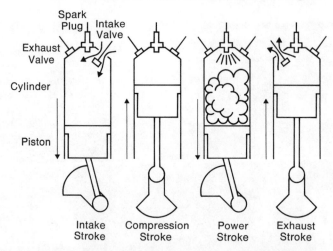

**Figure 3.**  This diagram shows the four strokes of the internal combustion engine. On the intake stroke, the piston moves down and draws in an air-gasoline mixture through the open intake valve. On the compression stroke, the piston moves up, compressing the gasoline-air mixture. Both valves are closed. At the end of the compression stroke, the gasoline-air mixture is exploded by a spark from the spark plug. The explosion forces the piston down in the power stroke. Both valves are still closed. On the exhaust stroke, the piston moves upward, driving the spent gases out through the exhaust valve.

producing and refining industry to keep them running. They also needed roads, which increased the demand for construction machinery, asphalt, concrete, drainage pipe, and highway designers. Service industries were created to sell and repair the autos, junk them, provide medical care for accident victims, bring lawsuits to recover losses, insure motorists against lawsuits, and so on. It is possible that the auto also played an important educational role by introducing millions of American youngsters to their first piece of complex machinery.

### Early Impact of the Internal Combustion Engine.

Autos powered by the internal combustion engine and the roads built for them constituted a very different kind of transportation system. Instead of the expensive tracks, tunnels, and electric-power systems required by railroads and trolleys, the auto needed only the comparatively cheap paved road. The owner put up the capital for the vehicle and assumed responsibility for driving and maintaining it. This meant labor costs were nearly zero, giving highway transportation an advantage over mass transit. The auto-highway system can be seen as an extension of the turnpike and canal, where users also provided the vehicle.

The internal combustion engine and cheap roads combined to produce a transportation system that gave fast, private, point-to-point, instantaneously available service. The auto was available to the owner any time of the day or night and would go anywhere there were roads. It is no wonder that early proponents of the auto saw it achieving miracles. Henry Ford — in ringing, Biblical style — wrote:

> I will build a motor car for the great multitude. It will be large enough for the family but small enough for the individual to run and care for. It will be constructed of the best materials, by the best men to be hired, after the simplest designs that modern engineering can devise. But it will be so low in price that no man making a good salary will be unable to own one — and enjoy with his family the blessing of hours of pleasure in God's great open spaces.

Despite Ford's emphasis here on the auto as a way for the city dweller to escape the city, the internal combustion engine had its largest initial impact on farms. Trucks and improved farm-to-market roads allowed farmers to get their crops to railroad depots and local markets more dependably and faster than before. This freed farmers from the necessity of locating near railroad depots or near the urban areas which consumed their food. When applied to tractors and other power equipment, the flexible, powerful internal combustion engine increased productivity — making it possible for farmers to cultivate more land with less human and animal labor. The auto also had a large impact on the farmers' social existence. The traditional isolation of the farm family had been lessened when the United States Post Office established rural free delivery of mail in 1896. Now the auto helped break down their physical isolation. With decent roads, a farm family in a relatively short time could be in a town 20 or 30 miles away.

In urban areas, the auto remained at first a recreation device — something the family piled into on Sundays for a drive into the surrounding countryside or for a visit to Grandma. Few used it for commuting or business. But as early as 1905, buses powered by the internal combustion engine began service in several cities and by 1923 had replaced the trolley in most smaller cities and were competing strongly in the larger ones. Buses moved on cheap, publicly maintained roads and therefore required a smaller investment than trolley systems; they could change their route in response to customer demand; and the same buses that carried people to work during the week could take them to outlying parks or beaches on weekends.

It has been charged that the automobile industry did not depend solely on the superiority of their product to win new business. A report[10] presented to the Senate Subcommittee on Antitrust and Monopoly states that General Motors starting in the 1920s and continuing almost to the present bought over 100 electric, surface rail systems in 45 cities. It then tore up the tracks and replaced the electric-powered trolley cars with diesel-powered buses made by General Motors. According to the report, the poor service given by the buses relative to the smoother riding, faster electric trolleys led to a switch to private autos. This led to more sales for the automobile industry since it takes 35 autos to replace one bus.

The same report states that General Motors, starting in the 1930s, used its influence with the railroads (it was and is the nation's largest user of rail freight) to convince various lines to abandon passenger service and convert from electric-powered trains to diesel locomotives, which General Motors manufactured. As a result, according to the report, railroad service deteriorated, encouraging passengers to travel between cities by bus (General Motors helped set up the Greyhound Bus Corporation) or by private auto. In a report also available from the Antitrust and Monopoly Subcommittee, General Motors has denied the above allegations.

**Suburbanization.** During the 1920s, 1930s, and 1940s, the auto and truck insinuated themselves into America but did not revolutionize it. In part, the reason was economic. The great depression of the 1930s froze the nation just as the auto was beginning to take hold. During World War II the auto industry converted to production of war materials, and gasoline was in tight supply. So until the early 1950s the auto — although important — was not yet defining the shape of the nation. There were still fairly sharp boundaries between cities and their surrounding countryside.

In the first half of the century, urban development was along mass-transit lines, with the central business district a concentrated, commercial, industrial, and transportation sector. The cities were "neat" enough so that planners saw them as a series of concentric rings, modified by the spoke-like pattern created by mass transit, surrounding the central business district. (See Figure 4.) The ring beyond the business district usually contained the poorest people living in the city's oldest housing. In some cities the inner ring also contained enclaves of wealthy families, who lived there so as to be close to the economic and cultural heart of the city. Further out, in the less accessible rings, were the middle-income groups. These rings were most densely populated along the mass-transit lines and sparsely populated elsewhere. Beyond the city proper were the suburban towns occupied by the wealthy people who could afford the daily trip by commuter railroad into the city. In general, these towns clustered around each stop of the commuter railroad, again forming a spoke-like pattern. The noise, heat, crowding, and fumes of the central city put steady pressure on the wealthy inhabitants of the inner ring to similarly move out to the suburbs.

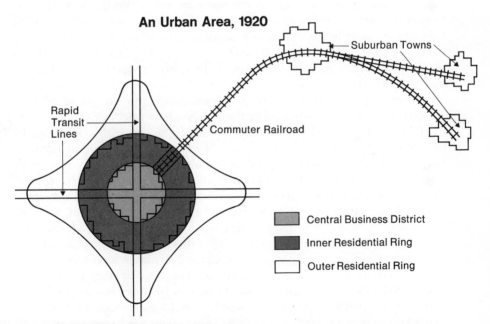

**An Urban Area, 1920**

Suburban Towns

Rapid Transit Lines

Commuter Railroad

Central Business District

Inner Residential Ring

Outer Residential Ring

**Figure 4.**  A model of a 1920 city is shown in the diagram. Note the radial, or star-like, pattern of residential development caused by the rapid-transit lines. Beyond the outer residential ring is the rural area, except where there are suburban towns.

The main effect of the auto and bus prior to World War II was to fill in the areas between the spokes of residential development along mass-transit lines. Within the cities, the buses and autos fed in people from relatively low density areas—which could not support a subway line—to the subway. The auto carried suburbanites to the commuter railroad, freeing them from living close to the stations.

But after 1945, U.S. productive capacity—freed from depression and war—was used to provide a large number of Americans with a one-family home standing on its own plot of land and with the cars and roads needed to serve that home. The drive to own a one-family home with one or two cars in the garage is powerful among all groups in the United States, and that drive was to change the look of the country. The new suburbs that mushroomed around the older cities could not be served by mass transit because the population densities were too low. To provide an area with even sporadic bus service requires four or five homes to the acre; rail transit needs even higher densities. In addition, suburban travel patterns are highly dispersed. As suburbs matured, their links to the local cities weakened and travel was likely to be in any direction. Fixed-route mass transit could not serve such travel needs; nor could it compete with the auto on the basis of speed, convenience, or privacy.

While many of the workers in the new suburbs of the 1950s commuted to jobs in the city, the suburbs from the beginning were well equipped with retail stores since the major department stores and supermarkets were quick to follow their customers out of the city. Usually these stores clustered together in centrally located shopping centers, with the stores surrounded by plenty of parking space. The first phase of suburbanization, then, was the construction of homes and stores, but most jobs remained in the city. Each morning there was a flow of commuters into the local city, with a corresponding flow out of the city in the evening. In the second phase, factories and then offices began to relocate in suburbs. In the central city, high real-estate values forced most factories to be multistory, which is inefficient because goods must be moved from floor to floor; manufacturing processes are most easily organized on a single level. Cheap suburban land allowed for sprawling, single-level, efficient plants with easy access to trucks bringing in and taking away goods.

But there were disadvantages in this exodus to suburbia. A factory that moved from a central city might find it hard to obtain adequate labor in the new suburban location. The need to have a car to commute to work would make the factory inaccessible to many of the poorer workers, who had used mass transit when the factory was in the city. Also, when the new plant was in the city, it was most probably located near or on a railroad line or port, which meant cheap shipment of goods. The suburban location often meant dependence on trucking, which is more expensive due to its higher labor and fuel requirements.

However, several factors tend to decrease rail's freight advantage over trucking. Railroads must build and maintain their tracks and pay real-estate taxes on the land these tracks occupy. But the federal, state, and local governments build and maintain the roads used by trucks, while fuel and other taxes paid by trucking firms do not seem to cover the total costs of these benefits. In addition, all of the nation's railroads are old and most are in a neglected, deteriorating state. They have not been maintained in the past and are subject to many accidents and equipment failures, which increase costs and decrease dependability and appeal to shippers.

A positive development for suburban factories and the various freight modes has been containerized and piggyback shipping. In containerization, a truck trailer is driven to the dock and loaded as a unit onto a specially designed cargo ship. At the other end it is unloaded and driven to its new destination. This is very efficient compared to the older technique of handling each box or crate individually. It also reduces theft, which is a major waterfront problem. In piggyback shipping, the truck trailer is driven to a railroad depot and then loaded as a unit on a freight car. The net sum of these techniques was to make it possible for factories not located near railroads or ports to ship their goods via the relatively inexpensive, long-distance rail and water modes.

**Air Travel.**  Autos and trucks were not the only transportation force working for the suburbanization of America. The post World War II growth of air travel also strongly affected the compactness of metropolitan areas. Because airports require large amounts of space, they were located in suburban or exurban areas, dependent on the auto to bring passengers to them. As air travel grew, the airports became centers of residential, commercial, and industrial development. Some development was directly related to air travel, for example, hotels and factories that shipped and received goods by air. Other businesses located near airports because air is a major means of travel between cities, making it convenient for executives and salesmen to be located there. Fifty years ago, these firms would have located near a downtown railroad terminal. This is another example of the way an area restructures itself to take advantage of a new transportation system.

**The Net Result: Metropolises.**  The net result of the movement of homes, stores, factories, and offices to the suburbs surrounding older cities has been to remake the face of America. The neat, spoke-like, urban patterns created by mass transit have been destroyed by the auto, which gives direct, point-to-point travel wherever there are roads. The new pattern, or nonpattern, is variously described as a metropolis, spread city, urban sprawl, or — in the U.S. Census Bureau's terms — a Metropolitan Statistical Area.

After the 1940s, population growth took place exclusively in the suburban areas around cities and in the new cities of the Southwest, which were all suburb. Between 1950 and 1960, the suburbs grew by 17 million people,[11] or almost 50 percent. At the same time, central cities, in terms of their 1950 areas, grew by only 767,000 people.[12] The small change in city populations actually conceals important shifts since most of those who could afford to left the cities for the suburbs. They were replaced by the aged, who needed the mass transit and urban services, and by the poor black and white people displaced from the countryside by mechanized farm machinery and from the coal fields of Appalachia by the shift from coal to other energy forms. At first the new suburbanites commuted back to the city for jobs, but increasingly the suburbs have become self-sufficient as all sorts of businesses have left the cities. In many areas, there is as much morning rush-hour commuting out of the city as into it—a phenomenon called reverse commuting.

**The City and the Highway.**   The movement of businesses and middle-class residents to the suburbs constituted a serious threat to the cities. They lost tax-paying residents, civic leadership, jobs, and cultural resources, leaving them with the aged and the poor and obsolete facilities. Cities responded by attempting to accommodate the auto in order to keep residents and businesses. Subway, bus, and even commuter railroads were neglected as resources flowed to highway travel. To make room for cars, urban centers were either razed and rebuilt from scratch or changed bit by bit; old buildings were demolished and replaced with highways, garages, parking lots, and high-rise offices.

But highways cannot be snaked through cities like thread through cloth. Limited-access roads—even when constructed without a median strip—take up a swath of land at least 100 feet wide, and much wider than that at interchanges. A single road may displace thousands of homes and businesses and leave a community physically divided. The community—after the road is built—finds itself with fewer tax-producing homes and businesses (the road does not pay taxes), more crowding, poverty, and noise, fouler air, and fewer resources with which to deal with the problems.

This situation is particularly true in many of the decayed residential or slum areas that ring the cities' central business areas. The roads which carry suburbanites to work pass through these neighborhoods. But while the suburbs and the central business area—revitalized by high-rise offices, multistory garages, and other new developments—may gain from the road, the inner residential ring will surely lose. The inhabitants of this ring—usually the aged and poor workers—are politically weak and economically impoverished. The office jobs in the renewed city require skills they do not have, and the manufacturing, retail, and service positions (for example, hospital orderly, auto mechanic) now located in the suburbs require auto transportation which they cannot afford.

It has been argued that the high price paid by inner-ring neighborhoods for roads connecting the central city with the suburbs may not in the long run even benefit the central business district. For one thing, these central congested areas are especially hard hit by the environmental problems caused by the auto. Cramming large numbers of cars into a tight space means air pollution, noise, and unattractive surroundings for pedestrians. But a more basic argument against shoehorning autos into a central business district is that autos are not compatible with central-city population concentrations. The auto requires so much space for roads, parking lots, and service stations that the central city cannot serve both the auto and the dense populations that are its strength. It is said that if our surviving cities continue to adapt to the auto by tearing down buildings and destroying remaining open space for roads and parking lots, they will lose their character and strength as cities without becoming accessible to the auto and as convenient as the suburbs.

**Halting Highway Construction.** Those who feel that America's cities are vital communication centers and information resources are heartened by the fairly recent phenomenon of "highway stopping." In 1972 legal and political moves by citizen groups and by local governments halted over 100 proposed highways and bridges, many of which would have been built through or close to cities. Opposition by local residents to large-scale highway projects has always existed, but in the past these objections were usually overridden in favor of a supposed greater public good. Over the past few years an erosion of public confidence in the ability of highway transportation to meet all of the nation's needs has developed. Some people have been aroused by the auto's environmental problems; others by its seeming destruction of cities and the unmanageable sprawl of its suburbs; and still others by motor-vehicle deaths and injuries.

In many communities these various interests came together in the late 1960s to form local coalitions to fight roads proposed for their areas. But while the construction of roads is in the hands of state or local governments, the ultimate force pushing the roads was usually the federal government through its control of the Federal Highway Trust Fund. Federal gasoline taxes are deposited in this fund, and until 1973 that money could only be spent on highway construction. Opponents of the auto decided that instead of fighting guerilla battles against innumerable local roads, it made more sense to attack the funding basis. Starting about 1970 serious political efforts were launched to persuade Congress to "open up" the Highway Trust Fund so that some of the money could be spent on mass transit. The pro–mass-transit lobbyists were an informal coalition of conservationists; representatives of the poor, the minorities, and the aged; big city and suburban community mayors and legislators; and the remaining mass-transit companies. Opposed to them was the so-called "road gang"—a grouping of auto, trucking, gasoline, tire, and highway-construction companies as well as public officials from rural areas. In the summer of 1973, after a protracted struggle, Congress voted a very complicated bill whose effect was to free over a period of three years about $1 billion in Fund money for mass transit. In addition, urban areas were given the right to not build controversial interstate highway sections; they could instead use the money for mass transit. This so-called "swapping provision" was vital, because it meant these areas would not lose the federal money by rejecting the road.

At present, it appears that America's surviving cities (for example, Boston, Philadelphia, San Francisco, Chicago, New York) will stop trying to cram more autos into their downtowns and instead emphasize renovation and construction of mass transit. The reversal of the auto trend has been accelerated by energy shortages and the Federal Clean Air Act, which requires that cities greatly improve the quality of their air. In many cases, this can be done only if emissions from individual autos as well as the number of autos on the street are greatly reduced.

**Communications vs. Transportation.**   Whether or not cities can survive and prosper by limiting the auto and emphasizing the benefits of compactness will not be immediately apparent. It took almost twenty-five years for the inherent weaknesses of the auto to become widely recognized; it may take another twenty-five years to see if those cities which do not accommodate the auto achieve a stronger position than auto-centered cities like Los Angeles and Phoenix. Or it may be that several kinds of urban forms will prosper, with people choosing to live in cities whose way of life suits them.

But it is also possible that the evolution will occur in a totally different direction with electronic communications replacing transportation for many purposes. In some ways, that has already happened. One can imagine the traffic jams on winter Sunday afternoons if all the TV football fans tried to drive to local games. Or the increase in travel if people who now watch movies on television went instead to the theater. Or the crunch on roads and in stores, banks, and motor-vehicle bureau offices if all the people who use the mails or phone to transact business did so in person.

Present use of communications can be compared to use of the auto before World War II — it is important but does not yet dominate our way of life. But communications could change America as drastically as the auto changed it. Such advanced communications technology already exists: a video-phone which allows two people to see and hear each other; conference-sized TV-type systems which allow meetings and seminars to take place between persons in different locations; facsimile equipment to transmit printed pages between two terminals; and an extensive cable-TV system with a large channel capacity and various types of programming.

The hardware itself does not determine the social context within which it would be used. Communications might, for example, simply supplement the existing system, eliminating some need for travel in business and personal life. Or it could theoretically lead to the withering away of cities, large office buildings, universities, and libraries. In this extreme, people would still come together in factories to produce goods but most white-collar jobs would be done via communications. An executive, from her home, could inspect an architect's plans for a new factory over TV, have a three-way video-phone conference with the architect and with the contractor who is to build the factory, and then dictate memos to a secretary—also home based—setting out the details of the morning's work. The dictated memos could be sent over facsimile links to others in the far-flung company who have need of the information and stored in the company's data bank, along with recordings of the morning's conferences.

Using such systems, university lecture halls could be replaced with a professor lecturing from home to students also located at home. Conference-type TV systems would make interaction possible and papers could be handed in and returned via facsimile links. The library would be transformed from a building housing books to a data storage and retrieval system, storing information on microfilm and in computer memory banks. Students and faculty would do research from their homes, communicating with the library via terminals and having papers and books displayed on a TV screen or printed out when needed as a permanent record via facsimile links.

More modestly, wider use of communications is seen as possibly helping to improve current population imbalances. Continued migration from rural areas to suburbs and cities has resulted at present in 75 percent of the people living on less than 10 percent of the land. People left, and still leave, rural areas because of lack of jobs, lack of educational and cultural opportunities, and inadequate medical care. Improved communications would help alleviate many of these problems. Multichannel cable-TV systems could bring cultural and sports events to isolated regions; rural students could have access to distant libraries and universities; dispersed medical specialists could consult with doctors on the scene and use instrumentation to examine patients and their data; and corporations could move some of their operations to rural areas without fear of losing employees because of a barren social and cultural environment.

There exists evidence that communications have already affected population patterns. One communications researcher, Richard L. Meier,[13] reports that telephone area codes, circulation territories of major newspapers, and the reception areas of major television stations all overlap in any one metropolitan area. According to Meier their common boundaries define the limits of a sprawling metropolitan region. The metropolitan region—as measured by population densities, work and shopping patterns, and people's personal sense of where they live—does not extend beyond these communications-determined boundaries.

## Conclusion

The preceding discussion of communications must be seen in the context of the history of transportation outlined earlier. We saw that transportation systems evolved to meet the shifting needs of a dynamic society. As the United States changed from a rural to an urban society, its means of transportation evolved from horse-drawn canal boats to railroads in rural areas, and from street railways to trolleys, subways, and finally to autos in urban areas.

The historical examination showed that transportation systems do more than fulfill existing needs—they are also forces for change. Street railways allowed the residential areas of the city to expand in a spoke-like pattern, and reinforced the importance of the central business district. The subway and el had the same effect as the street railway, while the auto and truck broke this pattern, causing urban areas to expand in a sprawling way. But more change is likely since society does not appear satisfied with the urban forms the auto, truck, and plane have created nor content to live with the environmental problems that accompany highway and air travel.

In addition, as the economic base of society evolves, transportation systems are put under pressure to change. In the nineteenth century, a steady increase in farm productivity produced a population shift from rural to urban areas. The labor force was no longer needed behind a plow and instead took its place in the factory. In our own time, industrial productivity has increased to the point where fewer and fewer people are needed in the factories. A majority now work in nonindustrial jobs as teachers, lawyers, doctors, beauticians, and salesmen. They are not as rigidly tied to a time clock or to a place as a factory worker, and the auto serves their more flexible travel needs better than mass transit. While canal barges and railroads still supply the heavy manufacturing industries such as iron and steel mills and auto plants, new industries such as computer and electronic-component manufacturers, medical and research centers, universities, and office complexes are well served by trucks and, increasingly, by air freight.

New transportation systems, then, do not totally replace existing systems in one sweep. Rather they supplement them and occupy new niches of their own. The auto and truck at first were used on a limited scale to perform a few specialized functions railroads could not efficiently handle. Only later, as new suburbs were built and cities altered to accommodate autos, did their use greatly expand. But mass transit and railroads continue to this day to serve the surviving nineteenth-century cities and heavy industry.

We can see the evolutionary process taking place today as the most advanced sectors of the economy come to depend more and more on electronic communications. But the end result will not be a twenty-first-century population permanently seated in front of a bank of communicators. If our survey of history has shown anything, it is that the twenty-first century will be a blend of the very new with surviving structures and institutions from the nineteenth and twentieth centuries.

To understand these evolutionary processes, we have here looked closely at the past and speculated about the distant future. In the next chapter we examine the present transportation situation and possibilities for change over the next several years. In contrast to the present chapter, Chapter 7 relies heavily on statistics to describe the existing situation and takes a close look at the physical laws constraining highways and mass transit in a search for clues to the short-term evolution of our transportation systems.

## Bibliography

*Source Notes*

1. Based on 100 million vehicles traveling an average of 10,000 miles per year at a cost (depreciation plus operating expenses) of fifteen cents per mile.

2. "Exploring Energy Choices." The Ford Foundation Energy Policy Project. New York: The Ford Foundation, 1974.

3. *Environmental Quality.* The Third Annual Report of the Council on Environmental Quality. Washington, D.C.: U.S. Government Printing Office, 1972.

4. *Fares, Please!* John Anderson Miller. New York: Dover Publications, 1960.

5. Ibid.

6. Ibid.

7. Ibid.

8. *The Transportation Revolution, 1815–1860.* George Rogers Taylor. New York: Harper and Row, 1951.

9. *American Cities.* Constance McLaughlin Green. London: The Athlone Press, 1957.

10. "American Ground Transport, A Proposal for Restructuring the Automobile, Truck, Bus and Rail Industries." Bradford C. Snell. Available from the United States Senate Subcommittee on Antitrust and Monopoly of the Committee on the Judiciary. Washington, D.C.: U.S. Government Printing Office, 1974.

11. *The Withering Away of the City.* York Willbern. Tuscaloosa, Alabama: University of Alabama Press, 1964.

12. Ibid.

13. *A Communications Theory of Urban Growth.* Richard L. Meier. Cambridge, Mass.: MIT Press, 1962.

*Further Reading*

### Transportation

HELEN LEAVITT. *Superhighway-Superhoax.* New York: Ballantine, 1970.
This book is written by a person who helped stop highway construction in Washington, D.C. A classic muckraking book with chapter titles such as "The Highwaymen" and "Neither the Quick Nor the Dead Are Safe," the last a reference to roads built through cemeteries.

JOHN ANDERSON MILLER.   *Fares, Please!* New York: Dover Publications, 1960.
This book is described exactly by its subtitle: A Popular History of Trolleys, Horsecars, Streetcars, Buses, Elevateds and Subways. Illustrated and enjoyable.

GEORGE ROGERS TAYLOR.   *The Transportation Revolution, 1815–1860.* New York: Harper and Row, 1951.
Taylor gives an historical examination of transportation in the United States from 1815–1860. He also gives valuable background to the period.

U.S. DEPARTMENT OF TRANSPORTATION.   *The Freeway in the City.* Washington, D.C.: U.S. Government Printing Office.
This large, profusely illustrated book shows what design choices are available in building roads through cities.

S. S. WILSON.   "Bicycle Technology." *Scientific American,* March 1973, p. 81.
An excellent blend of the technology, history, social impact, and future prospects of the bicycle are given in this article.

## Communications

*Communication.* Published by *Scientific American,* September 1972.
This issue contains eleven articles dealing with the biological and technological aspects of communications.

GEORGE GERBNER et al., eds.   *Communications, Technology and Social Change.* New York: John Wiley and Sons, 1973.
A collection of essays on the many aspects of telecommunications is contained in this book.

PETER C. GOLDMARK.   "The New Rural Society." 1973 Cornell University Lecture Series. (Available from: Department of Communication Arts, Cornell University, Ithaca, New York 14850.)
Dr. Goldmark, inventor of the LP record and past director of the Columbia Broadcasting System Laboratory, reports on his efforts to develop ways of strengthening rural areas through use of communications systems. See also the September 1972 *Scientific American* for his article "Communication and the Community."

RICHARD L. MEIER.   *A Communications Theory of Urban Growth.* Cambridge, Mass.: MIT Press, 1962.
This book is a very interesting collection of essays on the interaction between communications and urban areas.

NATIONAL ACADEMY OF ENGINEERING.   *Communications Technology for Urban Improvement.* Washington, D.C., June 1971.
This book presents a survey of possible applications of telecommunications to alleviate urban problems and guide future urban development in desired directions.

————. *Telecommunications Research in the United States and Selected Foreign Countries: A Preliminary Survey,* vol. i and ii. Washington, D.C., June 1973.
A survey of the state of telecommunications research and likely future developments is presented here.

## Urbanology

JACQUES ELLUL. *The Meaning of the City.* Grand Rapids, Michigan: Eerdmans, 1970.
Ellul is one of the great modern social theorists. In this extremely pessimistic book, he views the city as man's way of walling out God and nature.

CONSTANCE MCLAUGHLIN GREEN. *American Cities.* London: The Athlone Press, 1957.
The writer gives short histories here of both important and representative cities. She deals with many of the technological questions raised in this chapter. See especially the histories of Chicago and New Orleans.

JANE JACOBS. *The Death and Life of Great American Cities.* New York: Random House, 1961.
Ms. Jacobs' book helped change the way in which people look at cities. Basically, she is for random natural development and against planning.

_____. *The Economy of Cities.* New York: Random House, 1969.
In this controversial book, Ms. Jacobs presents her theories on the technological and economic functioning of cities.

LEWIS MUMFORD. *The City in History.* New York: Harcourt Brace Jovanovich, 1961.
This is a good book of Mumford's to start with.

_____. *The Urban Prospect.* New York: Harcourt Brace Jovanovich, 1968.
This book is a collection of essays by the dean of American urbanologists. Especially interesting is his indictment of the interstate highway system ("The Highway and the City") and his critique of Ms. Jacobs' *The Death and Life of Great American Cities* ("Home Remedies for Urban Cancer"). Mumford has been so right for so long that anyone interested in cities or the environment should read at least one of his twenty-plus books.

YORK WILLBERN. *The Withering Away of the City.* Tuscaloosa, Alabama: University of Alabama Press, 1964.
A short (138 pages) excellent treatment of the effects of suburbanization is presented in this book.

## Fiction

WILLA CATHER. *O Pioneers!* Boston: Houghton Mifflin, 1913.
Ms. Cather describes what it was like to live on the Nebraskan Great Plains before the turn of the century. This novel is relevant here for its excellent description of the isolated and hard life of the farmer.

JACK FINNEY. *Time and Again.* New York: Simon and Schuster, 1970.
This novel is about a man from the present who travels in time back to the 1880s. All sorts of technical information about urban life at that time is given. It is also a good novel.

E. M. FORSTER. "The Machine Stops."
This is a short story written in 1920 and set in a future world where everyone lives in their own room and communicates with each other via television and other communication means. Interesting speculation on the ultimate effect of man's evolving technology.

## Questions

1. The early, or ordinary, bicycle had a very large front wheel with the pedals directly attached to it, the way tricycles are today.
   a. What was the purpose of the large front wheel?
   b. How did the chain-driven bicycle eliminate the need for the large front wheel?

2. In many areas of the country the bicycle seems to be making a comeback. Do you see a possibility of the bicycle becoming an important part of the overall transportation system? Does the fact that the auto beat out the bicycle around the turn of the century indicate that the bicycle is not suited for general transportation purposes?

3. The text states that on the time scale of our individual experience, transportation systems seem permanent and unchanging. Do you agree? Have you discerned what you think is fundamental change in the way we move people or goods?

4. Describe as best you can the area in which you live. Is it rural, suburban, or central city? Are you aware of the population and area of your town, county, or city and of present population trends? If you are in or near a city, are you familiar with the shape of the pre–World War II city? Is a radial pattern following mass-transit lines still discernible? Is there any evidence of nineteenth-century transportation systems such as old canal beds? Are cobblestones occasionally visible at the bottom of potholes in streets now covered with asphalt?

5. Henry Ford, as the quotation cited earlier indicates, felt that the auto would allow man to work in cities and still enjoy the country. Have things worked out that way? If not, where did his vision of the future fail? Was he implicitly making assumptions about the future that have not been borne out?

6. Ford saw the auto as a tool, much like a good screwdriver. He once said people could buy the Model T in any color they wanted, so long as it was black. Is our present view of the auto similarly utilitarian? If our view has changed, is that in any way related to the way Ford's prediction (see question 5) has held up?

7. Highways were once commonly built through parks, along ocean and lake fronts, and in other scenic and wild areas. Present federal law has almost eliminated this practice. But it is argued that roads through such areas are needed. America, the argument runs, is a nation on wheels and banning roads in scenic areas means that only those willing or able to walk into those areas can see them. Opponents of this view claim the road destroys the very qualities that make the areas desirable and that little enjoyment or appreciation is gained from driving past something at 50 miles/hour. If the person stops at a "scenic turn-out," it is said, the presence of nearby moving vehicles will destroy his or her enjoyment of the view.
   What is your position on this argument? Is a middle ground available?

8. A large number of bus driver robberies led New York City to go over to an exact-fare system, in which the bus driver made no change and the passenger's fare dropped into a strongbox bolted to the floor of the bus. This stopped

bus robberies but holdups of taxicab drivers immediately increased. When taxis, too, converted to the strongbox system, the change booths in subways became the new targets. As of 1973, they also were being fortified.

    a. What do you suggest will happen once this fortification is complete?

    b. What does this say about technology (burglar alarms, outside lights, and so on) and crime?

    c. Can you think of other technological cycles in which one technological change led to an unforeseen and undesired response?

9. Do you make wide use of communications or – where you have a choice – do you prefer to travel to shop, pay bills, attend sports events?

10. What advantages and disadvantages do you see for the student in a "wired," or communications-centered, college?

11. The text mentions that street railways required plowed tracks, which interfered with the use of sleighs. Today, of course, all urban streets are plowed and horse-drawn sleighs are antiques.

    a. Speculate on why residents objected to the plowing of streets. After all, plowing would allow them to continue to use carriages and wagons, instead of switching to sleighs and sleds.

    b. What objections would the street-railway companies have to changing over to sleighs in winter weather?

    c. Speculate on the factors that eventually led to the plowing of all city streets.

12. Verify that the assumptions given in the Source Notes, number 1, yield $150 billion.

*But, properly, urban industrialism must be regarded as an experiment. And if the scientific spirit has taught us anything of value, it is that honest experiments may well fail.*

T. ROSZAK*

# 7 Transportation dynamics

Since the end of the Civil War the United States has been moving at an accelerating rate toward becoming an urban society. (See Figure 1.[1]) Before World War II society consisted of a concentrated central city, served internally by mass transit and externally by railroads, and a vast rural area dotted with small towns and villages. But after World War II, the urban and rural areas began to change. The central city remained, but the old residential rings surrounding the core lost their middle-class residents. These people began moving to the low-density, auto-centered suburbs which grew up in the former rural areas, supplanting the farms, the estates of the wealthy, the vacant lots, and the marshy areas. The drive behind this migration was, and still is, the desire for space and privacy offered by the one-family home combined with the convenience and speed of the auto, with which the one-family home meshes so well.

This flow of people into suburban areas is shown in Table 1 for the nation and in Figure 2[2] for the New York-New Jersey area. The urban fringe in Table 1 is

---

* From Roszak's book *Where the Wasteland Ends* (New York: Doubleday and Company, 1972).

suburbia and it almost tripled in population from 1950 to 1970, while central cities were holding steady at about 30 percent of the nation's population. The fact that the cities were holding steady in the face of the movement to the suburbs had two causes: many cities expanded physically by incorporating neighboring suburban areas (without that annexation they would have grown by only 767,000 people from 1950 to 1960), and the housing vacated by the new suburbanites was filled by poor rural people, mostly black, forced off southern farms by mechanization.

**Rural-to-Urban Transition**

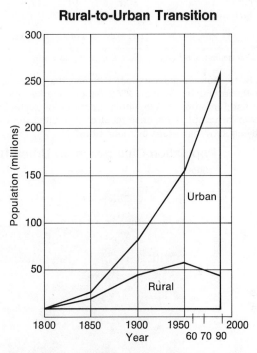

**Figure 1.** In this graph America's transition from a rural to an urban society is projected into the future. Urban areas are those with at least 2500 people.

As was emphasized in Chapter 6, the changing nature of urban areas strongly affects transportation. In the present chapter we describe the new urban forms and their effect on transportation needs. We then look at the abilities of different transportation systems to serve those needs, and at the various impacts the transportation systems have on cities and suburbs. We especially examine the land requirements of the various systems and the physical factors which determine those requirements. While urban form and transportation land needs are central to the problem of transportation, we shall also look at the environmental problems associated with different transportation systems. Wherever possible, this chapter will take a quantitative approach.

**Changing Population Patterns**

|  | 1950 | | 1960 | | 1970 | |
|---|---|---|---|---|---|---|
|  | *Population × 10³* | *%* | *Population × 10³* | *%* | *Population × 10³* | *%* |
| Rural | 54,479 | 36 | 54,054 | 30 | 53,887 | 27 |
| Urban (Total) | 96,847 | 64 | 125,269 | 70 | 149,325 | 73 |
|   Central City | 48,377 | 32 | 57,975 | 33 | 63,922 | 31 |
|   Urban Fringe | 20,872 | 14 | 37,873 | 21 | 54,525 | 27 |
|   Outside Urbanized Areas | 27,598 | 18 | 29,420 | 16 | 30,878 | 15 |
| Total | 151,326 | 100 | 179,323 | 100 | 203,212 | 100 |

SOURCE: *Statistical Abstract, 1971* (Washington, D.C.: U.S. Government Printing Office).

**Table 1.** Rural areas are those with less than 2500 people; urban areas are those with more than 2500 people. Marked changes occurred in the distribution of people within urban regions. The central city growth shown is deceptive because most of it resulted from the annexation of outlying suburban areas by older cities.

## Population Changes in an Urban Region

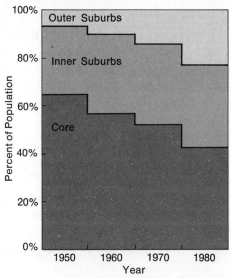

**Figure 2.** This graph shows the population changes in the New York-New Jersey metropolitan region. Since 1950 a steady decline has occurred in the percentage of the population living in the central city. The outer suburbs have grown rapidly during this period. This trend is expected to accelerate through the 1970s.

## Urban Passenger Travel

Travel Patterns. These population shifts of the past three decades had and continue to have a profound effect on urban (within a metropolitan area) transportation. In the central city, a person walks to the store, the

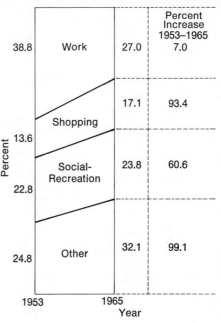

**Changing Urban Travel Patterns**

**Figure 3.** From 1953 to 1965 there was a relative decline in urban trips to and from work and a strong growth in trips for shopping, social-recreation and "other" (chauffeuring children, trips to the doctor). In 1953, 38.8% of all trips were to or from work. By 1965, that number had declined to 27.0%. But during this time the total number of trips to work had increased by 7.0%. In 1953 there were 2,481,000 daily trips to work and in 1965 there were 2,655,000 daily trips to work in the Detroit metropolitan area, where the above data were collected.

doctor's office, music lessons, school, and sometimes even to work. Those who don't walk go by bus or subway. But suburbs, with their low population density, cannot support a grocery store, doctor's office, bookshop, dance studio, and karate school every few blocks. Instead, shopping centers and "professional" buildings have been established along major roads so that people can drive to these places to shop, bowl, eat, and get their hair cut. This caused a great increase in the amount of travel, as shown in Figure 3.[3] All categories of travel grew, as the right column shows, but the fastest growing category was "other," which refers to such miscellaneous activities as chauffeuring children to friends and lessons, going to the doctor, and participating in civic activities.

The travel pattern established in the low-density suburbs spread out in all directions. There was never any force focusing it as the central business district focused early urban transportation. Thus it is difficult, if not impossible, for conventional mass transit to serve suburban travel needs. Moreover, few suburbanites would use mass transit even if it was available. The auto gives door-to-door service, lugs all the groceries a family can eat in a month, and is always on call. The result, shown in Table 2, is the already large and still growing dominance of the auto over all public transit. In a sense, Table 2 is misleading: in terms of the vehicle-miles traveled and passengers carried, mass transit is simply not in the same statistical league as the auto.

**Urban Passenger Travel**

| Travel Mode | Vehicle-miles × 10⁶ | | | Passengers × 10⁶ | | |
| --- | --- | --- | --- | --- | --- | --- |
| | *1960* | *1970* | *Change* | *1960* | *1970* | *Change* |
| Passenger Cars | 284,800 | 494,543 | 73.6% | N.A. | N.A. | N.A. |
| School Buses, Charter Buses, etc. | 1849 | 1810 | −2.1% | N.A. | N.A. | N.A. |
| Public Transit Buses | 1576 | 1409 | −10.6% | 5069 | 4058 | −19.9% |
| Subway and Elevated Train | 391 | 407 | 4.1% | 1670 | 1574 | −5.7% |
| Surface Rail | 75 | 34 | −54.7% | 335 | 172 | −48.7% |
| Trolley | 101 | 33 | −67.3% | 447 | 128 | −71.4% |
| Taxis | 5200 | 6800 | 30.8% | 1820 | 2378 | 30.7% |
| Commuter Rail for N.Y., Philadelphia, Chicago, Boston, and San Francisco | N.A. | N.A. | N.A. | 248 | 247 | −0.4% |

SOURCE: *1972 National Transportation Report,* U.S. Department of Transportation (Washington, D.C., 1972).

**Table 2.** The table shows that private auto and taxi use grew between 1960 and 1970 while mass-transit use of all kinds shrunk. To roughly translate passenger-car vehicle-miles into passengers carried (no official figures are given), we assume an average auto trip is 10 miles and that the auto carries 1.6 people. In 1960, then, autos carried about 46,000 × 10⁶ passengers, and in 1970, 79,000 × 10⁶ passengers. This means that in 1970 autos carried over 10 times as many passengers as all of mass transit combined. The distinction here between surface rail and trolley is not important. (N.A. in the table means the data are not available.)

**Auto Ownership**

| | *1960* | *1970* |
| --- | --- | --- |
| Autos per Capita | 0.32 | 0.39 |
| Autos per Household | 1.09 | 1.27 |
| Households with Autos (percent) | 75.5 | 79.6 |
| Households with Two or More Autos (percent) | 13.4 | 29.2 |
| Households without Autos (percent) | 24.5 | 20.4 |
| People per Household | 3.40 | 3.25 |

SOURCE: *1972 National Transportation Report.*

**Table 3.** Data for U.S. auto ownership on a per capita and per household basis in 1960 and 1970 are given in this chart.

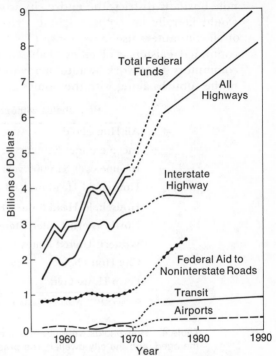

**Figure 4.** Until very recently, Federal spending on mass transit has been vanishingly small, while spending on roads has been very large. The projections shown are little more than guesses.

**The Economics of Transportation.** The creation of the suburbs and their transportation system was not achieved cheaply. The federal and state governments undertook to collect gasoline taxes and to build roads with the money collected. The federal funds invested over the past decade in highways—and the consequent neglect of transit—is shown in Figure 4.[4] The huge investment of public moneys in highways stimulated private citizens to buy autos to make use of those roads. Table 3 shows that in 1970 the average U.S. household owned 1.27 autos, up from 1.09 autos in 1960. This increase occurred while the number of people per household was dropping from 3.40 to 3.25. By 1970, the entire nation could fit into the front seats of its autos. But, according to Table 4, the poor and the aged had no cars to fit into.

The public and private concentration on auto travel meant financial troubles for buses, subways, and commuter railroad lines. In the past decades, many transit companies have gone under, and those that survive usually do so with subsidies from the local city. The cities subsidized mass transit because that was the only way they too could survive. As discussed earlier, those American cities that prospered did so as office centers, employing white-collar workers from the surrounding suburbs. Table 5 shows that great numbers of people commute into and out of the cities each day and highways could not carry them all without simultaneously wiping out the city. For 200,000 people to drive into Chicago's one-square-mile business district, the entire city would have to be paved over. There would literally be nothing left to drive to. So although only 9 percent of all commuters use mass transit (Table 6), that mass transit is vital to the continued existence of cities. Table 6 also shows that 81 percent of all commuters go to work by auto, many to the jobs that have been dispersing to the suburbs along with the homes and stores.

**Households without Autos, 1970**

| | |
|---|---|
| All Households | 20.4% |
| Income under $3000/year | 57.5% |
| Income over $15,000/year | 3.8% |
| Household Head over 64 years | 44.8% |
| Household Head 35 to 44 Years | 11.6% |
| Northeastern United States | 27.5% |
| Western United States | 14.9% |
| City Household | 34.0% |
| Farm Household | 12.8% |

SOURCE: *1972 National Transportation Report.*

**Table 4.** Households without autos are concentrated among the poor, the aged, and the city dweller. The practice of leasing autos somewhat overstates nonownership.

**Commuter Flow**

| City | Central Business District Area (square miles) | Approximate Number of Commuters |
|---|---|---|
| New York | 9.1 | More than 800,000 |
| Chicago | 1.0 | 200,000 to 250,000 |
| Philadelphia | 2.2 | 150,000 to 200,000 |
| Boston | 1.4 | 150,000 to 200,000 |
| Washington, D.C. | 6.1 | 150,000 to 200,000 |
| Los Angeles | 1.6 | 100,000 to 150,000 |
| San Francisco | 1.3 | 100,000 to 150,000 |
| Atlanta | 1.7 | 75,000 to 100,000 |
| New Orleans | 0.4 | 75,000 to 100,000 |

SOURCE: *Urban Rail Transit: Its Economics and Technology,* A. Scheffer Lang and Richard M. Soberman (Cambridge, Mass.: MIT Press, 1964).

**Table 5.** The table shows the hourly, evening, commuter rush-hour traffic which flows out of some major American cities. Although the data are from 1964, they are still fairly accurate.

**Some Data on Commuters**

| Mode | Percent of Commuters Using This Mode | Average Time for a One-way Morning Trip (min) | Average Speed (mi/hr) |
|---|---|---|---|
| Auto | 81 | 16 | 16–20 |
| Bus | 6 | 21 | 8–13 |
| Walk | 6 | 8 | 3 |
| Subway | | | 8–13 |
| Commuter R.R. | 3 | 41 | N.A. |
| Motorbike | | | N.A. |
| Bicycle | 2 | N.A. | 10 |
| Other | 2 | N.A. | N.A. |

**Table 6.** Even though mass transportation is used mostly to commute to work, it still carries only a small percentage of people to work. The information in the second and third columns was gathered in a 1971 Gallup poll and is reprinted here by permission. The average speed values are from a different source and were collected much earlier. (N.A. means the data are not available.)

### Travel to an Urban Business District, 1924-1965

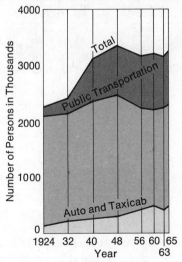

**Figure 5.** The total number of people entering New York City's central business district by auto each day has been increasing steadily. It is now about 15 percent of the total. More than half of the above trips are for commuting to work. During rush hours 93 percent of the travel to the central business district is by transit. This percentage drops sharply in nonrush hours. About 30 percent of all public transportation trips in the United States are made in New York.

**The City and the Auto.** While it may be impossible for all central-business-district workers to drive to work, a sizeable and growing fraction do so. Although Figure 5[5] is for all travelers to New York's central business district, it shows clearly that increasing numbers of cars are being forced into the downtown. As a result, New York and most central business districts are chronically congested, with resulting low speeds and high per-mile auto costs.

This photograph shows three major urban commuter highways leading into the central artery (in foreground) of Boston's busy central business district. The buildings in the foreground comprise Boston's financial district; the port of Boston Harbor can be seen in the right bottom corner. *Photo courtesy Massachusetts Department of Public Works.*

The chronic congestion and the high costs make rush-hour commuting by mass transit competitive with the auto. When rush-hour highways leading into the central business district are as clogged as central-business-district streets and avenues, then even relatively slow commuter railroads and subways are attractive. That is why some urban strategists urge that no effort be made to build more highway capacity or parking in cities. They say that any improvements in traffic flow will be quickly erased as even more people leave public transit and drive to work. So instead of improving traffic conditions, some cities are concentrating on discouraging auto travel by reducing parking, building carless pedestrian malls on former city streets, and closing roads through parks to motor vehicles.

But while mass transit can still attract the central-business-district commuter going to and from work, it cannot attract the nonrush-hour traveler. This leads to the pattern shown in Figure 6,[6] which gives data for the Chicago region but is typical of all urban areas. Mass transit carries most

## Hourly Use of Several Urban Transportation Modes

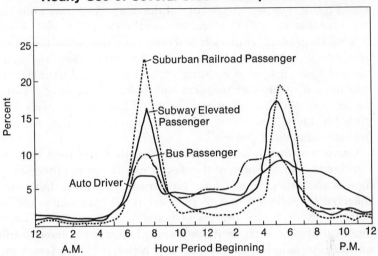

**Figure 6.** Use of rail transit peaks sharply during rush hours and then falls off drastically. Bus and especially auto use are much more regular. Rail transit is set up primarily to serve the person going to work while the bus and auto provide more flexible service. The data were collected in the Chicago region but are typical of most areas.

of its patrons during the morning and evening rush-hour periods while highways are used more uniformly throughout the day. This is a great economic handicap for transit because a large passenger-carrying capacity is used only a few hours a week. It is the familiar peak-hour load problem encountered in earlier chapters with elevators and aqueducts.

The peak-hour transportation situation is worsening because central business districts are losing or have already lost their factory jobs and have become office centers. This means most of the people wish to arrive at 9 A.M. and leave at 5 P.M., concentrating the rush hour into a briefer period of time. When cities were more heterogeneous, with a wide mix of jobs, the rush-hour period was spread out; factory workers arrived at 6 or 7 A.M. and left work in the early afternoon well before the office workers. Now the subways and buses carry fewer people overall during rush hours, but because the rush hours are more concentrated, the crowding is worse.

**Possibilities for Change.** Although highway and central-business-district motor vehicle congestion and mass-transit crowding maintain a tenuous equilibrium, it is not a very satisfactory state of affairs. It would be nice to untangle traffic congestion since this would reduce noise, air pollution, and jangled nerves. But if that's to be done, motor vehicle access to the central business district must be limited, and no one knows how to do this. It could be achieved by an outright ban on private auto use.

But it is said that if top-level executives could not be driven to work, they would move their companies out of the cities. And they would be followed by stores that cater to the wealthy and the departed office workers.

A more gradual approach is to improve transit to the point where it provides a reasonable alternative to the auto. Then the auto could be banned without fear of creating a ghost town. Unfortunately the kind of information needed to perform the delicate balancing act of improving transit and choking off motor vehicle access is not easily available. We probably know less about urban transportation than we do about the migratory habits of geese.

But it is difficult and expensive to gather the data that would allow intelligent change. Some of the data presented in the preceding tables and figures was taken from traffic and passenger counts, but much of it was collected by polling motorists stopped in toll plazas or at red lights, or by doing house-to-house surveys of people's travel patterns. Because of the money and time such methods require, most areas have insufficient data on which to plan improvements. The New York-New Jersey metropolitan region — one of the best studied in the nation — had its last full-scale urban transportation survey in 1963.

## Physical Capabilities of Urban Transportation

To see the extent to which existing transportation systems can be changed, we will examine their capabilities and limitations. In the previous discussions we have taken for granted that rail transit is suited to the high densities of cities and autos to the lower densities of suburbs. It was assumed that the auto cannot serve as the major transportation mode for a city without destroying the high densities and concentrated activity that make the city different from the suburbs. We now wish to look at the physical differences between rail transit and autos that lead to this conclusion.

Highway Passenger Capacities and Space Needs. We begin by calculating the passenger-carrying capacity of the modern, urban, interstate highway illustrated in Figure 7.[7] Because that highway may be built on very valuable urban real estate, it was designed as tightly as possible. A suburban or rural interstate road would have a much more generous median divider and buffer strips beyond the shoulders. We will compare the capacity of this highway with that of the San Francisco Bay region's commuter railroad, BART (Bay Area Rapid Transit), whose elevated section is shown in Figure 8.[8]

All transportation systems require a right-of-way, a stretch of land over which the vehicles can move. A highway lane and a railroad track are both 12 feet wide and are therefore said to have 12-foot rights-of-way.

## Land Needs for an Urban Highway

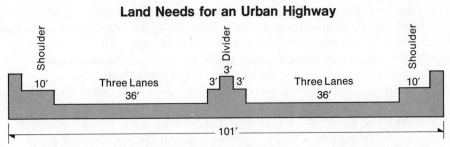

**Figure 7.** The diagram shows a cross section of a six-lane urban high-way meeting interstate specifications. Entrance and exit lanes will re-quire additional space.

## BART

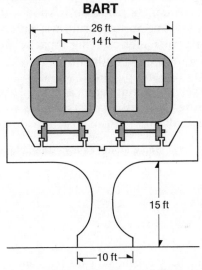

**Figure 8.** This diagram gives a cross section of an elevated section of BART.

In doing comparisons, we shall assume all rights-of-way (except subways, which are underground, and airport runways, which are about 200 feet wide) are 12 feet wide.

So the key difference between systems is not the size of a highway lane versus the size of a railroad track. The main distinction between systems is in their passenger-carrying capacities. The passenger-carrying capacity of a transportation artery is defined as the maximum number of passengers that can move past a given point per hour. To determine the passenger-carrying capacity of a highway lane, an observer stands by the side of the road during a peak-use period and counts the number of people who ride past in an hour. The concept of passenger capacity is similar to that of the flow capacity of an aqueduct. In both cases, what is measured is the movement past a point. In both cases, the total amount of water in the pipe or the total number of passengers on the transportation artery is irrelevant to the carrying capacity. In neither case does speed alone determine capacity. With an aqueduct, cross-sectional area is as important as speed. In the case of a highway lane or railroad track, the spacing between vehicles and the number of people per vehicle are crucial considerations.

Spacing between vehicles, or, more accurately, the time interval between consecutive vehicles passing a fixed point, is called headway. If a person standing alongside a highway is passed by a car every 1.5 seconds, the headway between cars is 1.5 seconds. If a trackside observer is passed by a train every 3 minutes, the headway is 3 minutes. Knowledge of headway immediately yields the vehicle-carrying capacity of the artery. Trains running on 3-minute headways yield a capacity of 20 trains per hour. If the number of passengers per train is known, then the hourly passenger capacity is also known. So the headway—without any information about speed—yields the passenger-carrying capacity. But as we shall see later on, headway is not always independent of speed.

With these definitions in mind, we will calculate a highway's hourly capacity. However, to do this requires several assumptions: that there are no trucks and buses on the road; that all autos are moving at 60 miles/hour; and that they are all obeying the spacing rule of one car length for each

### Some Motor-Vehicle Characteristics

| | |
|---|---|
| Autos | |
|    Weight | 2000–6000 lb |
|    Length | 14–19 ft |
|    Width | 5'8"–6'8" |
|    Height | 4'4"–4'10" |
|    Top Speed | 80–110 mi/hr |
| 0 to 60 mi/hr Acceleration Time for Autos | 12 sec |
| 0 to 40 mi/hr Acceleration Time for Single-Unit Trucks | 32 sec |
| Auto Braking Distance (60 mi/hr to rest) | |
|    Dry Pavement | 214 ft |
|    Wet Pavement | 300 ft |
| Total Auto Stopping Distance (reaction time plus braking) for 60 mi/hr to Rest | |
|    Dry Pavement | 346 ft |
|    Wet Pavement | 432 ft |
| Auto Braking Distance (30 mi/hr to rest) | |
|    Dry Pavement | 48 ft |
|    Wet Pavement | 73 ft |

**Table 7.** Some average motor-vehicle dimensions and performance characteristics are shown here. The slow acceleration characteristic of trucks affects entrance and exit lane lengths and other highway characteristics.

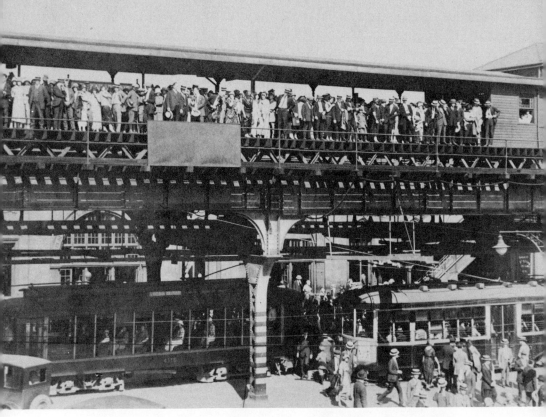

In this crowded central business district of the 1920s, trolley, elevated train, and auto had to share the same right-of-way. Today the trolley and the el are gone, but mass transit is still dominant in New York City. As can be seen, even in the 1920s commuter rush hours created unpleasant problems in the city. *Photo courtesy Museum of the City of New York.*

10-miles-per-hour of speed. Taking 20 feet as a generous auto length yields a separation between cars of 120 feet. Table 7, which lists some properties of motor vehicles, shows that 120 feet is appreciably less than the braking distance of a car moving at 60 miles/hour.

In fact, the one-car-length-per-10-miles-per-hour rule has little to do with braking distance: it is related to reaction time. When the lead auto's brake lights flash, the following driver takes about 1.5 seconds to register the information, decide to act on it, and then get a foot to the brake. During this 1.5 seconds, the car travels

$$d = (V)\,(t) = (88 \text{ ft/sec})\,(1.5 \text{ sec}) = 130 \text{ ft.}$$

Because the cars are originally 120 feet apart, the driver of the following car will begin to brake at approximately the same point the lead car's brakes were applied. In theory, this makes for smooth, coordinated slowing of a line of vehicles. In practice, some cars will be tailgating and have to make panic stops while other cars will have a large buffer space in front of them and the driver may only have to ease off the gas. Notice that if the lead car stops dead, the following car will slam into it just as the driver's foot reaches the brake.

To return to the ideal situation, the front-bumper-to-front-bumper distance between consecutive cars (see Figure 9) is 7 car lengths, or 140 feet. The headway is the time it takes a car going 60 miles/hour (88 feet/second) to travel 140 feet.

$$t = \frac{d}{V} = \frac{140 \text{ ft}}{88 \text{ ft/sec}} = 1.6 \text{ sec}$$

An observer alongside this highway lane would be passed by a car once every 1.6 seconds for an hourly flow of

$$\frac{3600 \text{ sec/hr}}{1.6 \text{ sec/auto}} = 2250 \text{ autos/hr.}$$

### An Air View of a Highway Lane

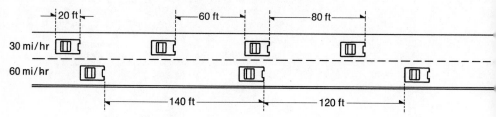

**Figure 9.** The top lane shows autos moving along a highway at 30 miles/hour. Under ideal conditions, they will maintain a 3-car-length, or 60-foot, separation. Front-bumper-to-front-bumper separation will therefore be 80 feet. The bottom lane's traffic is moving at 60 miles/hour, with traffic maintaining a 6-car-length separation.

To see how vehicle capacity changes with speed, we calculate the flow at 30 miles/hour (44 feet/second). The spacing between consecutive front bumpers is 4 car lengths, or 80 feet, yielding a headway of

$$t = \frac{d}{V} = \frac{80 \text{ ft}}{44 \text{ ft/sec}} = 1.8 \text{ sec.}$$

So the hourly flow is

$$\frac{3600 \text{ sec/hr}}{1.8 \text{ sec/auto}} = 2000 \text{ autos/hr.}$$

The theoretical vehicle capacity drops about 10% when the speed is halved. This relatively small change occurs because halving the speed also halves the separation between cars, according to the spacing rule. The headway does not quite remain constant because the front-bumper-to-front-bumper distance goes from 7 car lengths to 4 car lengths. It might seem that the vehicle capacity could be increased by running cars at 60 miles/hour with 3-car-lengths separation. That might work for a while, but eventually there would be a huge pileup, possibly disrupting traffic flow for hours.

Actually, our theoretical model gives too high a capacity. Highway flows rarely exceed 2000 cars/hour/lane[9] and this occurs only at fairly low speeds (25–30 miles/hour) on roads without grades, with few entrances and exits, without trucks or buses or drivers who are cutting in and out. The theory is also misleading in the sense that it shows volume increasing with speed while, actually, road flow tends to increase as speed decreases. Better mathematical models of highway flow are available, but they are beyond the level and intent of this text.

To calculate the passenger-carrying capacity of a highway lane, we must know the average number of occupants per car. The present national average is about 2. During nonrush hours—when families and shoppers go places together—auto occupancy is above 2, and during rush hours, occupancy is about 1.5, with 60% of the cars[10] containing only the commuter driving himself or herself to work. Car pools, which were once popular, were used less and less frequently during the 1960s as more people became able to own their own cars or as families got a second or even third car (see Table 3).

Since it is during rush hours that highways are used to capacity, the passenger flow of a road at 60 miles/hour is only 3000 people/lane/hour. The six-lane highway, if it were filled to capacity in both directions, could carry 18,000 people/hour. The one-way direction is 9000 people/hour. So auto occupancy is crucial. If the average number of occupants per car could be doubled to two during rush hours, it would be equivalent to building a new highway. In order to expand the capacity of highway facilities without new construction, the tolls on some roads and bridges have been reduced or eliminated, and exclusive lanes have been reserved for autos with three or more people.

What we have considered so far is the stripped-down highway, but there must also be entrance and exit lanes. If they are spaced every couple of miles, they will add appreciably to the road's space needs. If the entrance lanes are shortened, vehicles will come onto the road at low speeds, interrupting the flow of traffic, which may nullify any space saved with the shorter lane.

The limited-access highway under discussion is designed to bring the suburban commuter to the periphery of the central business district. Once off the road, the car will also need space on city streets and avenues. In addition, each car needs 300 square feet for parking and 200 square feet for its share of the space occupied by gas stations, auto showrooms, junkyards, and so on. All together, 20 to 40 percent[11] of urban land is devoted to the auto.

**Trucks and Buses.**   The theoretical and actual capacity of a highway is reduced by the presence of trucks, since they accelerate and brake at slower rates than cars, take up more space, and are generally less maneuverable (see Table 7). A highway that accommodates trucks must have longer entrance and exit lanes, thicker pavement, wider lanes and shoulders, and stronger dividers between opposing traffic flow. The net effect of trucks is to reduce lane capacity, make highways more massive and expensive, and increase noise levels (see Table 8).

Buses have some of the same liabilities as trucks—they are sluggish, large, and noisy. However, there is increasing likelihood that more and more buses will be found on highways, many of them in their own lanes.

**Some Common Noise Levels**

| | |
|---|---:|
| Uncomfortably Loud | |
|    Riveting Machine | 110 dB |
|    Rock and Roll Band | 108–114 dB |
|    Jet (flying over at 1000 feet) | 103 dB |
| Very Loud | |
|    Power Mower | 96 dB |
|    Interior of Subway Car (35 mi/hr) | 95 dB |
|    Motorcycle at 25 feet | 90 dB |
| Moderately Loud | |
|    Diesel Truck at 50 feet (40 mi/hr) | 84 dB |
|    Diesel Train at 100 feet (40–50 mi/hr) | 83 dB |
|    Passenger Car at 25 feet (65 mi/hr) | 77 dB |
| Quiet | |
|    Near Freeway Auto Traffic | 64 dB |
|    Light Traffic at 100 feet | 50 dB |

**Table 8.** Given here are some common noise levels measured in decibels (dB), a unit of sound. The designations "uncomfortably loud," "very loud," and so on, are subjective and not meant as a precise classification.

Buses are especially attractive as commuting vehicles in suburbs lacking commuter railroads. Forty-seat buses can economically pick up passengers on suburban streets and take a limited-access highway to a central city location. However, if the bus must share a highway lane with cars, it will crawl along at the same speed. This reduces the appeal of bus transport since the auto driver has the advantage of point-to-point, instantaneously available transportation, which makes up for its low speed en route.

The imbalance can be corrected by providing buses with their own uncongested highway lane. Exclusive bus lanes have been tried in a few locations with success. The advantage to the community is the large passenger capacity achieved by a bus lane, thus possibly eliminating the need for a new road and reducing auto traffic on side streets. Even assuming a conservative vehicle capacity of 800 buses/hour/lane[12] yields

(800 buses/hr/lane) (40 passengers/bus) = 32,000 passengers/hr/lane.

So the passenger-carrying capacity of a single highway lane reserved

This exclusive bus lane operates on a New Jersey commuter road to the Lincoln Tunnel and Manhattan. Two buses with a total of ninety passengers are here occupying the same lane space as roughly five cars with no more than ten people. Exclusive bus lanes are used today in several major cities in the United States as one solution to rush-hour traffic congestion. *Photo courtesy Port of New York Authority.*

exclusively for buses is over double the rush-hour capacity of a six-lane highway.

In addition, bus service comes close to approximating the auto's point-to-point service, and buses—unlike railroads—can make use of existing highways. Despite their dirty, lumbering image, buses use less energy (see Table 9) and produce less pollution per unit of travel than the auto.

**Transportation and Energy**

| Passenger | | Freight | |
|---|---|---|---|
| *Vehicle* | *Passenger-miles/gallon* | *Vehicle* | *Ton-miles of cargo/gallon* |
| Highway Bus | 125 | Pipeline | 300–500 |
| Commuter Railroad | 100 | Slow Freight | 420 |
| Subway | 75 | Fast Freight | 97 |
| Urban Bus | 40 | Truck (40 ton) | 50 |
| Auto | 32 | Jet Airplane | 8.3 |
| Boeing 747 | 22 | | |
| Supersonic Transport | 13.6 | | |
| Helicopter | 7.5 | | |

Source: "System Energy as a Factor in Considering Future Transportation," Richard A Rice (New York: American Society of Mechanical Engineers, Winter Annual Meeting, November 29 to December 3, 1970).

**Table 9.** The data here give the passenger- and cargo-carrying efficiencies of some transportation modes. Where a mode does not use gasoline, its energy consumption has been translated into the equivalent amount of gasoline.

For these reasons, many transportation planners see exclusive bus lanes playing a growing role in linking suburbs to cities. But it is unlikely that buses can take over the suburban nonwork trips now made by auto. These trips are made in all directions — not just to the central business district — and exclusive bus lanes could not be established in so many directions.

**A Bicycle Highway.** Environmental and energy problems make it useful to consider the advantages of converting a highway lane into a bicycle path. To calculate the passenger-carrying capacity of such a lane, we assume that the bicycles are 5 feet long, that they move at 10 miles/hour (15 feet/second), and that they stay 25 feet apart. The front-wheel-to-front-wheel separation is then 30 feet, for a headway of

$$t = \frac{d}{V} = \frac{30 \text{ ft}}{15 \text{ ft/sec}} = 2 \text{ sec}.$$

The number of bicycles per column will be

$$\frac{3600 \text{ sec/hr}}{2 \text{ sec/bicycle}} = 1800 \text{ bicycles/hr}.$$

If the lane can accommodate three columns of bikes, hourly capacity will be 5400 persons/hour, with little energy use and no noise or pollution. If adopted on a national scale, a major difficulty could be a resulting drop in fatal accidents and rise in healthful exercise, both of which could increase average life expectancy and contribute to the population problem.

Although among the cheapest modes of transportation, bicycle and jogging paths alongside highways subject the cyclist and jogger to noise and fumes. If a bicycle lane could accommodate three rows of bicycles, the hourly capacity of the lane would be 5400 persons per hour with little energy use and no noise or pollution produced. *Photo courtesy U.S. Department of Transportation.*

The real drawbacks of bicycle use in our culture are their low speed, difficulty on hills, and exposure to the elements. This has inspired an engineer at Carnegie University named Richard A. Rice to propose a wind tunnel for bicycles.[13] A wind of about 10 miles/hour would be kept blowing in an enclosed tunnel—perhaps made of glass for esthetic reasons—to move the cyclists along. Calculations show that the fans would use a minute amount of energy but would make possible 20-mile/hour speeds with minimal cycling. It is interesting to speculate on the kinds of makeshift bicycle sails and webbed clothing that would evolve to take advantage of the wind.

**Commuter Railroads.**    Before calculating the passenger capacity of the new BART system, let us look briefly at the general characteristics of commuter railroads. Commuter railroads are relatively high-speed, long-distance systems which link the central city to outlying suburbs. Typically commuter railroads run on headways of 15 minutes to a half hour during rush hours and less often at other times. The lines are set up to carry commuters to one or two central city stations. Often the commuter then must use subway or bus to reach work. In many cases the commuter must use two feeder systems: the bus or auto in suburbia and the bus or subway in the city. However, the high speeds made possible by widely spaced stations (about two miles) and the fact that the traveler can read or doze instead of driving give railroads some advantages over rush-hour clogged highways.

Some commuter railroads are still divisions of privately owned railroads which also handle freight and long-distance travel. When the railroads were hit by hard times following the 1940s, many companies tried to abandon passenger operations, which they said were financial drains on their freight operations. Critics of the railroads have charged that some lines purposely provided poor service to drive away passengers since the various government agencies regulating the railroads allow line abandonment only when use drops below certain levels. In any case, competition from autos, greater profits to be made moving boxes instead of people, and other economic pressures led to a decline in commuter railroads. But increasing public awareness of the physical impossibility of moving all central city commuters by auto has led to new efforts to preserve and even expand them. The most dramatic of these efforts is BART.

**BART.**    Constructed over roughly a 12-year period starting in 1962, at a cost of over $1.5 billion,[14] BART is a high-speed, 75-route-mile,[15] two-track line connecting parts of San Francisco, Alameda, and Contra Costa counties.[16] Its primary function is to link the downtown area of San Francisco to the suburban communities and smaller cities (for example, Berkeley and Oakland) surrounding it (see Figure 10). Construction of BART was almost entirely financed by a special real-estate tax voted on themselves by the residents of the three counties. The residents approved the tax even though the federal government—through the Interstate Highway Fund—would have built new roads and another bridge across San Francisco Bay at no direct dollar cost to the counties. Actually the main argument in favor of BART was that it would eliminate the need for more highways and bridges and thus prevent this federal largesse. The people of the Bay area felt that more roads would threaten the natural beauty of their area.

## BART System

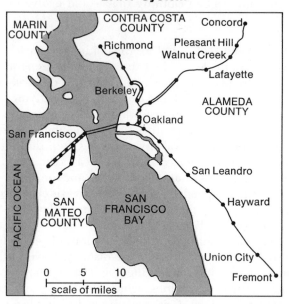

**Figure 10.** The map above shows the network line of the BART system. The solid line indicates that the tracks are aboveground. The upper fork in San Francisco is still in the planning stages.

When operating at peak capacity, computer-controlled BART trains will move at a top speed of 80 miles/hour on 90-second headways (40 trains/hour). To achieve an average speed of 50 miles/hour, the system will operate with a 20-second station-stop time during which passengers get on and off. This short station-stop time is made possible by the small headway, which prevents passengers from piling up at stations, and the lack of standees, which leaves aisles and doors clear. In its early stages, each train will have 6 cars with 72 seats each for an hourly passenger capacity of

$$(72 \text{ passengers/car}) \ (6 \text{ cars/train}) \ (40 \text{ trains/hr})$$
$$= 17{,}280 \text{ passengers/hr.}$$

If standees were allowed, the passenger capacity could be doubled or tripled. However, this would require longer station-stop times to load and unload passengers, which would reduce BART's average speed and make riding less comfortable. All of this would diminish BART's stated purpose – to persuade people to switch from cars to mass transit, thereby reducing the need for new roads and bridges.

## A BART Trip

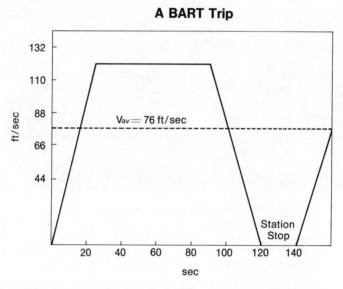

**Figure 11.** The solid line is the speed-time plot for a BART train traveling between stations 2 miles apart. The dotted line is the average speed achieved during the trip, including the 20-second station-stop time. The distance covered can be obtained by computing the area under the solid line.

The key elements in BART's ability to compete with the auto is the short headway – which offers almost instantaneous service – and the high average speed of 50 miles/hour – which compensates for the fact that the traveler must get to and from the station. We will show here how an 80-mile-per-hour top speed and a 20-second station-stop time translate into an average speed of 50 miles/hour. Figure 11 is a graph which gives velocity versus time for a typical 2-mile, station-to-station BART trip. Average acceleration is 4.4 feet/second² and deceleration 3.8 feet/second². To reach the top speed of 80 miles/hour (117 feet/second) takes

$$t = \frac{V_f - V_0}{a} = \frac{117 \text{ ft/sec}}{4.4 \text{ ft/sec}^2} = 27 \text{ sec}.$$

The distance covered while accelerating is

$$d = \tfrac{1}{2}(V_0 + V_f)t = \tfrac{1}{2}[0 + (117 \text{ ft/sec})](27 \text{ sec}) = 1580 \text{ ft}.$$

The time to decelerate is

$$t = \frac{V_f - V_0}{a} = \frac{(-117 \text{ ft/sec})}{(-3.8 \text{ ft/sec}^2)} = 31 \text{ sec}.$$

BART, the nation's first new urban mass transit system since 1907, has been in limited operation since September 1972. It has encountered serious initial operating difficulties and its ultimate success or failure is still to be determined. This photo shows a section of the new BART system with the Oakland skyline in the background. *Photo courtesy Bay Area Rapid Transit.*

The distance covered while decelerating is

$$d = \tfrac{1}{2}(V_0 + V_f)t = \tfrac{1}{2}\left[(117 \text{ ft/sec}) + 0\right](31 \text{ sec}) = 1814 \text{ ft.}$$

So a total 3394 feet are covered while changing speed, leaving (10,560 feet − 3394 feet), or 7166 feet, to be covered at the top speed of 117 feet/second. This takes

$$t = \frac{d}{V} = \frac{7166 \text{ ft}}{117 \text{ ft/sec}} = 61 \text{ sec}$$

which gives a total travel time of 119 seconds. To calculate the average speed we must add in the 20-second station-stop time, which gives

$$V_{\text{av}} = \frac{10,560 \text{ ft}}{139 \text{ sec}} = 76 \text{ ft/sec} = 52 \text{ mi/hr.}$$

In order to achieve the 52-mile-per-hour average speed, BART must move its trains along at 80 miles/hour and whisk them in and out of stations in 20 seconds.

Successfully competing with the auto also requires that the trains run on 90-second headways during rush hours. This physical performance must rest on an adequate economic base provided by the fares paid by the passengers. Most subway and many bus lines charge all users a single fare, regardless of trip length, which discourages short-distance riders from using the system. Almost all commuter railroads use a zone-fare system, in which the cost of the ticket varies with the trip distance. However, issuing and collecting tickets leads to higher labor costs while the one-fare system can be enforced with minimum labor by use of turnstiles or fare collection boxes. In an attempt to get the best of both worlds, BART has installed an automated but variable fare system, consisting of computer-controlled gates and magnetic-tape fare cards. To get the magnetic-tape fare card, a passenger inserts money into a vending machine. The amount of money paid into the machine is encoded on the tape. To enter a station, the card is inserted in an entrance gate, which records on the magnetic tape the station and time of entry and returns the card to the user. At the exit station, the passenger inserts the card in an exit gate, which "reads" the entry station from the card, computes and subtracts the correct fare from the total on the card, and returns the card to the passenger — all in less than a second. If the card has insufficient fare on it, the gate rejects it, and the passenger must go to a nearby machine to recharge the card. The gates require no more labor and operate nearly as quickly as those that accept coins.

At present, BART's future impact is not clear. It has taken much more time and money to build than originally expected and serious operating difficulties have crippled its initial operation. As late as mid-1974 the tunnel under the Bay could not be used because the system's computerized train control system did not operate properly.

More serious even than these technical difficulties is the possible impact of BART on San Francisco as a place to live and work. The Bay area residents who in 1962 voted for a $792 million bond issue to construct BART thought they were building a system that would relieve traffic congestion and eliminate the need for new highways. What they did not understand was the urban development potential of BART. Well before BART was near completion, office and high-rise apartment construction began along its route.

Many Bay area residents now fear that BART will lead to the "New Yorking" of San Francisco. They say that its relatively high passenger-carrying ability will allow businesses to erect skyscrapers in downtown San Francisco, destroying the relaxed, low-rise character of the city. This illustrates again that transportation technology — no matter how clever or well-intentioned — does not provide an automatic cure for urban problems. It is clear that BART can only succeed if its ability to move large numbers of people at high speeds is combined with effective controls on the development of San Francisco and the surrounding area.

**Commuter Railroads Versus Highways.** We calculated earlier that 3 interstate-highway lanes have a capacity of about 9000 people/hour while 1 BART track can carry 17,280 people/hour. Since BART can carry twice as many people on one-third the right-of-way, its space advantage is immediately 6 to 1. But a comparison of Figures 7 and 8 shows the advantage is greater because sections of BART are elevated (in other places it runs below ground or at grade) and has no shoulders or entrance and exit lanes. Nor does BART require a support network of gas stations and parking lots within the city. However, BART's suburban stations have parking lots to encourage commuters to drive to the station and then travel by train into San Francisco.

In addition to the space advantage, BART's other environmental impacts are also less than for the auto. BART is engineered to be quiet inside, unlike subways (see Table 8), and its outside noise is comparable to a freeway. Noise would be much lower if the trains ran on rubber rather than steel wheels. But this would introduce large frictional losses, requiring more powerful motors which would use more electricity, lowering the energy advantage rail transit has over the auto (see Table 9). The trade-off required here is another situation where the solution to one problem causes or aggravates other problems.

Although other commuter railroads are less advanced technologically than BART, they have the same general properties. Stations are fairly far apart and surrounded by parking lots, track capacities are on the order of 10,000 passengers/hour, and passengers are carried at fairly high speeds from low-density suburbs to the central business district. The major difference is that on older lines the relatively high passenger capacities are achieved using long, crowded trains running on much less frequent headways than BART's goal of 90 seconds.

**Subway Systems.** In contrast to commuter railroads, subway lines are high-capacity (about 60,000 persons/hour), low-speed, short-haul systems which bring people from high-density, residential neighborhoods into the central city. Unlike commuter railroads, subways are independent, self-contained operations usually run by the city within which they operate. Subway stations are generally one-half mile apart, which is much closer than commuter railroad stations, and most passengers either walk or ride buses to the station. The high passenger capacity is achieved by running trains on 2-minute headways, with each 10-car train carrying 2000 people:

$$(30 \text{ trains/hr})(10 \text{ cars/train})(200 \text{ passengers/car})$$
$$= 60,000 \text{ passengers/hr.}$$

On most subway systems, these high capacities are achieved at the cost of passenger comfort and speed. When 200 passengers are squeezed into a subway car (see Table 10), each person has less than 2 square feet of space, which is equivalent to a box 17 inches on a side. The crowding is aggravated by the low speeds at which subway trains move during rush hours. The low speeds result from the short distance between stations, low rates of acceleration and deceleration, and the long station-stop times caused by rush-hour congestion.

To see how these factors interact, we take the Chicago transit system as

**Data for Subway Cars**

|  | N.Y. IRT | Chicago | Toronto | Philadelphia |
|---|---|---|---|---|
| Length | 51 ft | 48 ft | 57 ft | 55 ft |
| Width | 8 ft 10 in. | 9 ft 4 in. | 10 ft 4 in. | 9 ft |
| Seats | 44 | 51 | 62 | 56 |
| Maximum Passengers | 200 | 181 | 220 | 190 |
| Area (ft²) | 400 | 368 | 525 | 445 |
| Maximum Speed (mi/hr) | 45 | 50 | 47 | 55 |
| Acceleration (mi/hr/sec) | 2.5 | 3.0 | 2.3 | 3.0 |

SOURCE: *Urban Rail Transit: Its Economics and Technology.*

**Table 10.** This table gives some data concerning selected North American subway cars.

an example. For safety and comfort, trains carrying standing passengers are limited to accelerations and decelerations of 3 miles/hour/second (4.4 feet/second²), as shown in Table 10. This means it takes the Chicago trains 17 seconds to reach their top speed of 50 miles/hour (73 feet/second):

$$t = \frac{V_f - V_0}{a} = \frac{73 \text{ ft/sec}}{4.4 \text{ ft/sec}^2} = 17 \text{ sec.}$$

During those 17 seconds the train goes

$$d = \tfrac{1}{2}(V_0 + V_f)t = \tfrac{1}{2}[0 + (73 \text{ ft/sec})](17 \text{ sec}) = 621 \text{ ft.}$$

If the train brakes to a halt at the same rate, this will also take 17 seconds and the train will go 621 feet for a total of 1242 feet while changing speed. The station-to-station distance is $\frac{1}{2}$ mile (2640 feet) so the distance traveled at the top speed is (2640 feet − 1242 feet), or 1398 feet. To go the 1398 feet takes

$$t = \frac{d}{V} = \frac{1398 \text{ ft}}{73 \text{ ft/sec}} = 19 \text{ sec}$$

for a total travel time of 53 seconds. During nonrush hours, when trains are uncrowded, station-stop times will be about 10 seconds, yielding an average speed of

$$V_{av} = \frac{d}{t} = \frac{2640 \text{ ft}}{63 \text{ sec}} = 42 \text{ ft/sec} = 29 \text{ mi/hr.}$$

But during rush hours, the station-stop times will be at least 30 seconds, for an average speed of

$$V_{av} = \frac{d}{t} = \frac{2640 \text{ ft}}{83 \text{ sec}} = 32 \text{ ft/sec} = 22 \text{ mi/hr.}$$

As we see, the average rush-hour speed is quite low. The low speed combined with rush-hour crowding, high noise levels, and the need for the passenger to get to and from the stations make subway travel extremely unattractive. And there are few ways to increase average speed and decrease crowding without at the same time reducing hourly track capacity.

Faster acceleration and deceleration rates would reduce the time spent traveling between stations but would be uncomfortable and even dangerous, so that option is out. Higher top speeds would not be uncomfortable providing the tracks were in good shape, but noise levels would increase and during the rush hours—when trains are moving on very low headways—these higher speeds would be dangerous. In fact, top speeds on most systems are reduced during rush hours because of the relatively close spacing of the trains.

Train loading and unloading times could be decreased by building cars with more doors. However, such cars would have fewer seats. Alternatively, all seats could be removed from existing cars, improving flow into and out of them and again decreasing station stop times. This would also increase the number of people each car could hold since seated passengers take up more room than standees. Because no more than one-third of rush-hour passengers get seats (see Table 10), and rush-hour subway users are largely a captive clientele having no feasible alternative, removal of seats would not necessarily drive them away, especially if speeds were increased.

But lack of seats would make subway travel that much less attractive to nonrush-hour passengers, who are very important economically to the system. It is very expensive to operate a system which needs a great deal of labor and equipment to handle rush-hour loads and then stands idle the rest of the time (see Figure 6). The need for a balanced load (passengers in this case) is characteristic of many physical systems, such as the urban water systems discussed earlier. Such need is the reason telephone and electric companies encourage off-hour and off-season use of their products. It is also why Florida and Aspen hotels are comparatively cheap in the summer and Cape Cod hotels cheap in the winter.

Station-stop times can also be shortened by decreasing the headways between trains, since then there will be more trains and space available per unit time to carry passengers away. But many subway systems are already operating under minimum headway conditions during rush hours. Capacity can be increased by adding more cars to each train. But in many cases this requires expensive lengthening of stations. It may also reduce train speed since the longer trains—with the same headways—will have less space between them.

Another alternative—which is possible only for a new subway system—is to have the stations spaced more than the one-half mile. With longer station spacing, trains will spend more time traveling at their maximum speed, increasing the average speed. The drawback is that fewer people along the route will be within walking distance of a station, and feeder systems will have to bring people further. The question is one of maximization. At what point are the passengers gained by the increased average speed outweighed by the passengers lost because of less accessible stations?

It is possible to have some of both worlds by building a three-track system with the middle track used for express trains stopping at every fifth station or so. Passengers within walking distance of an express stop could board one directly; others would change at the first express stop the local brought them to. Again, however, economics rears its dismal head. The system must have sufficient riders to use the capacity an express track would add. And express service must be frequent and well coordinated with local service; otherwise passengers will lose time waiting for the faster express.

## Intercity Travel

Travel between urban areas — called intercity travel — is much better documented than urban travel. Much of the intercity travel takes place along high-speed, often tolled, roads which are easy to survey. There are also good data concerning travel between cities by train, plane, and bus. Figure 12[17] shows the great increase in intercity travel that occurred between 1947 and 1970, all of which was accounted for by the automobile and airplane. Intercity bus travel held about constant while travel by train declined drastically. By 1970 rail travel between cities had almost vanished although creation of Amtrak — the national railroad company — and the energy problems have since reversed that trend.

The westbound traffic lanes for this section of Interstate 80 in Oregon are built into the Columbia River. The eastbound travel lanes and the Union Pacific Railroad use the available right-of-way on the south shore, to the right in the photo. Riverside construction provides the traveler with a scenic view but reduces use of the river for fishing, boating, and picnicking. *Photo courtesy U.S. Department of Transportation.*

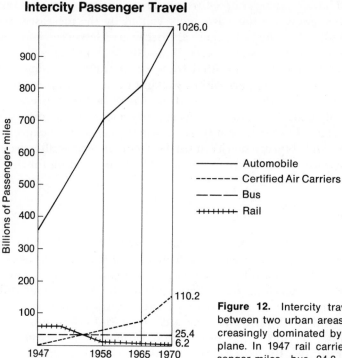

**Figure 12.** Intercity travel refers to trips between two urban areas. Such travel is increasingly dominated by the auto and airplane. In 1947 rail carried 40.8 × 10⁹ passenger-miles, bus 24.8 × 10⁹ passenger-miles, and air 7.5 × 10⁹ passenger-miles.

**Passenger Travel.** It would seem that travel between cities would be more favorable to mass transit than urban travel. When a person is going a few hundred miles, the need to get to a railroad station or bus terminal is less of a drawback than when one is traveling only a few miles to work. In a sense, Figure 12 supports this view because air travel—a form of mass transit—has grown greatly. But rail and bus lines have not done well and the reason is again suburbanization. Long-distance rail and bus travel are set up to carry passengers from the center of one city to the center of another. But people traveling between two urban areas are likely to start from one suburb and end up in another. If the cities are reasonably close together, the auto makes the most sense. Not only does it go at least as fast as the bus or train but on arrival the traveler has the car. When the trip is too long to drive, or time is at a premium, air travel takes over. Its high speed makes even a several-hundred-mile journey a matter of an hour or so. In addition, it connects much better with the auto. Unlike the central city train stations and bus depots, airports are well served by highways and surrounded by parking lots. A passenger can drive to the local airport, park the car, and rent another car at the destination airport.

One of the few railroad success stories of the past decade has been a railroad line that carries both autos and passengers from a suburb of

Washington, D.C., to Florida. Travelers drive their car – luggage and all – onto the train and at their destination drive the car away. This service is so popular that reservations are booked months in advance, indicating that rail transit can succeed where it is able to interface with the automobile. Other trends in this direction are park and ride depots, where passengers leave their autos in a suburban parking lot and board a train for a commuting trip to the local city or for a longer trip to another metropolitan area.

**Intercity Freight.**  The dispersal of people, offices, and factories that had such a large impact on passenger transportation also affected freight movement. Rail and inland water transport worked well when bulk agricultural products and raw materials like coal and iron ore moved from the countryside into a compact city, and industrial and consumer products were made and used in the city or shipped to other cities. But with suburbanization, railroad and water transport lost ground relative to the truck. The large number of intercity highways connecting cities gives trucks a great advantage over the more limited trains and barges.

The numbers in Figure 13 and Table 11 are the result of that advantage. The number of ton-miles (a unit analogous to passenger-miles) carried by

## Distribution of Intercity Freight Movement, 1947-1970

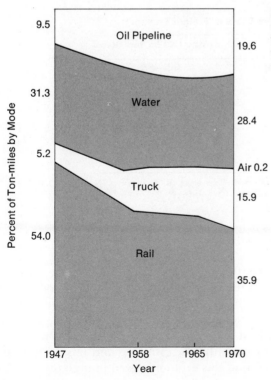

**Figure 13.**  The graph shows the percentage of intercity freight moved by five modes. A ton-mile is generated when one ton of freight is moved one mile.

truck increased from 5.2 percent of the market in 1947 to 15.9 percent of a much bigger market in 1970. In addition, trucks carried a large amount of urban freight since it usually does not pay to ship goods by rail within the same metropolitan area. Trucks achieved their gains despite the higher costs shown in Table 12.

### Intercity Freight Movement (billions of ton-miles)

| | *1947* | *1958* | *1965* | *1970* | *Percent Change 1958–1970* |
|---|---|---|---|---|---|
| Rail | 664.5 | 558.7 | 704.5 | 740.0 | 32.5 |
| Truck | 64.6 | 177.9 | 264.8 | 327.6 | 84.1 |
| Water | 385.0 | 452.2 | 506.3 | 586.3 | 29.7 |
| Oil Pipeline | 116.8 | 234.7 | 339.0 | 403.1 | 71.8 |
| Air | 0.1 | 0.7 | 2.0 | 3.9 | 457.1 |
| Total | 1231.0 | 1424.2 | 1816.6 | 2060.9 | 44.7 |

SOURCE: *1972 National Transportation Report.*

**Table 11.** The information presented as percentages in Figure 13 is presented here in terms of total ton-miles moved. Note that railroads carried more ton-miles of freight in 1970 than in 1947 despite the percentage decline shown in Figure 13.

### Relative Costs of Freight Transport

| *Mode* | *Relative Cost per Unit Moved* |
|---|---|
| Ocean Tanker | 0.5–0.8 |
| Pipeline | 1.0 |
| Barge | 1.0–3.0 |
| Rail | 4.0–8.0 |
| Truck | 6.0–8.0 |
| Plane | 128.0 |

SOURCE: *Transportation Engineering,* R. J. Paquette; N. Ashford; P. H. Wright (New York: Ronald Press, 1972), p. 89.

**Table 12.** Relative costs of freight movement are given here with pipeline costs taken arbitrarily as 1.0.

Suburbanization and the resulting growth in highway and air travel led to an accompanying growth in the use of oil for gasoline, diesel oil, and jet fuel. This, in turn, has caused the pipeline industry to grow. The nation is now crisscrossed by a network of pipelines carrying crude oil, gasoline, diesel fuel, and other liquids at a very low cost. So attractive is the mode that a few coal mines slurry coal (that is, grind up and mix with water) and ship it by pipeline. They find this economic even though the slurried coal must then be separated from the water. Work is also being done with slurried garbage, since a major solid-waste cost is incurred moving the garbage to dumps and incinerators.

Air transport is the smallest, most expensive, and fastest growing freight mode, presently holding less than 1 percent of the market. But that is a high value share, consisting of electronic components, spare parts for a broken computer, 500 mufflers for an auto-assembly plant that will have to shut down within hours if they don't arrive, and fresh flowers and strawberries for northern areas in winter and lobsters for Kansas all year round.

**Farms and Freight.** Agriculture provides another example of the way we have built increasing amounts of transportation into our system. One effect of the sprawl of suburbanization is the continuing conversion of farmland into homes, roads, and shopping centers. That conversion— combined with technological changes that make all but large, mechanized farms obsolete—has changed urban areas' sources of food. Before World War II, eastern cities like Boston, Philadelphia, and Washington got much of their food from relatively small vegetable farms, orchards, dairies, and chicken farms in the surrounding countryside. Today many of these farms and orchards are subdivisions and office sites. Eastern metropolises now get large quantities of fruit and vegetables from irrigated farms in California, Florida, Arizona, and Texas, wheat and corn from the Midwest, meat from Nebraska, Iowa, and Texas, and chicken and eggs from the South.[18] Nor is the Northeast unique. Most of the canned and frozen fruits and vegetables used in the United States come from a few fertile areas such as the San Joaquin Valley in California. The distribution of food across the nation takes large amounts of transportation, refrigeration, and packaging. And for the most part, these changes have occurred without our being aware of the side effects: no one purposely set out to put thousands of miles between the megalopolis of Boston-New York-Washington and its sources of food.

Transportation of both people and goods has increased because of fundamental changes in the way we do things. We live relatively far from jobs and shopping areas in residential patterns that defy the best efforts of mass transit. Our standards of comfort and convenience are such that even where mass transit would serve, we try not to use it. Our pace of life is such that air travel is just barely fast enough. Our goods are made and our food is grown far from their destinations. There are obvious advantages to all of these things or they would not have come about. But there are also disadvantages, which we shall now look at.

## Effects of Transportation on Environment

**Air Pollution.** Between them, the auto and truck emit about half of the nation's air pollution (see Table 13). As a result of that pollution, the air

**Millions of Tons of Air Pollutants, 1970**

| Source | Carbon Monoxide | Particulates | Sulfur Oxides | Hydrocarbons | Nitrogen Oxides | Total | Percent of Total |
|---|---|---|---|---|---|---|---|
| Transportation | 111.0 | 0.7 | 1.0 | 19.5 | 11.7 | 143.9 | 54 |
| Stationary Sources | 0.8 | 6.8 | 26.5 | 0.6 | 10.0 | 44.7 | 17 |
| Industrial Processes | 11.4 | 13.1 | 6.0 | 5.5 | 0.2 | 36.2 | 14 |
| Solid Waste Disposal | 7.2 | 1.4 | 0.1 | 2.0 | 0.4 | 11.1 | 4 |
| Miscellaneous | 16.8 | 3.4 | 0.3 | 7.1 | 0.4 | 28.0 | 11 |
| Total | 147.2 | 25.4 | 33.9 | 34.7 | 22.7 | 263.9 | 100 |
| Percent Change from 1969 | −4.5 | −7.4 | 0 | 0 | +4.5 | | |

SOURCE: *Environmental Quality,* 3rd Annual Report, Council on Environmental Quality (Washington, D.C., 1972).

**Table 13.** Almost all of the transportation pollutants—which in 1970 were 54% of the total—are due to the auto and truck. Comparing total weights of pollutants can be misleading. Sulfur oxides, which are mainly emitted by electric power plants (included with stationary sources), are more dangerous than carbon monoxide. However, power-plant pollutants are emitted from smokestacks high above the streets while auto fumes are emitted at street level. (Particulates are ash, cinders, and so on. Hydrocarbons are unburned gasoline, evaporated paint thinner, and the like.)

## Air Quality Comparison

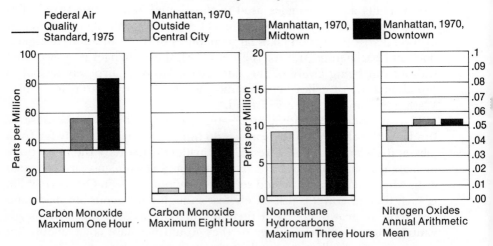

Federal Air Quality Standard, 1975 · Manhattan, 1970, Outside Central City · Manhattan, 1970, Midtown · Manhattan, 1970, Downtown

Carbon Monoxide Maximum One Hour · Carbon Monoxide Maximum Eight Hours · Nonmethane Hydrocarbons Maximum Three Hours · Nitrogen Oxides Annual Arithmetic Mean

**Figure 14.** New York City—whose air quality is typical of the nation's cities and many of its suburbs—will theoretically have to cut motor vehicle use by 50 percent to meet Federal Air Quality Standards. To meet the same standards, Los Angeles would have to cut motor vehicle use by 80 percent.

in most of our cities and suburbs is now and for at least the near future unhealthful (see Figure 14[19]). Because it is difficult to establish the precise relation between air pollutants and the deaths and diseases they cause, it is impossible to say "so-many thousand people died and so-many million were sickened last year because of air pollution." But our inability to unravel the statistics does not make the deaths and illnesses any less real.

Present automotive air-pollution work emphasizes emission controls on the existing internal combustion engine to reduce the pollutants shown in

### Automobile-generated Air Pollution (pounds/day)

| Source | No Controls | Year Car | | | | |
|---|---|---|---|---|---|---|
| | | *1968* | *1970* | *1972* | *1975* | *1976* |
| Exhaust Hydrocarbons | 0.86 | 0.37 | 0.23 | 0.20 | 0.03 | 0.03 |
| Carbon Monoxide | 7.3 | 3.3 | 2.3 | 2.0 | 0.3 | 0.27 |
| Crankcase Blow-by Hydrocarbons | 0.27 | 0 | 0 | 0 | 0 | 0 |
| Fuel Tank and Carburetor Hydrocarbons | 0.20 | 0.20 | 0.20 | 0.1 | 0.1 | 0.1 |
| Oxides of Nitrogen | 0.43 | 0.47 | 0.37 | 0.29 | 0.13 | 0.03 |
| Total | 9.06 | 4.34 | 3.10 | 2.59 | 0.56 | 0.43 |

**Table 14.** The data above are calculated assuming the auto just meets the emission standards for that year car and that it travels 30 miles per day, which is about the national average. Note that pre-1968 cars emit almost 10 pounds of pollution daily. This is not so incredible if one stops to ask where the gasoline that is regularly put in the car goes. Even an auto with its motor off pollutes through evaporation from the gas tank and carburetor. The controls imposed in 1968 to reduce carbon-monoxide and hydrocarbon emissions increased nitrogen-oxide emissions.

### Air-pollution Emissions per 100 Passenger-miles (pounds)

| Transportation Source | Hydro-carbons | Carbon Monoxide | Nitrogen Oxides | Sulfur Oxides | Ash | Total |
|---|---|---|---|---|---|---|
| Train (electric powered) | 0 | 0 | 0.014 | 0.056 | 0.014 | 0.084 |
| 1972–1974 Model Year Autos | 0.5 | 5 | 0.7 | 0 | 0 | 6.2 |

**Table 15.** Here we give a comparison of pounds of pollution emitted per 100 passenger-miles by an auto meeting 1972–1974 emission standards and a train powered by an electric power plant emitting average (for 1970) amounts of air pollution per unit of electricity generated. The auto emits about 73 times more pollution than does the train per 100 passenger-miles. Interpretation of this result is difficult because electric trains and autos emit different pollutants in different locations.

Table 14. Alternatives to cleaning up the internal combustion engine are to switch to a cleaner engine — possibly the rotary Wankel engine or a battery-powered car — or to change to an already operating, nonpolluting transportation mode such as the electric-powered train. The pollution advantage electric-powered trains enjoy over autos (see Table 15) has two causes: trains consume less energy per unit of travel, and the energy the trains do consume is produced by large, central, comparatively (to an auto) clean power plants.

### Energy Consumption, Oil Spills, Noise.

Table 9 shows that our auto-truck-air transportation system moves fewer people and less freight per gallon of gasoline (or its energy equivalent) than other modes. In addition to consuming resources at a great rate, indirect environmental problems arise. Nine million gallons of oil[20] are spilled into the nation's waters annually. Some of it washes up on beaches, where it coats and kills birds, and destroys fish and shellfish breeding areas. About half of our oil is refined into auto and truck fuel, so half of this damage should be charged to transportation.

We listed the direct air-pollution emissions by the auto, but there are also indirect ones. The oil refineries which turn the crude oil into gasoline and other products emit about 3.4 million tons of pollution annually. Although small compared with the auto's direct contribution of 144 million tons, it is significant.

Highway travel contributes to water pollution as well. It is estimated that several hundred million gallons of old crankcase oil are not recycled or re-refined. Some of this finds its way via sewers into rivers, lakes, and the ocean. In northern areas, deicing salt spread on highways is eventually washed away, raising the salt content of many water systems.

A complex problem is caused by the roughly 260,000 tons of lead[21] (0.01 pounds/gallon) used in gasoline each year to prevent engine knock

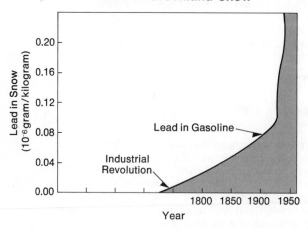

**Lead in Greenland Snow**

**Figure 15.** Analyses of Greenland snow show that lead content decreases with the depth at which the snow is found. By correlating depth with year, the picture here of lead content versus time is obtained. Rises in lead content are linked to the Industrial Revolution and the use of lead in gasoline. Lead is distributed worldwide by wind, evaporation, and rain.

and raise octane ratings. Much of this lead is emitted from auto exhausts, to eventually find its way into our air, water, food, and even Arctic snowfields. (See Figure 15.[22]) As a result of this exposure, we all carry a burden of lead, which can be detected in our blood, bones, teeth, and other parts of the body. Symptoms of lead poisoning begin to occur when lead concentrations in the blood reach 50 to 80 micrograms of lead per 100 grams of blood. Measurements of lead levels in exposed groups such as motorists, garage mechanics, and tunnel employees yield findings of 30 to 38 micrograms per 100 grams,[23] which some experts feel is uncomfortably close to the danger point.

In terms of space use and environmental impact there is really no comparison between highways and mass transit, especially subways. A single subway track can carry 20 times more people hourly than a highway lane. And the subway occupies no surface land, requires no parking space within the city, moves passengers at a very low energy and pollution cost, and does not expose nontravelers to noise. In addition, subways are much safer than any other transportation mode with the exception of elevators. The great advantage to urban communities of subways and other forms of mass transit is well known. Numerous public opinion polls show that a large majority of people favor the construction of mass transit. But the polls also show that the same majority have no intention of using mass transit themselves. They intend to travel by car on uncongested roads while other people go by train or subway.

This attitude is understandable in view of the great convenience and speed of autos and of the environmental impact on passengers of many old subway systems. In addition to terrible noise, the air in the older tunnels may be polluted with steel particles ground off the wheels and tracks. During the summer, the heat underground may be intense: much of this heat is generated during braking, when the train's energy of motion is dissipated as heat. During the winter, stations and even trains are likely to be drafty and cold. Socially, there is the lack of privacy, the unpleasing look of a tunnel bored through rock, and the danger of crime. All of these disadvantages discourage people from using the more environmentally acceptable subways and trains.

The powerful engines and high speeds of motor vehicles – even without horns and squealing tires – mean noise. On top of this, in our quest for convenience and to save a few steps, we have practically brought the auto into bed with us. As a result, most of us are exposed to varying degrees of highway and street noise. Table 8 lists the magnitudes of some typical noise sources. Unfortunately, even less is known about the health effects of noise than about the effects of air pollution. We know noise is annoying; that it can disturb sleep and prevent mental concentration; and that at high intensities it can damage hearing. But whether or not noise can cause or aggravate such tension-related diseases as ulcers and high blood pressure is not known.

Land Use. Unfortunately, even if the problems mentioned above should yield to new technology—and there is little sign of such yielding—we will still be faced with serious resource and land-use problems arising out of present urban forms. The central problem appears to be the sprawling way in which we use land, covering huge areas with suburban population densities. We have seen that these densities require autos, trucks, and highways, which in turn produce severe environmental problems.

But the sprawl itself has costs and dynamics that are only partly related to transportation. The economic aspects of sprawl are shown in Table 16.

**The Costs of Low Density**

|  | *Sprawl* | *Sprawl-Cluster* | *Closely Clustered* |
|---|---|---|---|
| Land Area (acres) | | | |
| Housing | 49,000 | 33,900 | 22,400 |
| Commercial | 3,200 | 2,800 | 2,500 |
| Industrial | 9,000 | 6,600 | 4,800 |
| Cost of Roads | $55,000,000 | $38,000,000 | $26,000,000 |
| School Bus Operation (20 years) | $24,000,000 | $15,000,000 | $ 9,000,000 |
| Cost of Water Facilities | $65,000,000 | $47,000,000 | $32,000,000 |
| Cost of Sewage Facilities | $84,000,000 | $63,000,000 | $39,000,000 |

SOURCE: *Environmental Plan for New York State,* New York State Department of Environmental Conservation, 1973.

**Table 16.** Listed above are the costs of four urban services under three different land-use conditions. The capital costs of roads and water and sewage facilities and the operating costs of school buses go up with decreasing density. Data are from an analysis of Howard County, Maryland, projected to 1985.

It lists the costs of providing four services—roads, school buses, water, and sewage—under the assumption of three density patterns: sprawl, sprawl-cluster, and cluster, listed in order of increasing population density. "Sprawl" consists of one-family homes; "sprawl-cluster" of a mix of one-family homes, townhouses, and garden apartments; and "cluster" of townhouses and garden apartments. As shown, costs of providing the urban services increase as the density decreases. This is because spreading people out means more miles of roads, greater distances traveled by school buses, and more miles of water and sewage pipe. There are other costs. Sprawl destroys watersheds, so communities have to go further for municipal water. Electric power companies need more miles of power lines and gas companies more miles of gas lines to reach customers. And the residents themselves must drive further to get to stores and services.

This not only adds to costs but to environmental damage. Covering land with roads means flooding problems; the extra travel built into the suburban system means more energy consumed and more air pollution produced; and the additional miles of gas and water pipe and power lines mean more consumption of resources. Beyond that, sprawl seems to create sprawl. We saw that the growth of urban areas has chased away farms. It has also destroyed open space suitable for recreation. This means people must go further to hike, ski, and picnic, adding to transportation needs.

Air pollution, water pollution, high energy consumption, pervasive transportation noise, and sprawling urbanization result from the way in which we use the auto, truck, and plane to bind together dispersed urban patterns. They are a by-product of our lifestyle—not some momentary technological malfunction. The problems are built into the system and it is not at all clear, or even likely, that they will be solved by anything short of large-scale and fundamental changes.

## Manhattan's West Side Highway: A Case Study

In our discussion of BART, we saw that a new mass-transit system contains the potential for disrupting a community. In the present case study, we wish to examine the potential effects of a proposed urban highway on the community and on its environment.

The city of New York, in 1972, set about deciding whether or not to spend $1.3 billion (about the cost of BART) to rebuild a 5-mile stretch of highway along the Hudson River on the west side of Manhattan Island. The money was no problem since 90 percent of it would come from the Interstate Highway Fund and the rest from state funds. The question was whether a new, 6-lane interstate road—even with exclusive bus lanes or rail transit—had any place in the nation's largest city.

The existing West Side Highway is a 10-mile, 40-year-old road which twists its way up the west side of Manhattan, more or less parallel to the Hudson River (see Figure 16). The part of the road designated for replacement is the lower, 5-mile, elevated portion, which connects the Brooklyn-Battery Tunnel to Brooklyn with the Lincoln Tunnel to New Jersey and runs along a now-abandoned waterfront lined with rotting piers. When built 40 years ago, the road was designed only for cars, and its narrow exits and entrances and weakened structural condition mean it can never accommodate trucks. It was elevated so that trucks going to the then-busy piers along the Hudson could drive under it. At present, the rusting, elevated road is an eyesore and acts as a psychological and visual barrier which separates Manhattan residents and workers from the Hudson—a magnificent if dirty river.

The upper 5-mile section of the road connects the Lincoln Tunnel with the George Washington Bridge. It was built mostly at grade and is in much better shape. It runs through a park, and there is easy access to the Hudson for the people of the mainly residential communities in that area. This section of the road is also not usable by trucks and the original plan was to rebuild the entire 10-mile road. However, the west side community bordering the upper section succeeded in getting the New York state legislature to pass a law barring reconstruction above the Lincoln Tunnel. They were satisfied with the existing road and park and could see no reason to allow the area to be torn up for a new road.

This was typical of road-building efforts in New York City. Several interstate-highway projects had been earlier blocked by community action and the federal highway money designated for these projects went unspent. As a result, New York City and New York state decided to put all of these funds into a rebuilt West Side Highway. When the planners came up with a $1.3 billion estimate for the 5-mile road (the average 5-mile interstate highway costs $10 million), the money was available.

Normally the road would have been designed by the New York State Department of Transportation, but like most state highway departments (the "transportation" name is cosmetic) this one thought in terms of concrete and traffic flow to the exclusion of communities and people. The state and city political leaders judged that if the road was to be built, the planning effort would have to involve the various communities and operate in an open and consulting manner. Usually roads are planned in secret and without community input and then sprung on a generally unprepared public: the result is pitched battles.

To avoid this, $7.5 million in federal-highway-planning money was used to hire an outside group of experts to plan the highway and to consult at

## Manhattan and the West Side Highway

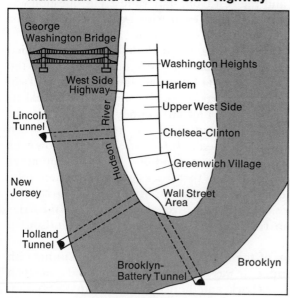

**Figure 16.** A sketch of Manhattan Island is shown here. The 10-mile West Side Highway originates in lower Manhattan at the Brooklyn-Battery Tunnel and goes north along the Hudson River, past the Holland and Lincoln Tunnels, to terminate at the George Washington Bridge. The highway defines the western border of such diverse communities as the financial district (Wall Street), Greenwich Village, old Hell's Kitchen (Chelsea-Clinton), the Upper West Side, Harlem, and Washington Heights. Rebuilding the road to provide these communities with the kinds of waterfront and land use patterns they desire, or at least can tolerate, is difficult indeed.

Residents of the apartments abutting the George Washington Bridge (which connects New York City and New Jersey across the Hudson River) live with constant noise and high levels of air pollution. Aided by the elaborate system of ramp approaches on each shore, the fourteen lanes of the bridge now carry nearly sixty million vehicles a year across the Hudson. *Photo courtesy Port Authority of New York and New Jersey.*

every step with a steering committee consisting of state and city officials as well as representatives of community groups. The planners held or attended innumerable public meetings and put out a wealth of published material as the work proceeded. As a result, the basic issues involved in the proposed highway became clear early on, even if the resolution of those issues did not.

The central elements were not the decaying road or the need for more highway capacity but rather the availability of the federal money and the potential value of the real estate on the west side if the old, blighting road was replaced by a more attractive one. With those two nontransportation factors as galvanizing forces, a variety of interests began jockeying for position and influence. The ecological picture of competing-helping organisms portrayed by biologists for natural systems is probably pretty simple compared to the human, political-economic system in a major city.

The obvious local forces were interested in the West Side Highway. New York's engineering and construction industry wanted the road built because of the billion dollars worth of jobs it would create. The real-estate industry wanted it because the proposed road would be built 700 feet out in the Hudson River and this landfill would create one billion dollars worth of riverfront property. In addition, demolition of the existing road would enhance the value of the adjoining property, much of which was owned by speculators. The trucking industry wanted the road because trucks are not allowed on the existing highway and they hoped the new road would reduce travel time. Less obvious industries were also concerned. A large wholesale meat market—which supplies much of Manhattan with fresh meat—was located alongside the highway. If land values boomed, the meat market would probably be forced to move to make way for offices and apartments. A large number of printing firms were also located near the road. Increasing land values would force them out too.

A variety of official New York City government agencies were concerned with the road-design project. The city's Environmental Protection Administration did not want the road to worsen the city's already bad air. The city's urban planners did not want it to block recreational and shipping access to the river. The Business Development Administration did not want the road to displace too many businesses. The Transportation Administration did not want the 5-year-long construction process to disrupt traffic. And the independent Port of New York Authority feared that the road's exclusive bus lanes would compete with the Authority's own bus terminals.

Citizen groups were also concerned. The Chelsea-Clinton community was politically controlled by longshoremen, who live there because it is near the once-active Hudson River docks. These docks, however, were put out of business years ago by containerized shipping, which they did not have the space to handle, and shipping experts saw little likelihood that they would ever again be used for shipping. Nevertheless, the longshoremen wanted the rebuilt highway to preserve the docks. Others in the Chelsea-Clinton area wanted the rebuilt waterfront to have parks rather than docks. But everyone feared that their side streets and avenues would be clogged with traffic feeding to and from the new superhighway. This fear was aggravated by the fact that the rebuilt, truck-carrying, high-capacity road would merge into the old, no-truck, low-capacity road in their neighborhood. They thought it likely that trucks and cars would pour off the new road onto their streets at that point. If the road were to be rebuilt, the Chelsea-Clinton residents wanted it rebuilt right up to the George Washington Bridge. This brought them into conflict with the Upper West Side community.

The Greenwich Village community—just to the south—was mainly residential and wanted a park-like waterfront. They did not want any exits or entrances in their community, thereby eliminating traffic feeding on or off the road through their streets. Some in the Village felt they were better off with the rusty old highway. Their major fear was that once the old highway was torn down, real-estate developers would put up high-rise office and apartment buildings, thereby destroying their low-rise, residential neighborhood. These people felt safest with the rusty old road; it kept the developers away.

The financial, or Wall Street, district below the Village has few residents and is controlled by the leaders of the financial community. They favored a new road because it would continue the refurbishing (some critics say destruction) of lower Manhattan that had started with the building of the twin towers of the World Trade Center. It would allow executives commuting to work by auto to reach their jobs more quickly. Finally, the exclusive bus lanes proposed for the road would ease the flow of workers into and out of the district.

In an attempt to satisfy the state and city, the communities, the business groups, the federal highway laws, and the Clean Air Act, the highway consultants came up with five alternatives, including three so-called no-build plans. These three would leave the road as is, repair it, or tear it down and replace it with a street-level boulevard. The more attractive of the two build alternatives consisted of a buried, six-lane highway with two additional lanes reserved exclusively for buses. The whole thing would be placed out in the river 700 feet from the existing shoreline; the land between the buried road and the shore would be filled in. It is the fill and the burying of the road that lead to the $1.3 billion price tag on this plan.

The advantages of this alternative is that the new land—estimated to be worth over $1 billion—could be used for parks, offices, apartments, or some combination of the three. The new road could be built without interfering with the existing West Side Highway; once built, the old one could be shut down and razed. So traffic disruption would be held to a minimum. The offshore road would have some piers, minimize noise, have no entrances or exits in the Village, and be able to handle some of the trucks now noisily using interior streets.

Many, however, object to any new road at all. They say a rebuilt highway will attract trucks and cars from a parallel tolled road in New Jersey (the New Jersey Turnpike). The resulting traffic jams, they say, will force vehicles to use city streets, thereby increasing the very noise, congestion, and pollution it was meant to alleviate. Critics also say the riverside land created by the road will inevitably be used for high-rise buildings, requiring more urban services, generating more traffic, using more energy, and creating more environmental problems.

They also point out that according to the West Side Highway Environmental Impact Statement[24] the new land created by landfill will be too noisy to be used as park land and offices or apartments built on this land will have to be sealed and air-conditioned to shut out the highway noise. Construction of the road, they say, will therefore set off a cycle of secondary environmental and energy-use impacts. Critics also say that the road has been planned in a vacuum since the New York City government has refused to formulate a specific land-use policy for the area through which the road and its associated mass transit will pass. This makes an analysis of future noise and air impacts difficult to do since the likely surrounding urban terrain is unknown.

Those who favor the road say that in a real-world situation one can never know everything possible about a proposed project. They also say that the pollution impacts of the road should not be viewed in isolation. New York City has general codes to control building and densities, and some of the communities fronting the road are politically active and could therefore help control the development. New York also has city-wide plans to reduce use of the automobile. If these traffic and density controls work, say the proponents, then a new West Side Highway will improve New York by removing a blighting, rusting structure and opening up the now-closed and ugly waterfront.

Just as with BART, the question of a rebuilt West Side Highway is not solely a technical or transportation or environmental problem. These are important aspects, but the total question is much larger. As of this writing, it is not clear what answer will be given to the issues posed by the West Side Highway. Public hearings still must be held on the five alternatives, the state and city must battle out ownership of the filled-in land, the inevitable lawsuits must be filed and countered, and so on.

## Future Transportation Systems

Earlier in this chapter subways and commuter railroads were described as slow, uncomfortable, and even environmentally hazardous to the user. But it is really not fair to judge the capabilities of a transportation mode on the performance of systems that were built 60 or 70 years ago. Such is the case with our subways and commuter railroads; they have been neglected for the past few decades while transportation resources flowed into highway travel. Technologically, there is no reason why a new subway system could not be quiet, clean, and relatively fast. The same goals should be even easier to achieve with commuter railroads.

As a result of the environmental and urban advantages mentioned earlier, it appears that political and financial backing is developing to improve and expand mass transit. In addition to San Francisco, the cities of

# RIDE WITH US TO TOWN
## ON OUR BUS "BIG SAM"

The sparse population and relatively long distances to be covered in rural areas make those who live there almost totally dependent on the auto. One possible approach to public transportation problems in rural areas is more efficient use of the bus. The people shown here are the first twenty members of the Green Eagle Rural Community Transportation Co-op which operates once a week, getting people to and from doctors, stores, and a visit to town. *Photo courtesy Office of Economic Opportunity.*

Washington, D.C., Denver, Atlanta, Baltimore, Honolulu, Miami, Pittsburgh, Toronto, and Montreal are planning, building, or have built new transit systems. After decades of steadily rising bus and train fares which drove travelers into autos, the early 1970s saw many cities and counties reverse this trend by slashing fares, subsidizing the losses out of general revenues. Increasingly, mass transit is being seen as a vital public service like water or sewage, essential to the well-being of the entire community and therefore the responsibility of the entire community. It would be unfortunate if the impression were given that rail transit will automatically save cities and highways automatically doom them. Railroads and highways are no more than urban tools; their usefulness depends on how skillfully they are used.

Before leaving the subject of transportation, we shall look at possible future technological developments. At one time it was assumed our problems would be solved with the invention of some miracle transportation system. We now realize that autos, jet planes, and existing, high-speed trains are all miracles from the perspective of 100 years ago and yet we still have problems. We have come to understand that foot trails and canoes may have served the needs of the Indians as well as or better than autos and jets serve our present needs. Very clever transportation innovations may turn out to be irrelevant to our lives—as with the helicopter—or to do more harm than good—as with snowmobiles and other wilderness-penetrating, all-terrain vehicles. But it is also possible that one or two developments discussed below will be successful and become integrated into existing systems.

**Dial-a-bus.** The dial-a-bus is one of several, experimental, demand-activated systems designed to serve low-density suburbs. Conventional bus systems serve fixed routes on fixed schedules. Demand-activated systems respond to travelers phoning (or otherwise signaling) for service. The bus takes the traveler to any destination within the area served. Dial-a-bus differs from taxi service because the same vehicle would serve many passengers. In one version, a central computer would process requests for service and monitor the positions of the buses. As new requests came in, bus routes would be modified so as to minimize passenger waiting and travel time. It is one of the few systems designed for the nonrush-hour traveler and would serve the shopper, the person going to the doctor, and the like. It is an attempt to combine the flexibility of the auto with the advantages of public transit.

The dial-a-bus system also emphasizes the possible interaction between transportation and communication since without good links between potential passengers, the central dispatcher, and the buses, the system cannot work. Good communications could also help existing systems. In high-rise buildings, for example, a panel informs the elevator dispatcher and waiting people where the elevators are and in what direction they are moving. This type of information system would be much more useful at train stations, at bus stops, and on highways to tell drivers what the speed conditions are ahead. At present, the only highway communication is what the driver may get in urban rush-hour periods over the radio from a traffic-monitoring helicopter pilot.

**Automated Highways.** On an automated highway, cars would be controlled electronically by a computerized system. Such automatic, centralized control could allow high speeds at almost bumper-to-bumper conditions, thereby increasing capacity. A completely automated highway is a long, expensive way off, but some small steps have already been taken. On a few limited-access roads, entrances to the road are con-

trolled by traffic lights. When traffic monitors indicate highway congestion, the lights seal the road off until traffic eases. As another alternative,
the entrance-ramp stop lights can be used to feed cars onto the highway at
a controlled rate to prevent traffic backing up near the ramp. These traffic-
limiting tactics are used because highway capacity decreases when a road
becomes too crowded.

**People Movers, Monorails, Pedi-cars.**   People-mover systems are best
described as horizontal elevators. Small unconnected cars holding two to
twelve people move along tracks. In systems with branchings, the passengers can choose a route by pushing one button and stop the vehicle by
pushing another button. People-mover speeds are low but passenger
capacities are higher than for a traffic lane on a typical urban street. They
are seen as useful for short-distance, central city trips.

Monorails are also fixed-route, tracked systems. The track is a single
rail from which the car is hung. Although monorails have captured the
public imagination, they appear to be impractical and are used only in
exhibitions about future transport systems and in amusement parks.

Pedi-cars are small, lightweight, enclosed vehicles powered by driver-
passenger pedaling. Possibly they will prove to be practical, all-weather
vehicles for short urban trips, especially if pedaling is boosted by a battery-
powered electric motor.

**High-speed Trains.**  These include the hundred-plus mile-per-hour
hover train—which rides on an air cushion—and the 2000-mile-per-hour
tube train, which moves through an evacuated tube—the way a bullet
moves through a gun barrel—under the impetus of gas pressure behind it.
Work on the hover train is quite advanced, especially in Europe, but the
tube train is little more than an idea at this point. If developed, it would be
a substitute for long-distance air travel. It would not pay to use a 2000-
mile-per-hour vehicle for a mere 500-mile trip.

## Conclusion

It is difficult to draw sweeping conclusions in the midst of the political,
economic, and technological turmoil which currently envelops transportation. The efforts by various levels of government to control air pollution
and other environmental insults, the rapidly changing energy picture, and
the continued suburbanization of the nation do not allow for easy answers.

But at least some past mistakes are clear. We attempted to force two
transportation modes—the auto and the plane—to do the work that should
have been shared by several modes, each operating in their areas of
strength. When problems of safety, highway congestion, noise and air
pollution inevitably arose, we responded with separate, uncoordinated
actions. For example, safety measures in transportation increased overall

weight and therefore fuel consumption, making energy conservation and pollution control that much more difficult.

The failure of add-on technical solutions was followed by increases of support for mass transit and some timid steps toward land-use controls. In 1974 the federal government issued regulations which banned large-scale developments such as sports arenas and shopping centers unless it could be shown they would not adversely affect air quality in the local area. Unlike air-bags and pollution-control devices, construction of more mass transit and rules that discourage suburbanization mean fundamental changes in life-style. Moreover, they represent a much more permanent and long-term commitment. Pollution and safety devices can be conceived, implemented, and abandoned all within a few years. Mass-transit and land-use changes will be with us for decades.

Major long-term decisions about life-style and urban forms cannot be made on the basis of dirty air and noise alone. Making things cleaner and quieter are negative goals which must be achieved within a positive vision of what the rebuilt society will be like. The importance of air pollution, noise, and highway danger is that it impels us to act. But it most certainly does not tell us how to act.

## Bibliography

*Source Notes*

1. U.S. Bureau of the Census.

2. U.S. Bureau of the Census. Tri-State Regional Planning Commission.

3. *1972 National Transportation Report.* U.S. Department of Transportation. Washington, D.C., 1972.

4. "National Transportation Planning Manual A." U.S. Department of Transportation. Washington, D.C., 1970.

5. Regional Plan Association, New York City.

6. *1972 National Transportation Report.*

7. *Preliminary Analysis of Alternative Program Packages.* West Side Highway Project, October 1972.

8. *Regional Rapid Transit for Bay Area.* Parsons, Brinkerhoff, Quade and Douglas, Inc.

9. *Highway Transportation.* U.S. Department of Transportation, Federal Highway Administration. Washington, D.C., November 1970.

10. *1972 National Transportation Report.*

11. *Urban Rail Transit: Its Economics and Technology.* A. Scheffer Lang and Richard M. Soberman. Cambridge, Mass.: MIT Press, 1964.

12. The *1972 National Transportation Report* gives 1200 buses/lane/hour; the November 1970 issue of *Highway Transportation* gives 1000 buses/lane/hour.

13. "New Perspectives in Transport Technology." R. A. Rice. Transportation Research Institute. Pittsburgh, Pa.: Carnegie-Mellon University, February 1972.

14. *The New York Times*. Wallace Turner. 2 April 1974, p. 38.

15. "BART System Gives Focus to Regional Plan." *Engineering News-Record*, 7 September 1972, p. 22.

16. "Rapid Transit: A Real Alternative to the Auto for the Bay Area?" *Science*, vol. 171 (19 March 1971), p. 1125.

17. *1972 National Transportation Report.*

18. "The Immovable Feast: Transportation, the Energy Crisis, and Rising Food Prices for the Consumer," part 2. Prepared for the Committee on Agriculture and Forestry, U.S. Senate. Washington, D.C.: U.S. Government Printing Office, 1974.

19. New York City Environmental Protection Administration.

20. *Environmental Quality, 3rd Annual Report.* Council on Environmental Quality. Washington, D.C.: U.S. Government Printing Office, 1972.

21. "Air Pollution, the Case of Air-borne Lead." Glenn Paulson. In *Ecology and Pollution*. Philadelphia: North American Publishing Co., 1972.

22. *Chemist*, vol. 7 (1971), p. 55.

23. "Air Pollution, the Case of Air-borne Lead."

24. *West Side Highway Project Environmental Impact Statement.* U.S. Department of Transportation. New York, 1974.

*Further Reading*

### Transportation

JANICE CROSSLAND. "Cars, Fuel, and Pollution." *Environment* (March 1974), p. 15.
A discussion of the auto industry's efforts, or nonefforts, to solve the air pollution problem is presented here.

MATTHEW EDEL. "Autos, Energy, and Pollution." *Environment* (October 1973), p. 10.
Edel discusses urban transportation and urban sprawl from a social science point of view.

ROBERT HERMAN and KEITH GARDELS. "Vehicular Traffic Flow." *Scientific American* (December 1966), p. 35.
This is an interesting discussion of the factors determining highway capacity.

A. SCHEFFER LANG and RICHARD M. SOBERMAN. *Urban Rail Transit: Its Economics and Technology.* Cambridge, Mass.: MIT Press, 1964.
A comprehensive technical description of urban rail transit is given here.

J. R. MEYER; J. F. KAIN; M. WOHL. *The Urban Transportation Problem.* Cambridge, Mass.: MIT Press, 1965.
This is a classic study of urban transportation. It has a lot of useful information but never, anywhere, mentions air pollution or noise.

JOHN NEWMAN. "A Ride for Everyone." *Environment* (June 1974), p. 11. DANIEL ROOS. "Doorstep Transit." *Environment* (June 1974), p. 19.
These two articles discuss experimental urban transportation systems.

RADNOR J. PAQUETTE; NORMAN ASHFORD; PAUL H. WRIGHT. *Transportation Engineering.* New York: Ronald Press, 1972.
This is an excellent book combining the urban planning and engineering aspects of transportation. It covers all transportation modes for people and freight and provides a wealth of data.

STEPHEN ZWERLING. "BART." *Environment* (December 1973), p. 14.
This article discusses the possible effects of BART on the urban development of San Francisco. The author's thesis is that BART was created by San Francisco's business and political leaders in order to "Manhattanize" the Bay area.

### Technical Reports

The following reports were found useful in preparing the preceding chapter, but may not be found in all libraries. However, these reports are being churned out at such a rapid rate that the same kind of information can probably be obtained from other, similar reports.

*A Study for the Development of Stewart Airport.* Available from: Metropolitan Transportation Authority, 1700 Broadway, New York, New York 10014. Published in 1973.
This is a self-serving study but has lots of data and pictures.

*Jamaica Bay and Kennedy Airport.* National Academy of Sciences. Washington, D.C.: National Academy of Engineering, 1971.
A pioneering, multidisciplinary case study of the impact on Jamaica Bay and its environs of expanding Kennedy Airport is given in this report.

*1972 National Transportation Report.* U.S. Department of Transportation. Washington, D.C.: U.S. Government Printing Office, 1972.
This report is bursting with data on all aspects of transportation. This is the first in a series of reports of this kind that the U.S.D.O.T. is required by law to publish.

## Questions and Problems

1. Verify from other data in Table 3 that the number of people per household is as stated there.

2. In general, old people tend to live in cities rather than suburbs. Can you suggest why?

3. From Figure 3 and the caption, calculate how many shopping trips were made daily in the Detroit area in 1953 and 1965.

4. Assume a bus line carries 120,000 passengers daily, charging $0.50 per ride. How much additional revenue will a fare hike to $0.55 bring in? It is known that a 10% fare hike usually causes a 6% drop in the number of riders.

5. In the text, 300 square feet is taken as the parking space needed per auto. Draw a diagram of a parking lot and show approximately where this number comes from.

6. The text states that each car requires 200 square feet for its gas station-junk-yard-auto showroom support system. In order to verify this number for your own area, what kind of information would you need?

7. Is it logical to say that a car needs 300 square feet of parking space at both origin and destination? Could the two spaces serve two cars?

8. In recent years several programs have been introduced which change the typical workday or workweek. These include the 4-day week with its 10-hour day; the German program called Gleitende Arbeitszeit (gliding time) in which workers can start any time between 7 A.M. and 11 A.M., producing leaving times between 3 P.M. and 7 P.M.; and an effort to spread out the starting and leaving times of large companies concentrated in a given area.
   a. What implications do these programs have for transit and highways?
   b. What significance does it have for the personal lives of the workers?
   c. Which program would you prefer?

9. What are the relative advantages and disadvantages of the two methods of representing the freight data used in Table 11 and Figure 13?

10. When a pipeline was opened in 1973 on Long Island, N.Y., the wholesale price of heating oil dropped from $0.15 to $0.145 per gallon because pipeline transport is cheaper than truck transport. Using the cost data in Table 12, calculate how much of the original price was due to truck transport and how much of the $0.145 price is due to pipeline transport. Take the truck-pipeline cost ratio as 6 to 1.

11. It has been suggested that the harder a driver brakes, the brighter the brake lights should shine. What purpose would this serve?

12. Assume you are driving a 12-foot-long car. If you are traveling 40 miles/hour, how far behind the lead car should you stay?

13. Why is it safer for a bicyclist to ride with auto traffic while a pedestrian is advised to walk against the traffic? Assume for purposes of discussion an auto speed of 45 miles/hour, a cycling speed of 15 miles/hour, and a walking speed of 3 miles/hour.

14. In Table 7, what reaction time is assumed in auto braking?

15. Assume you are designing an interstate highway, which must therefore accommodate both trucks and cars. Using Table 7, calculate how long your entrance lane must be if the most sluggish vehicle is to get up to 40 miles/hour before entering traffic. Assume constant acceleration.

16. Assume you are driving at 60 miles/hour (88 feet/second), 6 car lengths (120 feet) behind a leading car. Also assume your reaction time is 1 second and your auto and the lead auto decelerate at the same rate of 20 feet/second$^2$.
   a. How far from the lead auto will you be 1 second after seeing its brake lights flash? Take that as the moment when your foot reaches the brake.
   b. How far will you be when you both come to rest?
   c. What would have happened if your reaction time was 2 seconds? Would you have collided? Where?

17. You are on a two-lane, undivided, 60-mile-per-hour highway behind a 40-foot truck traveling at 40 miles/hour. How far must the oncoming lane be clear for you to pass? For simplicity, assume your car accelerates at 3 miles/hour/second independent of speed and that oncoming traffic is moving at 60 miles/hour. Make any necessary assumptions.

18. Can you think of nontechnical ways (that is, methods which do not involve altering the magnetic tape) by which the BART fare-collection system can be thwarted? Schemes may involve more than one person.

19. Would your plan work if the BART exit gate examined the entrance time recorded by the entrance gate and rejected cards if the trip had taken more than a plausible length of time?

20. Would your scheme work if the gates will not let you exit at the station of entry recorded on the card?

21. Tests show that for passages or sidewalks over 4 feet in width there is a flow of 27 people/minute/foot of width. Using this figure, calculate the hourly passenger-carrying capacity of a 12-foot-wide sidewalk.

22. Assume one station on a subway line during rush hours receives 30,000 people in a half hour. How many 12-foot-wide passageways are necessary to accommodate this flow?

23. A conveyor belt, or horizontal escalator, has been described as a mass-transit line with zero headway.
    a. What is meant by that?
    b. Why are belt speeds generally limited to 3 miles/hour?
    c. Can you think of ways to increase a belt-system's speed? For discussion purposes, assume you have a 12-foot right-of-way.
    d. Making some reasonable assumptions, calculate the hourly passenger capacity of a 12-foot-wide belt system.
    e. What would be the hourly per-lane vehicle capacity of an automated highway in which the cars ran bumper to bumper at 60 miles/hour?

24. One of the BART stations is at Candlestick Park, home of the baseball Giants and football 49'ers. BART designers installed a limited number of gates at this station so that passengers could not move onto the platforms faster than the trains could take them away.
    a. Why is a bottleneck desirable at this location?
    b. If a BART gate can accommodate 40 passengers per minute, how many gates should there be when BART is running at a capacity of 6-car trains on 90-second headways? Assume all passengers are going in the same direction and that the trains arrive empty.

25. From the information given in Table 10 on subway cars, which system would you expect to give (a) the best service to the passenger? (b) The greatest track capacity?

26. For constant train speed, decreasing headway reduces the distance between trains. To test this, assume a subway system's trains move at 30 miles/hour on 4-minute headways.

    a. Calculate the distance between 10-car trains if the cars are 50-feet long. Disregard the effects of stations, acceleration, braking, and so on.

    b. Assume the speed is kept at 30 miles/hour but headway is decreased to 3 minutes. What is the new separation?

27. Assume a subway system is built with a top acceleration and braking rate of 3 miles/hour/second but an unlimited peak speed.

    a. What is the maximum speed it could reach traveling between two stations $\frac{1}{2}$ mile apart?

    b. How much time would this save over the Chicago system, which is limited to 50 miles/hour?

28. Use the data in Table 9 to solve the following problems.

    a. Calculate how far a 4000-pound auto can be shipped by slow freight train on a gallon of gasoline.

    b. How far would the same gallon take the car if it were aboard a 40-ton truck?

    c. About how far could the car be driven on that gallon?

    d. Does the auto train to Florida make sense from an energy and pollution point of view? Do you think it generally makes sense?

29. If all the intercity freight shipped by truck in 1970 (see Table 11) had been sent by slow freight instead, how many gallons of gasoline would the nation have saved that year?

30. Assume the United States used about $110 \times 10^9$ gallons of gasoline and diesel fuel for transportation (auto, truck, train, pipeline, and so on) in 1970.

    a. What percent of yearly transportation fuel use would the system described in problem 29 save?

    b. If transportation takes 25% of our energy, what percent of total energy use would that save?

31. As oil companies have begun manufacturing unleaded gasoline, they have encountered transportation and storage problems since the unleaded gasoline is shipped and stored in pipelines and tanks also used for leaded gasoline.

    a. Assume a gasoline must have less than 0.05 grams of lead per gallon of gasoline to be considered unleaded and that a certain brand of leaded gasoline has 4 grams of lead per gallon. A gasoline station is going to put 5000 gallons of unleaded gas into a tank that previously held leaded gasoline. It is estimated that 40 gallons of leaded gasoline remain at the bottom of the tank. Will that put the 5000 gallons of unleaded gasoline over the 0.05 grams/gallon limit?

    b. Mixing is likely to occur when unleaded gasoline is shipped through a pipeline sandwiched between two shipments of leaded gasoline. To separate out the unleaded fuel a valve must be opened in the pipeline at just the right moment and closed at just the right moment. Assuming you have all sorts of resources at your disposal (for example, glass pipelines, delicate scales, radio communication with people upstream of you), can you think of methods involving physical measurements or observations that will let you remove the desired section, or tender, of gasoline from the pipeline?

32. A U.S. Department of Transportation publication titled "America's Lifelines" says that the pavement in the interstate highway system would make a parking lot 20 miles by 20 miles with space for about 50 million cars. (You might want to check their calculation.) It goes on to say that the dirt and rock excavated could bury Connecticut knee-deep. The concrete used could build six sidewalks to the moon and the culverts and drain pipes could make storm water and sewer systems for six cities the size of Chicago.

Such comparisons are common in descriptions of large technological projects. Do you find them useful in understanding a project? Or do they strike you as useless or misleading? Is it possible that the very size of the projects is the point?

If you wish to see where these comparisons come from, you might be interested in making up one of your own. For a start, calculate the height of a 12-foot-thick, world-girdling wall built out of the sand and gravel the 40,000-mile system requires. Each mile of the system uses 60,000 tons of sand and gravel. Each ton has a volume of 10 cubic feet. The earth's circumference can be taken as 24,000 miles.

33. A highway engineer in the May 1971 issue of *Highway User* writes:

> A return to the horse and mule is obviously out of the question. . . . The average horse produces 35 pounds of solid and 18.5 pounds of liquid excrement per day. . . . If we were to maintain our present standard of living by means of live instead of mechanical horses, there would be one ton of solid waste and one-half ton of liquid waste per person per day. Viewed in this light, our pollution problem has already been solved.

a. How many horses is the writer assuming per person?
b. Speculate as to how the writer came up with this number.
c. Is the assumption on which this number is based logical to you?
d. What is meant by the statement "our pollution problem has already been solved"? Do you agree?

34. The same article also contains the statement:

> An additional benefit caused by our conversion to high-speed mechanized transportation has been the elimination of the need for 90 million acres of pasture land to feed all the horses and mules that were necessary to serve our transport needs of the early 20th century. This is twice the total area of all the rights-of-way of all the public roads in the United States, including the three million miles of roads that existed before World War I.

a. Are there trade-offs involved here which have not been mentioned? Should the pasture area be compared to the road area or is it analogous to other components of the transportation system?
b. Assuming it is valid to compare pastures to roads, does the impact of the road extend beyond its own official area? What of the impact of the pastures?

*The planet itself seemed less impressive, in its old-fashioned, deliberate, annual or daily revolution, than this huge wheel. . . . Before the end, one began to pray to it; inherited instinct taught the natural expression of man before silent and infinite force. Among the thousand symbols of ultimate energy, the dynamo was not so human as some, but it was the most expressive.*

HENRY ADAMS *

# 8 Introduction to energy

In this chapter we apply to energy the qualitative and quantitative reasoning used earlier to describe water and transportation systems.

Not very long ago the statistical and physical descriptions to follow would have been unnecessary. When people chopped their own wood or fed coal chunks into their fire, a quantitative description of the energy they used was redundant. But today our energy flows silently and unobserved into the home, office, and factory, through gas lines, from oil storage tanks refilled automatically by the local oil company, and as electricity — perhaps the most mysterious energy form of all.

To discover how much fuel we use we must consult bills, cryptically labeled and devoid of obvious physical meaning. We no longer think of energy as cords of wood or tons of coal; instead we say that our electric or gas bill was so many dollars. The point of this chapter is to look behind the dollar costs to the physical reality the costs represent — or obscure. We begin with a brief description of the history of our use of energy and then move to the physical laws and numbers that describe our present state.

---

* From Adams' book *The Education of Henry Adams* in a chapter titled "The Dynamo and the Virgin" (New York: Random House, 1918).

**213**

## A Brief Chronology of Early Energy Use

Hunting, Fire, and Agriculture. Anthropologists believe that between 10 and 15 million years ago our ancestors diverged from the modern ape's ancestors. The human-like creatures, or hominids, over the next several million years evolved from tree-living to ground-living vegetarians. This evolution was accompanied by important changes in brain size, teeth, carriage, and diet. During this time the total consumption of energy remained the food the hominids ate — perhaps 2000 kilocalories a day. (The kilocalorie, abbreviated kcal., is a unit of food energy which we shall later define precisely.)

Roughly 3 million years ago the hominids turned to hunting. This represented an expansion of diet and an increase in the amount of energy controlled since the game animals fed off vegetation the hominids could not directly consume. Hunting men also used language and had the ability to work together on a hunt but were otherwise not markedly different from the animals they lived among.

About 500,000 years ago hominids distinguished themselves from other animals by gaining an additional energy source — fire. Fire allowed them to survive in climates which would otherwise be too cold and enabled them to greatly expand their diet by cooking foods which were inedible raw. Some have suggested that fire is at least partly responsible for our social nature. Without fire, a watch had to be kept all night against large cats and other predators. But the smell of fire — probably because of forest fires — terrifies most animals and left humans free to sit around the fire and grunt or talk.

Fire doubled the amount of energy hominids controlled, to about 5000 kilocalories per person per day, but did not at first radically alter their lives. They remained a hunting and food-gathering people, living in small groups and, at most, establishing semipermanent base camps from which to forage. Anthropologists estimate modern humans appeared about 50,000 years ago — still a hunter and food gatherer. Until 10,000 years ago the world's entire human population, about 10 million people, was living a hunting existence. About this time the first signs of settled agricultural communities are found. The cultural transition from hunting to agriculture was slow but irreversible, and eventually the settled agricultural communities became dominant.

Cultivation of crops and raising domesticated animals require more skill and knowledge than does a nomadic life. Seed must be stored from season to season and then planted at the proper time. Where rainfall is scarce, an irrigation system must be built and maintained, and water allotted in the proper amounts to the different fields. The crops must be harvested at the correct time. In addition, walls or fences may be needed to protect crops from wild animals, and soldiers and fortifications maintained to protect against enemies. A settled agricultural community was therefore quite complex and required specialization to handle the complexity. Because it was producing a dependable supply of food and often even a surplus, the agricultural community could support the priests—who were in charge of storing the seed, determining when to plant and harvest, and allotting irrigation water—and the political-military organization needed for defense. The existence of settled communities, which produced food surpluses, also created the conditions for the growth of crafts and trade. Since some people were freed from agricultural tasks, they could mine ore, smelt metal, make pottery; these products could then be traded with neighboring communities.

Fire, agriculture, domestic animals, and the growth of crafts led to a large increase in the amount of energy consumed by each person. About 5000 years ago it is estimated that the primitive agricultural human controlled 12,000 kilocalories per person per day. This per-capita increase was accompanied by a large population growth. As a result, this increasing control over energy could not be reversed without disaster. The expanded population—even if it were willing to return to a hunting and food-gathering existence—could not do so without most people dying from famine. A wandering existence cannot support the population densities an agricultural system can.

Wind and Water Power.   The next step in our expanding control of energy was the use of river currents to float rafts and other cargo-carrying craft downstream. This was followed by the harnessing of wind by sailboats, invented about 6000 B.C.[1] in Mesopotamia. The raft and sailboat were then used in trade.

However, the energy advance with the greatest implications for modern society was the waterwheel, believed invented about 50 B.C.[2] by the Romans. (See Figure 1.) The energy of the flowing stream turns the

**Figure 1.**   A sketch of a 22-foot-diameter, 3-foot-wide, overshot waterwheel (meaning the water hits the wheel at the top) dating from 1882 is shown here. Note that the intricate transmission allows the power to be drawn off in several places. *Sketch courtesy Smithsonian Institution.*

waterwheel, which operates any of a number of machines. Among its earliest applications were the grinding of grain into flour, the sawing of marble and wood, and the pumping of irrigation water out of streams or canals into fields. The waterwheel was the first nonbiological engine used by humans. We can look at succeeding evolution as consisting of the development of more powerful engines hooked to bigger and more efficient machines.

This type of sturdy wooden windmill was used to grind grain as late as the eighteenth century. As shown here, the vanes radiate from a horizontal shaft that transmits power through gears to the mill below, on the second level in this sketch. *Sketch courtesy Smithsonian Institution.*

The flow of air was harnessed in Europe at the end of the twelfth century[3] with the development of the windmill. Used initially to grind grain and pump water, windmills were eventually adapted to wood cutting, cloth making, and other tasks. Notice that in all these examples there are two elements: the engine (waterwheel or windmill) and the machine (grist mill, saw mill) the engine drives.

In most places the waterwheel proved more dependable than the windmill. By the fourteenth century the waterwheel was in limited use in technologically advanced areas of western Europe, and two centuries later its use had spread throughout Europe. In metal making alone, the waterwheel was used to pump water out of flooded mines, ventilate mine shafts, crush and grind ore, and operate the bellows which force-fed air into the hot fires used to refine ore into metal. It was used in other industries to cut wood, make cloth, work bellows in glass factories, and pump drinking water into cities. Waterwheels and windmills provided the only nonmuscle source of energy in Europe for several centuries and helped lay the foundation for today's industrial society. Due to the expanding energy sources, the advanced agricultural person in fourteenth-century western Europe controlled about 25,000 kilocalories/person/day.

Our increasing control over energy and the greater power of our engines (see Table 1) took place against a backdrop of increasing urbanization and industrialization. By the seventeenth century, these developments in western Europe had put a tremendous strain on forests. The urban populations required large amounts of wood for cooking and heating, and the industries of the day needed wood to make metal, glass, and pottery. The invention of the cannon in the fifteenth century had especially strained forests: cannons were heavy and it took several tons of wood to produce one ton of iron.

**Average Engine Power, 1700**

| Engine | Horsepower |
|---|---|
| Man | 0.1 |
| Ox | 0.5 |
| Horse | 1.0 |
| Windmill | 40.0 |
| Waterwheel | 80.0 |

**Table 1.** For comparison, auto engines generate up to several hundred horsepower, and large electric power plants generate over one million horsepower.

As wood became scarce and expensive, coal began to be used in the home, in glass and brick factories, and in breweries. Ironically, metal makers continued to use wood since the impurities in coal produced an inferior iron. The conversion to coal created new problems, including air pollution and unhealthful and dangerous working conditions for miners; both of these problems are still with us. An additional problem was the flooding of coal mines. As we saw earlier, there is a large amount of water underground, and mines that penetrated the water table or intersected an underground stream became flooded. Some mines were kept dry by man-and-horse-operated pumps and others by waterwheel-operated pumps. But mines were not always near suitable streams, and on the European continent a device was developed to transmit power over a distance of several miles from the waterwheel to the mine. Called a Stangekunst, it was a series of linked bars which transmitted the energy by a push-pull motion. For some reason, England never adopted the Stangekunst; thus in England there was a need for a new power source.

The saying "necessity is the mother of invention" is often interpreted to mean that needs will inevitably be met, but it also happens that necessity leads to stagnation or disaster. History is strewn with cultures whose farming practices destroyed their soil's fertility or that allowed their irrigation systems to silt up and become useless. And for every victorious nation that wins a battle by using a new weapon (the stirrup, the crossbow, the atomic bomb), there is a defeated nation that fails to develop the needed defense. But in the case of England and its flooded coal mines, invention followed necessity. In 1698 England found its needed power resource when Thomas Savery (1650–1715) invented the first steam engine.

## The Steam Engine

The early steam engine—whose only moving parts were valves—operated like a giant soda straw (see Figure 2). It consisted of a boiler

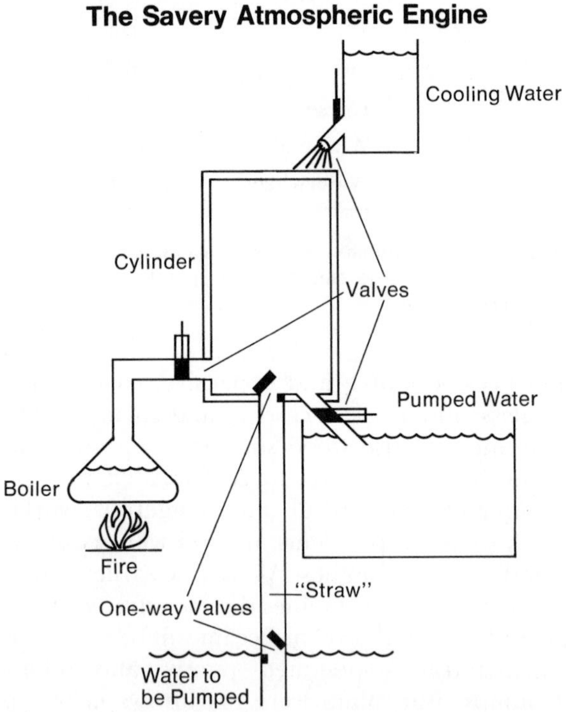

**The Savery Atmospheric Engine**

**Figure 2.** The Savery engine raised water by creating a vacuum in the cylinder. The vacuum occurred when steam admitted from the boiler was condensed as a result of the cooling of the cylinder by the cooling water spilled over it. This reduced the vacuum in the cylinder and "straw," allowing atmospheric pressure to force water up the straw.

to generate steam and a cylinder. Steam generated in the boiler was admitted to the cylinder and then condensed into water by a spray of cold water against the outside walls of the cylinder. Condensed water occupies about 1/1600th of the volume occupied by steam; the condensation therefore created a vacuum in the cylinder. Atmospheric pressure, pushing on the water in the mine, forced it up the pipe into the cylinder. It is this lifting that is the object of the engine. The pumped water is then removed from the cylinder and a new charge of steam admitted, starting the operation over again.

Although from our perspective it seems a simple and obvious idea, the steam engine was a revolutionary concept for the time. For thousands of years heat had been used to cook food, refine metal, and perform similar tasks; but not until Savery's invention could thermal energy be turned into mechanical energy. Until that invention, all mechanical work was done by muscle, wind, or water power. However, the Savery engine did not lead to the immediate disappearance of windmills and waterwheels. The engine was used only to pump water out of mines, and even there its use was limited since, at the maximum, atmospheric pressure can pump water up 34 feet; a typical height for the Savery engine was 20 feet.

A great improvement over the Savery engine was achieved by Thomas Newcomen (1663–1729), who in 1712 invented the reciprocating steam engine. Unlike the Savery engine, the Newcomen engine had several moving parts (see Figure 3). But the operating principle was the same.

## The Newcomen Atmospheric Engine

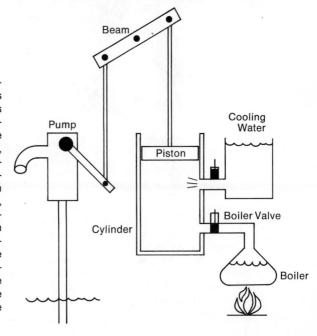

**Figure 3.** The Newcomen engine is shown about to begin its power stroke. Cooling water is being sprayed into the cylinder, which will condense the steam. Atmospheric pressure, pushing on the top of the piston, will force it down, operating the pump. When the piston reaches the end of its stroke, the boiler valve will open automatically, breaking the vacuum and allowing the counterweighted beam to raise the piston. The boiler did not generate enough steam to push the piston up. In fact, raising the piston drew steam into the cylinder.

Steam generated in a boiler filled a cylinder. The steam was then condensed by a spray of cold water, creating a vacuum. Atmospheric pressure pushed down on the piston, moving it and powering the pump to which it was attached. Then additional steam was admitted to the cylinder, breaking the vacuum and allowing the piston to be raised by the counterweighted beam. After it had been raised, cold water was again sprayed into the cylinder, repeating the cycle.

The valves on Newcomen's later engines were automatically opened and closed as the beam changed position, reducing labor needs. A small engine by present standards, it nevertheless represented a great advance for the day. One particular Newcomen engine (they came in all sizes) pumped out in 48 hours a dock which had previously taken 20 horses

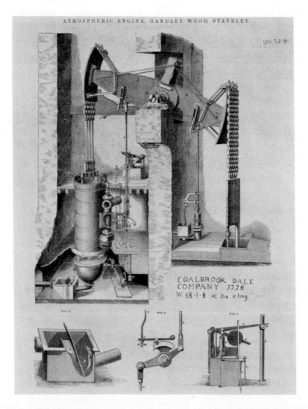

This atmospheric engine was used to pump water out of a coal mine. Steam entered the cylinder from below as the counter weighted pump plunger (at the right) moved the piston to the extreme upper end of its stroke. The steam was then condensed to water, creating a vacuum. Atmospheric pressure then forced the piston to the bottom of the cylinder, which raised the pump plunger. The intricate arrangement of rods and levers automatically opened and closed the valves. *Sketch courtesy Smithsonian Institution.*

and 50 men a week. Because of our familiarity with the reciprocating internal combustion engine, Newcomen's engine may also seem obvious. But it was not obvious when he conceived and built it. In addition, he faced enormous practical difficulties. The brass cylinders, for example, had to be finished by hand, and the seal between the cast iron piston and the cylinder was extremely difficult to achieve. The wooden pipes of the day and the low-melting-point solder used to join pieces of metal were other sources of difficulty.

The early steam engines depended on atmospheric pressure to push on the water to be raised (the Savery engine) or the piston to be moved (the Newcomen engine). The role of steam was essentially negative: it was condensed to provide a vacuum on one side of a surface. Air pressure on the other side then exerted a force which moved the surface. Air can be thought of as a multitude of tiny, quickly moving particles. The incessant beating of these gas molecules against a surface exerts a force on it. At sea level, this force exerted by air molecules banging against a surface is equal to 14.7 pounds/square inch.

Normally we do not notice the force due to air pressure because it is acting equally on all sides of an object, leaving it in equilibrium. But if a situation is created where the air pressure acts on only one side of an object, then an unbalanced force is observed. In both the Savery and Newcomen engines, steam was condensed to eliminate pressure on one side of a surface. With the Savery engine, atmospheric pressure acting on the surface of the water in the mine (see Figure 2) was not counteracted by pressure in the engine's "straw." As a result, the water moved upward in the "straw." In the Newcomen engine, the unbalanced atmospheric pressure acted on the piston, whose movement was then used to operate pumps. However, the use of atmospheric pressure limited the power of a steam engine since the greatest possible pressure difference was 14.7 pounds/square inch. At higher altitudes, where air pressure is even less, the pressure difference and resulting engine power was further reduced. This limitation was not removed until James Watt's inventions drastically modified the steam engine.

**The Watt Steam Engine.** For 60 years, the Newcomen engine remained dominant. Its major use was to keep coal mines dry, but it was also employed to pump municipal water from rivers into towns. Because the Newcomen engines produced reciprocating, or back and forth, motion, they were difficult to apply to other jobs: the machines of the day were built for the rotary motion of the waterwheel and windmill. In some cases a steam engine was used to pump water up into a tank, from where it would spill down, turning a waterwheel and producing rotary motion. But this pumped waterfall was not an efficient energy source. (See Figure 4 on the next page.)

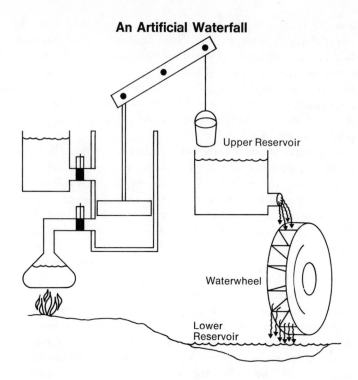

**An Artificial Waterfall**

**Figure 4.** A Newcomen engine is used to lift water to an upper reservoir. It then spilled down, turning the waterwheel and producing the desired rotary motion.

Major advances in steam engine design were made by James Watt (1736–1819), a Scottish instrument maker. He introduced four fundamental changes: the condenser, the use of steam pressure instead of atmospheric pressure to push the piston, a fly-ball governor, and the crank. The condenser resulted from his observation that it took several charges of steam, with each charge equal to the volume of the cylinder, to fill a Newcomen-engine cylinder. He reasoned that the first few volumes of steam were condensed by the cylinder and piston, which had been cooled by the spray of water. Only after the cylinder and piston had been reheated could the steam enter the cylinder without being condensed. Watt's solution was a separate section to condense the steam (see Figure 5). Since the cylinder walls and piston were no longer being heated and cooled each cycle, the condenser saved a large amount of steam and fuel.

Watt's second innovation led to a larger pressure difference acting on the piston. In this development, a vacuum is established on one side of the piston as in earlier engines. But instead of applying air pressure to the other side, Watt introduced relatively high-pressure steam to push the

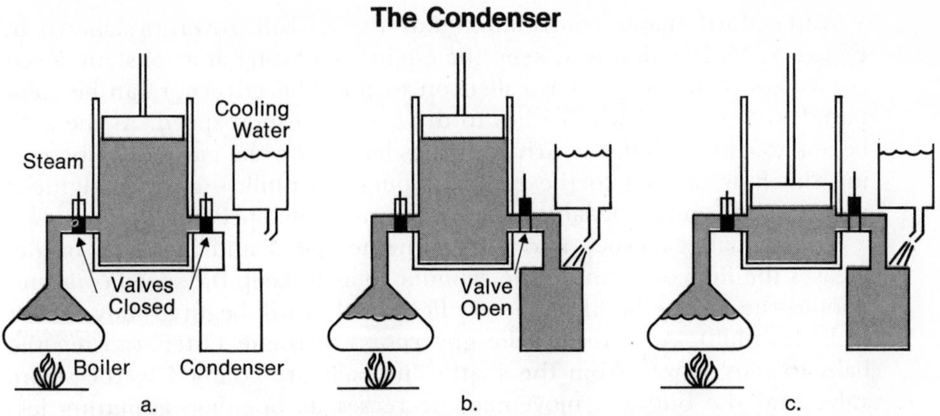

## The Condenser

**Figure 5.** a. The cylinder is filled with steam and the condenser and boiler valves are sealed off. b. The condenser valve is opened and steam flows into the condenser. c. Some steam has been condensed; atmospheric pressure is pushing the piston down. The steam still in the cylinder will also be condensed.

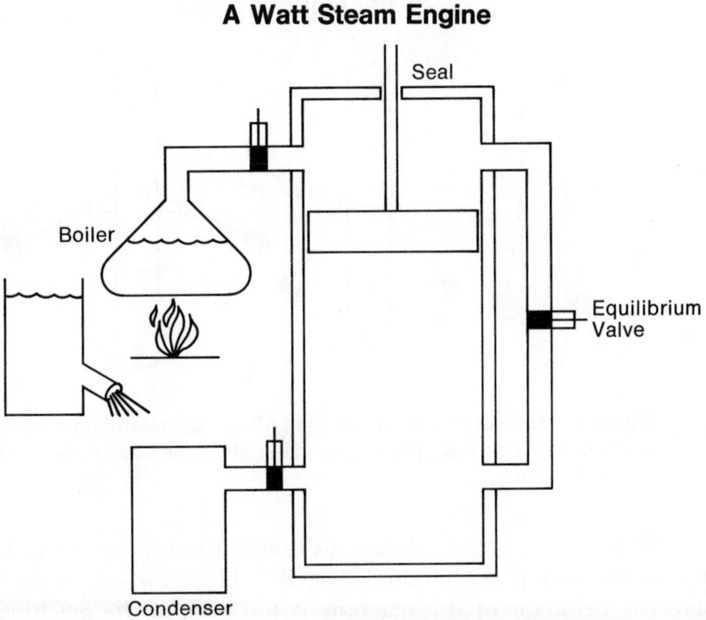

## A Watt Steam Engine

**Figure 6.** In this engine, a vacuum is created below the piston by condensing steam, and steam instead of atmospheric pressure is used to push the piston down. At the end of the power stroke, the equilibrium valve is opened to admit steam to the lower part of the cylinder, breaking the vacuum. This allows the piston to be raised. The seal keeps the steam from escaping.

piston down (see Figure 6). With this development, steam engines could be made more compact and powerful as the technology developed to handle higher temperatures and pressures.

Watt's third major contribution was the fly-ball governor, shown in Figure 7. Its function is to keep the engine operating at a constant speed regardless of the work it is called on to do. The governor can be compared to a motorist who wishes to drive at a constant speed. As the auto begins to climb a hill, the driver pushes harder on the gas pedal, increasing the flow of fuel to the engine. Going downhill, the driver lightens the pressure on the pedal to prevent the car from speeding up.

The fly-ball governor also senses engine speed and increases or decreases the flow of steam to the cylinder so as to keep the speed constant. Should the engine be lifting a very light load, it will begin to move faster (roll downhill). As a result, the governor will rotate faster, causing the balls to move away from the shaft. The balls are coupled to the steam valve and the outward movement decreases its opening, admitting less steam to the engine cylinder. Reducing the steam flow reduces the push on the piston, slowing the engine. If the load being lifted is heavy, the engine will tend to slow, causing the balls to move closer to the shaft.

## A Fly-ball Governor

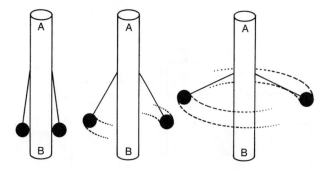

**Figure 7.** The speed with which shaft AB rotates determines the position of the balls. Their position, in turn, determines the size of the opening of the steam valve.

This will open the steam valve wider, admitting more steam to the cylinder and increasing the engine's speed. This is an example of feedback, where the behavior of the machine is fed back to the machine to modify its functioning.

Watt's fourth invention speeded the application of steam power to other tasks besides pumping water. He adapted the crank, which converts reciprocal motion to rotary motion, to the steam engine. With the crank, the steam engine could be applied to a variety of tasks, including sawing wood, boring holes in metal, cloth manufacturing, and in the beginning of the nineteenth century, to powering trains, boats, cable cars, and automobiles.

Although steam-generated energy—especially after Watt's improvements—was an immense advance over human or animal labor and more dependable than wind or water power, it was not directly accessible to most people. Steam engines were difficult and dangerous to operate, required skilled workmen to keep them in repair, used large amounts of fuel, and were dirty and noisy. This confined their use to factories, ships, train locomotives, and municipal water systems. People used the products manufactured with steam power, but did not make direct use of steam-generated energy.

**The Modern Steam Engine.**   Today the reciprocating steam engine has been replaced by the steam turbine. Instead of the back and forth motion of the piston, the turbine produces rotary motion. It can be thought of as a windmill, with the wind consisting of steam at a temperature of 1000°F and a pressure of over 2000 pounds/square inch.[4] The steam is produced by burning either powdered coal, oil, or natural gas in a furnace. Nuclear plants "burn" uranium. The heat from the fuel produces the high-temperature, high-pressure steam.

The turbine is a series of wheels with blades or buckets against which the steam pushes. Steam from the boiler hits the buckets on the first turbine wheel at 200 miles/hour. Within one-thirtieth of a second, the steam has pushed on roughly 5000 buckets mounted on 24 wheels which are spinning the turbine at 30 or 60 revolutions per second. During this one-thirtieth of a second, the steam's temperature drops to 100°F and its pressure to below atmospheric pressure.[5]

The steam used to drive a modern electric turbine is generated in an immense boiler of this type. The walls are pipes containing the water that is boiled into steam. The man suspended from the pulley is cleaning the burners. *Photo courtesy Florida Power Corporation.*

From the last turbine wheel, the exhausted steam enters the condenser, where cool water reduces it to water. Even this stage squeezes out an extra bit of energy since the vacuum created by the condensation increases the pressure difference between the boiler and condenser. The condenser itself is a chamber containing approximately 400 miles of one-inch-diameter pipe. Cooling water withdrawn from a river or lake flows through the pipe, condensing the steam in the chamber. The condensed steam is recirculated to the boiler, to be heated again into steam; the cooling water is returned to the river or lake. (See Figure 8.)

### A Steam Electric Plant

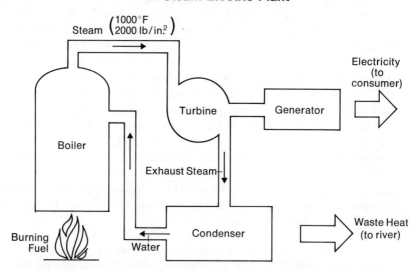

**Figure 8.** The diagram indicates the steam and energy flow through a modern steam electric plant.

A steam turbine can be immensely powerful. Some turbines are rated at 1 million kilowatts—large enough to supply the needs of a city of 700,000 people. The furnace feeding such a turbine consumes almost 300 pounds of coal each second and the turbine generates enough power to lift a 100-ton railroad car straight up at over 2000 miles/hour. But there is little call for such applications and the energy instead goes to power refrigerators, air-conditioners, electric-powered trains, radios, and street lights. A million-kilowatt turbine can simultaneously power 5 million 100-watt light bulbs, 500,000 refrigerators, and 500,000 color television sets.

## Electric Power

The Electric Dynamo. The first step toward expanding the use of steam power took place about 1867[6] with the improvement of the electric

## The Dynamo

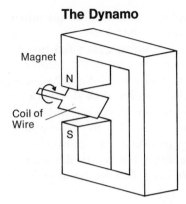

Magnet

Coil of Wire

**Figure 9.** If the closed loop of wire is rotated between the pole faces of the magnet, a current will flow through the wire.

Shown here is a turbine being serviced in a power plant. In operation, the turbine is enclosed in a shell to contain the steam. The shaft of the turbine is spun by jets of steam (flowing from nozzles at the periphery of the cylinder) which hit the turbine blades. The work created by the rotary motion is transformed to electric energy by the generator connected to the turbine and visible here at the rear. *Photo courtesy Florida Power Corporation.*

dynamo, or electric generator. The dynamo is a coil of copper wire mounted so that it can be spun between the poles of a magnet (see Figure 9). The rotation of the coil produces an electric current which is transmitted through a wire. The current can be thought of as a flow of energy. The dynamo transforms the energy expended in spinning the coil into electric energy. At first the electric energy could be recovered only as heat, by connecting, for example, an 1867 version of an electric iron or toaster into the circuit.

But in 1870,[7] a second major development occurred. It was discovered that if two electric generators are properly connected, turning the coil of one causes the other's coil to turn. The effort expended turning the first generator's coil appears as the rotary motion of the second generator's coil. The second generator is called an electric motor. The generator-motor combination meant that the energy produced by the steam engine could be transmitted through copper wire to distant sites and used there as a source of mechanical work. You may recall that the generator-motor made it possible for the electric trolley to replace the more clumsy and expensive cable car. Both used steam energy, but the trolley transmitted that energy as electricity while the cable car relied on the more primitive method of a moving cable.

The invention of the dynamo, its modification into the electric motor, and the invention of the electric light bulb solved the problem of getting steam-generated energy into the home. Under the control of Thomas A. Edison (1847–1931)—the American engineer who invented the light bulb and phonograph—steam-driven electric power plants were built in most major American cities by 1900. The energy generated by the large, noisy, and dangerous steam engines was sent silently through copper wires to the customers' homes. At first the energy was used mainly to provide light, but as the radio, phonograph, vacuum cleaner, and washing machine were invented, increasing amounts of electric energy went to power appliances. Factories installed electric-powered machinery, freeing them from the bother of maintaining steam engines or locating near water power. The development of electricity allowed power generation to be concentrated in a comparatively small number of centrally located plants, with the energy shipped to users through overhead and underground wires.

In broad outline, this is the situation as it exists today. Electric energy is still generated in large power plants by steam, or at dams using water power, and transmitted to homes and factories. Of course there have been changes. The reciprocating steam engine has been replaced by the steam turbine, the scale of energy production has increased greatly, and the electricity is transmitted over longer distances at much higher voltages than 90 years ago. The electric energy itself is used to power things that weren't dreamed of in 1880 when Edison built his first power plant in New York City—televisions, computers, electric razors, and movie projectors. But despite the changes, we still have a system in which coal or oil is burned to provide steam to spin a dynamo coil.

Almost since its introduction, the amount of electric energy used in the United States has doubled every ten years. The doubling has meant that the benefits of this energy have been available to increasing numbers of people in increasing amounts. It has also meant that the problems associated with the production and transmission of electric energy have been increasing. Whether the problems have increased faster than the benefits and whether each further increase in the production of electricity makes us richer or poorer are, as yet, unanswered questions. But there is no doubt that the production of electricity is not an unalloyed good.

In the following chapters we shall try to measure the benefits and costs of electricity by relating, for example, the quantity of electric energy produced to the acres of land strip mined for coal, to the gallons of thermally polluted water, and to the weight of air pollution created by generating the electricity. To do these comparisons we must first have a better understanding of the physical operation of electricity.

**A Physical Model for Electricity.** Electricity occupies such a central position in the discussion to follow that it is helpful to introduce a physical model to describe it. The model does not explain electricity: it provides a way of remembering its behavior and may even enable you to reason about electrical phenomena. One useful analogy to consider is water flowing under pressure in a pipe. The amount of water flowing past a point in the pipe is analogous to the electric current, and the water pressure is analogous to the voltage. The water pump plays the same role as the electric generator. Pumping the water in one section of the pipe causes the water in the entire pipe to move. In the same way, a dynamo located 20 miles from a home can cause an electric current in the home.

The analogy can be taken a step further, as illustrated by the model in Figure 10. The model consists of a piston placed in a water pipe, which forms a closed loop several miles long. Also in the pipe are small waterwheels linked to machines outside the pipe; and some areas of the pipe are partially blocked.

## A Water Model for Electricity

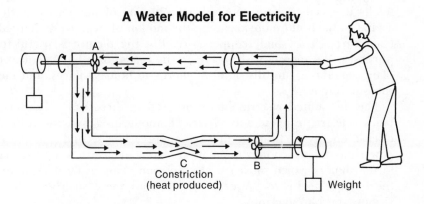

C
Constriction
(heat produced)                    Weight

**Figure 10.** The movement of the piston to the left causes the water to circulate counter clockwise through the loop. Its motion spins the propeller-like waterwheels at A and B, lifting the weight, while heat is generated at C. The piston corresponds to an electric generator, the waterwheels to motors, and the constriction to a toaster or light bulb.

When the piston is moved, water throughout the pipe moves with it because the water is incompressible. Some of the energy expended in moving the piston is dissipated as heat generated by the friction of the water rubbing against the pipe walls. The rest appears as work done by the waterwheels and as friction-generated heat when the water pushes its way through the partially blocked portions of the pipe.

Electrically, the piston corresponds to the generator, the water pipe to the wire which conducts the electric energy from power plant to user, the waterwheels to the refrigerator, dishwasher, and elevator motors connected to the generator, and the constricted portions of the pipe to heat devices such as light bulbs and toasters. The water corresponds to the electrically charged electrons whose incompressible flow constitutes the electric current. When the electrons in the coil of wire rotating between the dynamo's magnetic poles experience a push, the push is transmitted almost instantaneously throughout the wire and all the electrons move. The push on the electrons in the dynamo coil occurs because electrons moving in a magnetic field experience a force. By continuously rotating the wire coil in the magnetic field, a force is maintained on the electrons. Then the electrons in the wire connected to the coil move in concert with the coil electrons, just as all the water in our pipe system moves with the water in the pump. And, like the water, the electrons' movement through the copper wire results in frictional losses. The further the electricity must be sent, the greater are these transmission losses. It is for this reason that most electric power is generated in local power plants.

This model may make electricity plausible, but it actually, technically, explains nothing. Compared to the easily understood picture of the piston pushing on water, the action of the magnetic field on the electrons is totally unspecified here. Similarly, the motion of water moving through a pipe is much more obvious than the motion of negatively charged electrons through a "solid" copper wire. But the picture is useful for our purposes. We merely wish to create the image of a large central power plant generating and distributing energy to homes, offices, and factories surrounding it.

The distributed electric energy is used in three ways. Toasters, light bulbs, electric ranges, and electric home-heating systems convert the electric energy to heat, or thermal energy. The second major use is to power motors, which may range in size from an electric tooth-brush motor to the motors which move an electric train along at 60 miles/hour. The third major use is to power electronic equipment such as radios, televisions, and phonographs.

For a specific example, let us look at a light bulb. Turning on a light bulb consists of connecting the filament of the light bulb to the coil of the dynamo. The connection may be through miles of underground and aboveground wire, but it is a direct connection; in theory one could trace the connection from the home to the power plant. Once connected, the electrons in the filament move approximately in step with those in the dynamo. The filament wire, however, has a high resistance to the movement of electrons, and forcing electrons through the filament results in the release of heat energy, just as vigorously rubbing your hands together releases heat. This heat raises the temperature of the filament, causing it to glow and emit light. Toasters, electric ranges and ovens, electric blankets, hair dryers, and electric heaters all work on the same principle although the temperatures reached and the amount of heat and light given off will be different.

**From Coal to Electricity.**   To many people, electricity is intangible. It seems to come out of and go into thin air. But behind the sockets from which the electric energy quietly and cleanly flows is a network of coal mines, oil and gas wells, coal trains, tankers, pipelines, refineries, storage tanks, power plants, and power transmission grids. Associated with this network are a multitude of environmental and land-use problems not even hinted at when we turn on a light bulb or toaster.

The intangibility, then, is all in our minds. The mere act of playing a color television for $1\frac{1}{2}$ hours or burning a 100-watt light bulb for 10 hours results in the burning of a pound of coal or an equivalent quantity of oil or natural gas. The typical home in 1970 consumed the equivalent of 4 tons of coal a year—about 20 pounds/day—in the form of electric energy. The nation as a whole that year consumed, as electricity, 320 million tons of coal, 12 billion gallons of oil, and 3.4 trillion ($10^{12}$) cubic feet of natural gas.

**Thermal Pollution.**   The function of an electric power plant is to burn a fuel, transforming its stored chemical energy into electrical energy. But as with all physical processes, there are side effects. In a later chapter we shall consider the air and water pollution and the land disturbance associated with energy production and use. For now we wish only to look at a more subtle side effect—the waste heat emitted by power plants as they generate electricity.

The source of the waste heat is familiar from the discussion of early steam engines, which used cool water to condense steam to make a vacuum. Because of their small size, these engines used comparatively little cooling water. But today's power plants literally run rivers through their condensers to carry off waste heat. At present, about one-sixth of all U.S. runoff water is used to cool steam electric plants. For this reason, power plants are always located on a river, ocean, or natural or artificial lake. A million-kilowatt plant operating at peak capacity requires about 12,000 gallons/second of cooling water. If the plant is located on a river, the water is drawn in upstream and discharged downstream, 10 to 30 degrees warmer.

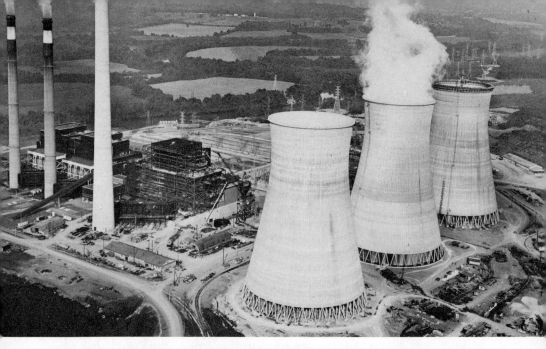

Three immense (300 feet wide and 437 feet high) cooling towers are used to transfer the power plant's waste heat directly to the atmosphere. Hot water from the condensers is pumped part way up the towers then allowed to cascade down, cooling the water and releasing heat to the atmosphere. The cooled water is then returned to the river. *Photo courtesy Tennessee Valley Authority.*

Even if the water is withdrawn from a large river, there will usually be a biological effect. The withdrawal of 12,000 gallons/second can result in the battering of large fish against the screens covering the intake pipes. Small fish, fish eggs, and plants drawn into the condenser may be killed by the high temperatures. In addition, the steady discharge of heat to a river or lake raises its overall temperature, perhaps driving out desirable cold-water fish, such as trout and salmon, and encouraging less desirable fish and excessive algae growth.[8] At present, no definitive statement can be made about waste heat. The impact varies with the size of the river, the size of the plant, the season of the year, the care with which the intake pipes were positioned, and the amount of chemicals fed through the condenser to discourage algae growth.

Those who see the waste heat as harmful call it thermal pollution. They have pressured electric utilities to construct cooling towers,[9] which transfer the waste heat immediately to the air. Some utilities claim that the waste heat enriches biological systems in some circumstances by extending the growing seasons of fish and shellfish into cold months. Fish are attracted during the winter to the warm water released by the plants, but if the turbine is shut down for repair or maintenance, the sudden cooling of the water can thermally shock and kill the fish.

The problem of disposing of waste heat raises this question: Why not eliminate it by doing away with the condenser and converting all of the fuel's energy into electricity? For the answer we must turn to two fundamental physical laws.

## The Conservation and Entropy Laws

The Conservation of Energy.   The first law we will consider is the law of conservation of energy. The energy conservation law says that energy can neither be created nor destroyed. If we start with a pound of coal containing 10,000 BTU (an energy unit to be defined later) of stored energy, we will still have 10,000 BTU after the coal has been burned. But the energy will be dispersed as hot smokestack gas, waste heat carried off by cooling water, and electricity. The sum of these different energies will be 10,000 BTU.

The conservation law says that you cannot make 15,000 BTU of electricity out of 10,000 BTU of coal energy, but it does not say why 10,000 BTU of coal energy cannot be converted to 10,000 BTU of electrical energy. If such 100% conversion could be accomplished, there would be no waste heat.

The Second Law.   The explanation of the inherent inefficiency of steam electric plants is provided by the second law of thermodynamics. The second law states that to convert heat energy into mechanical energy (for example, lifting a bucket of water or spinning a generator coil to produce electricity) the heat must "flow" from a high-temperature source (the boiler) to a low-temperature "sink" (the condenser). (See Figure 11.)

## The Second Law of Thermodynamics

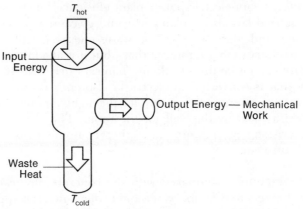

**Figure 11.**   This schematic diagram shows the flow of energy through a heat engine. Energy enters the engine as heat at a high temperature, $T_{hot}$. Some of this heat is converted to mechanical work while the rest is dumped as waste heat into a heat "sink" at temperature $T_{cold}$.

Unless the thermal energy can flow between two different temperatures, no mechanical work is done. And it is mechanical work produced from the steam that spins the generator coil to produce electricity. An analogy is provided by a waterwheel. To turn a waterwheel requires that water flow from a higher to a lower level. Without a height difference, no energy can be extracted from the water. Thus, for example, the water in the ocean cannot be used to spin waterwheels because it is all at the same level. Similarly, heat needs a temperature difference to "flow" between. Using the ocean again as an example, the thermal energy it contains is useless without a lower temperature "sink." We therefore burn coal or oil or natural gas to provide a high-temperature energy source and use the ocean or a river or lake as the low-temperature "sink."

The most efficient steam engines convert 40 percent of the input energy to mechanical work. At each step some energy "leaks" out so that the other 60 percent is wasted. While some of the energy goes up the stack as heated gas or is lost as friction in the generator, most of it is lost in the condenser. This loss is determined — again according to the second law — by the temperature difference between the input steam and the condenser. The higher the input steam temperature and the lower the condenser temperature, the greater the efficiency. The maximum input temperature is determined by the metallurgical properties of the turbines. The condenser temperature is determined by the water temperature, which is the only practical coolant. A power plant could simply exhaust its steam directly to the atmosphere after passing through the turbine, but this would be less efficient than using a condenser and it would fill the area with a cloud of steam. Refrigerating the coolant water would increase a plant's efficiency, but also consume more energy than would be recovered by the increased efficiency. However, when nature does the refrigerating during the winter, steam-electric-power-plant efficiencies increase.

The second law also explains why energy cannot be recycled like aluminum cans and glass bottles. The waste energy is still there — the law of energy conservation guarantees that — but it is at a lower temperature and therefore cannot be used to do mechanical work. The 40 percent of input energy that is converted to electricity also ends up as degraded, or low-temperature, energy. For example, the light emitted by a light bulb is absorbed as heat by the walls of the room. The electric energy pumped into television sets, motors, and other equipment also ends up as low-temperature energy.

**A Summation.** Compared with the concrete physical models used in earlier chapters to describe water and traffic flows, the approach to electric current and energy is abstract. One physical model or analogy follows another as we seek to depict the conversion of something called heat into something called electricity into something called mechanical work. And all of these models and analogies are built on quicksand because we have not precisely defined temperature or heat or energy.

But the objective here is not to create the kind of concise, rigorous, quantitative picture of the world which is the province of physics. The aim instead is to introduce those few physical terms and models which will be useful in constructing a picture of the way energy systems function. The second law of thermodynamics is brought into the discussion so the reader knows that there is a law which requires the production of waste heat, given current methods of producing electricity. The analogy to a waterwheel is developed more as a memory device than as an explanation of how physicists understand the law.

## A Quantitative Look

Having hopefully created a verbal framework, we now wish to apply numbers to the production and use of energy. Again the aim is descriptive rather than explanatory. By calculating the pounds of coal or cubic feet of natural gas it takes to operate a light bulb or lift an elevator, we may succeed in making concrete what is now abstract. We are assuming, then, the underlying physical principles which determine the efficiency of a generator or the energy content of a pound of coal. We are interested in the technological and environmental consequences of those principles.

**Thermal Energy.** Our first quantitative step is to define a unit of thermal energy so that we may measure energy the way we measure distance and time. The unit of thermal energy is the British Thermal Unit (BTU). One BTU is the amount of heat energy which raises the temperature of 1 pound of water 1°F. For example, if 20 BTU of heat energy are added to 1 pound of water, its temperature will rise 20°F. The kilocalorie is the unit of heat energy in the metric system. One kilocalorie equals 4 BTU. The kilocalorie is defined as the quantity of heat which raises the temperature of 1 kilogram of water 1° Centigrade. It is most familiar as a measurement of food energy.

**Example 1.** A pot holding 8 pounds of water at 40°F receives 200 BTU of heat. What is the final temperature?

The final temperature can be found informally by noting that each pound of water will receive 25 BTU [(200 BTU) ÷ (8 lb) = 25 BTU/lb]. This produces a 25°F temperature rise, for a final temperature of 65°F.

We can proceed more formally by defining the heat capacity, $C$, of water as

$$C = 1 \text{ BTU/lb/°F}$$

which restates concisely the way a pound of water responds to the addition of 1 BTU of heat. Using $C$, we can write a relation between the heat, $Q$, flowing into or out of the water, the weight, $w$, of the water, and its temperature change, $T$. The relation is

$$Q = C(w)(T).$$

To solve the above example, we use the values of $Q = 200$ BTU and $w = 8$ pounds to obtain

$$T = \frac{Q}{(C)(w)} = \frac{200 \text{ BTU}}{(1 \text{ BTU/lb/°F})(8 \text{ lb})} = 25°\text{F}.$$

**Example 2.** A piece of bread is burned beneath a pot containing 10 pounds of water. If the water temperature rises from 40°F to 60°F, what was the energy content of the bread in BTU and kcal?

$$Q = C(w)(T) = (1 \text{ BTU/lb/°F})(10 \text{ lb})(20°\text{F}) = 200 \text{ BTU}$$

$$= 200 \text{ BTU}\left(\frac{1 \text{ kcal}}{4 \text{ BTU}}\right) = 50 \text{ kcal}$$

The above is the procedure by which the energy content of food is determined. If you consume 3000 kilocalories (12,000 BTU) of food energy in a day, you have eaten enough energy to raise the temperature of 1000 pounds of water 12°F.

The BTU is most familiar to us from its use to classify air-conditioners. A 6000-BTU air-conditioner has the capacity to remove 6000 BTU of heat energy per hour from inside a room and exhaust it to the outside. Hot-water heaters are also specified by the BTU per hour they can deliver to the water being heated. A typical home hot-water heater has a heat-delivery capacity of 50,000 BTU/hour, which can produce 40 gallons of hot water per hour.

**Example 3.** To see where the hot-water-heater rating comes from, assume the water enters the heater at 40°F and leaves at 160°F, for a temperature change of 120°F. One gallon of water weighs 8.3 pounds. Thus the total water heated per hour is (40 gal)(8.3 lb/gal) = 332 lb. The heat needed is

$$Q = (C)(w)(T) = (1 \text{ BTU/lb/°F})(332 \text{ lb})(120°\text{F}) = 39,840 \text{ BTU}.$$

Ideally, then, the heater needs about 40,000 BTU/hour. But the heaters are no more than 80% efficient, with 20% of the heat going up the flue with the combustion gases. The 80% efficiency means that 50,000 BTU/hour are needed to deliver 40,000 BTU/hour to the water.

**Example 4.** Calculate the BTU required to convert 5 pounds of water, initially at 52°F, to steam.

Water boils at 212°F at sea-level pressure, so the first step is to calculate the heat needed to bring the water to 212°F. To achieve the 160°F increase requires

$$Q = C(w)(T) = (1 \text{ BTU/lb/°F})(5 \text{ lb})(160°F) = 800 \text{ BTU}.$$

At sea-level atmospheric pressures, the water cannot be raised above 212°F. As heat is added to the 212°F water, it boils into steam at 212°F. The heat needed to convert the water into steam—called the heat of vaporization—is 980 BTU per pound of water. To boil the 5 pounds of water into steam requires

$$Q = (\text{heat of vaporization})(\text{weight of water})$$
$$= (980 \text{ BTU/lb})(5 \text{ lb}) = 4900 \text{ BTU}.$$

Thus the total heat needed is 5700 BTU. When the steam condenses to water at 212°F, it releases 980 BTU per pound of steam condensed, which is the main source of the heat carried off from power-plant condensers. The heat of vaporization of 980 BTU also explains why steam gives a much more serious burn than an equal weight of boiling water.

**The Energy Content of Fuels.**  We now use the BTU-water-thermometer "yardstick" to measure the energy content of different fuels. This can be done by burning a pound of coal, a cubic foot of natural gas, and a gallon of gasoline under vats of water and measuring the temperature increase. Such experiments show the following results.

A pound of coal yields 10,000 BTU.
A gallon of gasoline yields 140,000 BTU.
A cubic foot of natural gas yields 1000 BTU.

These numbers vary with the quality of the fuel. Poor grade coal yields 8000 BTU/pound while anthracite yields 14,000 BTU/pound. In this text we shall take 10,000 BTU/pound as the average energy content of coal. One pound of average coal therefore equals ten cubic feet of natural gas and one-fourteenth of a gallon of gasoline.

Knowing the energy content of the three fuels, we can compare the cost and environmental impact of equal amounts of energy derived from different fuels. A person, or company, buying fuel to heat a building is interested in obtaining the largest amount of BTU's per dollar. (A rough rule of thumb is that energy costs about $2 per $10^6$ BTU.) Environmentalists, on the other hand, are interested in the quantity of pollutants emitted per unit of energy released.

**Example 5.**  A person owns a home heated by a furnace that can be converted to burn coal or oil. If 10,000-BTU-per-pound coal sells for $10 a ton, and 100,000-BTU-per-gallon heating oil sells for $0.20 a gallon, which fuel is cheaper?

The ton of coal yields

$$Q = (2 \times 10^3 \text{ lb})(10^4 \text{ BTU/lb}) = 2 \times 10^7 \text{ BTU} = 20 \times 10^6 \text{ BTU}$$

or 20 million BTU/ton. At $10 a ton, the cost per million BTU is

$$\frac{\$10}{20 \times 10^6 \text{ BTU}} = \$0.50/10^6 \text{ BTU}$$

or 50¢ per million BTU. The cost of the petroleum per million BTU is

$$\frac{\$0.20}{10^5 \text{ BTU}} = \$2.00/10^6 \text{ BTU}$$

or $2.00 per million BTU. So the coal is cheaper by $1.50 per million BTU.

**Example 6.** Assume fuel oil is 3% sulfur by weight and coal 1.5% sulfur. Which will emit more sulfur dioxide per unit of energy? Assume the fuel oil weighs 6 pounds/gallon.

To obtain $10^5$ BTU you must burn 6 pounds of fuel oil and 10 pounds of coal. The 6 pounds of fuel oil contain

$$(0.03)(6 \text{ lb}) = 0.18 \text{ lb}$$

of sulfur. The 10 pounds of coal contain

$$(0.015)(10 \text{ lb}) = 0.15 \text{ lb}$$

of sulfur. So the coal will emit less sulfur dioxide per unit of energy. (The sulfur dioxide is formed when the fuel is burned: sulfur + oxygen → sulfur dioxide.)

**Work and Potential Energy.** Now that we have a measure of heat and of the energy content of fuel, we wish to relate them to the work done by a steam turbine. Because it provides a simple example, the work we shall consider is the lifting of a weight. To lift a 1000-pound weight requires that the steam engine exert a 1000-pound force upward. If it lifts the weight 20 feet into the air, the work done is

$$\text{work} = (\text{force})(\text{distance}) = (F)(d) = (1000 \text{ lb})(20 \text{ ft}) = 20,000 \text{ ft-lb.}$$

The foot-pound is the unit of energy used to measure mechanical work. Work is done whenever a force is exerted parallel to the direction of motion. If a 20-pound force is used to drag a box 30 feet across the floor, the work done is

$$W = (F)(d) = (20 \text{ lb})(30 \text{ ft}) = 600 \text{ ft-lb.}$$

But if a person walks across a room carrying a 20-pound object, no work is done because the force required to support the object is exerted in the upward direction and the motion is perpendicular to it, in the horizontal direction. (See Figure 12.)

## Some Examples of Work

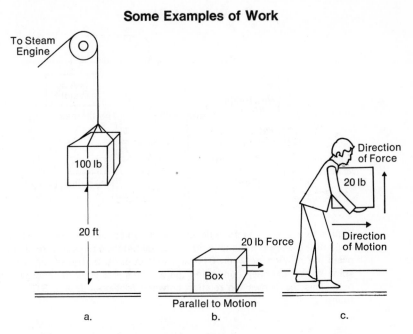

**Figure 12.** In a and b, work is done because the force is exerted in the direction of motion. But in c, no work is done because the motion is perpendicular to the force.

Returning to the weight-lifting example, we wish to know what happens to the energy the steam engine expends lifting the weight. The answer is that the energy is converted into the gravitational potential energy of the weight. That is, the weight is said to have increased potential energy (P.E.) by virtue of its increased height. Intuitively this makes sense because if the weight is allowed to fall freely back to earth, the potential energy is transformed into energy of motion and then into noise and crushing energy as the weight hits the ground. More accurately, the change in potential energy is defined as

$$\text{P.E.} = (\text{weight})(\text{distance}) = (1000 \text{ lb})(20 \text{ ft}) = 20,000 \text{ ft-lb.}$$

**BTU and Foot-pounds.** The energy used to lift the weight originally came from burning fuel. We now wish to know how much heat it takes to do a given amount of work. We back into this by first converting work into heat since work can be converted into heat with 100% efficiency, but heat, from the second law, cannot be converted into work with 100% efficiency. Experiments such as those in Figure 13 show that

$$778 \text{ ft-lb} = 1 \text{ BTU.}$$

We can use this relation to calculate how many foot-pounds of work a 40% efficient steam engine can squeeze out of a pound of coal. At 40%

## Work into Heat

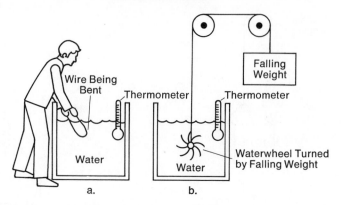

**Figure 13.** a. Work is done flexing a wire, which generates heat. Knowledge of the work done, the weight of water, and the temperature change gives the relation between BTU and foot-pounds. b. The falling weight spins the waterwheel, converting the weight's lost potential energy into heat. This too allows the relation between foot-pounds and BTU to be found.

efficiency, 4000 of the 10,000 BTU will be converted into work. That is equivalent to

$$(4000 \text{ BTU})(778 \text{ ft-lb/BTU}) = 3.1 \times 10^6 \text{ ft-lb.}$$

Let us assume we use the electric energy generated from this pound of coal to lift a 4000-pound elevator. We can calculate how high the $3.1 \times 10^6$ foot-pounds of energy can lift the elevator by writing

$$W = (F)(d).$$
$$d = \frac{W}{F} = \frac{3.1 \times 10^6 \text{ ft-lb}}{4 \times 10^3 \text{ lb}} = 770 \text{ ft}$$

To lift the elevator we have converted some of the heat energy released by the coal into the mechanical energy of the spinning coil. That energy is then converted with very close to 100% efficiency into electrical energy and the electrical energy is converted with close to 100% efficiency to mechanical energy by an electric motor. We could also use the electric energy to produce heat by connecting it to an iron, toaster, or hot-water heater. In that case we would get 4000 BTU of heat from the original 10,000 BTU of heat released by the coal.

To see the significance of this heat loss, we return to the hot-water heater considered earlier. In that example, 50,000 BTU of heat were released by burning gas to deliver 40,000 BTU to the hot water. But if the hot-water heater is electrical, then 100,000 BTU of heat must be used in the power plant to deliver 40,000 BTU to the heater. There are no further losses because the electric heat is delivered with almost 100% efficiency to the water by the electric coils. This calculation provides part of the reason why electric heat—whether it is used for space heating, cooking, clothes drying, or hot water—is expensive compared to the heat produced by burning a fuel directly in the home.

**Kilowatt-hours.** Neither the electric company nor anyone else measures electric energy in foot-pounds or BTU. Instead, electric meters record energy use in kilowatt-hours (kw-hr). The relations between kilowatt-hours and BTU and foot-pounds are

$$1 \text{ kw-hr} = 3413 \text{ BTU}$$
$$1 \text{ kw-hr} = 2.7 \times 10^6 \text{ ft-lb.}$$

To test these two conversion relations, we could perform the experiments shown in Figure 14. In the first experiment an electric heater is

### Electricity into Heat and Work

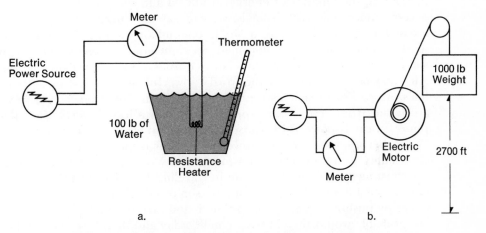

**Figure 14.** a. 100 pounds of water are heated from 40°F to 74.13°F by 1 kilowatt-hour of electricity. b. The same quantity of electricity is used to raise a 1000-pound weight 2700 feet. In both cases, the electric power meter determines when 1 kilowatt-hour of electricity has been used.

used to warm 100 pounds of water initially at 40°F. It is found that when the meter shows 1 kilowatt-hour of electricity has been consumed, the water temperature has risen to 74.13°F, a temperature change of 34.13°F. The heat released to the water by the kilowatt-hour of electric energy is therefore

$$Q = C(W)(T) = (1 \text{ BTU/lb/°F})(100 \text{ lb})(34.13°F)$$
$$= 3413 \text{ BTU} = 1 \text{ kw-hr.}$$

In the second experiment, an electric motor is used to lift a 1000-pound weight. It is found that when the meter reads 1 kilowatt-hour, the weight is 2700 feet above the ground. The work done is therefore

$$W = (F)(d) = (10^3 \text{ lb})(2.7 \times 10^3 \text{ ft}) = 2.7 \times 10^6 \text{ ft-lb}$$
$$= 1 \text{ kw-hr.}$$

It should be kept in mind that although we have used the straight-forward examples of lifting a weight and heating water, the same analysis could be applied to the operation of an electric fan, air-conditioner, food blender, or light bulb. In these cases, the measurement of the work done or heat produced is more difficult, but the principle is the same.

**Power.** The steam engine and electric generator have greatly increased the energy at our disposal. Instead of being limited to the energy contained in our food or in a wood-burning fire, we now have energy converters that consume hundreds of pounds of coal per second and deliver the energy output into every home, office, and factory. In addition to the increase in the amount of energy produced and consumed, we have also become more powerful. That is, we can expend energy at a greatly increased rate. For example, a single one-million-kilowatt generator can work as fast as several million men. So eight hours of energy output by such a generator is equivalent to a day's output of several million laborers. An everyday illustration of the word "powerful" is provided by automobiles. All cars can reach a speed of 60 miles/hour. But a powerful car can accelerate from rest to that speed faster than a less powerful car. The powerful car is powerful because it can expend energy at a high rate.

Another approach to the concept of power comes from comparing a car's ability to use energy and a man's ability to use energy. An average car consumes 1 gallon of gasoline in traveling 12 miles. That gallon contains about 140,000 BTU. A strong person could also move a car 12 miles, either by pushing it or by dismantling it and carrying each piece 12 miles. He probably would travel about 1 mile a day and therefore take 12 days to do the job. If he were consuming 3000 kilocalories/day, his energy consumption would be 36,000 kilocalories, or 144,000 BTU, about the same amount of energy as the auto engine consumed. But the auto engine moved the car at 60 miles/hour and used the 35,000 kilocalories in 12 minutes. It is much more powerful than the human engine.

Power, $P$, is defined as

$$P = \frac{\text{work}}{\text{time}} = \frac{W}{t}.$$

The unit for power is foot-pound/second.

**Example 7.** Assume a man lifts a 50-pound weight 4 feet in the air in 8 seconds. What is the power output?

The work done is

$$W = (F)(d) = (50 \text{ lb})(4 \text{ ft}) = 200 \text{ ft-lb}.$$

The power is therefore

$$P = \frac{W}{t} = \frac{200 \text{ ft-lb}}{8 \text{ sec}} = 25 \text{ ft-lb/sec}.$$

While the foot-pound/second is the easiest power unit to understand, the two most common power units are horsepower and watt or kilowatt (1000 watts). Automobile engines, diesel engines, and some electric motors are rated in horsepower (hp), which is based on the rate at which an average horse can work. James Watt originated the unit so that he could describe to prospective purchasers how many horses his steam engine would replace.

$$1 \text{ hp} = 550 \text{ ft-lb/sec}$$

The watt (w) or kilowatt (kw) are used to rate electric power plants and the power needs of electric appliances. The most common use is the rating of light bulbs as 60 watts, 100 watts, and so on.

$$1 \text{ w} = 0.737 \text{ ft-lb/sec}$$
$$1 \text{ kw} = 737 \text{ ft-lb/sec}$$

If the power rating of a device is known, the amount of energy it uses can be calculated from the formula

$$W = (P)(t).$$

For example, in 1 hour a 1-kilowatt (1000-watt) light bulb uses

$$W = (P)(t) = (1 \text{ kw})(1 \text{ hr}) = 1 \text{ kw-hr}.$$

Or the result can be obtained in foot-pounds by noting that 1 kilowatt is 737 foot-pounds/second and 1 hour is 3600 seconds. Therefore

$$W = (P)(t) = (737 \text{ ft-lb/sec})(3600 \text{ sec}) = 2.7 \times 10^6 \text{ ft-lb}$$

as we saw earlier.

The electric company could bill customers for the number of foot-pounds used, or even in terms of the coal or oil it takes to generate the electricity. However, it is much more convenient to bill in kilowatt-hours. Charging for kilowatts, of course, would not make any sense. It would be analogous to an auto-rental firm charging for the speed at which you drove the car instead of for the distance, which is the product of speed and time.

A kilowatt-hour of electricity is consumed when a device rated at 1 kilowatt is operated for 1 hour, or when a 100-watt (0.1-kilowatt) device is operated for 10 hours, or a 500-watt device for 2 hours.

$$W = (P)(t) = (1 \text{ kw})(1 \text{ hr}) = (0.1 \text{ kw})(10 \text{ hr}) = (0.5 \text{ kw})(2 \text{ hr})$$
$$= 1 \text{ kw-hr}$$

**Example 8.** Calculate the kilowatt-hours of energy it takes to run a 500-watt color TV 3 hours a day for a month (500 watts = 0.5 kilowatts).

$$W = (P)(t) = (0.5 \text{ kw})(3 \text{ hr/day})(30 \text{ days}) = 45 \text{ kw-hr}$$

If the electricity costs 4 cents/kilowatt-hour, then the cost of running the set for a month is

$$(\$0.04/\text{kw-hr})(45 \text{ kw-hr}) = \$1.80$$

The size motor or engine a machine needs depends on the job to be done. To move a full-sized American car along a road at 60 miles/hour takes a force of about 250 pounds. That force is exerted by the reaction to the tires pushing on the ground. To determine what horsepower engine is needed to produce this force, we must calculate the work done per second. Since 60 miles/hour = 88 feet/second, the work done in 1 second in exerting the 250-pound force is

$$W = (F)(d) = (250 \text{ lb})(88 \text{ ft}) = 22,000 \text{ ft-lb}.$$
$$P = \frac{W}{t} = 22,000 \text{ ft-lb/sec} = (22,000 \text{ ft-lb/sec})\left(\frac{1 \text{ hp}}{550 \text{ ft-lb/sec}}\right) = 40 \text{ hp}$$

High rates of acceleration or higher speeds would require greater power, but a car that puts out 40 horsepower at the tires is adequate for most purposes.

## Water Power

Historically, water power provided the base from which our modern energy system has grown. But the use of water power has changed both qualitatively and quantitatively since the days of wooden waterwheels. The early waterwheels were powered by the flow of the stream or river they were placed in and rarely generated more than 10 kilowatts of power. Today concrete dams are used to back up rivers, simultaneously creating a large height difference and a method of storing the water until it is needed. Massive water turbines — capable of generating on the order of 10,000 kilowatts each — use the gravitational potential energy of the falling water to spin generators which produce electricity.

In 1970 water power produced about 15 percent of the nation's electric energy, but this percentage decreases each year. The reason is that most of the good hydroelectric sites have already been used. Our increasing demand for electricity is being met by steam-powered turbines, which are adaptable to almost any location.

The Glen Canyon Dam, completed in the mid-1960s, concentrates 710 feet of the Colorado River's gradient at this one point in Arizona. Backed up behind the dam is the twenty-seven million acre-foot Lake Powell, most of which is situated in Utah. The potential energy of the dammed water is converted to electric energy at the hydroelectric station at the base of the dam. *Photo courtesy Nancy Wakeman, University of California at Berkeley.*

Water power requires a height difference through which the water can fall. The sun will continue to shine for billions of years, evaporating water from the ocean or land and thereby "pumping" water up to high altitudes. In this sense, water power is a replenishable resource which is fully renewed each year. It is unlike the fossil fuels, which are renewed only on a scale of millions of years. But despite this eternal pumping of water by the sun, water power will also be used up within several hundred years because eventually all of our existing reservoirs will silt up. The height difference created by the dam will remain, but because the reservoirs are silted up there will be no control of the water flow. At times of peak flow there may be more water than the turbines can handle, and it will generally be impossible to match electric power production to power demand.

Although water power depends on a huge heat-engine cycle—in which the sun evaporates water which later falls on elevated land areas as precipitation—the production of energy by turbines is not limited by the second law of thermodynamics. In theory, the gravitational potential energy of the falling water could be converted to electricity with 100% efficiency. (The immense amount of energy available can be seen in the Grand Canyon: that huge gorge was made by water power as the flowing Colorado River cut its way through the earth's surface.) But in practice, friction reduces the efficiency to about 80%. The energy generated by a water turbine depends on the amount of water flowing through it and the height the water falls through.

**Example 9.** Assume there is a 100-foot drop between a reservoir and the bottom of the dam forming the reservoir. If 1000 cubic feet flow through the dam's turbines each second, what is the dam's power output?

Since 1 cubic foot of water weighs 62.4 pounds, the per-second flow is

$$(10^3 \text{ ft}^3/\text{sec}) (62.4 \text{ lb/ft}^3) = 6.24 \times 10^4 \text{ lb/sec}.$$

The potential energy available to be converted into electrical energy each second is

$$\text{P.E.} = (w)(h) = (6.24 \times 10^4 \text{ lb})(100 \text{ ft}) = 6.24 \times 10^6 \text{ ft-lb}.$$

The power is $6.24 \times 10^6$ foot-pounds/second:

$$P = (6.24 \times 10^6 \text{ ft-lb/sec})\left(\frac{1 \text{ kw}}{737 \text{ ft-lb/sec}}\right) = 8.5 \times 10^3 \text{ kw}.$$

If the turbine-generator system that converts this water power to electric power is 80% efficient, the output will be

$$P = (8.5 \times 10^3 \text{ kw})(0.8) = 6.8 \times 10^3 \text{ kw}.$$

**Niagara Falls.** Let us now look at a very untypical hydroelectric facility, Niagara Falls. The important thing about the Niagara River is that it drains the four upper Great Lakes. This ensures it of a large and fairly steady flow of water, averaging 195,000 cubic feet/second. Because it is fed by the lakes, the Niagara River flow varies far less than most rivers from season to season, and it can generate a steady amount of electricity without a large reservoir to regulate the flow.

To calculate the electric power the Falls can generate, we must know the height difference and water flow. The Falls are 167 feet high. In addition, there is a 50-foot drop at rapids above the Falls and a 98-foot drop at rapids below the Falls: a total drop of 315 feet within a few miles (see Figure 15).

To generate electric power at the Falls, water is diverted into two huge pipes whose openings are in the river $2\frac{1}{2}$ miles above the Falls. The water is carried by the pipes beneath the city of Niagara Falls to the powerhouse 4 miles below the Falls where the electricity is generated. A maximum amount of electric energy could be made by diverting all of the Falls' water into these pipes. But tourism is important to the Falls area; if all the water went through the pipes, the tourist trade—like the Falls—would dry up. Therefore the United States and Canada, which jointly generate the electric power, signed a treaty guaranteeing a flow of 100,000 cubic feet/second over the Falls in the tourist season and 50,000 cubic feet/second at other times. This leaves an average of about 130,000 cubic feet/second to be used for electric power. To calculate the average electric power this water can generate, we first calculate the weight of the water available per second.

The American side of Niagara Falls, 167 feet high and with a curving crest line of about 1000 feet, is shown here with Rainbow Bridge in the background. Ironically, to tap the power of the Falls, water must be diverted underground, away from the Falls, into enormous tunnels carrying the water to downstream power plants. The 35-mile-long Niagara River, seen in the background, drains the four Upper Great Lakes. *Photo courtesy Niagara Falls Area Chamber of Commerce.*

## Niagara Falls

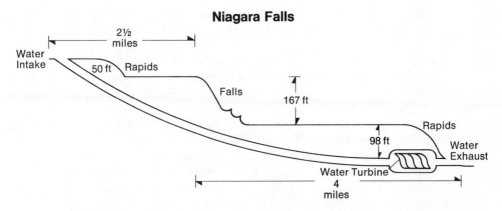

**Figure 15.** This schematic diagram shows the hydroelectric system underlying the Falls.

weight/second $= (1.3 \times 10^5 \text{ ft}^3/\text{sec})(62.4 \text{ lb/ft}^3) = 8.1 \times 10^6 \text{ lb/sec}$

Since the drop, or head, is 315 feet, the power is

$$(\text{weight/sec})(h) = (8.1 \times 10^6 \text{ lb/sec})(315 \text{ ft}) = 2.6 \times 10^9 \text{ ft-lb/sec}$$

$$= (2.6 \times 10^9 \text{ ft-lb/sec})\left(\frac{1 \text{ kw}}{737 \text{ ft-lb/sec}}\right) = 3.5 \times 10^6 \text{ kw.}$$

If the system is 80% efficient, the electric power produced will be

$$P = (3.5 \times 10^6 \text{ kw})(0.8) = 2.8 \times 10^6 \text{ kw}$$

which is in the same ballpark as the actual Niagara Power Project rating of $2.4 \times 10^6$ kilowatts.

**Conclusion.** The fact that Niagara Falls is both a "natural wonder" and an important source of energy raises questions about the way in which our technology interacts with nature. Presumably Niagara Falls attracts visitors from all over the world because of its beauty and because it is an example of untamed thundering power. Does the fact that the Falls can almost be turned on and off like a water faucet detract from its appeal? Is the real "wonder" not the Falls but the systems of valves and pipes which allow a few technicians to divert 150,000 cubic feet/second of water away from the Falls and into two underground pipes?

There can be no right answer to these questions. Those who value the Falls as spectacle will say there has been little loss. Water still cascades over the Falls in a spectacular way. In fact, diversion of some of the water has slowed the rate at which its energy was eroding the Falls and moving it upstream. This means the observation platforms and other tourist areas won't have to be moved for a long time. But those who feel that the Falls' value was as a living example of natural forces at work will judge that when man gained the ability to turn them on and off they lost a vital element.

As our environmental awareness continues to develop, this type of question will be confronted more often. Now the environmental problems are dirty air and water, cut forests, strip-mined land, and oil spills. But as society eliminates these obvious blights, we will be faced with the more difficult question of what kind of clean world we want. For example, if timber is cut down carefully, should it be allowed or must our forests be left to develop naturally? If offshore oil can be extracted without oil spills, should the drilling be allowed or does the very presence of the platforms degrade the area? The environmental movement is now more or less united against the various pollutants. But as progress is made, splits will widen between preservationists—who generally wish to leave things as they are—and conservationists—who wish to use resources and nature in ways they judge to be nondestructive.

These questions about the meaning of nature are intimately connected to questions about the meaning of our technology. For example, some will deplore the "engineering" of the Falls but say that the value of the energy generated outweighs the loss. Others will state that the very mastery of the Falls is an important and desirable achievement as an example of man's ability to control the natural world. We seem to delight in the large scale on which much of our technology operates. The builders of the Hoover Dam, for example, proudly pointed out that it contains enough concrete—4.4 million cubic yards—to build a highway lane from San Francisco to Boston.

Another aspect of Niagara Falls is how the energy generated is used. Much of the electric energy goes to manufacture aluminum, which is then turned into pots and pans, construction material, beer and soda cans, and airplane and train bodies. Other products using Niagara Falls power are liquid chlorine, which sanitizes municipal drinking water and backyard pools, and graphite, which is a lubricant and the "lead" in lead pencils. The electricity not used by industry is sent to homes, offices, hospitals, and stores. In the home it may be used to refrigerate food, power an electric can opener, or operate a television. In a hospital the electricity may provide light for a life-saving operation—or for a death-dealing blunder.

Our society has never tried to measure how important these uses are, or whether some of them should be foregone in favor of a freely running Niagara Falls or less oil consumed. The policy is to provide as much electricity and other energy as a person or institution can afford. However, environmental and supply problems may force a change in that policy. In the following chapter we will look in detail at the ways in which our society uses energy. This examination may help provide the context needed to answer the kinds of questions raised by Niagara Falls.

## Bibliography

*Source Notes*

1. *The Columbia Encyclopedia.* New York: Columbia University Press, 1950.

2. *Technology in Western Civilization,* vol. 1. Melvin Kranzberg and Carroll W. Pursell, Jr., eds. New York: Oxford University Press, 1967.

3. Ibid.

4. *Thermal Pollution—1968,* part 1. Hearings before the Subcommittee on Air and Water Pollution of the Committee on Public Works, U.S. Senate. Washington, D.C.: U.S. Government Printing Office, 1968.

5. Ibid.

6. *Technology in Western Civilization.*

7. Ibid.

8. "Impact of Waste Heat on Aquatic Ecology." Clarence A. Carlson, Jr. In *Power Generation and Environmental Change*. David A. Berkowitz and Arthur M. Squires. eds. Cambridge, Mass.: MIT Press, 1971. Page 351.

9. Alternate Technologies for Discharging Waste Heat." William H. Steigelmann. In *Power Generation and Environmental Change*. Page 394.

*Further Reading*

HENRY ADAMS. *The Education of Henry Adams*. New York: Random House, 1918. The autobiography of Henry Adams (1838–1918) has been described as the "most important autobiography" written in America. It is relevant here for the profound impact the electric dynamo and physics had on the author, as indicated in this chapter's opening quotation.

MELVIN KRANZBERG and CARROLL W. PURSELL, JR., eds. *Technology in Western Civilization,* vol. 1. New York: Oxford University Press, 1967. This book gives a history of the development of modern industrial society from earliest times to 1900.

T. A. L. PATON. *Power from Water*. London: J. Guthrie Brown, Leonard Hill, Ltd., 1961. This book gives a short history of waterwheels before moving on to modern dams.

L. T. C. ROLT. *Thomas Newcomen*. London: David and Charles Publishers, Ltd., 1963. Ostensibly a biography of Thomas Newcomen, this book is more a concise, well-illustrated history of the development of the Newcomen engine.

JOHN F. SANDFORT. *Heat Engines*. New York: Doubleday (Anchor Books), 1962. Sandfort presents an excellent blend of the history of steam engines and the development of thermodynamics.

CHARLES SINGER et al., eds. *A History of Technology,* vol. iv. London: Oxford University Press, 1958. This is the definitive study of the development of technology. Volume iv covers the industrial revolution.

ROBERT SOULARD. *A History of the Machine*. New York: Hawthorn Books, 1963. This book is filled with pictures of machinery from the time of the pyramids to the present.

## Questions and Problems

1. Complete Figure 5 by showing the entire cycle. Be sure to indicate when the valves are open and when closed.

2. Thomas Edison located his first electric power plant in New York's financial district (the Wall Street area). Can you think of a nontechnological reason for him to have chosen that site?

3. Rank in order of importance the following developments: agriculture, the wheel, pottery, the steam engine, fire, heart transplants, and television. State

explicitly the standards on which your judgments are based. Add any important developments you think have been omitted.

4. There are certain types of bacteria which feed off petroleum, producing edible food. Many oil companies are looking for methods of producing cattle feed from oil. Assume a process has been developed which transforms oil into food for humans with 80% efficiency. If the average car burns 2.5 gallons of gasoline daily, how many people could be fed each day with this energy? (Assume 140,000 BTU/gallon; 4 BTU = 1 kcal; 3000 kcal/person/day.)

5. A person's doctor tells him he must cut his food intake in order to lose weight. He loves to eat and hates to exercise, so he decides to burn the energy off by sitting in a bathtub of cold water. If he gets in a bathtub with 200 pounds of 52°F water and uses body heat to warm it to 62°F, how many kilocalories has he burned up? (4 BTU = 1 kcal)

6. An average American consumes about 3000 kilocalories of food energy daily. Assume 2700 kilocalories go for maintenance (for example, pumping the blood, maintaining body temperature) and weight gain. How many foot-pounds of work can be done with the remaining 300 kilocalories?

7. In Figure 13a, the person flexing the wire does 4000 foot-pounds of work. If the wire is immersed in $\frac{1}{2}$ pound of water, what will the temperature rise be?

8. In Figure 13b, assume a 2000-pound weight falls 50 feet. If the paddle wheel is immersed in 2 pounds of water, what will the temperature change be?

9. A college classroom of 1000 square feet is lighted by eighty 40-watt fluorescent light bulbs.
   a. How many kilowatt-hours of electricity are consumed in a typical 10-hour day?
   b. If that electricity is generated in a 40% efficient coal-burning power plant, how much coal is consumed in a day to light the room? (Assume $10^4$ BTU per pound of coal, and that 1 kw-hr = 3400 BTU.)

10. Calculate from bills or by some other means the amount of electricity consumed in your home in a year. Assume the electricity is generated by a 40% efficient power plant and calculate the amount of coal ($10^4$ BTU/lb) consumed yearly.

11. An electric motor is to be used to lift a 2000-pound weight at 10 feet/second. What size motor is needed? Give the answer in kilowatts and horsepower.

12. How fast can a 4-horsepower motor raise a 100-pound weight?

13. The text states that a million-kilowatt electric power plant generates enough power to lift a 100-ton railroad freight car straight up at a speed of more than 2000 miles/hour. Check this statement.

14. A turbine at the Bonneville Dam on the Columbia River in Washington uses 13,600 cubic feet/second of water falling through a 50-foot drop. If the turbine-generator system is 80% efficient, what is the turbine's maximum power output?

15. Grand Coulee Dam, also on the Columbia River, has a present power capacity of 2 million kilowatts. To produce the same power in a 40% efficient steam electric plant, how many pounds of 10,000-BTU-per-pound coal would have to be burned each second? (The amount of BTU a plant needs to produce 1 kilowatt-hour is called the plant's heat rate.)

16. How much water must flow each second through an 80% efficient turbine having a 250-foot drop to power a 10-car subway train drawing 6000 kilowatts?

17. For water from the Colorado River to reach Los Angeles via the Colorado Aqueduct, it must be pumped 1600 feet above the river's elevation.
    a. Calculate how many kilowatt-hours it takes to pump one person's daily supply of water (150 gallons or 20 cubic feet) to Los Angeles. (1 ft³ = 62.4 lb)
    b. The electricity to pump the water is generated by the Hoover Dam. How many cubic feet of water must flow through the dam to generate the electricity? Assume a 600-foot drop and 80% efficiency. Is there any relation between the dam's effective height of 480 feet (80% of 600 feet), the 1600 feet the water must be raised, and the water needed to flow through the dam?

18. Average yearly runoff in the United States is 9 inches, and the average altitude of the United States is 1000 feet above sea level. Assume 80% of the potential energy relative to sea level could be squeezed out of this runoff water in the course of a year.
    a. How many kilowatt-hours would be generated? U.S. land area is $3.6 \times 10^6$ square miles.
    b. What would be the average power output in kilowatts? (1 yr $= 3.2 \times 10^7$ sec $= 8760$ hr)
    c. Compare your answers with the following information. The Federal Power Commission in 1968 estimated that the United States has $51 \times 10^6$ kilowatts of developed hydroelectric power and $130 \times 10^6$ kilowatts of undeveloped power. In 1968, the hydroelectric power produced $222 \times 10^9$ kilowatt-hours of electricity. Are your results of the same order of magnitude? Are the differences in the expected direction?

19. In this chapter we oversimplified by saying that the modern steam turbine's 40% efficiency results from the second law of thermodynamics. On the basis of the boiler and condenser temperatures, the maximum theoretical efficiency is 53%. But the turbine can achieve only 89% of that maximum. Losses also occur in the furnace, which extracts 88% of the fuel's chemical energy (the rest goes up the smokestack as hot gases, water vapor, and unburned fuel), and in the generator, which converts 99% of the input mechanical energy to electricity. Show that this works out to the 40% efficiency cited.

20. Assume there is a million-kilowatt plant operating at 40% efficiency with 20% of the input heat going up the smokestack and 40% being discharged through the condenser.
    a. Calculate how much water (in pounds and in gallons) flows through the condenser per second and per hour if the temperature rise is 20°F. (1 gallon = 8.3 pounds)

b. If the water is pumped halfway to the top of a 400-foot-high cooling tower, how much work is done per second and per hour?

c. What percent of the plant's electric power goes into pumping water up the tower?

21. A hydroelectric dam with a 400-foot height drop, or head, generates 10,000 kilowatts of power.

a. Calculate how many pounds of water it uses per second if the efficiency is 75%.

b. Compare that water use with the cooling water needed by a 10,000-kilowatt fossil-fuel plant which operates at 40% efficiency. Assume 70% of the waste heat is exhausted through the condenser; the rest goes out through the stack. Assume a 15°F temperature rise for the cooling water. (1 kw-hr = 3400 BTU)

*At the beginning of this foreword I stated that this book has a purpose. That purpose is to arouse the reader to an awareness of technological necessity and what it means. It is a call to the sleeper to awake.*

JACQUES ELLUL*

# 9 Energy use in the United States

In the last chapter we took a narrow view of energy, examining the use of steam and water power to generate electric energy. Hopefully we established a physical understanding of energy that will now permit us to create a statistical and physical picture of how energy is used in the United States. In following chapters we shall look at the environmental and resource problems that go with this use.

## Growth and More Growth

As Figure 1 shows, the past, present, and projected future course of U.S. energy use is growth. In 1900 we used 10 quadrillion (a quadrillion is $10^{15}$) BTU of energy, which corresponds to a trillion ($10^{12}$) pounds of coal. By 1970 we were using almost 70 quadrillion BTU, or the equivalent of 7 trillion pounds of coal. During this time population increased by less than a factor of 3, from 76 million to 203 million.

The United States contains approximately 6 percent of the world's population and consumes 35 percent of

* From Ellul's book *The Technological Society* (New York: A. A. Knopf, 1970).

254

### Twentieth-Century Energy Use in the United States

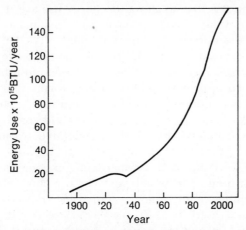

**Figure 1.** Past and projected future energy use are plotted here for the twentieth century. Starting about 1960, the yearly rate of growth accelerated from 3% to over 4%.

### Per-person Income versus Per-person Energy Consumption

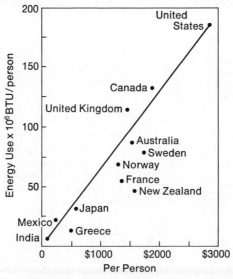

**Figure 2.** This graph shows a plot of per-person energy use versus per-person income. Although there is a clear relation between energy use and wealth, there is also wide variation among many nations having the same income but very different energy consumption. The chart is based on 1961 data but the pattern shown remains true.

the energy used worldwide each year. The possible significance of this consumption is shown in Figure 2, where per-person energy use is plotted against per-person income for several nations. It is clear that the prosperous nations use a great deal more energy than poor nations. A straight line has been drawn connecting India and the United States to illustrate one interpretation — that wealth and energy use are directly related. But several of the developed nations have yearly per-person incomes of about \$1500 and yet use different amounts of energy. The United Kingdom uses roughly three times as much energy per person as New Zealand but has a lower per-person income. So Figure 2 is open to other interpretations.

Energy is used in primary and secondary forms. The primary category includes the consumption of gasoline by autos, of natural gas by stoves, hot-water heaters, and furnaces, and of oil and coal by factories. Secondary use refers to electricity which is generated by an electric utility in a central power plant for transmission to the ultimate user. As shown in Figure 3, electricity use has been increasing exponentially, with the number of kilowatt-hours consumed per year doubling each decade.[1] If the doubling continues, eight times as much electricity will be used in the year 2000 as was used in 1970. As a result of this rapid growth, an increasing amount of our total energy goes to generate electricity.

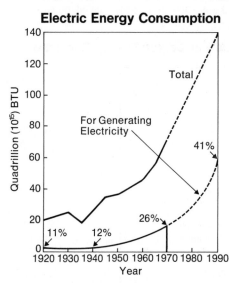

**Figure 3.** The upper line is total energy used and the lower line is the amount used to make electricity. The United States is using increasing percentages of its energy to produce electricity.

**Fuel Use.** So far we have looked at the use of BTU or kilowatt-hours without reference to the fuels from which they are obtained. Figure 4[2] shows the fuel sources for 1971, projected through to 1990. The greatest growth is expected in nuclear energy, while petroleum and natural gas use are expected to shrink in percentage terms although their use in absolute terms will increase. None of the projections assume any sizeable contributions from such sources as geothermal or solar energy. They also assume that energy growth will continue in the future as it has in the past. Such projections have been correct for most of this century. But environmental and resource problems indicate that the 1970s may be a very different decade.

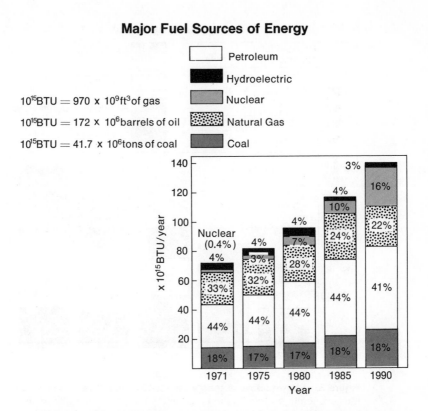

**Figure 4.** This graph shows U.S. energy use by source. The two cleanest energy sources — hydroelectric power and natural gas — are expected to shrink in the future.

**Energy-use Categories.** Energy production is much easier to categorize than energy use. Figure 5[3] classifies energy use according to BTU consumption in four economic sectors: residential/commercial (mainly homes and offices), industry, electric utilities, and transportation. The graph shows the predicted increasing amount of energy we will consume as electricity. Since utilities produce energy for use by the three remaining sectors, Figure 5 also shows the utility energy reassigned to them. Transportation remains unchanged because at present little of its energy is electricity and it is assumed that this situation will continue into the future. Increased use of rail transit or widespread adoption of the electric car would throw these projections off.

Figure 6 fills out the numbers in Figure 5 by showing some of the ways the United States used energy in 1973. Heating, cooling, and providing hot water are the major ways in which homes and offices consume energy. Notice that 5.5 percent of our fuels are not used for energy. Instead, the petrochemical industry uses the oil and gas as raw materials for the manufacture of plastics, synthetic fibers, chemicals, and drugs.

## Energy Use by Sector

|  | Residential/Commercial | Industry |
|---|---|---|
| 1971 | 57% | 43% |
| 1975 | 58% | 42% |
| 1980 | 59% | 41% |
| 1985 | 55% | 45% |
| 1990 | 53% | 47% |

- Electric Utilities
- Industry
- Residential/Commercial
- Transportation

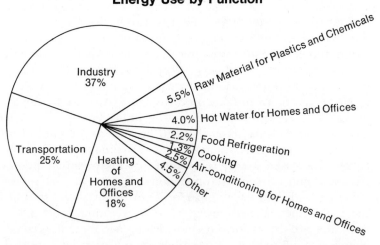

**Figure 5.** Shown above is energy use for 1971 and projected to 1990 for four economic sectors. In the upper left corner, the electricity produced by the utilities is distributed to the residential/commercial and industrial sectors. In 1971, 57% of all electricity went to the residential/commercial sector and 43% to industry.

## Energy Use by Function

**Figure 6.** This diagram shows a more detailed breakdown of energy use by function for 1973. Space heating uses the most energy in the home and office and therefore presents the greatest opportunity for conservation.

The three end-use categories listed in Figure 5 – home/office, industry, and transportation – are convenient categories. They are standard economic groups, and the energy-use figures are usually obtained by looking at the amount of money different sectors of the economy spend on energy. However, the classifications sometimes appear a bit arbitrary. The gasoline used in the family car is assigned to transportation rather than to the home while the energy used to make the car is assigned to industry, as is the energy used to extract crude oil from a well and refine it into gasoline. Similarly, the electricity used by running a TV in the home goes to the residential sector but the energy used to make the television goes to industry. The energy consumed by a freight train carrying iron ore to a steel mill is assigned to the transportation sector, but the energy then used to process the ore into steel is assigned to industry, even if the steel is fabricated into a railroad locomotive. Nevertheless, these three categories – home, industry, transportation – provide convenient breakdowns of energy use, and thus it is these three categories that we will use to study energy use in the United States.

## Energy Use in the Home

Residential energy use has been growing rapidly because of three trends: an increasing number of households, the steady introduction of new electricity-using appliances such as air-conditioners and color television sets, and the growing replacement of gas- or oil-fueled hot-water heaters, clothes dryers, and home furnaces by electric-powered devices.

**Appliances.** Most electric appliances have similar histories. When first introduced, the radio, refrigerator, air-conditioner, and dishwasher were luxuries which few people could afford. With time, prices dropped and increasing numbers of people bought them. Within a few years they ceased being curiosities or luxuries and became necessities which everyone had. In business jargon, the market for the various appliances became saturated.

Theoretically electricity growth should stop once everyone has a new device. But the pattern has been that as one device saturated, a new one would come onto the market. At present, color television is beginning to saturate America's households, along with air-conditioners and dishwashers. Before that it was black and white television sets, refrigerators, and – way back – radios. And existing appliances may use even more energy as improved models come onto the market. Color television sets consume about 60 percent more electricity per hour of use than do black and white sets. Frost-free refrigerators use 67 percent[4] more electric energy than ordinary refrigerators of the same size. A family will often replace their old refrigerator with a larger model having the frost-free option, resulting perhaps in a doubling of the electric energy used for refrigeration.

The air-conditioner is a relatively new appliance which has caused important changes in our pattern of electricity use. Formerly, periods of peak power demand occurred in the winter, when the days are short and people spend most of their time indoors. Summers—with long daylight hours and decreased need for lighting—were times of low energy use. But as a result of air-conditioning, hot summer days are the times of peak power use and the associated brownouts and blackouts. A climbing thermometer means a climbing demand for electricity as air-conditioners work to keep apartments, houses, and offices cool.

**Electricity into Heat.** Another trend which has added to residential demand is the use of electricity to generate heat. Gas stoves are replaced by electric ranges, gas clothes dryers by electric dryers, and gas- or oil-fueled furnaces by electric heat. This trend is separate from the use of televisions or air-conditioners because the electric-heat devices perform the same function as the original fuel-powered device. The shift toward electric devices is a result of their greater consumer appeal. In most cases, an electric appliance is initially cheaper, as in the case of electric heat for homes. An electric heating system requires no more than a few baseboard units connected to the power box. In addition to the low initial cost, electric heat gives great flexibility since the temperature of each room can be adjusted as easily as lights are turned on and off. And the electricity is generated in a central, often distant, power plant so no fuel is burned or dirt produced in the home.

By comparison, an oil- or gas-fueled heating system is complex. The simple electric power box is replaced by a furnace—and in the case of oil, there is in addition a storage tank. The baseboard units containing heating wires are replaced by a system of steam or hot-water pipes leading to radiators or hot-water units in each room. To control the temperature on a room-by-room basis, the heating units must be opened or closed one by one. The initial cost of an oil- or gas-heat unit is higher than the initial cost of an electric-heat unit and the oil or gas heat is neither as clean nor as flexible.

But electric heat is so expensive to operate that the initial cost advantage is quickly burned up. This economic fact can be partly traced to the second law of thermodynamics. When oil or gas is burned in a home furnace, up to 80 percent[5] of the fuel's energy is used to heat the house, with the rest going out the flue as hot gases or unburned fuel. In comparison, the most efficient electric power plants convert only 40 percent of their energy content into electricity. By the time the electricity has been transmitted to the home, another 5 percent or so has been lost and the conversion efficiency is down to 35 percent. So even though the resistance wires in the baseboard units convert the electricity to heat with 100 percent efficiency, no more than 35 percent of the fuel's energy is available to heat the house. The same rule holds for all devices which convert electric energy into heat:

electric ranges, dryers, and toasters all use more energy than would gas units. The cost of electric-generated heat is also pushed up by the fact that it costs more to transport energy as electricity than as gas.

**Matching Power Demand to Load.** Thus far, we have looked at electric energy use independent of the power plant which produces it. That is easy to do since the power plant and its mountains of coal or oil or gas storage tanks are usually well out of sight. But anyone who uses electricity is in constant touch with the plant. When you turn on an appliance, you are demanding energy from the plant. That demand is sensed by the spinning turbine — which slows down ever so slightly. Speed sensors — like Watt's fly-ball governor — detect this slowing and feed a bit more coal to the furnace, increasing the flow of steam through the turbine and moving its speed back to normal. Turning off an appliance slightly decreases the turbine's load and causes it to speed up, reducing the fuel fed to the furnace. At any given moment, the power generated by the turbine must be precisely equal to the demand being put on it.

A coal pile, smokestack, cooling tower, and power grid are outlined in relief against an overcast sky over Ohio's Muskingum River. An additional power-generating unit can be seen under construction to the right of the smokestack. *Photo courtesy American Electric Power Company.*

Occasionally this balance is threatened. Several years ago the performer Tiny Tim married a Miss Vicki on the Johnny Carson Show at 11:30 P.M., eastern standard time. At that hour, New York City's turbines are loafing along since businesses are closed and many people are asleep. Suddenly technicians at Consolidated Edison, the local utility, noted that power demand was climbing swiftly as millions of New Yorkers turned on their television sets to watch the wedding. However, turbines cannot be turned on and off like water faucets, and Con Edison was just barely able to produce the steam to meet the demand. If they had been unable to meet the demand, they would have had to shut the system down since a turbine-generator system cannot turn at a low rate without suffering serious damage. When all those people turned on their television sets, it was as if they were collectively reaching out and putting their hands on the huge spinning turbines. The turbines had to either generate enough power to resist that drag or fold.

**The Northeast Power Blackout.** A large-scale shutdown took place in 1965 when a huge power failure blacked out the Northeast United States and Canada, including the cities of Boston, Philadelphia, New York, Ottawa, and Montreal. The problem started as a failure in a transmission line carrying power out of Niagara Falls. That failure resonated throughout the entire interconnected system causing utilities throughout the Northeast to fold. Some shut down because without the electricity flowing in via the power grids from outside utilities they were unable to meet local demand for power. So they had to shut down their turbines. Others suddenly found their turbines disconnected from their loads; these had to be shut down to keep them from speeding up and being damaged.

The shutdown occurred about 5 P.M. on a weekday, trapping people in elevators, underground in subways, on streets without traffic signals, and on operating tables. And it was not until the following morning that the Northeast had power again. The situation can be compared to a man carrying a 100-pound pack: he is okay as long as he keeps walking, but should he fall it is difficult to get up. It is the same with the turbine. Light switches, refrigerators, elevators, street lights, and water pumps were switched on and ready to go all through the blackout. Bringing the entire load on line from a standing start was impossible so the utilities had to spend hours disconnecting neighborhoods from the power system since people did not (or could not) respond to radio appeals to disconnect all their appliances. Once the turbines were going, these areas and their loads were connected back to the system one by one.

Ironically, the utilities that crashed were all hooked together via power grids to provide greater dependability, the idea being that if one utility is short of power it can call on others in the local pool for help. Also, power demand peaks at different times in different places, reducing the total capacity needed by any one utility. Usually the system works. But in this instance it failed catastrophically and unpredictably. Before the blackout occurred no one had predicted that such an event was even a remote possibility.

The blackout and the chronic electric-power shortages that developed in some areas in the late 1960s have resulted in changes in the system. The interconnections are now more dependable and better understood. Many utilities can automatically shed a load, disconnecting entire neighborhoods from the system to reduce power demand and avoid a catastrophic shut-down. And even before that needs to be done, they can reduce system voltage, which results in appliances using less energy. But utilities still do not have the flexibility of the telephone system—which simply denies users access to the system (no dial tone) until circuits are available.

Blackouts are spectacular, but utilities face a more chronic load problem. As we saw with water and transportation, a system is most efficient when it is run at peak capacity around the clock. But electric utilities don't come close to operating at peak output. Power demand varies with the time of the day and with the season. Utilities therefore encourage power-use patterns that will smooth out their load. They advertise that people should "light a light and stop a thief" to encourage nighttime use of electricity. In earlier years they encouraged use of air-conditioners since peak power use occurred in the winter. When summer demand for power surged ahead of winter use, they began encouraging electric heat. Despite these efforts, most utilities have the same kind of rush-hour problems as roads, subways, and water systems. Their turbines and transmission systems are called on to perform at peak capacity for one hot afternoon in August and the rest of the time only part of the capacity is used.

**Powering Energy Growth.** We have been discussing the dynamics of electric energy use—the way in which demand for energy surges and lapses. We now return to a look at the total amount of energy used, independent of the rate at which it is consumed. Statistically, the average household in 1970 used 7000 kilowatt-hours of electricity.[6] An additional 130 million BTU of energy was used per household that year for space heating, cooking, and hot water. If the average home was all electric, it used a total of 33,000 kilowatt-hours of electricity in 1970. An all-electric home uses electricity to cook, heat water, and heat the home as well as to power all the usual electric appliances.

To indicate what this energy buys, Table 1 shows the amount of electricity or the number of BTU some typical appliances use per year. A 15-cubic-foot refrigerator in an average year would use 1137 kilowatt-hours. If electricity costs $0.04/kilowatt-hour, it would cost $45.48 to run the refrigerator for a year. If the refrigerator is frost free, it would use 1897 kilowatt-hours, and cost $75.88 to run. Some appliances interact with each other, causing additional energy to be used. For example, a dishwasher uses 363 kilowatt-hours of electricity per year to run its pumps.

**Yearly Energy Use by Appliance**

| Appliance | Kilowatt-hours | Resource BTU ($\times 10^7$) |
|---|---|---|
| Space Heat (oil or natural gas) | | 9.09 |
| Space Heat (electric) | 15,000 | 15.30 |
| Gas Range | | 1.06 |
| Electric Range (12,207 w) | 1175 | 1.20 |
| Gas Hot Water | | 2.72 |
| Electric Hot Water (2475 w) | 4661 | 4.75 |
| Dishwasher (1200 w) | | |
|    Direct Power | 363 | 0.37 |
|    Extra Hot Water (gas) | | 0.97 |
|    Extra Hot Water (electric) | 1629 | 1.66 |
| 15 ft³ Refrigerator-freezer (341 w) | 1137 | 1.16 |
|    with Frost-free Option (440 w) | 1897 | 1.91 |
| 12 ft³ Refrigerator (241 w) | 728 | 0.74 |
| B & W TV (237 w) | 362 | 0.37 |
| Color TV (332 w) | 502 | 0.51 |
| Room Air-conditioner (1566 w) | 1389 | 1.43 |
| Central Air-conditioning | 3350 | 3.42 |
| Lighting | 600 | 0.61 |

SOURCE: "Power Consumption and Human Welfare," Barry Commoner (Philadelphia: American Association for the Advancement of Science, 29 December 1971).

**Table 1.** Some typical appliances and the energy they use in a year in an average U.S. household are given here. If the appliance is electrical, the energy used is given both in kilowatt-hours and in resource BTU—the amount of energy used at the power plant to generate the electricity. If the appliance is powered by fuel burned in the home, the fuel's energy is listed under resource BTU.

This replaces the few hundred kilocalories of food energy a human dishwasher would use. But the automatic dishwasher also uses 13.5 gallons of hot water per load of dishes, instead of the estimated 3 gallons hand washing takes. In a year, therefore, the dishwasher requires almost 10 million extra BTU of heat to make the additional hot water. If the hot water is supplied by an electric hot-water heater rather than a gas or oil heater, the energy consumed to make the hot water goes to 17 million extra BTU.

This pattern is repeated over and over again. It appears there is no limit to the amount of energy we can use, just as we seemingly have an insatiable demand for transportation. As long as the cost of energy remained low, its use was bound to expand. For one thing, low cost encouraged people to skimp on thermal insulation of homes and refrigerators and on the efficiency of air-conditioners. On a larger scale, cheap energy allowed apartment complexes to be built close together and without adequate natural ventilation. The apartments were then air-conditioned to make them livable in hot weather. On balance, such buildings are cheap to construct because they pack more units to an acre, permit lower ceilings, smaller windows, and less insulation. But because of energy demands, these buildings are expensive to maintain and run.

The market for new energy-using luxuries in the home is probably infinite. In addition to such obvious things as the totally air-conditioned, humidified, filtered home, it would be nice to have electric-heating coils buried in the driveway and sidewalk to melt snow. After all, we have already replaced the shovel with the energy-consuming, but convenient, snow blower. Energy use is especially likely to increase in the recreational area. Formerly, ice-skating was a winter sport which used naturally frozen ponds and lakes. But most ponds and lakes in urban areas are now gone, and ice-skating has moved indoors. The ice is made by refrigeration — which takes energy — and some of the rinks stay open all year around. The natural environment has been replaced by a predictable, artificial environment which allows us to skate when and where we wish. Tennis — once a summer sport — has followed a similar trend, moving indoors to allow year-round play. The courts are heated in the winter and air-conditioned in the summer. Skiing, of course, early went this general route with the adoption of snow-making machinery which uses a fair amount of energy.

This photo shows the enclosed, air-conditioned, plastic-domed Astrodome in Houston, Texas. Inside the twenty-story-high stadium are three and one-half acres of playing field and 46,000 seats. The stadium lights alone consume enough power to light a town of 9000 people. *Photo courtesy Houston Astrodome.*

Overall, skiing is a large energy user since ski slopes are usually far from urban areas, which encourages long-distance travel on weekends. Their separation from urban areas is not an accident. Hills close to cities quickly become covered with homes.

If urbanization and generous energy use continue, we can expect a growing movement of recreation indoors. Covered sports arenas such as the Houston Astrodome, with its air-conditioned, all-weather capability, will be the rule rather than the exception. Pools and ice-skating rinks are increasingly found in high-rise buildings. Perhaps the amusement park and county fair of the future will be an immense high-rise containing health clubs and gymnasiums, swimming pools, ice-skating rinks, tennis courts, football fields, and "nature" trails.

**Conserving Residential Energy.** The point of such futurism is not to predict the year 2000 but to project existing trends and show the logic and momentum of the past. Such projections assume low energy costs and ignore environmental problems such as strip mining and air pollution. But if price rises and environmental concern continue, then there will be pressure to reduce energy use. In theory this can be done by changes in life-style or by doing more with less. Most likely we will first attempt to keep our life-style intact by using energy more efficiently. To see what kinds of savings are possible, Table 2 shows the energy used to fuel various household functions in 1960 and 1968 and lists the growth rate between those years. Space and water heating are the big energy users, but it is

**Energy Use in the Home, 1960 and 1968**

| | Use ($\times 10^{12}$ BTU) | | Yearly Growth Rate | Percent of Total Energy Use | |
|---|---|---|---|---|---|
| | 1960 | 1968 | | 1960 | 1968 |
| Space Heating | 4848 | 6675 | 4.1 | 11.3 | 11.0 |
| Water Heating | 1159 | 1736 | 5.2 | 2.7 | 2.9 |
| Cooking | 556 | 637 | 1.7 | 1.3 | 1.1 |
| Clothes Drying | 93 | 208 | 10.6 | 0.2 | 0.3 |
| Refrigeration | 369 | 692 | 8.2 | 0.9 | 1.1 |
| Air-conditioning | 134 | 427 | 15.6 | 0.3 | 0.7 |
| Other | 809 | 1241 | 5.5 | 1.9 | 2.1 |
| Total | 7968 | 11,616 | 4.8 (average) | 18.6 | 19.2 |

Source: *The Potential for Energy Conservation,* Executive Office of the President, Office of Emergency Preparedness (Washington, D.C.: U.S. Government Printing Office, 1972).

**Table 2.** Shown above is the residential use of energy in 1960 and 1968, the growth rate between those two years, and the percent of all energy use represented by the various categories.

**Possible Yearly Energy Savings by 1980**

| | Use (× 10¹² BTU/yr) | Savings (× 10¹² BTU/yr) | Percent Saved | Percent Saved of Total National Energy Use |
|---|---|---|---|---|
| Space Heating | 8600 | 1100 | 13 | 1.1 |
| Cooling — Better Insulation / Better equipment | 2400 | 1100 / 200 | 54 | 1.3 |
| Water Heating | 3200 | 250 | 8 | 0.3 |
| Cooking | 780 | 58 | 7 | 0.05 |
| Refrigeration | 500 | 100 | 20 | 0.1 |
| Other (lights, etc.) | 2000 | 500 | 25 | 0.6 |
| Total | 17,480 | 3308 | 19 | 3.45 |

SOURCE: *The Potential for Energy Conservation.*

**Table 3.** This chart shows possible energy savings in the residential sector based on technological improvements rather than changes in consumption or life-style. The final column is calculated assuming total energy consumption of 96 × 10¹⁵ BTU in 1980.

air-conditioning and refrigeration that are growing most rapidly. Table 3 shows the amount of energy homes will be using by 1980 if anticipated growth occurs and the savings possible if various conservation steps are taken. Energy conservation could reduce residential use 19 percent below the projections for 1980, but total use will still be larger than at present.

The overall 19 percent savings are based on a series of conservation steps outlined in a federal government report titled *The Potential for Energy Conservation.* The report suggests such things as spark-ignition devices on stoves and gas dryers to eliminate continuous-burning pilot lights, better wall insulation, lower winter, and higher summer, home and office temperatures, better methods for keeping air-conditioner and refrigerator condenser coils clean, and ways for using the exhaust heat from hot-water heaters to help warm the house. The report also stresses more efficient appliance design. At present, some 6000-BTU-per-hour air-conditioners consume as much electricity as efficient 12,000-BTU-per-hour units. Also helpful would be the invention of a fluorescent light bulb that could fit an incandescent, or mazda, fixture. Other hints are to keep fireplace dampers closed to prevent heat loss, to use light colors on the roof and exterior walls of a home to aid in cooling, and to use pots that fit tightly over stove burners.

## Transportation and Energy Use

Significant energy savings are also possible in transportation. This is a critical area because one-quarter of all U.S. energy goes to transportation in the form of petroleum (gasoline, diesel fuel, and jet-plane fuel), which is in short supply. Figure 5 shows that the percentage of transportation's share of energy is projected to decline slightly in the future, but in absolute terms its consumption will increase from 8.5 million barrels per day in 1971 to 15 million barrels per day in 1990. The large amount of transportation energy is due to factors covered in Chapter 7—the dispersion of people, stores, offices, and industry to suburbs which can only be served by the auto and truck. This has been accompanied by a decline in railroad, subway, and bus transit, and the growth of air travel for movement between cities. As we saw in Chapter 7, the auto, truck, and plane are less efficient energy users than rail and water transportation.

The auto, for example, grew less and less efficient through the 1960s and early 1970s (see Table 4). In part this was because autos have been getting heavier: a 2500-pound vehicle gets twice as many miles to the gallon[7] as a 5000-pound vehicle. And increasingly autos are built with various accessories which not only increase their weight but may directly consume extra fuel. A car with an automatic transmission uses 5 to 6 percent more gasoline than a car with a standard shift.[8] An auto air-conditioner in use will drop gas mileage by 10 to 20 percent. According to the U.S. Environmental Protection Agency, the various pollution-control devices in use by 1973 imposed an additional 7 percent fuel penalty, bringing the goal of clean air into conflict with energy conservation.

#### Motor-vehicle Gasoline Efficiency (miles/gallon)

|        | 1940  | 1945  | 1950  | 1960  | 1968  | 1969  | 1970  | 1971  |
|--------|-------|-------|-------|-------|-------|-------|-------|-------|
| Autos  | 15.29 | 15.04 | 14.95 | 14.28 | 13.91 | 13.75 | 13.58 | 13.73 |
| Buses  | 6.09  | 5.48  | 5.57  | 5.26  | 5.33  | 5.32  | 5.34  | 5.38  |
| Trucks | 9.68  | 9.09  | 8.57  | 7.96  | 8.37  | 8.36  | 8.39  | 8.38  |

SOURCE: *Statistical Abstract of the United States, 1971* (Washington, D.C.: U.S. Government Printing Office).

**Table 4.** The above data show a long-term decline in fuel-use efficiency by all types of motor vehicles. In the case of autos, this decline is aggravated by an accompanying decrease in passenger occupancy.

Another area of concern is speed. In cities and many suburbs, traffic is chronically congested, causing low speeds and stop-and-go driving. This causes low gasoline mileage and large amounts of air pollution. At the other end of the speed spectrum, rural interstate highways allow more and more driving at speeds above 50 miles/hour, which also consumes large amounts of gasoline. High speeds hurt because air and chassis resistance increase rapidly with speed[9] (see Figure 7). For this reason, national highway speeds were decreased in the fall of 1973 when the United States first encountered severe fuel shortages.

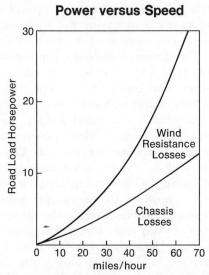

**Figure 7.** Horsepower needs, as measured at the tires, increase rapidly as speed increases. This means high gasoline consumption at high speeds.

**Conserving Transportation Energy.** One painless approach to gasoline conservation requires convincing large numbers of drivers to change their driving habits. Even moderately fast stops and starts waste gasoline. Some professional drivers in car economy runs drive barefoot, and to encourage gentle driving, may pretend there is an egg between their foot and the gas pedal. Going around curves quickly sloshes gas out of the carburetor, and it is better to keep a steady foot on the gas pedal and let the speed drop than to climb a hill at a constant speed. Gas mileage can also be improved by keeping the car tuned and tires inflated to a proper pressure. It is estimated that radial tires improve gas mileage 10 percent because they are stiff and reduce rolling friction. A very helpful device would be a dynamic gas meter, which would indicate on a continuous basis the rate at which gasoline was being used. That way a driver would quickly be able to eliminate wasteful habits.

It is possible that changes in auto design will produce energy savings, but the battery-powered, or electric, car—which is the one most frequently suggested—would not result in significant energy savings. That is because the batteries must be charged with electricity generated in a power plant. These plants at best have only 40 percent efficiency and when transmission and battery-charging losses are taken into account, the electric car is about 20 percent efficient,[10] a figure similar to that for the internal combustion engine. But the electric car would conserve petroleum if the electricity was generated from coal or nuclear energy. The greatest handicap is the electric car's limited range. A pound of gasoline has roughly 100 times more energy than a pound of lead storage batteries, and gasoline is about ten times more concentrated an energy source than even exotic batteries. This means the electric car goes a much shorter distance between refueling than a gasoline-powered car.

Possible long-term solutions are of the type discussed earlier in the chapter on transportation. There we were concerned with auto-caused land-use patterns, noise, air pollution, physical danger, and the esthetic impact of paving over large areas of land. Here we are concerned with excessive energy use, but the problems are related. The tremendous scale and speed of highway and air travel require large amounts of space and huge expenditures of energy. The burning of this energy causes noise, pollution, and general annoyance for all except — possibly — the users. So the solution to both sets of problems lies in the same direction.

The possibilities of even short-range changes in transportation patterns were revealed in late 1973 when gasoline use fell roughly 20 percent in response to an Arab oil embargo and a shortage of U.S. oil-refining capacity. The lower speeds and curtailed travel also resulted in a pronounced reduction in highway deaths. In air travel, consolidation of flights to save fuel resulted in more people per plane with a resultant drop in fuel use.

Less driving and increased use of smaller cars can have large indirect effects. Small cars require less material, which means less energy spent in mining, shipping, and fabricating metals and other substances. The material reduction could prove especially important since the United States is dependent on foreign countries for many metals important to U.S. industry. The reduction in fuel use also has secondary fuel effects. It takes energy to produce energy. Exploration for oil deposits, construction of tankers and pipelines to bring that oil to refineries, construction and operation of refineries, and the storage and distribution of the refined product all use material and energy. So a reduction in transportation energy use reverberates throughout society. However, it is much easier to predict the physical results of such reductions than the economic and social results. The economy of the United States for the last three decades has been one of continuing growth. Much of that growth has been in the form of more and larger cars using more fuel. We have no experience with a situation where this growth stalled or where contraction occurred over a significant period of time.

## Industry and Energy

Until now we have looked only at energy operating costs. We have added up such things as the energy needed to run a car, power a television and dishwasher, and heat a home. But there is a second major aspect to energy use: the energy needed to produce an object. We call this the energy capital cost. To construct a car, energy is needed to mine and process the iron and copper, to machine and form the refined metal, to manufacture and process the plastic dashboards and steering wheels, and to assemble the various parts into the complete car. Any consumer product—from a beer can to a yacht—has energy costs built into it. To produce a gallon of home heating oil requires the expenditure of energy at the oil well, pipeline, and refinery. This energy use—like the energy consumed to make the car, television, or beer can—is assigned to the industrial sector while the operating costs (gasoline for the car, electricity for the refrigerator to cool the beer) are assigned to the transportation or commercial/residential sectors.

Table 5 looks at energy consumption in the industrial sector. The major industrial uses of energy are the production of metals (iron, aluminum, copper, and so on) from their ores, the manufacture of chemicals and chemical products, the refining of crude oil into gasoline, heating oil, and other fuels, and the production of food, paper, cement, glass, and similar products. Most industrial energy is consumed in converting raw material such as iron ore or wood into intermediate material such as steel or paper. The subsequent conversion of the steel or paper into a car or magazine takes comparatively little energy. Paper manufacturers use much more energy than do printing firms, and steel makers use more energy than auto companies.

**Energy Consumption in the Industrial Sector, 1971**

|  | $\times 10^{15}$ *BTU/yr* | *Percent of Industrial Energy Use* |
|---|---|---|
| Primary Metal Production | 4.70 | 24.0 |
| Chemical-Petrochemical Sector | 3.70 | 18.0 |
| Petroleum Refining | 2.20 | 11.0 |
| Highway and Building Materials | 2.00 | 10.0 |
| Cement | 0.86 | 4.3 |
| Glass | 0.32 | 1.6 |
| Concrete | 0.30 | 1.5 |
| Clay | 0.28 | 1.4 |
| Other | 0.24 | 1.2 |
| Paper | 1.80 | 9.0 |
| Food | 1.60 | 8.0 |
| Subtotal | 16.00 | 80.0 |
| All Other Industries | 4.00 | 20.0 |
| Total | 20.00 | 100.0 |

Source: *The Potential for Energy Conservation.*

**Table 5.** The industries above are ranked according to consumption. The energy figures do not include electricity use.

Agriculture and Energy. One of the most dramatic examples of industrial energy use is provided by agriculture. Table 5 shows that food production consumes 8 percent of our fossil-fuel energy (other studies suggest 12 percent[11] to 13 percent[12]) although theoretically it could require none since the sun powers the growth of plants. The increasing use of fossil-fuel energy on the farm is at the heart of the large population shift from country to city. When the nation was young, almost everyone was involved with food production. But as agriculture became mechanized — first with horse-drawn mechanical seeders and reapers and then with tractor-drawn implements — fewer people were needed to raise food. This trend was accelerated by insecticides, fertilizers, irrigation projects, scientific breeding of plants and animals, and improved soil-conservation practices. As a result, today only 2 out of each 100 Americans[13] are farm workers; yet these farmers feed themselves, the rest of America, and a significant number of people abroad.

This great productivity is often referred to as a miracle but it has its origin in some hard, though not obvious, facts. First, while only 2 percent of all Americans work on farms, several times that many are engaged in food production. These "others" build, sell, and service tractors, manufacture fertilizer and insecticides, run the trains and barge fleets that carry food and farm materials, and build the refrigerators needed to store the food. The once-isolated farmer has been plugged into a sophisticated industrial system which depends on him for large quantities of food and on which he depends for industrial products and technical information. For example, most dairy farmers feed their cows a computer-determined diet. The computer — based on a cow's weight, milk output and quality, and the cost of different feeds — determines what diet each cow should receive to maximize milk output and minimize cost. Most farmers have access to a central computer at a local college or government agency. Among other scientific-technical services for the farmer are weather and economic forecasting, medical and biological research, soil analysis, and advice on seeds, fertilizers, and insecticides.

The emphasis on mechanization has put the small family farm at an increasing disadvantage relative to the large, well-capitalized farm. This, in part, has forced 22.5 million people to leave the farm between 1940 and 1970,[14] a flow which continues even today. In part this is a result of government policy. One typical example of the direction of government-sponsored research is the effort to develop hard tomatoes. Soft tomatoes bruise easily and can only be picked by hand, but hard tomatoes are pickable by machine. This mechanization will increase labor productivity and force out of business small growers, who will be unable to afford the mechanical pickers, and the farm workers who had formerly picked the tomatoes. It also means that the consumer will be forced to shift from the tasty soft tomato to the less tasty hard tomato.

A second result of the agro-industrial approach to farming is "oily potatoes." To grow, harvest, process, ship, and store the average American's 3000 kilocalories of daily food energy requires a large amount of fossil-fuel energy. And as food output per man-hour of work continues to increase and elaborate packaging and frozen foods become more common, the fossil-fuel subsidy grows.

An agriculture energy accounting is provided by Table 6, which shows energy inputs and outputs to corn production. The key figure is the bottom line, which shows the ratio of food energy produced to fossil-fuel energy used. That ratio has progressively declined as machinery, gasoline, chemical fertilizers, and herbicides have been substituted for human labor, manure, and crop rotation. In primitive agriculture, where all work is done by man and animals, the ratio would be very large since the only energy input would be from human and animal labor and the sun.

Table 6 is a conservative statement of food production's energy needs since it shows only farm-related energy expenditures. The paper cited in source note 12 in the Bibliography takes a broader look at the energy inputs to food, including off-farm processing, transportation, refrigeration, retail selling, and so on. The authors' conclusion is that it takes five to ten kilocalories of fossil-fuel energy to deliver one kilocalorie of food

**Fossil-fuel Input to Corn (kilocalories per acre)**

|  | 1945 | 1954 | 1964 | 1970 |
|---|---|---|---|---|
| Labor | 12,500 | 9,300 | 7,600 | 4,900 |
| Machinery | 180,000 | 300,000 | 420,000 | 420,000 |
| Gasoline | 543,400 | 688,300 | 760,700 | 797,000 |
| Fertilizer | 74,600 | 295,400 | 582,600 | 1,055,900 |
| Insecticides and Herbicides | 0 | 4,400 | 15,200 | 22,000 |
| Drying | 10,000 | 60,000 | 120,000 | 120,000 |
| Electricity | 32,000 | 100,000 | 203,000 | 310,000 |
| Transportation | 20,000 | 45,000 | 70,000 | 70,000 |
| Other | 52,900 | 45,900 | 62,800 | 97,000 |
| Total Energy Input | 925,000 | 1,548,300 | 2,241,900 | 2,896,800 |
| Corn Yield (bushels/acre) | 34 | 41 | 68 | 81 |
| Corn Yield (kcal/acre) | 3,427,200 | 4,132,800 | 6,854,400 | 8,164,800 |
| Output kcal per Input kcal | 3.70 | 2.67 | 3.06 | 2.82 |

SOURCE: "Food Production and the Energy Crisis," David Pimentel, et al. (*Science*, vol. 182 [2 November 1973]), pp. 443–449.

**Table 6.** Since 1945, the fossil-fuel input per acre of corn has tripled but energy output per acre has increased by only a factor of 2.4. This is demonstrated by the bottom line, which shows that in 1945 1 kilocalorie of input energy yielded 3.70 kilocalories of corn energy; in 1970 that kilocalorie only yielded 2.82 kilocalories of corn energy.

(Farm labor energy is based on 21,770 kilocalories/week/worker and a 40-hour week. Each acre in 1970 required 9 hours of human labor. Gasoline energy is 36,225 kilocalories/gallon. Corn energy is 1800 kilocalories/pound. A bushel of corn weighs 56 pounds. The energy value of farm machinery is assumed the same as an auto. It takes 32,000,000 kilocalories to build a 3400-pound auto.)

energy to the consumer. They estimate that it would take 80 percent of the world's total fossil-fuel energy to supply the world's population with food using the American agricultural system.

The dependence of modern agriculture on our industrial system was illustrated by a series of events in the winter of 1972–73. In the preceding summer the United States had sold 21.1 million tons of grain to the Soviet Union. A disagreement over which nation's ships were to carry the grain to Russia resulted in a late shipping start. When the grain-laden railroad cars from the Midwest finally converged on Louisiana ports, they were caught in a massive traffic jam. The port's loading facilities were unable to keep up with the arriving railroad cars, which for weeks had to sit fully loaded on sidings while empty ships waited offshore for loading berths. In some cases, spot shortages of diesel fuel caused by that winter's energy crunch prevented cars from being moved at all for periods of time. Because the amount of grain to be moved was so large, grain cars were in short supply and the railroads substituted cars normally reserved for fertilizer shipments. As a result of the jam in Louisiana, these cars were tied up longer than expected, creating a car shortage in the spring when it came time to ship fertilizer. The shortage that same winter of natural gas in certain areas also prevented the manufacture of some fertilizer and the drying of some grain.

**Conserving Industrial Energy.**   The agricultural pattern of increasing energy use holds for industry in general. Machine power has replaced manpower and high-energy substances like aluminum, detergents, and synthetic fibers have replaced steel, stone, soap, wood, wool, and cotton.[15] Industrial energy can be saved in several ways, but the painless path is to have industry achieve the savings internally by use of more efficient processes and equipment.

It might be thought that if large-scale savings were possible by use of greater internal efficiency, industry would already have introduced the improvements. However, until recently energy was so cheap it did not pay industry to put great effort into saving it. But with energy prices rising, the economic picture has changed to make conservation more attractive. Energy experts believe that over a period of years internal economies will save 10 to 15 percent of industry's projected energy use. The largest savings are likely to come in the steel industry. At present steel is made by either the open-hearth or the basic-oxygen methods. In 1970 each method was producing about half of the nation's steel, but the basic-oxygen method uses much less energy than the open-hearth method per unit output. Overall, the steel industry now uses 6 percent of all U.S. energy. Complete conversion to the basic-oxygen method could reduce that figure to 3 percent, resulting in a 3-percent reduction in the nation's total energy use.[16]

Such large reductions are not foreseen in other industries. No major technological breakthroughs are likely in the chemical or petrochemical industries, although housekeeping savings of 10 percent are achievable. The petrochemical industry is especially dependent on energy because most of its products (for example, bowling balls, plastic combs, drugs, antifreeze, synthetic fibers) are made with petroleum as the raw material and natural gas as the source of processing energy. This means the petrochemical industry is dependent on the two scarcest fossil fuels. It is possible that this raw material-fuel double squeeze will price some petrochemical products out of the market, reducing one rapidly growing area of energy use.

It is likely that industrial energy can be saved by using materials more sparingly. One study of high-rise office buildings estimated that careful design, more man-hours of construction work in assembling materials, and more realistic safety standards could cut the material used in the typical building by 50 percent.[17] According to this study, buildings are presently designed to provide unnecessarily large safety factors and to permit rapid construction with minimum use of manpower. Only in ships, planes, and bridges is material used sparingly. In buildings, for example, instead of using a beam which is thick where it must provide most strength and thin elsewhere, the beam is made uniformly thick. In the same way, during construction the builders will pour an extra 5 or 10 percent concrete over what the design specifies, to play it safe. The design, of course, already includes a generous safety allowance and the creation of extra weight creates a need for additional weight to support it. If beams were made lighter and less concrete was poured, additional savings would become possible since there would be less building to support.

**Life-style and Garbage.** The second approach to conserving industrial energy requires changes in life-style. The big energy-conserving change would be a shift from autos to mass transit and communications. This would conserve both operating and industrial energy since building trains, railroad tracks, and communication facilities is much cheaper energetically than building an equivalent amount of autos and roads. Other industrial energy savings would result if people used fewer air-conditioners, dishwashers, and other appliances. Since these are electrically powered, not only would manufacturing and operating energy be saved, but also the energy needed to build the power plants and transmission systems that supply the electricity.

Industrial energy can be saved in a second and separate way by reusing or recycling consumer products. This would also help to solve the solid-waste problem. Municipal garbage alone amounts to about three pounds per person per day[18] and its disposal requires a large amount of land for dumps. Most garbage is generated in urban areas and suitable dump sites are growing scarce. This has forced some cities and suburbs to ship their garbage long distances or to incinerate it, which causes air pollution.

All garbage contains material such as paper, metal, glass, and plastic which was originally obtained from wood, metal ore, sand, and petroleum, respectively. Throwing the object away means its replacement must be made out of new raw material. If the discarded object was returned to the steel or paper mill, the need for raw material would be reduced. This is called recycling; it refers to the reuse of the material but not of the object itself. Newspapers and glass are commonly recycled.

A higher goal is to reuse the discarded object, which occurs when a deposit bottle is returned to the supermarket, a burned-out electric motor or generator is rebuilt, or an old apartment house or office building is renovated instead of demolished and replaced. With reuse, the raw material, the processing energy, and some of the manufacturing energy is saved. Over the past several decades, recycling has become less and less common and reuse has just about vanished. In general, we prefer to throw away or knock down and start all over as part of our start-from-scratch ethic.

The land needs of the auto go beyond highways and parking lots, as this junkyard indicates. *Photo courtesy U.S. Department of Transportation.*

Both reuse and recycling are partly design problems. Modern objects are not made with reuse, rebuilding, or recycling in mind. Light bulbs do not have replaceable filaments, fountain pens have been replaced by throw-away plastic ballpoint pens, and all sorts of containers from wine bottles to egg boxes are made to be used only once. Some objects become useless in more subtle ways: they are designed to become obsolete within a few years. Sometimes the built-in aging is physical, as with toasters, lawn mowers, and dishwashers that break down after a few years of use. In other cases the obsolescence occurs because the object begins to look old. We can all spot a 10-year-old auto or TV because the newer versions make the older ones look out of place and old-fashioned.

The auto companies are particularly good at working both sides of the obsolescence street. Autos become very expensive to maintain after several years, and a 5-year-old auto looks old no matter what its condition. The auto companies usually introduce major style changes every three years, which are meant to make all earlier models look obsolete. Although social, economic, and physical reasons may work against renovation and reuse, the materials the objects are made of should be recyclable. But at present garbage is a mix of paper, cardboard, plastics, metals, and discarded food. If separate, these materials would have some value, but to separate them after they are mixed together usually costs more than it is worth. One possibility is to have the material kept separate in the home or office. But this runs counter to the convenience ethic, and such separation would take up valuable household or office space.

Not only is garbage usually combined into a difficult-to-separate mix, but the individual products themselves may be made of an undesirable combination of materials. The most common soft-drink and beer containers have steel sides and bottom and an aluminum top for the tab. The auto is largely steel, but mixed in is 200 pounds of nonferrous metals[19] such as copper wiring and cast-zinc door handles. A light bulb consists of a tungsten filament, a glass bulb, and an aluminum base, all intimately joined. The ordinary tin can is steel, coated outside with tin and inside with tin, zinc, or lacquer, and soldered with a tin-lead alloy. This makes scrap tin cans much less valuable than if they were made of a single metal. Recycled tin cans are used mainly in copper refining, not in steel making.

**Beverage Containers.**   Although a fairly small part of our national solid-waste and energy problems, disposable beer and soft-drink containers have become symbols of what is seen by some to be a wasteful, polluting, throw-away economy. One-way bottles and cans litter picnic spots, parks, beaches, and roadsides. Tabs from aluminum-top cans are found literally everywhere, and all projections agree that their use will continue to increase.

The problem, therefore, has esthetic, raw-material, and energy components. It would seem on the face of it that the most conserving approach would be recycling or reuse of the object. Disposal of the object as garbage would seem the most wasteful solution. That seemingly obvious conclusion is only partly true. In many cases it is both energetically and economically cheaper to discard rather than recycle. The complexity of the situation can be seen by looking at returnable and one-way bottles. If a bottle is discarded after use, it finds its way more or less directly to a dump. If the bottle is of the deposit type, however, it must be returned to the store, sorted, shipped back to the bottling plant, cleaned, and refilled. The deposit-type bottle must be stronger than the one-way bottle in order to survive the many round trips. And finally, the returnable bottle eventually wears out or breaks and has to be discarded or recycled. So the returnable bottle has economic and physical costs the one-way bottle does not.

A detailed energy study of beverage containers has been done by Bruce Hannon,[20] an engineer at the University of Illinois. He added up the energy costs of different approaches to soft-drink and beer containers and concluded that it is both economically and energetically cheaper to use returnable bottles. He also found that in terms of total energy consumed, it makes little difference whether a one-way bottle is recycled or just thrown away. Table 7 compares the energy costs of returnable bottles with one-way bottles. The one-way bottles consume three times as much energy per gallon of beverage handled as the returnable bottles. The calculations are based on a conservative assumption of eight round trips per returnable

**BTU and Bottled Soft Drinks (per gallon)**

| Operation | Returnable 8 Trips (BTU) | Throw-away |
|---|---|---|
| Obtaining Raw Materials | 990 | 5,195 |
| Transporting Raw Materials | 124 | 650 |
| Making Container | 7,738 | 40,624 |
| Making Cap | 1,935 | 1,935 |
| Transportation to Bottler | 361 | 1,895 |
| Bottling | 6,100 | 6,100 |
| Transportation to Store | 1,880 | 1,235 |
| Waste Collection | 89 | 468 |
| Total (not recycled) | 19,217 | 58,112 |
| Total (30% recycled) | 19,970 | 62,035 |

SOURCE: "Bottles, Cans, Energy," Bruce M. Hannon (*Environment*, March 1972), p. 11.

**Table 7.** Listed above are the number of BTU it takes to bottle a gallon of soft drinks in a returnable bottle assumed to make 8 round trips and in throw-away bottles. The bottles hold 16 ounces. The returnable bottles weigh 1 pound and the throw-aways 0.65 pounds.

bottle. The 1971 national average was fifteen round trips per bottle-life-time, and it was once forty round trips during its six-month lifetime. The energy costs for the returnable containers are low because they have been averaged over eight trips. Even transportation costs for returnable bottles are not high because the truck which delivers one-way bottles to a store returns empty to the bottling plant. Little additional energy is consumed if it returns loaded with empties. Table 7 also shows that if either type of bottle is recycled, energy costs rise. Material is saved by recycling, but sand, limestone, soda ash, and feldspar are neither scarce nor valuable.

Beverages are also sold in cans. Some are all aluminum but most have steel walls and bottom and an aluminum lid to make the pull-off tab possible. Table 8 shows the energy used for steel-aluminum cans per gallon of beverage sold in 12-ounce cans. The one-way, steel-aluminum

**BTU and Canned Soft Drinks (per gallon)**

| Operation | BTU per gallon |
| --- | --- |
| Mining (2.5 lb of ore per lb of steel) | 1,570 |
| Ore Transportation (1000 miles by barge) | 560 |
| Making Ore into Steel | 27,600 |
| Making the Aluminum Lid (12% of can weight) | 12,040 |
| Transporting the Steel 392 miles | 230 |
| Making the Cans | 3,040 |
| Transportation to the Bottler | 190 |
| Transportation to the Retailer | 6,400 |
| Waste Collection | 110 |
| Total for Can System | 51,740 |

SOURCE: "Bottles, Cans, Energy."

**Table 8.** Shown here are the energy costs of bottling a gallon of soft drinks in 12-ounce steel cans with aluminum tops. There are 10 cans to the pound. An all-aluminum can would require 33% more energy. There are 20 aluminum 12-ounce cans to the pound.

can consumes roughly three times as much energy as a deposit bottle, and an all-aluminum can consumes about one-third more energy than the aluminum-steel combination. Unlike glass bottles, recycling of aluminum cans is energetically profitable. It takes about 1500 BTU to recycle an aluminum 12-ounce can,[21] which is about 4500 BTU less than it takes to manufacture one from ore. In more concrete terms, it takes almost two pounds of coal (or its energy equivalent) to make three aluminum cans from ore.

Because throw-away containers are more expensive in dollars, BTU, and raw materials, it is logical to ask where they came from. Current use of throw-aways started with an attempt by the metal-can industry to get a chunk of the beverage-container market, then dominated by returnable bottles. The returnables were making forty round trips in six months, which meant replacement of all returnables by throw-aways would result in eighty times more sales. With a huge market at stake, the metal-container industry invested large sums in advertising the convenience of their product. The American public – never adverse to convenience – responded, and the bottle makers countered by introducing their own disposable product. They could have launched an advertising campaign stressing the cheapness of returnable bottles and the public benefit of limiting litter and solid-waste costs. It is not known if such a campaign would have succeeded because it was never undertaken. The bottle makers had the same economic interest in increasing sales volume the can makers had.

As a result of the litter caused by the disposables, volunteer organizations have set up recycling centers, and a few states – led by Oregon – have passed laws restricting one-way bottles. The industry has responded by saying that eliminating one-way containers will eliminate jobs. They have also set up the Keep America Beautiful organization, whose theme is that people and not one-way containers cause litter. Industry has established its own recycling centers, but except for all-aluminum cans, recycling is such an uneconomic activity that it only works with the help of large amounts of donated labor.

## A Case Study: Office Buildings

We close the chapter with a long and – the reader should be warned – involved examination of commercial energy use, specifically in office buildings. We have set the stage for this examination with the earlier description of the evolution of the central city into the home of high-rise office buildings which workers commute to via mass transit and auto. The high-rises symbolize the shift of the labor force from factory, or production, work to office, or service, work. The modern labor force, instead of pushing shovels or crates, now pushes paper, pens, telephones, and scalpels. We are not producing less goods, but with machines and large inputs of energy, factories are making more with fewer people. Just as the factory and mill are the physical homes of industrial work, the office building is the home of service work. The air-conditioned, fluorescent-lighted, glass-walled or sealed-window building houses not only conventional white-collar activities but also hospitals, schools, research institutions, and semi-industrial operations such as the assembly of electronic instruments.

**The Office-Building System.** We have already discussed the evolution of central-business-district office buildings from eight- or ten-story struc-

The concrete screen on the western exposure of the United Fund Building in Philadelphia keeps the high summer sun from penetrating the glass walls but admits the lower winter sun. *Photo courtesy Mitchell/Giurgola Associates Architects.*

tures with massive walls to soaring skyscrapers served by elevators. After World War II these buildings evolved once again, as the gray stone buildings with setbacks were succeeded by boxier buildings with glass walls. The new buildings function as differently as they look. Air, which enters and leaves older buildings through windows and by infiltrating walls, is drawn into new buildings by huge intake fans and ducts. The air is then heated or cooled, humidified or dehumidified, and circulated via another system of fans and ducts throughout the building. At the same time, exhaust fans and ducts remove "old" air from within the building and dump it outside.

To help the system function, the building's exterior walls are sealed as tightly as possible against air leakage, which means the building is dependent on the ventilation system. If the building has windows, they are invariably kept locked or sealed so that inhabitants cannot open them and "unbalance" the heating and cooling system. In central cities, this system has certain economic advantages. Because the building is no longer dependent on air entering through windows and the outer wall, it can be made as bulky as desired with all the "breathing" done by the air-handling system. Totally sealed buildings no longer require court yards or indentations to bring air to interior parts of a structure, which allows more office space to be squeezed onto a plot of ground.

**Energy Costs.** Operating costs for the sealed building are high. In many respects, the building fights itself. The glass walls which are the mark of the modern building allow sunlight to pour in, straining the air-conditioning. The bright, uniform illumination in such buildings produces still more heat. People, equipment, and lights produce so much heat that if the outside temperature is above 65°F, a modern sealed building must be air-conditioned. This requires energy an older building would not need. Prestigious buildings are tall buildings, which also creates an energy drain since elevators are needed to deliver people to the upper floors.

Sealed office buildings are used in rural and suburban sites as well as the central city because they are prestigious and because architects and the building industry are geared to design and build such structures. When a company or college or school board attempts to have a different building put up, they encounter higher costs and delays.

**Energy and Power Use.** We now make the discussion more specific by taking as a case study a 50-story office building containing 1 million square feet of space (20,000 square feet per floor). Figure 8 shows an aerial view of the 100-foot by 200-foot building. Before giving figures on energy use in this building, we should point out that wide variations occur from building to building. One study suggests that similar office buildings may differ by as much as a factor of seven in the energy they use.

We have already discussed several variables with respect to residential energy use. Some buildings are poorly insulated, are kept very warm in the winter and very cold in the summer, and may have inefficient heating, cooling, and ventilating systems. The ventilation of buildings is still more art than science. Many health codes require that a building's air be changed three times each hour although there is no firm basis for this rule.[22] Such changes use large amounts of energy because the incoming air must be heated or cooled to the interior temperature and then must be pushed through the building by the fans. If the building is cheaply constructed, the ventilation ducts are probably small. This saved on construction costs but requires more powerful fans and therefore a greater expenditure of

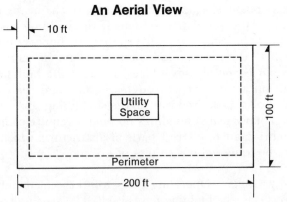

**Figure 8.** This diagram gives an aerial view of one floor of the 50-story building. A total of 5600 square feet per floor is within 10 feet of an outer wall.

energy. In addition the air must be pushed through the smaller ducts at a greater speed, creating an intrusive hum which larger ducts would avoid.

Air changes are one variable; there are others. In some buildings, lights are left on 24 hours a day; in others they are used only during working hours. If construction was done with an eye to saving money, there may be only one light switch per floor, which means that all of a floor must be lighted if any one section is in use. Areas near windows often have no need for artificial light, but in most buildings the lights in this perimeter area cannot be independently turned off. Another factor in the energy use of a building is its age. As a building gets older, its equipment functions less efficiently, requiring more energy to do the same job. If the building was built cheaply in the first place, deterioration will occur more rapidly.

With that array of cautions in mind, we look at Table 9, which lists possible electric-energy use and power requirements for the sealed, 50-story, million-square-foot building. The largest electric-energy consumer is lighting, which requires 36.3% of the building's power capacity and uses 45.0% of its electric energy. The next largest user is air-conditioning, which requires 30.1% of the power and uses 17.2% of the energy.

**Typical Electric-Power and Energy Use in a Million-Square-Foot Building**

|  | Demand (kw) | Percent of Demand | Energy ($10^3$ kw-hr) | Percent of Energy |
|---|---|---|---|---|
| Lighting | 3,800 | 36.3 | 9,880 | 45.0 |
| Advertising | 450 | 4.3 | 1,310 | 6.0 |
| Elevatoring | 630 | 6.1 | 1,970 | 9.0 |
| Refrigerating | 3,150 | 30.1 | 3,780 | 17.2 |
| Air Handling | 780 | 7.5 | 1,750 | 8.0 |
| Pumps, Motors | 700 | 6.7 | 800 | 3.6 |
| Office Equipment, Misc. | 950 | 9.0 | 2,470 | 11.2 |
| Total | 10,460 | 100.0 | 21,960 | 100.0 |

SOURCE: "Architecture and Energy," Flack and Kurtz, Consulting Engineers, New York City.

**Table 9.** A typical pattern of electric-power demand and electric-energy use in a 50-story building is shown here. Energy use is per year.

Air-conditioning consumes little energy relative to its power capacity because it is used only a few months a year. Another energy cost resulting from the sealed nature of the building is air handling, which needs 7.5% of the power and uses 8.0% of the energy. The 50-story height requires that 9.0% of the building's electric energy be used to operate elevators. All together, the building consumes almost 22 million kilowatt-hours of electricity yearly. At $0.02/kilowatt-hour, this is an annual bill of $440,000.

**Lighting Energy.** Lighting is the easiest energy use to quantify since it does not vary with the height or bulk of the building or the outside temperature. A modern, brightly lighted, uniformly illuminated building requires a power input of 4 watts/square foot for lights and an additional 1 watt/square foot to operate typewriters and other office equipment. Looking just at lights, a million-square-foot building having 950,000 square feet of lighted space (the rest is elevator shafts, utility rooms, and the like) requires

$$(4 \text{ w/ft}^2) \ (9.5 \times 10^5 \text{ ft}^2) = 3.8 \times 10^6 \text{ w} = 3.8 \times 10^3 \text{ kw}.$$

If we conservatively assume the building is lighted 10 hours per day, 5 days a week, 52 weeks a year, the lights will be on 2600 hours/year for an energy consumption of

$$\begin{aligned} \text{energy} &= (\text{power}) \ (\text{time}) = (3.8 \times 10^3 \text{ kw}) \ (2.6 \times 10^3 \text{ hr}) \\ &= 9.88 \times 10^6 \text{ kw-hr.} \end{aligned}$$

At \$0.02/kilowatt-hour, this is a lighting bill of \$197,000.

Lighting energy can be reduced if natural light is used. In general, space within 10 feet of the windows can be lighted using natural light. If the lights within this perimeter area can be turned off, appreciable savings are possible. Each floor of the 50-story building has 5600 square feet of its 20,000 square feet within the perimeter area, for a building-wide total of 280,000 square feet. This represents almost 30 percent of the total lighted square footage in the building. If the perimeter lights were kept off an appreciable amount of the time, significant lighting and cooling savings would be possible. During the winter, slightly more energy would have to be used for heating to make up for the lighting loss. But the heating energy—which is not subject to the second law of thermodynamics—is generated more efficiently than the electricity used for the lights. Until recently, however, electric costs were so low that few buildings were designed to allow perimeter-area lights to be operated independently of interior-area lights. Even buildings with glass walls are usually lighted throughout.

**Lighting Standards.** Another possible area of savings is in the lighting levels used in buildings. Over the last several decades, lighting levels have increased sharply in office buildings, schools, and hospitals. Such institutions are several times more brightly lighted today than they were twenty or thirty years ago. Table 10 shows that lighting levels have tripled in twenty years in one typical urban school system. Adding to the higher lighting levels is the trend toward more uniform illumination of buildings. Today entire buildings, including corridors and storage areas, are more brightly illuminated than work areas were thirty years ago. The electricity used for lighting has not increased quite as sharply as the preceding would indicate because of the introduction of fluorescent bulbs, which supply about three times more light per input kilowatt-hour than incandescent bulbs.

The present lighting levels are based on recommendations made by the Illuminating Engineering Society (IES). It is general adherence to their specifications that give new buildings their bright, white, uniformly illuminated look. However, some disagree with these standards. They say the brightness and lack of contrasting light levels gives the effect of a snow-field and suggest that only work areas be brightly lighted, leaving other areas at lower levels. Since dimly lit buildings are not esthetically appealing, it is proposed that research and experimentation be done by architects and interior designers to find ways to light a building in a healthful, appealing way that still saves energy.

**Lighting Levels in an Urban
School System, 1952–1971**

| Year | *Lighting Levels (in foot candles)* |
|------|------------------------------------|
| 1952 | 20 |
| 1957 | 30 |
| 1971 | 60 |

SOURCE: "Architecture and Energy." Richard G. Stein (Philadelphia: American Association for the Advancement of Science, 29 December 1971).

**Table 10.** The above figures are for classroom use in a school system but are typical of office buildings. Libraries in this same school system in 1971 required 70 foot candles, and a drafting room 100 foot candles.

It has been suggested that there may be economic reasons for the high illumination levels recommended by the IES. Companies such as Westinghouse and General Electric are influential in the IES and it is in their interest to have high light levels; they not only make lighting fixtures and bulbs, but the electric generators, power lines, and transformers which then supply the electricity. Higher light levels therefore have a multiplying effect on their business.

**Temperature Control.** We have already hinted at the complexity of heating and cooling a building. The outside temperature and humidity, the sunlight and wind, the tightness of the building's outer wall and its heat-conducting ability, and the amount of energy released inside the building all influence the heating and cooling of a building. To start with the obvious, Figure 9 shows a typical temperature pattern for the Northeast[23] and indicates when the building must be heated or cooled. So much heat is generated in the building that no heating is needed when the temperature is between 55 and 65 degrees.

A building must be designed to handle the highest and lowest temperatures the area receives. In our case, we assume the building must maintain a 72°F interior temperature under external conditions that range from 0°F to 95°F. The maximum heating load is defined as the amount of heat the building's furnaces must generate to keep the building at 72°F when it is 0°F outside. The maximum cooling load is the amount of heat the building's air-conditioning system must exhaust to keep the building at 72°F when it is 95°F outside.

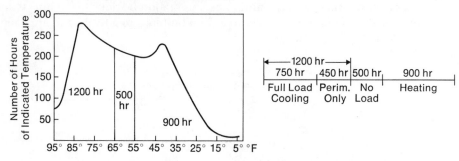

### A Temperature Distribution

**Figure 9.** The graph shows the temperature distribution for a city in the New York-Philadelphia region. This assumes a 2600-hour year (10 hours per day, 5 days per week, 52 weeks per year). The diagram on the right indicates the number of hours of air-conditioning and heating that would be needed. For 500 hours of the work-year, the temperature outside will be between 55°F and 65°F and no heating or cooling would be needed.

To illustrate how different designs and operating procedures influence the energy needs of the 50-story building, Table 11 lists cooling load, cooling energy, and lighting energy for five different conditions. Table 12 lists the heating load and heating energy for similar conditions. A building whose outer walls are 40 percent windows is compared with one whose walls are 20 percent windows and with one which is windowless. For the two cases with windows, the cooling load is calculated with perimeter lights on and off.

Cooling load and cooling energy needs drop as the amount of window space drops. This is primarily due to a decrease in the amount of sunlight entering the building. Turning off the perimeter lights causes a further drop in cooling load because the air-conditioning no longer has to fight the heat given off by these lights.

To check the cooling load decrease shown in Table 11, we recall that the building uses 4 watts of lighting-energy power per square foot of floor space. There are 280,000 square feet of perimeter space so the total power reduction is

$$(4 \text{ w/ft}^2)(2.8 \times 10^5 \text{ ft}^2) = 11.2 \times 10^5 \text{ w} = 11.2 \times 10^2 \text{ kw}.$$

$$\text{heat} = (11.2 \times 10^2 \text{ kw})(1 \text{ hr}) = 11.2 \times 10^2 \text{ kw-hr}$$
$$= (11.2 \times 10^2 \text{ kw-hr})(3.4 \times 10^3 \text{ BTU/kw-hr}) = 3.8 \times 10^6 \text{ BTU}$$

**Cooling and Lighting Energy Demands for Three Building Designs**

| | Cooling Load (10⁶ BTU/hr) | kw-hr (× 10³) for Cooling | kw-hrs (× 10³) for Lighting | Total kw-hr (× 10³) |
|---|---|---|---|---|
| 40% Windows Lights On | 38 | 3780 | 9880 | 13,660 |
| 40% Windows Lights Off | 34 | 3400 | 6970 | 10,410 |
| 20% Windows Lights On | 34 | 3400 | 9880 | 13,320 |
| 20% Windows Lights Off | 30 | 3020 | 6970 | 9,990 |
| 0% Windows | 31 | 3160 | 9880 | 13,040 |

SOURCE: "Architecture and Energy," Flack and Kurtz.

**Table 11.** The least cooling and lighting electrical energy is used by the building with 20% windows and perimeter lights off. It uses 3,670,000 kilowatt-hours less than the highest energy user—the building with 40% windows and perimeter lights on.

**Heating Energy Demands for Three Building Designs**

| | Heating Load (10⁶ BTU/hr) | Heating Energy (× 10⁹ BTU) | Hot Water (× 10⁹ BTU) |
|---|---|---|---|
| 40% Windows | 22.7 | 50.2 | 4.3 |
| 20% Windows | 16.4 | 36.5 | 4.3 |
| 0% Windows; 72°F | 13.4 | 30.3 | 4.3 |
| 0% Windows; 67°F Winter Temperature | 12.5 | 27.9 | 4.3 |

SOURCE: "Architecture and Energy," Flack and Kurtz.

**Table 12.** The heating load and energy is calculated without regard to the effect of perimeter lights due to the need to maintain a fairly constant temperature at night and on weekends, when lights and equipment are off and no people are in the building. Note that there are 2600 hours in our assumed work year and 8760 hours in the total year.

This heat figure rounds to the 4-million-BTU-per-hour drop in cooling load shown in Table 11.

Although the windowless building has no entering sunlight, it must use perimeter lights, so its cooling load and cooling energy are a little higher than the building with 20 percent windows and perimeter lights off. The windowless building has a low heating load since there is no heat loss through windows, but its total consumption of heating energy and electric energy (at 10⁴ BTU to generate 1 kilowatt-hour) is 160 billion BTU. The building with 20 percent windows and perimeter lights off uses only 137 billion BTU.

It is surprising to note that the winter heating load is significantly less than the summer cooling load (see Tables 11 and 12) despite the fact that the heating system must fight a 72°F difference (assuming a 0°F coldest day) while the cooling system must overcome only a 23°F difference (assuming a 95°F hottest day). One major reason for the comparatively large cooling load is the heat given off by lights, people, and equipment. We have already mentioned that lights and equipment require 5 watts/square foot. If we assume 1 person per 100 square feet, this raises the total to 6 watts/square foot since people give off about 100 watts each. (See Table 13 for more exact data.) All of this power is converted to heat for a total of

$$(10^6 \text{ ft}^2)(6 \text{ w/ft}^2) = 6 \times 10^6 \text{ w} = 6000 \text{ kw}.$$

In an hour, the heat added to the building by lights, equipment, and people is 6000 kilowatt-hours, or

$$(6000 \text{ kw-hr})(3400 \text{ BTU/kw-hr}) = 20{,}400{,}000 \text{ BTU}.$$

During the winter this 20-million-BTU-per-hour heat input aids the building's heating system. The system is also helped by sunlight entering through windows. But in the summer, both of these heat inputs are liabilities and must be removed by the air-conditioning.

So effective are lights, equipment, people, and sunlight in warming a building, that the heating system's peak load occurs on cold winter nights, when the building is empty of people, the lights are off, and the sun is not shining. Those heat-input losses are somewhat balanced by the fact that there is no need to change the building's air every hour or half-hour since no one is there to breathe it. Therefore the large amount of heat needed to warm 10 million cubic feet of air (the volume of our million-square-foot building) is not needed. For all these reasons, the cooling load in a typical office building is greater than the heating load.

There are several other complications to be mentioned. The bulky building we are working with has so much volume relative to its surface area that heat-conduction losses through the outer wall are negligible. In addition, the amount of air seeping through the walls varies greatly depending on wind speed, wall construction, type of window used, and the air pressure maintained within the building by the ventilation system. As a rule of thumb, we can assume one air change per hour due to air seepage, or infiltration, but this can vary widely.

Fluorescent light bulbs present another problem. To light a 100-watt fluorescent bulb takes 120 watts of power because of heat losses in the ballast, or fixture. This heat is transferred to the air near the ceiling and is likely to be immediately pulled out of the room and through ceiling ducts and exhausted from the building without ever affecting the air-conditioning load.

The information in Table 13 is provided for those who wish to do a detailed calculation of this or a similar building's heating and cooling loads. The window and wall U-values (coefficients of heat transmission) tell how much heat flows by conduction through the walls and windows. For example, if the interior temperature is 72°F and the outside temperature is 52°F, the quantity of heat flowing through 1000 square feet of wall in 2 hours is

$$Q = (U)(\text{area})(\text{time})(\text{temperature difference})$$
$$= (0.15 \text{ BTU/hr/ft}^2/°F)(10^3 \text{ ft}^2)(20°F)(2 \text{ hr}) = 6000 \text{ BTU.}$$

### Data on Building Heat Gain and Loss

| | |
|---|---|
| Lighting | 4 w/ft² |
| Equipment | 1 w/ft² |
| Heat Generated per Office Worker | |
|    Sensible Heat | 195 BTU/hr |
|    Latent Heat | 205 BTU/hr |
|    Total | 400 BTU/hr |
| Wall Heat Transfer | U = 0.15 BTU/hr/ft²/°F |
| Window Solar Gain | 45 BTU/hr/ft² |
| Window Heat Transfer | U = 0.5 BTU/hr/ft²/°F |
| Air Changes | 0.3 ft³/min per ft² of floor space |
| Volumetric Heat Capacity of Air | 0.018 BTU/ft³/°F |

Source: "Architecture and Energy," Flack and Kurtz; and *Guide and Data Book* (New York: American Society of Heating, Refrigeration and Air-Conditioning Engineers [ASHRAE]).

**Table 13.** Some data needed to calculate total heating and cooling loads for a typical office building are given here. In most buildings, between 100 square feet and 200 square feet are allocated per worker. Latent heat refers to the water vapor given off by each person: it affects only cooling loads. (The ASHRAE *Guide* should be consulted for more detailed information.)

The U-values for the walls and windows do not include the effect of air leaking through cracks or of sunlight shining through the glass. The solar-heat load varies a great deal since it depends on cloudiness, amount of shading, height of the sun in the sky, and exposure. Table 13 assumes 45 BTU/hr/ft² of window area as a typical summer figure, averaged over all four exposures.

Table 13 also gives the heat capacity per cubic foot of air, which is needed when calculating the heat needed to raise or lower the temperature of ventilation or infiltration air, and the contribution to the cooling load caused by the building's inhabitants. The loading comes in two parts: sensible heat and latent heat. The sensible heat is the number of BTU given off by the person. The latent heat is a result of the water vapor people put into the air by breathing and perspiring. When this vapor is condensed from the air (dehumidified), it gives up about 1076 BTU per pound of water condensed. If the air were cooled without being dehumidified, it would feel damp and clammy. Because warm air can hold more water vapor than cool air, warming of air during the winter often makes it uncomfortably dry, requiring humidification.

**Thirty-three Small Buildings.** We now examine the energy effects of splitting the 50-story building into 33 three-story buildings, each containing 30,000 square feet, or 10,000 square feet per floor (100 feet by 100 feet). The largest energy saving will be in powering elevators since a three-story building requires little elevator use. In addition, substantial amounts of space occupied in the 50-story building by elevator banks will be available for office use in the smaller buildings. But a larger view of the transportation picture modifies this gain. Three-story buildings do not provide sufficient density for mass transit. Such offices are likely to be found in suburban locations surrounded by parking lots. So the million square feet of office space take up more room than is at first realized, and the energy saved by reducing elevator use will disappear because auto transportation will replace mass transit. The worst combination from an energy viewpoint would be a 50-story office building served by autos.

The three-story buildings can be lighted more efficiently than the 50-story building because a larger proportion of their collective floor space will be within 10 feet of an exterior wall. In fact, the 33 three-story buildings will have 80,000 square feet more space within the perimeter area than the one large building. While this can result in appreciable savings on lighting, the small buildings lose out on heating and cooling. These losses occur for the same reason that the lighting gains occur: the buildings have large window, wall, and roof areas, all of which leak heat. For example, the 33 small buildings have sixteen times as much roof area as the 50-story building.

When the use of energy for lights, elevators, cooling, and heating are added up, it turns out that the large building is most efficient. Under present conditions – where almost all buildings use artificial lights in the perimeter areas – the 50-story building has an especially large advantage.

While the calculations we have done are useful, we have not been complete even within the narrow bounds of energy use. Dense urban concentrations represented by 50-story office buildings mean that water, electricity, and food must come from long distances and then be shoehorned into the city. Anyone who has ever watched an urban street being torn up knows they are underlain with gas pipes, water and sewage lines, building foundations, electric, telephone, and telegraph cables, and steam lines. Cities and public utilities devote a large amount of effort to keeping track of the underground networks. So bringing in services to areas of dense concentration is economically and physically expensive. At the same time, the concentration and intensity of use has economic and physical advantages. We have not measured these costs and benefits.

**Toward the Future.**   The sealed, total-environment, fluorescent-light building is a comparatively recent development which has problems aside from energy use. Many of these buildings have difficulties with air circulation and air-conditioning. In some cases an entire building may be too warm or muggy; in other cases one part of a building may be too warm and another part too cold. Some occupants of large office buildings complain even when their building is operating as designed. Among the complaints are the lack of windows, supposedly stale air, the 60-second flutter of fluorescent lights, building sway, and noise from elevator shafts.

In view of these complaints it is interesting to try to imagine the building of the future. Will esthetics and energy problems move us toward low buildings that use windows which open for ventilation and a siesta or lengthy summer vacation as a substitute for air-conditioning? Or will present modern buildings evolve into more comfortable and efficient structures? Without getting into science fiction, one can imagine several technically achievable changes. Sophisticated light and temperature sensors and controllers can be visualized. Offices could be equipped with light sensors which would adjust artificial light to maintain a desired light level. This would be especially useful in perimeter areas, where natural light is a variable factor. If the light sensors were hooked up to mechanically operated blinds or shades on the windows, they could adjust the shades to admit enough light for work but not so much that glare would bother people or put an unnecessary load on the air-conditioning. Other sensors — perhaps similar to the ultrasonic burglar alarms which detect movement — could be used to turn off the lights when the room is unoccupied.

In a more advanced building, the output from light, temperature, and occupancy sensors could be fed into a central computer which would decide what the most energy-efficient combination of artificial and natural light inputs would be. On winter nights, for example, all the blinds would be drawn to conserve heat. The same kind of feedback system could be used to monitor the temperature, humidity, and air quality in the building and adjust ducts, fans, filters, coolers, and humidifiers to achieve a desired state. At present, no attempt is made to monitor air quality and modern buildings are likely to exhaust perfectly good air in order to draw in polluted air from outside.

**High-rises and Fires.**   Past experience indicates that care must be exercised in designing automatic equipment. Several years ago, elevators in some high-rise buildings were equipped with heat-sensitive call and floor-selection buttons and with photoelectric sensors on the doors. The call buttons were activated by the heat of a person's finger. The photoelectric detector was set so that the door remained open if the light beam was broken. A person getting on the elevator at the last moment stopped the closing door without physically touching it.

This very clever system unfortunately turned into a death trap in a fire. In several cases, the heat from a fire activated the call buttons on that floor. When the elevator arrived, the smoke obscured the photoelectric device's light beam, making the circuit think a person was in the way. So the door remained open, trapping the elevator occupants on the very floor that had the fire. Most cities now ban such systems but some fear that high-rises are themselves huge fire traps. Although the buildings will not burn, they are filled with flammable desks, furniture, rugs, and paper. The fear is that if a large fire got started, a chimney effect would spread it throughout the building; and some high-rise fires in the 1970s lent support to this fear. Unfortunately, there is still too little known about the behavior of large buildings in fires.

## Conclusion

It would be nice to end this chapter on a definite note and declare—for instance—that U.S. energy needs can be reduced 20 percent below 1985 projections. We could then go on to the following chapters on energy production with a clear goal in mind. But if the preceding examination did anything, it showed the complexity of our energy-use situation. Out of this complexity and the trillions of individual, corporate, and government decisions made yearly has emerged a constantly growing demand for energy. We have seen how this growth is built into our homes, our food, our transportation, and our industry.

The most optimistic statement we can make is that until now we have not looked at the world in terms of energy conservation. Therefore it is possible that once we begin searching for more efficient homes, factories, power plants, and trucks, large savings will occur. But we must also recognize that the homes, offices, transportation systems, and farms designed in times of cheap plentiful energy will be with us far into the future. The sealed office building and mechanized farm will not disappear because energy supplies are growing tight and expensive. Present buildings and transportation systems can be expected to last about 30 years. The same 30 years can be taken as a measure of a generation. People who grew up during a time of unlimited energy use are the same people who must change their habits of consumption and production to adapt to new conditions.

It is in this area of social and political action that least can be said. Energy use, after all, is a means to an end and not an end in itself. So through all of this we must keep in mind that whatever means we choose to use and to produce energy, they must be consistent with the kind of life we wish to lead, just as that way of life must be consistent with the boundaries the physical world imposes.

There is irony in our present situation. As we shall discuss in the following chapter, our generous use of energy has caused various environmental problems. But at the cost of quiet surroundings, clean air, and damage to water and landscape, we have obtained a large amount of control over the natural environment and great savings in time and labor. However, if present energy-resource problems persist, we may be forced to practice strict budgeting and bookkeeping to limit energy use. We would still have the various environmental costs, but we could lose many of the benefits our formerly extravagant energy consumption brought us. Just possibly we could be left with the worst of both possible worlds: tight energy supplies and a deteriorating environment.

## Bibliography

*Source Notes*

1. *The 1970 National Power Survey.* Federal Power Commission. Washington, D.C.: U.S. Government Printing Office.

2. *The Potential for Energy Conservation.* Executive Office of the President, Office of Emergency Preparedness. Washington, D.C.: U.S. Government Printing Office, 1972.

3. Ibid.

4. *The User's Guide to the Environment.* Paul Swatek.  New York: Ballantine Books, Inc., 1970.

5. Ibid.

6. *The 1970 National Power Survey.*

7. "Fuel Economy and Emission Control." U.S. Environmental Protection Agency. Washington, D.C.: U.S. Government Printing Office, 1970.

8. Ibid.

9. "Electric or Nuclear Power for Automobiles." Victor Wouk.  Philadelphia: American Association for the Advancement of Science, 28 January 1967.

10. "Lost Power." D. P. Grimmer and K. Lusczynski.  *Environment,* April 1972.

11. "Food-Related Energy Requirements." Eric Hirst.  *Science,* vol. 184 (12 April 1974), p. 184.

12. "Energy Use in the U.S. Food System." John S. Steinhart and Carol E. Steinhart.  *Science,* vol. 184 (19 April 1974), p. 307.

13. "Food Production and the Energy Crisis." David Pimentel et al.  *Science,* vol. 182 (2 November 1973), p. 443.

14. "Farming with Petroleum." Michael J. Perelman. *Environment,* October 1972.

15. *The Closing Circle.* Barry Commoner. New York: Bantam Books, 1971.

16. *The Potential for Energy Conservation.*

17. "A Matter of Design." Richard G. Stein. *Environment,* October 1972.

18. "Municipal Solid Waste." National Center for Resource Recovery. Bulletin 3, no. 2. (Available from: NCRR, 1211 Connecticut Ave., N.W., Washington, D.C. 20036.)

19. "Taking It Apart." Edward M. Dickson. *Environment,* July/August 1972.

20. "Bottles, Cans, Energy." Bruce M. Hannon. *Environment,* March 1972.

21. "Energy and Well-Being." A. B. Makhijani and A. J. Lichtenberg. *Environment,* June 1972.

22. "A Matter of Design."

23. "Architecture and Energy." Flack and Kurtz, Consulting Engineers. New York.

*Further Reading*

EDWARD M. DICKSON. "Taking It Apart." *Environment,* vol. 14 (July/August 1972), pp. 36–41.
This article takes a look at the problems and possibilities of recycling.

JAMES MARSTON FITCH. *American Building,* vol. 1. Boston: Houghton Mifflin Company, 1966.
This book presents a study of the evolution of American architecture. The author skillfully combines the technological, social, and esthetic factors.

D. P. GRIMMER and K. LUSCZYNSKI. "Lost Power." *Environment,* vol. 14 (April 1972), pp. 14–22.
This article examines the efficiency with which we use energy.

MICHAEL J. PERELMAN and KEVIN P. SHEA. "The Big Farm." *Environment,* vol. 14 (December 1972), pp. 10–15.

MICHAEL J. PERELMAN. "Farming with Petroleum." *Environment,* vol. 14 (October 1972), pp. 8–13.
These two articles take a look at modern agriculture's use of energy and material.

JAMES T. PETERSON. "Energy and the Weather." *Environment,* vol. 15 (October 1973), pp. 4–9.
Peterson discusses the effect of energy use on urban weather in this article.

DAVID J. ROSE. "Energy Policy in the U.S." *Scientific American,* January 1974, pp. 20–29.
This article gives an excellent survey of the energy options open to the United States.

*Scientific American.* "Energy and Power." September 1971.
This entire issue containing eleven articles is devoted to the production and use of energy in society.

RICHARD G. STEIN. "Architecture and Energy." *Architectural Forum,* July/August 1973, pp. 38–58.
This article presents a comprehensive review of energy use in buildings.

## Questions and Problems

1. The average U.S. household in 1970 used 7000 kilowatt-hours of electricity and the average all-electric home used 33,000 kilowatt-hours. Compare electric energy use in your home to these figures by consulting old bills. Can you simply take one bill and multiply by 12? Could a bill from 12 months ago somehow give you total electric energy use?

2. Use the data in Table 1 to calculate your electric bill theoretically.

3. Is electric and heat energy used sparingly or wastefully in your home or dorm? Is the building well insulated, outside doors weather stripped, storm windows used, temperatures kept low in the winter, and the like?

4. Go through your dwelling and classify appliances as luxuries, conveniences, or necessities. Be sure you are clear on your definition of the three terms. Is it always easy to distinguish? Can you imagine any of the conveniences evolving into necessities?

5. Explain the difference between a power and an energy shortage. Which causes electric brownouts on hot summer days? Which causes gasoline shortages?

6. Making an assumption, compare the nation's total automotive power with the nation's electric power capacity of 360 million kilowatts. Does this comparison say anything about the feasibility of widespread use of electric cars? Would electric cars help or hurt the electric-power peak-hour problem? Power demand peaks seasonally in the summer and during daylight hours all year around.

7. The Northeast power blackout came as a surprise to almost everyone concerned. Can you think of other, more recent, technological surprises? Is there a common theme to these unexpected occurrences?

8. Refer to the data given in Figure 4.
   a. Calculate how many tons of coal the nation used in 1971, assuming $10^4$ BTU per pound.
   b. If 40% of that coal was obtained by strip mining, how many square miles of land were stripped? Assume average land yields 2 million tons of coal per square mile stripped.

9. Refer to the data given in Figure 4.
   a. Calculate how much petroleum the nation used in an average day in 1971.
   b. The Trans-Alaska Pipeline has a design capacity of 2 million barrels per day. The equivalent of how many such pipelines will be required to supply the nation with petroleum in 1980?

10. Use Figure 5 to calculate the total amount of energy used in the industrial and commercial/residential sectors in 1971 by calculating how much electric energy they used.

11. At 3 pounds per day, how many pounds of household garbage do you generate in a year?

12. Table 6 lists the energy it takes to construct a car. How does this compare with the energy a car uses during its 100,000-mile lifetime?

13. Assume you wish to repeat Hannon's study of energy costs for bottles. You have access to glass makers, bottlers, truckers, and retail stores. What kind of information would you request of each one? You should ask for the data in a form convenient to the company being questioned. Do not, for example, ask the bottler for the number of BTU it takes to bottle a gallon of beverage. The company would not collect that kind of information.

14. From Table 8, express in ton-miles/gallon of gasoline the energy cost of transporting steel by rail. Assume 140,000 BTU/gallon of gasoline. Note that a gallon of beverage is 128 ounces.

15. Is recycling or reuse of newspapers, bottles, and the like easier for the suburbanite living in a one-family home or for the apartment dweller? Do projections that an increasing proportion of the population will be living in multiple dwellings bear on the solid-waste problem? Is it correct to describe solid waste as a systems problem? If so, outline the systems nature of the problem.

16. Is your school or office located in a sealed, fluorescent-light building? Is that construction appropriate to the location? Can you determine the factors that determined its shape and functioning?

    In general, does the building "work"? Is its temperature and humidity control good? Is noise between adjoining areas a problem? Does the building encourage interactions between people and yet allow for isolated work? Is it aging well? Is elevator service satisfactory?

17. Use the data given in Figure 8.
    a. Verify that the perimeter area is 5600 square feet/floor.
    b. Calculate the total perimeter area for the 33 small buildings considered earlier and compare with that of the 50-story building.
    c. Compare the total roof and wall area for the 33 small buildings with the roof and wall area for the 50-story building. How is this calculation relevant for heating, cooling, and lighting?

18. Assume a building is heated electrically. Does it make energy sense to conserve on lighting? Do costs beyond those for electricity make it profitable to turn off the lights?

19. A company must decide whether to turn off its 25,000, 40-watt fluorescent lights from 6 P.M. to 8 A.M. and on weekends, or to let them burn around the clock. Turning the lights on and off once a day reduces their 10,000-hour continuous-burning lifetime to 7000 hours. (Remember that it takes 48 watts to power a 40-watt fluorescent bulb.)

a. At $0.02/kilowatt-hour, calculate the electric energy cost difference between the two approaches over 417 days (10,000 hours).

b. Assume the fluorescent tubes cost $2.00 each and calculate the cost difference for tubes between the two approaches.

c. Making some assumptions, calculate the difference in the labor cost of replacing tubes between the two approaches. Would you replace them as they burned out or take some other approach?

20. Use Table 11 to calculate the rate (in BTU/hour/square foot) at which sunlight enters the building's windows at the time of peak cooling load. Assume the floor-to-floor height is 10 feet.

21. Use Table 13 to calculate the heat it takes to warm to 72°F a volume of air equal to the building's volume when outside temperature is 2°F. How does your result compare with the building's (20 percent windows) heat load shown in Table 12?

22. Assume the 50-story building's average U-factor over walls and windows is 0.3 BTU/hour/square foot/°F and calculate the hourly heat loss when the exterior temperature is 2°F. How does this compare with the building's heat load (20 percent windows) shown in Table 12?

23. The sum of the heat loads calculated in problems 21 and 22 exceeds the heating load listed in Table 12 for the building with 20 percent windows. Explain the discrepancy.

*Coal has always cursed the land in which it lies. When men begin to wrest it from the earth, it leaves a legacy of foul streams, hideous slag heaps and polluted air. It peoples this transformed land with blind and crippled men and with orphans. It is an extractive industry which takes all away and restores nothing. It mars but never beautifies. It corrupts but never purifies.*

HARRY M. CAUDILL*

# 10 Energy, fossil fuels, and the environment

Until now, we have taken the sources of energy for granted. Our emphasis in Chapter 8 was on the technological developments which enabled man to tap increasing amounts of fossil-fuel energy at ever greater rates. In the last chapter we looked at the ways we now use energy and at projections of future use. In this and the following two chapters we examine the energy resources available to meet projected demands.

This examination will be far more tentative than that of the preceding chapters. It has been said that "resources are not; they become." Resources become through technical, social, and economic changes. Wood was useless as an energy source until man learned to control fire. Many coal beds were inaccessible until the steam engine was developed as a pumping machine. In our own day the natural gas that often flows out of the ground with oil was disposed of by burning it off (called "flaring") until construction of a national network of gas pipelines allowed it to be distributed to consumers. At present, high prices for oil have created interest in western oil shale — rock containing solid petroleum

---

* From Caudill's book *Night Comes to the Cumberlands* (Boston: Little, Brown and Co., 1962).

locked within it. Nuclear reactors have turned once-useless uranium into a valuable energy source.

Technical changes take place in an economic and social context that is often more complex and difficult to understand than the physical context. Rises in the price of oil in the early 1970s were in part triggered by production cutbacks on the part of Middle Eastern nations. But some say the higher prices were mainly caused by the action of the multinational oil companies (for example, Exxon, Mobil, Shell, British Petroleum). They preferred to develop cheap Middle Eastern oil, which can be pumped out of the ground and brought to a tanker for about one-ninth of a cent per gallon.[1] This, it is said, led them to neglect exploration and production in the United States because of the greater expense and the need for environmental safeguards. In any case, it is indisputable that U.S. production of oil peaked about 1970 at eleven million barrels (bbl) per day[2] and began declining thereafter, while consumption—stimulated in part by auto and oil company advertising—continued to rise.

Natural gas presents another difficult situation. Gas shortages originating in the early 1970s were attributed to the low prices imposed by federal regulations. This was said to have discouraged oil and gas companies from exploring for additional reserves. The situation was aggravated by a huge increase in gas use, encouraged by its low price and environmental cleanliness. But here too there were charges of manipulation. It has been said that the market was being controlled not only by federal price regulations but also by owners of gas reserves, who were holding the gas off the market until prices rose.

Estimates of future energy supplies, then, require more than a knowledge of likely technological developments and possible discoveries of unknown fuel deposits. The estimates must also be based on future world economic conditions, foreign relations among nations, and future public attitudes toward environmental problems and family size. If the people who predict future energy needs and reserves tried to take all of the above into consideration, they would never get out of bed in the morning. So they initially simplify the situation by assuming that energy prices will remain about the same, that no unexpected technical developments will occur, and that discoveries of new fossil-fuel deposits will occur at about the same rate as in the past.

**Estimating Fossil-fuel Reserves.** Best measured of all the fossil fuels is coal. It is found in beds formed within the past 600 million years. These beds—which are the remains of ancient buried forests—may run more or less continuously under large areas of land. By drilling test holes at widely separated points, the amount of coal and its energy content can be closely estimated. The result of such estimates for the United States and the world is shown in Table 1. Coal is the nation's most abundant fuel supply. Much of the United States in the Rocky Mountain region is underlain with coal,

### The World's Initial Supply of Minable Coal

| Geographic Area | Coal ($\times 10^9$ tons) |
| --- | --- |
| U.S.S.R. | 4740 |
| U.S. | 1630 |
| Asia | 750 |
| Canada | 660 |
| Western Europe | 415 |
| Africa | 120 |
| Australia, New Zealand | 70 |
| South and Central America | 15 |
| Total | 8400 |

SOURCE: "Energy Resources," M. King Hubbert, in *Resources and Man* (San Francisco: W. H. Freeman and Company, 1969).

**Table 1.** The world's estimated total initial supply of minable coal is given on the last line of this chart. So far about 2 percent of that initial supply has been consumed. The United States uses about 600 million tons yearly. At that rate, the nation's coal would last for 2700 years. Our growth rate cuts that time to a few hundred years.

and at present rates of use it is estimated the United States has several hundred years' supply. However, this prediction must be hedged with several constraints. If we should run short of other fossil fuels and turn to coal, it would last a shorter period of time. Coal is also the dirtiest of fuels — both to mine and to burn. A growing environmental concern could therefore limit the amount of coal used.

Predictions about oil reserves are more difficult to make for both technical and nontechnical reasons. The people who know most about oil reserves are the oil companies. They, however, consider this information a secret to be kept from their competitors, and therefore from everybody else. In addition, oil reserves fluctuate with the prices of its end products — gasoline, heating oil, kerosene, and the like. When oil prices rise, marginal wells which had been shut down may be brought back into production. More significantly, only about 30 to 40 percent of the oil in a deposit is brought to the surface.[3] The rest remains in the ground, much like water in a rock sponge. As the price of crude oil rises, it becomes economically feasible to "squeeze" the sponge by such means as pumping water underground at high pressures to fracture the rock and collect the oil.[4] Increasing oil prices also encourage more exploration and the tapping of difficult-to-reach deposits, such as those found offshore or in Alaska.

Compared with coal, oil is found in relatively small isolated pools, a few hundred feet to several miles underground. It is generally agreed that much of the oil on the U.S. mainland has already been found, and most attention now centers on Alaskan and offshore deposits. Although the California and Gulf of Mexico continental-shelf areas have been explored, the eastern coastal areas from Maine to Florida until 1974 had not been touched. Nor had the deeper, outer continental shelves on either coast been explored.

Estimates of yet-to-be-discovered petroleum fields are made from a knowledge of the geology of unexplored areas and from past success in exploratory drilling. In 1945 it took twenty-six wildcat wells (a well drilled in an area with no record of previous oil finds) to discover a new field. By 1963 the number of wells required had risen to sixty-five. This number plus estimates of the rate at which exploratory wells are likely to be drilled yield one estimate of future discoveries. A more detailed approach is based on the oil found per foot of exploratory well drilled. Around 1900, about 200 barrels of oil were found per foot drilled. By the 1920s the ratio had declined to 170 barrels/foot. It is now about 35 barrels/foot. The decline of this ratio indicates that oil is becoming much harder to find.

The estimated oil reserves listed in Table 2 are based on this and other information. It is thought that the United States, exclusive of Alaska, initially contained 200 billion barrels of recoverable petroleum. Production of petroleum in the United States peaked in 1970 at about 11 million barrels per day, compared to consumption of 15 million barrels per day. In 1973 oil production had dropped slightly, but demand was up to 17 million barrels/day.[5] By 1980 it is estimated that 130 billion of the nation's initial 200 billion barrels of petroleum will have been pumped out and burned. The remaining 70 billion barrels will be increasingly difficult to mine because the easy, cheap oil had been removed first. The additional 30 to 50 billion barrels believed to be contained in Alaska, and not counted in the 200 billion estimate, will stretch out the production picture for the

**The World's Initial Supply of Petroleum**

| Geographic Area | Oil ($\times 10^9$ barrels) |
| --- | --- |
| Middle East | 600 |
| Communist Bloc Nations | 500 |
| Africa | 250 |
| South America | 225 |
| United States (not including Alaska) | 200 |
| Asia | 200 |
| Canada | 95 |
| Europe | 20 |
| Total | 2090 |

SOURCE: "Energy Resources."

**Table 2.** Worldwide it is estimated that about 10 percent of the above initial supply has been mined. But the United States is estimated to have already used half of its initial supply of 200 billion barrels. In the early 1970s, the United States was using about 6 billion barrels of petroleum yearly.

United States but not change it appreciably. The general picture is that 80 percent of all U.S. oil will be used between 1935 and 2000.

The natural gas picture is much the same. In fact natural gas is often found associated with oil. As a rule, 6000 cubic feet of natural gas[6] are found for every barrel of oil found, so the same geological and drilling analyses can be applied to natural gas. It is estimated that U.S. production of natural gas will peak about 1980. Total initial U.S. natural gas supply is estimated to have been 1300 trillion cubic feet; we will have used about 600 trillion cubic feet of this initial supply by 1980, leaving another 700 trillion cubic feet in the ground.[7] In 1973 we used about 24 trillion cubic feet.

## Oil

The steady growth in U.S. petroleum use and the shrinkage in domestic production have caused the nation to become partially dependent on oil imported from Canada, South America, and the Middle East. In 1969 about 22 percent of the oil consumed in the United States came from foreign sources. In 1974, 35 percent was imported. It is predicted that by 1985 oil imports to the United States will rise to 19 million barrels/day, or about two-thirds of our oil consumption and one-third of our total energy consumption. The Arab oil embargo of 1973–1974 illustrated the political and economic dangers of dependence on foreign oil and launched the United States in quest of energy self-sufficiency. Since U.S. land areas have been thoroughly searched for oil, this quest led to more intense exploration of offshore areas. But while imported oil and offshore oil may be different politically and economically, they have some environmental characteristics in common.

**Oil Spills.** Both offshore oil and imported oil pose a threat to the world's oceans because they inevitably lead to the spilling of oil into water. It is estimated at present that about one million tons of oil[8] (there are about seven barrels/ton) find their way into ocean water each year. Oil is not foreign to the oceans. It has always seeped into the water from undersea deposits, and the plant life in the ocean produces a certain quantity of hydrocarbons. There are microscopic organisms in the water which feed on the hydrocarbons—oil included—converting them into harmless materials. But the danger is that oil spills, concentrated mostly in the biologically rich coastal regions, will overwhelm the seas' ability to assimilate them. In addition, oil spills have ugly effects, coating beaches, boats, and swimmers with oily muck.

There are several sources of ocean oil. About half is believed to come from ships discharging ballast water. Ballast water is sea water pumped into empty fuel tanks of ships for weight and balance. The quantity varies from ship to ship, depending on the size of its oil tanks and the roughness

An increasing quantity of the oil produced in the United States will come from offshore deposits, increasing the risks and numbers of oil spills. *Photo courtesy Mobil Oil Corporation.*

of the sea on any particular trip: in bad seas ships usually take on more water for stability. The biggest offenders are oil tankers—which are nothing more than huge floating cans. Large tankers may take on thousands of tons of water for ballast and discharge it mixed with oil from their tanks. New methods of treating the ballast before it is pumped out have reduced the amount of oil entering the ocean, but in 1969 it was conservatively estimated at about 500,000 tons annually. As shipping of oil increases, the amount of ballast oil dumped will also increase.

The other major source of oil spills is tanker collisions or sinkings. Probably the best-known tanker accident was the 1967 grounding and break-up of the fully laden *Torrey Canyon,* with the spilling of 118,000 tons of crude oil into the sea near the English Channel. Although a large tanker at the time of its sinking, the *Torrey Canyon* would now be dwarfed by the much larger supertankers (500,000 tons deadweight). Although it takes a huge loss like the *Torrey Canyon* to make headlines, tanker accidents occur regularly, involving smaller but cumulatively serious losses. In addition to collisions, there are a large number of loading and unloading accidents, as when a poorly attached or strained hose breaks, discharging oil into the water. Tanker accidents and oil spills are much like auto accidents — statistical inevitabilities rather than avoidable occurrences given the technology in use. Tanker spills are estimated to add another 500,000 tons of oil to ocean water annually.

A smaller class of accidents consists of spills from offshore oil wells. The most spectacular accident of this type occurred off the coast of Santa Barbara when an oil-gas well under high pressure broke loose, spilling an estimated three million gallons of crude oil into the water. This spill — because it dragged on for over three months and devastated the beautiful seashore of a prosperous California town — attracted a great deal of attention.

Oil can threaten a coastal area even if a drop is never spilled into the local water. If a large offshore deposit of oil is found, there will be pressure to build storage tanks, oil refineries, and petrochemical plants along the coast near the strike. This development can destroy the coastal area for recreation. The establishment of an unloading facility for large oil tankers can spur the same kind of development.[9] When this is added to the ever-present threat of actual oil spills, many coastal areas are impelled to oppose offshore wells and ports. Delaware, for example, passed a law in 1972 which effectively forbade any sort of industrial development on its coast.

Arctic Oil.   The nation's shrinking petroleum reserves and higher prices for foreign crude oil have led to intensive efforts to develop U.S. oil. But these yet-untapped reserves are found mainly in inaccessible, environmentally difficult locations. The large oil reserve found on the North Slope of Alaska in 1968 is typical of the problems encountered. The 10 to 12 billion barrels of oil discovered off Prudhoe Bay (see Figure 1) illustrates many of the increasingly difficult energy decisions the nation will have to make. The 10 billion barrels represented a three-year supply of oil at 1970's rate of use, and it is believed that Alaska may ultimately contain 50 billion barrels, approximately equal to the lower 48 states' total reserves.

Far from being universally hailed, the discovery set off a five-year-long conflict between the oil companies and the environmental movement over how, or whether, the oil was to be moved from the north of Alaska to the lower 48. The conservationists saw and still see Alaska as the last true wilderness in the United States — a fragile, ice-locked land with an abundance and variety of wildlife, threatened by the oil wells and the development that could follow the wells. The oil companies see immensely important and potentially huge oil reserves remaining forever unused because of what they think is an overconcern for wilderness. At the extremes, the oil people see their opponents as preservationists who care more about trees than people. The conservationists see the oil people as rapists who would destroy every living thing for a barrel of oil.

**TAPS**

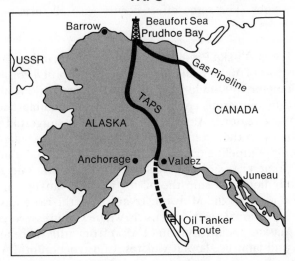

**Figure 1.** Reserves of 10 to 12 billion barrels of oil were discovered in 1968 off Prudhoe Bay on Alaska's North Slope. The oil will be brought to Port Valdez via the 800-mile-long TAPS pipeline and then transported further south by tanker. An overland pipeline through Canada may be built to bring the associated natural gas south.

To understand why the Arctic resources are difficult to get at, it is necessary to know something about the area. Prudhoe Bay, where the oil was found, is on the Beaufort Sea (an arm of the Arctic Ocean) about 1300 miles from the North Pole. While the oil strike is close to water, it is ice-locked and impassable to ships much of the year. On land the nearest road is 360 miles to the south across a mountain range. Although subzero temperatures, a six-month night, and mountain ranges present difficulties, the main problem is the permafrost — the soil type found in much of northern Alaska. As the name implies, it is a permanently frozen mixture of ice, gravel, and sand overlain with a mat of vegetation. In summer, the very top of the permafrost melts, giving the vegetation necessary water and making thousands of square miles soggy and unstable.[10]

If the permafrost were a dead lump of ice which melts a bit each summer, there would be little difficulty. But it is far from dead. During the summer, water and solid-water mixtures flow slowly in sheets beneath the covering mat of vegetation. When a jeep or truck is driven across the permafrost, breaking the vegetation mat, a process of erosion and land movement begins. The five-foot-wide track cut by the vehicle widens and deepens as water and material flow in the open wound. Large-scale land movement may begin. Because the Arctic growing season is short, such scars are slow to heal. The damage done and the litter left by exploration activities in the Arctic during World War II are still fresh and visible.

The permafrost can damage as well as be damaged. A road built over it will sink in some places and rise in others as the ground adjusts to the road's weight. The same effect occurs with all sorts of structures unless great care is taken.

The Trans-Alaska Pipeline.  To move the Prudhoe Bay oil south to the all-year port of Valdez, the oil companies proposed construction of a four-foot diameter, 800-mile-long pipeline. Construction of the pipeline was opposed by numerous environmental groups and blocked in the courts for a variety of reasons. Among the alternatives suggested was a proposal to leave the oil in the ground until techniques were available to ship it safely or to build a pipeline overland through Canada to the midwestern United States. Some critics of the Alaskan pipeline route said the oil companies eventually hoped to ship the oil to Japan by tanker[11] and therefore were against a route to the Midwest. In any case, the issue was resolved in 1973 during a national energy crunch when Congress voted to exempt the Trans-Alaska Pipeline System (TAPS) from adherence to various environmental and land-use laws it violates. Construction of TAPS got underway in 1974.

Compared with TAPS, this pipeline, which is being laid underground through a mountain valley, is a relatively small one. *Photo courtesy Mobil Oil Corporation.*

The oil which the pipeline is to move was discovered in three pools lying between one and two miles underground. These pools are estimated to contain 10 to 12 billion barrels, but it is also believed that there are yet-undiscovered deposits on the North Slope containing several times as much oil. According to the Environmental Impact Statement prepared by the Department of the Interior, the oil in the found reservoirs is at 200°F and under a pressure of 4000 pounds/square inch. Dissolved in the hot, pressurized oil is natural gas in a ratio of 850 cubic feet per barrel of oil. As the oil-gas mixture flows to the surface through wells, its pressure drops and the natural gas bubbles out of the solution. The gas-free oil at the surface weighs 56 pounds/cubic foot, or 6.3 barrels/ton. Because of the high underground pressure, the oil will gush out of each well drilled at a rate of 10,000 barrels/day, considerably higher than the national average of 17 barrels/day/well. When the Prudhoe Bay field is working at top capacity, it will have about 200 wells, producing 2 million barrels of oil per 24-hour day. The oil will then flow south at 10 feet/second through the $3 billion, four-foot diameter pipeline laid across the permafrost, under and over streams and rivers, and over mountain gorges and passes. The Environmental Impact Statement also says that to move the fluid at this speed over the mountains will take 12 power plants generating a total of 430,000 horsepower of pumping power.

At Port Valdez, 800 miles to the south of Prudhoe Bay, the pipeline will empty into one of fifteen storage tanks, each of which is 62 feet high and 250 feet in diameter with a capacity of 500,000 barrels. From these hilltop tanks the oil will flow by gravity into one of a fleet of tankers (costing $1.7 billion) which will ferry the oil to Seattle, Los Angeles, and possibly Japan. Port Valdez will be able to load five tankers simultaneously, with each of them taking on about 100,000 barrels/hour. The tanker fleet—a seagoing extension of the pipeline—will consist of eight supertankers holding 250,000 tons each, sixteen tankers in the 120,000-ton size, and seventeen smaller tankers ranging from 90,000 tons to 45,000 tons.

TAPS is complicated by the hot (150°F–170°F) oil it will carry since the heat flowing out of the pipeline will aggravate the normally difficult task of building on permafrost. Were the pipeline to be buried for its entire route, one could visualize a several-hundred-mile-long mud-filled ditch blocking the migration of caribou and other animals. Actually, an entirely underground construction of the pipeline would be impossible. If the pipe were buried on certain hillsides, the melting would cause large earth movements which would rip apart the pipe. The current plan is to elevate 350 miles of the pipe several feet aboveground with the remaining 450 miles buried.

Whether buried or elevated, the pipeline will consume an estimated 46.5 million cubic yards of gravel. Where buried, it will be laid on a thick bed of gravel for support. Where elevated, the support structure will stand on gravel pads rather than directly on the permafrost. The pipeline will also require the construction of a 360-mile-long gravel road stretching south from Prudhoe Bay until it connects with already existing roads at the Yukon River. It is this new road which will open up presently inaccessible areas. Gravel will also be used to build three permanent and four temporary airfields. The removal of this gravel is likely to cause environmental damage. Much of it will be mined from river beds, thus destroying fish-spawning sites, increasing siltation, and possibly changing the courses of streams and rivers. Removing land sources of gravel is likely to cause erosion and further land movement.

**Pipeline Breaks.** Once built, TAPS will pose an entirely different threat. With 2 million barrels of oil flowing through it daily, the danger is that corrosion, shifting of the permafrost, or an earthquake will break the pipe, spilling thousands of barrels of hot oil. If the oil remains on the land, the damage would be comparatively small. But if it should spill into a river, the fish and other life in the river system could be destroyed. One guard against such spills is the care with which the system is built. But the Environmental Impact Statement describing the project says that in the lifetime of the system spills are almost inevitable.

To minimize the effects of any spill, the flow through the pipeline will be continuously monitored by an array of pressure, speed, and temperature detectors, with the readings sent to a central station via radio, microwave, and telephone systems. In theory, leaks as small as 31 barrels/hour should be detectable. If a large break occurred, steps would be taken to immediately shut down the line. The pipeline is fitted with 94 block valves which can be slammed into place by remote control, isolating sections of the line and minimizing the spilled oil. Under static conditions, with the oil just sitting in the line, a maximum of 60,000 barrels of oil could spill.

But the oil will not be just sitting in the line; it will be flowing at 10 feet/second, powered by 430,000 horsepower pumps. The 800 miles of moving oil will have an incredible momentum, and the system could not be shut down in a second. If the 94 block valves were dropped without first braking the oil, the line, its pumps, and the valving would probably be destroyed by the resulting shock waves, or water hammer. So it will take ten minutes to shut down the system and close the block valves. The Impact Statement does not list the spill expected under these dynamic conditions.

**Port Valdez.** If we are to have an overview of TAPS, we must also look at the problems posed by tankers loading at Valdez. Almost inevitably, the daily loading of 2 million barrels of oil and the movement of tankers into and out of the port will result in spills and collisions. The two main questions are these: How serious will the spills be and how efficiently will they be contained and cleaned? Similarly, with present technological and economic constraints, oil will enter the port water with the ballast water. However, it is planned that ships will discharge oily ballast water into land-based tanks for treatment. The treated water will then be dumped into the sea. This will reduce the amount of oil entering the water, but the long-term build-up may still be serious.

Other Considerations.   There are a great many interesting details connected with the construction of TAPS. Crude oil is a mixture of many petroleum fractions. Among these are various waxes such as paraffin which will condense out of the cooling oil and coat the pipeline walls. Eventually the coating would get quite thick and obstruct the line, just as deposits of fat in a person's blood vessels can close them down and bring on a heart attack. To prevent pipeline blockage, the pump stations can launch or receive a "pig," a device which moves through the pipeline scraping wax off the walls. It is carried along by and gets its scraping power from the flowing oil. Without it the pipeline would eventually become an 800-mile-long candle.

The fuel used by the twelve pumping stations is also of interest. The stations south of the Yukon River will extract oil from the pipeline, refine out of it a sort of kerosene, and use the kerosene to power the pumps. The stations north of the Yukon will be fed natural gas through a 10-inch pipeline originating at the Prudhoe Bay field.

A 765,000-volt transmission line is shown here crossing an open corn field. *Photo courtesy American Electric Power Company.*

Moving Energy. The North Slope oil deposit is a dramatic example of an energy source being far from the consumer, but this is an increasingly common problem. So a vital part of any evaluation of an energy resource is a calculation of how much of the energy must be used to move the remaining energy to the consumer. If it takes a huge amount of fuel to power the pumps for TAPS and the engines of the tankers moving between Valdez and the refineries, then it might not pay to extract the energy. To illustrate the various ways of moving energy and the costs attached, we consider below several alternative methods of getting North Slope oil to the lower 48 states.

To move oil through a pipeline requires an average of 1 gallon of gasoline (or its energy equivalent) for each 300 ton-miles. To calculate how much fuel is required to move the daily allotment of crude oil, we first calculate the weight of the 2 million barrels to be moved daily. The Alaskan crude has a density of 6.3 barrels/ton, or 56 pounds/cubic foot. Therefore the 2 million barrels weigh

$$(2 \times 10^6 \text{ bbl}) (1 \text{ ton}/6.3 \text{ bbl}) = 3 \times 10^5 \text{ tons}.$$

The ton-miles generated daily are

$$(3 \times 10^5 \text{ tons}) (8 \times 10^2 \text{ miles}) = 2.4 \times 10^8 \text{ ton-miles}.$$

The fuel used at 1 gallon/300 ton-miles is

$$\text{fuel} = (2.4 \times 10^8 \text{ ton-miles}) (1 \text{ gal}/300 \text{ ton-miles}) = 8 \times 10^5 \text{ gal}$$
$$= (8 \times 10^5 \text{ gal}) (1 \text{ bbl}/42 \text{ gal}) = 19,000 \text{ bbl}.$$

So the percentage of oil needed to ship the oil is

$$\frac{1.9 \times 10^4 \text{ bbl}}{2 \times 10^6 \text{ bbl}} = 0.95 \times 10^{-2} = 0.95\%.$$

About 1% of the oil's energy is used shipping it to Valdez. The much longer trip by tanker from Valdez to the West Coast—at an energy consumption rate of 250 ton-miles/gallon—will raise the total energy shipping cost to about 5%.

For an overall energy cost, we must consider several other factors. It takes energy to find and remove petroleum from underground. Finding oil involves the energy cost of drilling exploration and production wells and the energy needed to pump the oil when it does not flow out itself. This discovery and removal process has about a 4% energy cost.[12] The crude oil, after transport, is refined into gasoline, diesel fuel, kerosene, and other products at about 87% efficiency. This means 13% of the input energy is lost to refining. Once refined, the fuel must be shipped again. If this is done by truck, the efficiency is only 50 ton-miles/gallon. There are also evaporative and small spill losses at the end point when, for example, the gasoline is pumped into a car. Finally, the auto can only extract about 25% of the energy in the gasoline that reaches it.

**Moving Energy Electrically.**   A second way to move the 2 million barrels of oil is as electricity. If this approach were adopted, power plants at Prudhoe would generate electricity which would then be shipped via electric power grids through Canada to the United States. To see what power capacity the plants would require we note that the energy content of 2 million barrels of oil is

$$(2 \times 10^6 \text{ bbl})(5.8 \times 10^6 \text{ BTU/bbl}) = 1.2 \times 10^{13} \text{ BTU}.$$

Assuming the power plants require $10^4$ BTU/kilowatt-hour, they will produce

$$\frac{1.2 \times 10^{13} \text{ BTU}}{10^4 \text{ BTU/kw-hr}} = 1.2 \times 10^9 \text{ kw-hr}.$$

The power output is

$$\text{power} = \frac{\text{energy}}{\text{time}} = \frac{1.2 \times 10^9 \text{ kw-hr}}{24 \text{ hr}} = 50 \times 10^6 \text{ kw}$$
$$= 50{,}000 \text{ megawatts}.$$

For comparison, the entire installed power capacity of the United States in 1970 was 340,000 megawatts. Since this total is projected to double by 1980, the 50,000 megawatts could conceivably be absorbed. But it is enough power to supply twelve cities the size of Chicago.

Once the power is generated, it must be transported to load centers over electric power grids. These are complicated systems and we shall not attempt to describe their functioning in detail. Instead, we treat them with the information summarized in Figures 2 and 3.[13] These show the power a line can carry and the losses per 100 miles of line. We opt for a 765,000-volt grid carrying 3000 megawatts of power. To transport 50,000

## Power-carrying Capacities of Transmission Lines

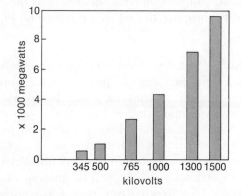

**Figure 2.**   The power-carrying capacity of transmission lines increases approximately with the square of the voltage. The highest voltage lines commercially available are 765 kilovolts.

**Power Losses**

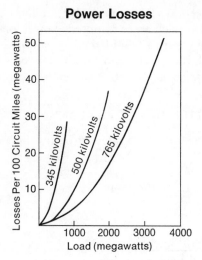

**Figure 3.** The flow of power through a line results in losses. For a 765-kilovolt line carrying 3000 megawatts, the losses are about 30 megawatts per 100 miles of circuit.

megawatts would require seventeen such grids, with each grid carrying 3000 megawatts. The right-of-way for a single grid is 100 feet, but the seventeen grids could be placed within a single right-of-way at the sacrifice of some reliability. The environmental impact would be similar in many ways to TAPS. A large amount of gravel would be required for support structures and access roads, and airfields would have to be built. There would be no oil spill or melting danger, however.

For this electric-energy situation, energy losses would be high. As shown in Figure 3, each 100 miles of circuit would cause a 30-megawatt loss. If the distance via grid to the U.S. load centers was 3000 miles, there would be a 900-megawatt loss for each circuit, or about 30% of the original load of 3000 megawatts. This loss comes on top of the 60% loss incurred when the oil's energy is converted into electricity. The 40% generating efficiency and 70% transmitting efficiency lead to an overall efficiency of $(0.4 \times 0.7)$ = 0.28, or 28%. In comparison with the 30% loss incurred shipping the energy electrically, shipping the oil that distance by pipeline would only cost 3% or 4%.

Solid Petroleum. So far we have been talking of liquid petroleum — oil which occurs as a fluid contained in porous rock. Because it is a liquid it can be pumped out of the ground like water. But petroleum is also found as a very thick viscous liquid that will not flow. Such deposits are called tar-sands, and Alberta, Canada, alone is estimated to have 300 billion barrels of oil locked up in this form, compared to Canada's estimated reserves of 95 billion barrels of liquid petroleum. Petroleum also occurs in a solid form locked up in oil shale. The amount of petroleum in this form is also great. The Green River rock formation — which underlies 25,000 square miles of Colorado, Utah, and Wyoming — is believed to hold 600 billion barrels. All together, the United States is thought to have 1800 billion barrels of oil shale. However, the problems connected with obtaining this oil appear much greater than those surrounding Arctic oil.

Until the sharp price rises in crude oil occurred in late 1973, there was no economic possibility of extracting oil from shale. But when the price rose from roughly $3 per barrel to $10 per barrel and up, the economic picture changed. The heart of the technical and economic picture is the fact that a ton of Green River oil shale contains a maximum of 100 gallons of oil, with 35 gallons[14] being a reasonable average. This means that to produce 2 million barrels of oil daily would require mining about 1.4 million tons of rock each day. Once the rock is mined, it must be crushed into small pieces and fed into a retort, which can be visualized as a huge steel pot. The shale is heated in the retort from 800°F to 1000°F, which transforms the shale's organic matter into oil and some low-energy (100 BTU/cubic foot) gas. The gas is used to supply heat to the retort, and the 35 gallons of oil obtained from each ton of rock must then be refined into end products. So even before there is oil to refine, a huge and expensive mining, crushing, and retorting process must be carried out. (See Figure 4[15] on the next page.)

The potential environmental impacts are enormous. The cheapest way to mine the shale is by strip mining, which would disturb vast areas of the West. The retort process also has environmental consequences. Whatever processes are finally developed are likely to produce air pollution and may require cooling water. This is a serious problem in the arid West. In addition, the shale will yield about 5 gallons of water per ton processed. This water will contain various pollutants which will have to be removed before the water can be disposed of or used. However, the removed water will help compensate for the water lost in cooling.

A major problem involves the retorted shale. Although it will be lighter because of the lost oil and water, its volume will be twelve percent greater. If mined by underground methods, all of the spent shale will not fit underground. If stripped, it will be larger than the surface pits. This expansion and the powdery nature of the waste rock raise serious disposal and land-reclamation problems.

One possibility which would eliminate many of the above problems is to carry out the retort process underground. In such a procedure, hot steam or combustible gases would be driven underground via wells to heat the oil shale in place. The retorted, liquefied petroleum would then be recovered via other wells; this would eliminate mining the shale and the environmental problems associated with it. But, at present, underground retorting seems impractical. The shale formations are relatively impermeable, which makes it hard to heat large quantities of rock. It is also difficult to control the heating process. It has been suggested that the rock be fractured by an underground nuclear explosion to increase its permeability but this raises various other problems.

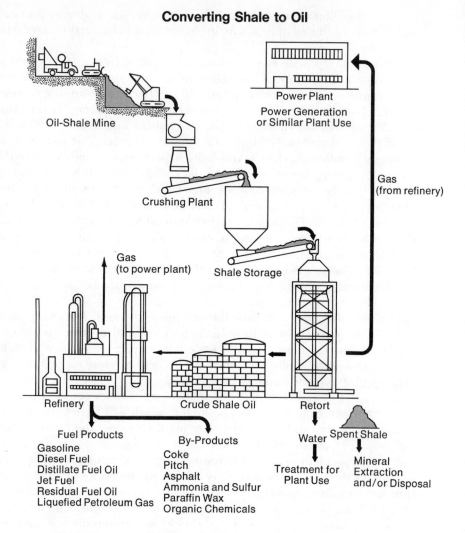

**Converting Shale to Oil**

Oil-Shale Mine

Crushing Plant

Power Plant
Power Generation
or Similar Plant Use

Gas
(from refinery)

Gas
(to power plant)    Shale Storage

Refinery          Crude Shale Oil          Retort

Water    Spent Shale

**Fuel Products**
Gasoline
Diesel Fuel
Distillate Fuel Oil
Jet Fuel
Residual Fuel Oil
Liquefied Petroleum Gas

**By-Products**
Coke
Pitch
Asphalt
Ammonia and Sulfur
Paraffin Wax
Organic Chemicals

Treatment for
Plant Use

Mineral
Extraction
and/or Disposal

**Figure 4.** The processes involved in obtaining fuels and by-products
from oil shale are shown here.

## Natural Gas

The use of natural gas has increased greatly due to its cleanliness, ease
of transmission, and, until 1973, to a very low government-controlled
price. As a result of increased use and lack of incentives to find and,
where found, to release gas to the interstate market, proved reserves in
the United States had dropped by 1972 to an eleven-year reserve at 1972's
rate of use. In addition, actual shortages had appeared in the early 1970s
so that some gas distributors refused to take on new customers, denied old

customers permission to connect new gas appliances, and in cold weather often had to cut off gas supplies to industrial customers on interruptible contracts.

Evaluation of U.S. natural-gas reserves is difficult because—as with oil—such information is held by the oil and gas companies as a trade secret. It may be, for example, that the gas shortages of the early 1970s were totally economic—caused by a refusal of those owning the gas to sell it at prevailing prices. Or perhaps a lack of exploration in preceding years had resulted in an actual physical shortage of gas. Or, less likely, maybe the nation had already exhausted its gas supply. The federal government's approach to the problem was three-fold: it allowed prices to rise, it encouraged imports, and it undertook research to increase natural-gas reserves.

Until the early 1970s almost all natural gas used in the United States originated in the United States or Canada and was shipped by pipeline. But with the shortage of natural gas many companies have begun building tankers with capacities of almost 3 million cubic feet[16] to carry liquefied natural gas (LNG) from the Middle East and Russia. At ordinary temperatures and at atmospheric pressure, natural gas is—redundantly—a gas. But when cooled to 259°F below zero, it condenses to a liquid, just as steam condenses to water below 212°F. In this condensed state, natural gas occupies about one six-hundredth of the volume it occupies as a gas. The huge volume reduction makes it feasible for ocean-going tankers to carry LNG from the Middle East or Russia to the United States. But the refrigeration required to liquefy the gas and the need to transport it by tanker will make this gas more expensive than domestic gas shipped by pipeline.

The gas now used in the United States is found in loose, porous rock through which it moves easily. But a great deal of gas is also locked up in impermeable rock, in much the same way as shale locks up oil. The U.S. Atomic Energy Commission has set off several nuclear explosions in this gas-holding rock in the hope of fracturing it and freeing the gas. Critics of the program object that the gas produced will be radioactive, that the blasts may trigger earthquakes, that radioactive material may escape from underground, or that ground water will be contaminated. One particular blast in Colorado was fought by oil-shale interests, since the gas-bearing rock was beneath a rich shale deposit. It was feared that the blast would affect later efforts to mine the shale. At present it appears nuclear explosives will not be widely used to free natural gas.

**Arctic Gas.** One new source of natural gas is the North Slope of Alaska—the gas produced at Prudhoe Bay with the oil. At first this gas will be pumped back into the ground since Alaskan state law prohibits disposal burn-off and there will be no way to ship the gas south. There are presently several alternatives being considered to move the gas. One possibility is an all overland pipeline through Alaskia and Canada to the United States. This pipeline would be four feet in diameter and have many problems. However, there would be no oil-spill problem, and it appears the gas can be cooled before shipment so the pipeline could be laid in the permafrost.

A second possibility is to build a gas pipeline parallel to TAPS. This would eliminate the need to tear up a whole new section of the Arctic, but no one knows what to do with the gas at Port Valdez. At present, the only possibility is to liquefy the gas, thereby greatly reducing its volume, and send it south by tanker. But a huge amount of money would be needed to build the liquefaction plant and a fleet of tankers. For this reason, the overland route is the favored solution at this writing.

## Coal

Looming over all discussions of oil shale, liquefied natural gas, and imported oil are the nation's vast reserves of coal. Until 1970 coal was seen as a dirty and inconvenient fuel, difficult to ship, store, and use. In the recent past, industry and homes switched from coal to other fuels whenever possible. The nation's railroads converted to diesel trains after World War II and many homes in the United States converted during the same period from coal-powered heating furnaces to gas or oil furnaces. Rising environmental concern in the late 1960s tended to cause even electric power utilities to convert from coal to gas or oil.

This does not mean coal was not being mined. In 1970, 18 percent of U.S. energy came from coal, and 58 percent of all fossil fuel consumed by electric utilities was coal. But this was a decrease from 66 percent in 1960 and without the energy problems of the 1970s this decrease would have continued.

Mining Coal. Coal occurs in seams which may run underground for thousands of square miles. Much of the United States in the Rocky Mountain region is underlain with thick seams of coal, as is the Appalachian range in the eastern United States, and parts of Kentucky, Indiana, Illinois, and Ohio. Until recently, coal could be mined only by digging vertical or sloping shafts into the ground until the seam was reached. The miners then dug out the coal, following the seam wherever it led. A well-worked mine would have miles of underground tunnels honeycombing the ground.

As might be guessed, the underground mining of coal can be a dirty, dangerous, and unhealthful job. Since coal mining began, hundreds of thousands of miners have been killed or injured by collapsing tunnels, explosions, equipment accidents, and lung diseases resulting from breathing rock and coal dust. Coal mining can also damage the surface above the mines. As abandoned mine tunnels collapse, the land above may subside. Enormous amounts of rock and dirt are removed from mines and piled in slag heaps on the surface. Often this material is washed by rain into local streams and rivers, polluting them. Occasionally the heaps slide down a hillside, burying whatever is in their path. Or a lake may pile up behind the slag heap and, when the heap finally gives way, flood the valley below. Water seeping through abandoned mines becomes acidic because of a reaction with the coal. This red acidic water eventually flows into and pollutes the ground and surface water.

So tunnel-mined coal is not cheap in human or environmental terms. But it does not completely ravage the land. Towns, forests, and farms exist above coal mines without harm. However, a new and growing method of obtaining coal (see Table 3)—called strip or surface mining—is much more damaging. In strip mining, huge machines, called draglines, come in to remove the overburden of soil, rocks, and trees. One of the largest of these shovels is named Big Muskie. It can pick up 325 tons of rock and soil at one time. At present it is slowly eating its way through the area around Cumberland, Ohio (see Table 4). The draglines pick up the soil and rock and place it to one side. Then smaller bulldozers come in to load the exposed coal onto trucks, which carry it to a nearby power plant or to trains for shipment to more distant power plants. The pits thus dug may be as deep as 200 feet.

**U.S. Coal Use**

|  | 1950 | 1955 | 1960 | 1965 | 1966 | 1969 |
|---|---|---|---|---|---|---|
| Coal Used per year ($\times 10^6$ tons) | 560 | 491 | 434 | 527 | 527 | 571 |
| Percent from Underground Mines | 76 | 75 | 70 | 68 | 66 | 65 |
| Percent Strip Mined | 24 | 25 | 30 | 32 | 34 | 35 |

SOURCE: *Statistical Abstract 1971* (Washington, D.C.: U.S. Government Printing Office).

**Table 3.** Coal use in the United States has just barely held its own since 1950, despite a huge growth in overall energy use. But during this time the percentage of strip-mined coal has greatly increased.

Coal lying within a few feet of the earth's surface can only be mined by stripping since the roof of a shallow tunnel would collapse. But much of the deeper lying coal now stripped could be mined by underground means. And coal is so abundant that the reserves close to the surface would not be missed were they left in the ground. So there is no resource or physical necessity for strip mining. But in most cases stripping is cheaper than tunnel mining. The bulldozers needed for strip mining cost less than the

**U.S. Strip Mining in 1969**

| State | Coal Produced (× 1000 tons) | Acres (mi²) Disturbed | tons/mi² |
|---|---|---|---|
| Illinois | 34,670 | 6,711 (10.5) | 3,300,000 |
| Indiana | 17,976 | 3,335 (5.05) | 3,420,000 |
| Kentucky | 44,714 | 12,200 (19) | 2,350,000 |
| New Mexico | 3,636 | 250 (0.4) | 9,080,000 |
| North Dakota | 4,705 | 330 (0.5) | 8,940,000 |
| Ohio | 32,616 | 10,629 (16.5) | 1,976,000 |
| Pennsylvania | 27,171 | 12,308 (19.4) | 1,208,000 |
| Virginia | 5,182 | 2,258 (3.6) | 1,432,000 |
| Wyoming | 4,481 | 154 (0.24) | 17,920,000 |
| West Virginia | 19,388 | 15,711 (24.5) | 7,790,000 |

SOURCE: *The Strip Mining of America* (Sierra Club, 1971).

**Table 4.** The amount of coal produced by strip mining in various states and the land disturbed producing that coal are listed here. At present, eastern states are most intensively stripped, but as the last column shows, it is the western states that are richest in coal.

tunneling and ventilating equipment needed for underground mining. Tunnel mining also requires a larger and more skilled work force than strip mining. The result is that a ton of strip-mined coal is about 40% cheaper than a ton of tunnel-mined coal.

Strip-mining critics say it is cheaper in part because all of the costs are not included in its price. Unreclaimed strip-mined land may be unusable for decades, possibly centuries, after the stripping. It cannot be used for farming, grazing, hunting, or fishing because the grass cover has been removed, the topsoil lost, the woods knocked down, and the streams polluted. The area is ugly and the ground unstable so no one wants to build homes or offices on the site. Strip-mined land was perhaps best characterized by the executive of a company which intends to strip mine in the southwestern United States. He suggested to local residents that they plan on attracting tourists to old strip-mine sites by promoting them as man-made badlands.

Strip-mine critics maintain that, at the least, stripped land should be stabilized against erosion and ideally should be returned to its original state. The effects of stripping can extend far beyond the land actually mined. The loose dirt, not retained by trees or grass, washes into streams with the rain. This increases the silt they carry and may block them or cover their beds, killing fish eggs and other underwater life. The silt which doesn't reach the streams may wash over neighboring land, burying it under infertile dirt. In many cases, the area stripped is mountainous, and disturbing the landscape sets into motion a cycle of erosion which can continue for decades. Red acidic water is also produced in strip mines and the disturbance of the land often disrupts the water table, destroying wells. Often the coal vein itself served as the water-bearing aquifer.

Perhaps the most tragic effects of strip mining have occurred in the mountains of Appalachia. There, the grandfathers and great-grandfathers of the people now farming or living on the land had sold the mineral rights to their land. This means they gave the companies which bought the rights the power to remove any minerals under their land. At the time these now-dead men sold the rights, the only way to extract coal was by tunnel mining, which does not greatly interfere with the land above. But the courts have interpreted the mineral deeds to mean that the holders of the mineral rights can remove the coal by surface mining, even if this destroys the land and the buildings on the land. Many Kentucky and West Virginia farmers and landowners have had to stand by and watch the big machines destroy forever their farmland and pastures to get at the coal lying beneath. Some have fought back in the mountain tradition — with rifles — and a few have won in the courts. But most of those who fought lost their fight, and only recently has a movement begun in the state legislatures and in Congress to control strip mining. As late as mid-1974, the Congress was still debating possible federal requirements for reclamation of stripped land.

**Air Pollution.**   Strip-mined land is only the first of the problems resulting from the use of coal. The typical pound of coal is mostly carbon but is also 2.5 percent sulfur and 10 percent ash. In addition, coal contains a variety of trace metals such as mercury, cadmium, beryllium, and the radioactive elements uranium and thorium. Several things happen when coal is burned in a power plant: the carbon and oxygen combine to form carbon dioxide ($CO_2$) and release energy; the sulfur combines with oxygen to form sulfur dioxide ($SO_2$), which is a dangerous pollutant; oxygen in the air fed to the fire combines with nitrogen in the air to form harmful oxides of nitrogen ($NO_x$); and the inert mineral matter is released from the coal as ash.

From the furnace where the coal is burned, all of the hot gases plus some of the ash rise up the smokestack and enter the surrounding air. The purpose of the stacks, which may be several hundred feet high, is to disperse the pollutants. By releasing them high above the ground, it is hoped they will be thoroughly mixed with and diluted by the air by the time they descend to ground level. This is the oldest form of pollution control — dispersion and dilution. But such methods work only when comparatively small quantities of pollutants are released to the atmosphere and when weather conditions are right. We are releasing pollutants in such huge quantities that the concentration of these materials in the best of weather is too high. And when the winds die and the air turns stagnant, the concentrations of pollutants can build to dangerous levels.

The situation is analogous to water pollution: the air in the nation can be thought of as a river which more or less flows west to east. Into this flowing stream of air, industries, autos, and homes pour all manner of chemicals and particles, just as riverside plants and towns dump their wastes into the water. In the air, the emitted chemicals and particles mix together and react chemically to form new substances. Eventually (in a few hours to a few weeks) the material settles or is washed by rain out of the air onto the ground, just as river-borne silt and other solid materials eventually settle to the bottom of a reservoir or delta. When the air pollution settles out, it becomes surface pollution, which corrodes metals, eats away at rubber tires, dirties clothing and buildings, and destroys vegetation.

Just as rivers may rush strongly or slowly, so the flow of air is variable. Occasionally the air stagnates and sits quietly over a particular area. Usually this stagnation is caused by a temperature inversion, in which the air temperature increases with height, trapping the lower air near the surface and preventing mixing. When air is stagnant over an urban area it is a prescription for trouble. Factories, homes, and autos continue to pour out their pollutants. But the pollutants are not carried away by surface winds or mixed by vertical motion of the air; they just sit there, building in concentration. Since the quality of air in urban areas is nearly always marginal, an inversion can spell disaster. And inversion-caused disasters have struck several times in the past 25 years. The best-known cases occurred in London, England (December 3–9, 1952), Donora, Pennsylvania (October 26–31, 1948), and New York City (November 20–26, 1966). In each case, stagnant air laden with chemicals and particulates greatly increased the amount of illness and death, almost as if the areas were being subjected to a poison-gas attack. In addition to these spectacular occurrences, there is mounting evidence that we are living in a continuing air-pollution crisis since it seems that the present quality of our air increases diseases such as bronchitis, emphysema, cancer, and heart disease.[17]

In at least one sense, air pollution is more difficult to deal with than water pollution. Polluted water stays within the boundaries of the river, lake, or ocean. But air pollution has no such bounds. The air flowing into a city may already be burdened with the pollutants emitted by a factory or power plant upwind of it. The most dramatic case of traveling pollution is alleged to have happened in Sweden. Sweden was early very conscious of environmental dangers and cleaned up much of its air pollution. Despite this, it was subject to black snows and acid rains, obviously caused by air pollution. Sweden charged that it was receiving the fallout from British industry, which had solved its own air-pollution problems by building huge smokestacks 1000 feet high or more. According to Sweden, these stacks lofted the pollution so high it did not descend until it was over Sweden.

All fuels emit air pollutants but coal is a worse offender than natural gas or oil. A coal-burning electric power plant is capable of producing large amounts of air pollution. An average-sized plant of 500,000 kilowatts consumes almost 500,000 pounds of coal per hour. If there are no pollution controls on the plant, 50,000 pounds of pollution can be emitted hourly to the atmosphere. Once out of the smokestack, the ash, or particulates, the sulfur dioxide, and the oxides of nitrogen begin to chemically react with each other and with constituents of the air.

**Particulates.** Particulates are the most noticeable of all pollutants. The ash and soot (unburned carbon) given off by coal-burning plants range in size from several hundred microns to less than a micron. (A micron is one-millionth of a meter, or about one four-hundred-thousandth of an inch.) The large particles settle out almost immediately, dirtying and making gritty whatever they touch. But the small light particles present the biggest problem. Because one-micron particles are about the same size as a light wave, they are very efficient scatterers of light. They produce haze and are a major cause of the gloomy look of polluted areas.

It is also feared that small, high-flying particles may ultimately change our climate by shielding us from some of the sun's rays. The reflection by these particles of incoming sunlight back into space can reduce the amount of solar energy reaching the earth, thus lowering the temperature. It is known, for example, that the earth's average temperature drops for a year or so following a volcanic eruption that discharges large amounts of particles into the upper atmosphere. It is also known that the earth's average temperature has been dropping for the past 35 years. But we do not know enough to say that it is our contribution to the airborne dirt that has caused this drop.[18]

The small, micron-sized particles also present a major threat to health. The tiny particles are invariably found associated with sulfur dioxide adsorbed on their surfaces. The combination is natural because plants or factories that emit particulates are also likely to emit sulfur dioxide. When we inhale air containing the particles, the adsorbed sulfur dioxide helps immobilize the respiratory system's defenses against such particles; so they penetrate the lungs' air sacs and interfere with breathing.

**Sulfur Dioxide (SO$_2$).** The sulfur in coal is emitted to the atmosphere as sulfur dioxide, which can discolor leaves and even defoliate certain trees and shrubs. It is a major cause of damage to various crops, including wheat, oats, and rye. This makes air pollution still another factor in driving farms and gardens away from urban areas, depriving cities of green belts. Sulfur dioxide illustrates how the atmosphere can act as an immense reaction vessel. While floating in the air, sulfur dioxide is oxidized to sulfur trioxide (SO$_3$). The sulfur trioxide then combines with water vapor to form corrosive sulfuric acid, which attacks vegetation, discolors or dissolves paint, and is injurious to health.

**Oxides of Nitrogen ($NO_x$).**  In the burning of coal or in any high-temperature fire, nitrogen and oxygen combine to form a mix of various nitrogen oxides. The major constituent is nitric oxide (NO), which is oxidized to nitrogen dioxide ($NO_2$) once in the air. Nitrogen dioxide is a dangerous pollutant which does its dirty work in several ways. By itself it irritates the respiratory system, and high levels of nitrogen dioxide are associated with increased cases of respiratory disease. But the most dangerous effect results from its role in smog and ozone ($O_3$) formation, which occur when air containing nitrogen dioxide and unburned hydrocarbons (mostly gasoline from cars) is exposed to sunlight. The complex set of reactions that occur produce the smog and ozone, which irritate the eyes, cause breathing difficulty, aggravate cases of asthma, and damage vegetation.

Like sulfur dioxide, nitrogen dioxide can also be oxidized in the atmosphere to form an acid. When these acids fall out on the land, they act to increase the acidity of rivers, lakes, and the soil. The change in river and lake acidity can change the fish and plant populations, while increasing soil acidity reduces and then completely destroys its fertility. The situation is especially serious in the Scandinavian countries, with their proximity to the heavy industry of northern Europe.

**Present Controls on Coal-burning Plants.**  The most serious pollutant given off by burning coal is sulfur dioxide. The simplest way to reduce sulfur dioxide emissions is to burn low-sulfur coal, but the average coal burned in the United States in 1970 had 2.7 percent sulfur (low-sulfur coal contains less than 1 percent sulfur). About 70 percent of the nation's coal has less than 1 percent sulfur, but this coal is mostly found in the western United States, far from the major coal-consuming centers of the Northeast and Great Lakes states. At present it is too expensive to ship this coal east, but if oil and natural gas prices continue to rise, it may become economical. Or, new economic and technological developments may allow the electricity to be generated in the West and transmitted east by power grids. However, the western coal is not problem free. Most of it is intermediate or high in ash, some containing as much as 20 percent ash.

Another way to reduce the sulfur dioxide emissions is to remove the sulfur from coal before burning. Washing pulverized coal removes about 50 percent of the sulfur and some ash. But the remaining sulfur and ash can still cause a lot of air pollution. For these reasons, attention has centered on methods of removing the sulfur dioxide from the flue gas before it is released from the smokestack. But this is terribly difficult and at least until 1974 there were no satisfactory methods for removing sulfur dioxide. The problem can be compared to purifying a river after the sewage has been dumped into it. A huge amount of water must be treated to remove a small proportion of pollutant. Only a few experimental plants have any kind of sulfur-dioxide control system. The rest pour all of their sulfur dioxide into the atmosphere. As Figure 5 shows, this situation is expected to continue. If stiff sulfur-dioxide regulations are promulgated, power plants will have to install control devices. But with present techniques, this would greatly increase the cost of electricity.

### Emissions of Sulfur

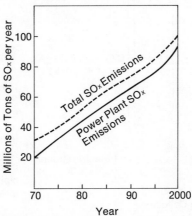

**Figure 5.** The graph shows projections of sulfur oxide emissions to the year 2000. Most emissions come from power plants with the rest mainly due to metal refining. Sulfur oxides are emitted by both oil-and coal-burning plants.

By contrast with sulfur-dioxide control, it is technically possible and economically reasonable to remove over 99% by weight of the particulate matter from flue gas. This high rate of purification is achieved with an electrostatic precipitator, shown in Figure 6. A central wire at a high voltage sprays out a cloud of electric charge. This charge is picked up by the ash particles in the hot flue gas; the particles are then attracted to the outer wall by the strong electric field. They collect there until they are shaken or brushed off by a mechanical scraper. But precipitators are not perfect. Ironically, they do not work well with the ash from low-sulfur coal, which has a high electrical resistance, since the electric charge is not attracted to the sulfur-free ash as well as it is to high-sulfur ash.[19] A second problem is that precipitators are very inefficient collectors of small-diameter particles, as shown in Figure 7. It is the small-diameter particles that are most damaging to health, interfere most with light, and stay aloft the longest.

Precipitators also add to the price of electricity. It costs money to build and maintain them and it takes a certain amount of electricity to sweep the current of charged particles out of the gas. Once the ash is collected, it must be disposed of, which can be quite a problem since coal may be 20 percent ash. Some progress is being made in finding uses for the ash, but at present most is buried in landfills.

## An Electrostatic Precipitator

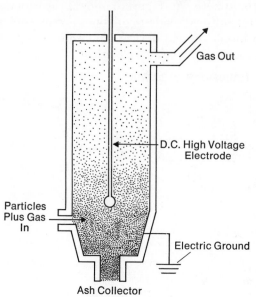

Gas Out

D.C. High Voltage Electrode

Particles Plus Gas In

Electric Ground

Ash Collector

**Figure 6.** A discharge of electrons from the negatively charged central wire (−100,000 volts) creates negative ions. The ions attach themselves to the ash particles, which are forced by the electric field to the outer wall of the precipitator, to be then shaken loose into the ash collector.

## Particle Sizes and Precipitator Efficiency

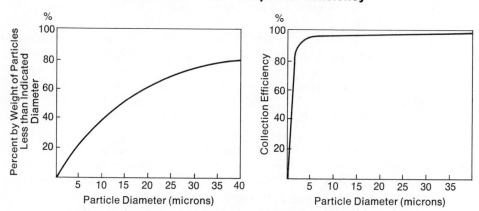

**Figure 7.** The curve on the left indicates the percentage of particles less than a given diameter. Significantly, about 20% by weight of particles emitted are smaller than 5 microns in diameter. The figure on the right shows that precipitator collection efficiency falls drastically for particles less than 5 microns in diameter.

**A Quantitative Look.** Because of the immense quantity of particulates a power plant can produce, even plants using precipitators or scrubbers of 90 or 95 percent efficiency can be very dirty. To see this, let us look at a million-kilowatt power plant. Such a plant at peak capacity consumes 1 million pounds of coal hourly in generating its 1 million kilowatt-hours

This cut-away of an electrostatic precipitator shows the series of plates which collect the particulates. The larger particles are easily separated and collected at the bottom. However, the electrostatic precipitator does not effectively remove small particles. *Photo courtesy American Electric Power Company.*

of energy. Although the coal may be 20% ash, we assume it is average U.S. coal with 10% ash. The plant will then produce

$$\text{ash} = (0.1)(10^6 \text{ lb/hr}) = 100,000 \text{ lb/hr}.$$

If half of the ash, or 50,000 pounds, goes up the stack (the rest falls as bottom ash), and the precipitator is 90% efficient, the ash emitted to the atmosphere is

$$(0.1)(50,000 \text{ lb/hr}) = 5000 \text{ lb/hr}$$

so that 2.5 tons of ash will be pumped into the atmosphere hourly.

As mentioned, when sulfur in the coal burns it combines with oxygen to form sulfur dioxide. Because each sulfur atom combines with two oxygen atoms, the sulfur dioxide emitted is heavier than the original sulfur. It so happens that an atom of sulfur is twice as heavy as an atom of oxygen. (Sulfur has an atomic weight of 32 and oxygen of 16.) Therefore the resulting sulfur dioxide is twice as heavy as the original sulfur, and burning 1 pound of sulfur produces 2 pounds of sulfur dioxide. If the million-kilowatt power plant is burning coal of 2.5% sulfur, then the coal burned contains

$$\text{sulfur} = (0.025)(10^6 \text{ lb/hr}) = 25{,}000 \text{ lb/hr.}$$

The 25,000 pounds/hour of sulfur will be oxidized to 50,000 pounds of sulfur dioxide. Since most plants have no sulfur-dioxide devices, all of this will be emitted to the atmosphere.

## Energy from Coal

### Electricity from Coal.

As mentioned earlier, all through the 1940s, 1950s, and 1960s, residences, utilities, and industries converted from coal to oil or natural gas. Natural gas emits practically no pollutants, but combustion of heating oil to make electricity or to heat homes produces sulfur dioxide, oxides of nitrogen, and some ash. However, modern oil refineries can remove most of the sulfur from oil for a price, so there is no technological reason why oil cannot burn clean. Therefore, if in the 1970s, the trend for electric utilities and industry is away from gas and oil and toward coal, we can expect a worsening air-pollution situation.

That a trend toward coal exists is indicated by a complex of plants being built in the Four Corners region formed by Utah, New Mexico, Colorado, and Arizona. These plants use strip-mined coal from the immediate area to generate electricity used "locally" in such cities as Tucson and Albuquerque and also exported hundreds of miles to Southern California. Most famous is the Four Corners plant near Farmington, New Mexico, whose smoke plume was said to be visible to astronauts in space. It has a capacity of 2 million kilowatts and burns coal that is low in sulfur (about 0.7%) but contains 21% ash.[20] It is said to have singlehandedly degraded the quality of thousands of square miles of clean desert air. Although Los Angeles uses some power from this plant, the plant itself is so dirty it could not legally be built in that city. Plants already existing, being built, or planned for the Four Corners area could add about 10,000,000 additional kilowatts of capacity. Together they would burn 10 million pounds of strip-mined coal per hour and produce at least 1 million pounds of ash hourly. Even if only 1% of this ash got into the air, it would constitute a serious problem. Total lack of sulfur-dixoide controls means that even 0.7%-sulfur coal would emit 140,000 pounds/hour of sulfur dioxide.

Several issues are raised by this proliferation of power plants. The fact that the plants are too dirty to operate in an urban area like Los Angeles indicates that pollution problems are being solved by spreading the dirt around. Should areas with very clean air be kept clean, or should policy be to allow clean air to be dirtied somewhat in order to take the strain off already impacted areas? Another problem revolves around water. The Southwest is an arid region and its water is much in demand. Should the water be used – as in the past – for agriculture or be diverted to industrial uses such as power generation? In power generation, water is not only needed for direct use as a coolant but also for irrigation to reclaim the stripped land.

**The North Central Power Study.**   That the Four Corners development is not an isolated occurrence is demonstrated by the North Central Power Study, which proposed in 1972 a huge electric-power complex centered in Wyoming, Montana, and North Dakota. By strip mining some of that area's 600 billion tons of coal, power plants in this sparsely populated, low-power-use region would produce and transmit 50,000 megawatts of electricity to load centers in thirteen states (see Figure 8) spread over one million square miles of the central United States.[21] Wyoming and Montana coal and water would provide energy for Minneapolis-St. Paul, St. Louis, Kansas City, Omaha, Des Moines, and scores of smaller cities.

## The North Central Power Study

**Figure 8.**   The above map shows the thirteen-state region covered by the North Central Power Study. If built, the project would generate 50,000 megawatts of power at the two locations indicated by G and distribute this power via massive grids to load centers indicated by L. The size of the generating complexes and load centers is roughly indicated by the letter size.

Because the power would be generated in the western part of the area supplied, and most of the power load is in the east, huge transmission grids, covering thousands of miles and costing billions of dollars, would have to be built. However, the utilities making the study estimate that this will be cheaper than shipping the coal to smaller power plants located throughout the thirteen states. By concentrating generating capacity in a small region, the utilities hope to minimize transportation costs and take advantage of economies of scale, even without further technical advances. In addition, this location minimizes and eases the number of environmental battles that must be fought since the states of Montana, Wyoming, and North Dakota have less restrictive environmental codes than more developed areas.

### New Approaches to Coal-generated Electricity.

The prospect of large amounts of strip-mined coal being used to generate electricity is a bleak one. As we mentioned earlier, even in 1974 the U.S. Congress had still been unable to decide on a law requiring reclamation of strip-mined land. In addition, only limited progress has been made in developing techniques to clean air pollution from the plants. Most efforts have been aimed at improvement of the electrostatic precipitator and at the development of other add-on devices to control sulfur dioxide and oxides of nitrogen.

But some engineers are critical of this add-on approach. They say the result will be more cumbersome and less efficient power plants, resulting in more expensive and less dependable power. To the critics the add-on approach lacks unity and esthetic appeal. These engineers urge that electric power plants be completely redesigned with the intent of building systems that are small, efficient, and clean.

Two major factors stand in the way of such a development. First, at least until recently, there has been very little research money available to design and build such plants. The electric utilities spend next to nothing on research. In 1970 they devoted only 0.23 percent[22] of their gross income to all research and development. This is one-tenth of what American industry on the average spends and one-eighth of what the utilities spent advertising their product—which is already fairly well known. Nor has the federal government put significant funds into coal-related research. Its research money goes to weapons development, advanced technology such as space probes and nuclear power, and basic (unapplied) research in the various scientific disciplines.

The second reason new systems may not be developed is due to an unwillingness on the part of the electric industry to change the heart of the power plant—the pulverized-fuel furnace. In the pulverized-fuel furnace, pulverized coal is blown into a large, hot fire that is burning in a large chamber. The heat released boils the water in the rows of metal tubes which are the walls of the giant chamber. A 500,000-kilowatt plant requires a furnace about 35 feet by 65 feet by 140 feet high. The pulverized-fuel furnace, adopted in the 1920s, took over from systems in which coal was burned on grates. The grate furnaces were unable to burn coal fast enough to feed heat to the big boilers then coming into use. The grates also became easily clogged with ash, which interfered with the burning. The pulverized-fuel system solved both problems. The fine pulverized coal could be sprayed into the fire at a high rate. And the fire burning in mid-air could not become clogged. The heavier ash fell as bottom ash while lighter material went up the flue with the gases. It is the large amount of ash flying upward that has created present problems.

Now that the emission of particulates and other pollutants is recognized as a serious problem, it is urged that the burning process be re-examined in its entirety. One attractive possibility is the fluidized-bed furnace in which chunks of coal interact with a rising stream of steam and air (see Figure 9). The speed of the gas stream is kept just large enough to suspend the coal without blowing it away or allowing it to fall. The interaction produces a gas consisting of hydrogen and carbon monoxide, which is then burned to provide heat for a boiler. The system has several advantages. Since the coal is not pulverized, the ash is heavier and less likely to go up the flue. If the reaction is held to 2000°F, the resulting ash clumps together and falls to the moving belt, which eliminates the need for an electrostatic precipitator. In addition, the reaction produces hydrogen sulfide, which is easier to remove than sulfur dioxide. The comparatively low-flame temperature also minimizes the quantity of nitrogen oxides produced.

### A New Approach to Coal Burning

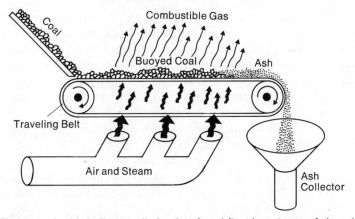

**Figure 9.** In this boiler, small chunks of coal float in a stream of air and steam entering from below. If the reaction temperature is held at 2000°F, the ash clumps together and falls to the moving belt. The coal-steam-air interaction produces carbon monoxide and hydrogen, which are then burned in a boiler to produce heat. The two-step process has important pollution advantages.

Another new approach is use of a two-stage engine consisting of a gas turbine and a steam turbine. A gas turbine is similar to a steam turbine in design, but the gas turbine is spun directly by hot gases resulting from combustion. Coal burned in a fluidized-bed furnace under several atmospheres of pressure produces high-pressure gases that spin a gas turbine. Having passed through the gas turbine, the hot gases are then used to boil water into steam; the steam is used to power a steam turbine. In theory, this two-stage process could generate electricity with 50 percent efficiency, which is 25 percent greater than present top efficiencies. Such a system would have the practical effect of expanding coal supplies by 25 percent, illustrating again how difficult it is to make predictions about the amount of energy available.

**Gas and Gasoline from Coal.**   Some coal experts suggest that processes be developed to convert coal into synthetic natural gas and gasoline. This would free coal from its present limited use as a heat source for power plants and metal refineries and enable it to be used to heat homes, cook food, and power automobiles, reducing pressure on oil and natural-gas supplies. Such coal-conversion plants would also produce by-products which could be used by the chemical industry as a starting material in the manufacture of synthetics.

It appears that coal can be gasified or liquefied with roughly 75 percent efficiency, which means that 25 percent of the coal's initial energy will be lost in the conversion process. Economic methods of converting coal to synthetic natural gas (1000 BTU/cubic foot) seem possible quite soon, but coal liquefaction to produce gasoline appears further off. While gasification would produce a low-sulfur fuel that could be transported in the existing gas pipeline network, there would still be environmental impacts. The coal would probably be strip mined and the conversion process would produce air pollution and require cooling water. Many of the problems are similar to those encountered with oil shale. A method of gasifying the coal while still underground would eliminate many of these problems. Land disturbance would be minimized and deep or thin beds of coal could be used that at present cannot be mined economically. Underground gasification might also increase the amount of coal removed from each bed. Present mining techniques require that roughly half the coal in a bed be left in the form of pillars to support the mine roof.

It is also possible that coal beds will in the future yield large quantities of natural gas, or methane, which is often found associated with coal. This gas is a nuisance in mines, being responsible for many fires and explosions. In the usual practice, the gas is flushed out of mine shafts and exhausted to the outside. Recent investigations show the nation's coal beds contain about 260 trillion cubic feet of natural gas, which is as much natural gas as in all other known deposits. It represents about ten years' supply at present rates of use. If this gas can be tapped, it would double domestic gas reserves.

## Conclusion

Seemingly, there are a large number of ways to meet future fossil-fuel energy needs. Petroleum and natural gas can be imported via tanker; oil shale and natural gas can be cooked and blasted out of their imprisoning rock; offshore and Arctic oil can be developed; and coal can be converted into electricity or gasified and liquefied. But there is a sameness to this diversity: they are all expensive, environmentally destructive sources of energy. The cheap, easy energy is gone.

Moreover, we grew fat on the earlier cheap flow of energy and built ever-growing demand into the system. We now must either cut back on energy use, as discussed in the last chapter, or develop new energy sources to meet growing demand. This chapter discussed meeting that demand with new sources of fossil fuel. In the following chapter we look at nuclear energy, which some have hailed as the cheap, abundant fuel of the future and others have called the ultimate energy disaster. The nuclear-energy chapter is followed with an examination of such "natural" sources as solar and tidal energy.

The technical details raised here and to be raised in later chapters are complex and fascinating. There are an infinite number of ways to arrange and rearrange strip-mined coal, oil shale, offshore oil, imported oil, and natural gas to meet our energy needs. Complex models of energy systems can be created to maximize BTU output and minimize unwanted effects. But through this technical work we must keep in mind that we are not talking of some abstract machine but rather of the visual and physical environment we live in and of the air and water we breathe and drink.

## Bibliography

*Source Notes*

1. "Snake Oil from the Oil Companies." *Consumer Report,* February 1974, p. 122.

2. "Energy Policy in the U.S." David J. Rose. *Scientific American,* January 1974, p. 20.

3. "Prognosis for Expanded U.S. Production of Crude Oil." R. R. Berg; J. C. Calhoun, Jr.; R. L. Whiting. *Science,* vol. 184 (19 April 1974), p. 331.

4. "The Secondary Recovery of Petroleum." Noel de Nevers. *Scientific American,* July 1965, p. 34.

5. "Low-Cost, Abundant Energy: Paradise Lost?" Hans H. Landsberg. *Science,* vol. 184 (19 April 1974), p. 247.

6. "Energy Resources." M. King Hubbert. In *Resources and Man.* San Franciso: W. H. Freeman, 1969. Page 157.

7. Ibid.

8. "The Black Tide." Julian McCaull. *Environment,* November 1969, p. 2.

9. *Potential Onshore Effects of Deepwater Oil Terminal-Related Industrial Development*, volumes i–iv. Report to the Council on Environmental Quality by A. D. Little, Inc., 1974.

10. *Trans-Alaska Pipeline*, part 2. Hearings before the Committee on Interior and Insular Affairs. U.S. Senate, 16 October 1969. Washington, D.C.: U.S. Government Printing Office.

11. "The Wrong Route." Charles J. Cicchetti. *Environment*, June 1973, p. 4.

12. "Lost Power." D. P. Grimmer and K. Lusczynski. *Environment*, April 1972, p. 14.

13. *The 1970 National Power Survey*, part 1. Federal Power Commission. Washington, D.C.: U.S. Government Printing Office.

14. *Final Environmental Impact Statement for the Prototype Oil Shale Leasing Program*, vol. 1. U.S. Department of the Interior, 1973.

15. Ibid.

16. "Cold Cargo." James A. Fay and James J. MacKenzie. *Environment*, November 1972, p. 21.

17. "Air Pollution and Human Health." Lester B. Lave and Eugene B. Seskin. *Science*, vol. 169 (21 August 1970), p. 723.

18. "A Perspective on Climatic Change." Reid A. Bryson. *Science*, vol. 184 (17 May 1974), p. 753.

19. "Clean Power from Coal at a Profit." Arthur M. Squires. In *Power Generation and Environmental Change*. David A. Berkowitz and Arthur M. Squires, eds. Cambridge, Mass.: MIT Press, 1971. Page 175.

20. *Problems of Electric Power Production in the Southwest*. Report of the Committee on Interior and Insular Affairs, U.S. Senate. Washington, D.C.: U.S. Government Printing Office, 1972.

21. *North Central Power Study*, volumes i and ii. Coordinating Committee, North Central Power Study, 1971. (Available from: Bureau of Reclamation, U.S. Department of Interior, Washington, D.C. 20240.)

22. *The Price of Power—Electric Utilities and the Environment*. The Council on Economic Priorities. New York, 1972.

*Further Reading*

RICHARD CARTWRIGHT AUSTIN and PETER BORRELLI. *The Strip Mining of America*. Sierra Club, 1971.
An examination of the technological and environmental aspects of strip mining is given in this book.

HARRY M. CAUDILL. *Night Comes to the Cumberlands*. Boston: Little, Brown and Co., 1962.
Caudill presents a fine portrayal of the impact on the Appalachian mountains and its people of underground and strip mining.

M. KING HUBBERT. "Energy Resources." In *Resources and Man*. Committee on Resources and Man. San Francisco: W. H. Freeman, 1969.
This is an informative article on our fossil-fuel and nuclear-fuel reserves.

HARRY PERRY. "The Gasification of Coal." *Scientific American*, March 1974, p. 19.
This article describes several methods of converting coal into pipeline gas.

ARTHUR M. SQUIRES. "Clean Power from Dirty Fuels." *Scientific American*, October 1972, p. 26.
This article describes various methods of obtaining clean power from coal.

U.S. DEPARTMENT OF THE INTERIOR. *Final Environmental Impact Statement for the Prototype Oil Shale Leasing Program*. Six volumes, 1973.
Volume 1 describes current technology and overall environmental impact of the oil-shale program.

## Problems

1. Assume exploratory well drilling in the United States averages 100 barrels per foot drilled. How many miles of exploratory wells must be drilled to find the total U.S. supply of oil, which is estimated at 200 billion barrels?

2. If natural gas occurs in the ratio of 6000 cubic feet per barrel of oil, how many trillion ($10^{12}$) cubic feet of natural gas did the United States initially have? Assume the initial oil supply was 200 billion barrels.

3. The average U.S. oil well produces oil at a rate of 17 barrels/day. Assume that the oil is transported and converted to end products with 80% efficiency, and that half of the end products are gasoline.
   a. How many cars can the average oil well keep fueled if the average car travels 30 miles/day and gets 12 miles/gallon? (A barrel of oil contains 42 gallons.)
   b. Under the above conditions (80% efficiency and half of the oil converted to gasoline), how many autos could TAPS fuel daily when running at full capacity?
   c. Calculate how many less miles each of the nation's approximately 100 million cars would have to travel to save the gasoline yielded by one million barrels of crude oil.
   d. If the cars continue to travel 30 miles/day, by how much would average gasoline mileage have to increase to save the same amount of gasoline yielded by one million barrels of crude oil?

4. Assume that the density of Alaskan crude is 56 pounds/cubic foot and that there are 6.3 barrels/ton.
   a. What is the volume of a barrel of Alaskan oil?
   b. Verify that the 4-foot diameter pipeline can carry 2 million barrels/day of oil at 10 feet/second.
   c. How long will it take oil to travel the 800 miles from Prudhoe Bay to Port Valdez through the pipeline?

5. The TAPS tanker fleet will have a total capacity of 5.2 million tons. How long is it assumed the typical tanker round trip will take when TAPS is running at capacity? (There are 6.3 barrels per ton of oil.)

6. The various TAPS flow monitors are said to be able to detect a leak of 31 barrels/hour. What percent of the maximum hourly flow is that?

7. TAPS is equipped with 94 block valves, equally spaced.
   a. How much oil is contained in the length of pipe between two valves? (See problem 4.)
   b. Suppose the oil is moving at 10 feet/second when a major break in the line occurs, and it takes 10 minutes to shut the block valves. Make some rough estimates and calculate how much oil would leak out.

8. Assume the TAPS walls become coated with wax so that its effective diameter is reduced 25%, from 4 feet to 3 feet.
   a. If the maximum speed remains at 10 feet/second, what is the pipeline's new daily capacity?
   b. How fast must the oil move through the constricted pipeline if it is to maintain a 2-million-barrels-per-day capacity?

9. Assume Alaskan oil suffers a 5% energy loss due to shipping, a 13% loss due to refining, and a 4% loss due to exploration and recovery. What is the total energy efficiency?

10. Assume a cargo of oil is shipped 2000 miles by pipeline at an energy cost of 300 ton-miles/gallon and 3500 miles by tanker at 250 ton-miles/gallon. What is the average transportation efficiency, in ton-miles/gallon, at which this oil is moved?

11. Compare the energy content of a ton of oil shale (35 gallons/ton, $1.3 \times 10^5$ BTU/gallon) with a ton of coal ($10^4$ BTU/pound). What implications does this have for environmental problems?

12. Compare the energy-carrying capacity of an oil tanker containing 300,000 tons of crude oil (6.3 barrels/ton, $5.8 \times 10^6$ BTU/barrel) with a liquefied-natural-gas tanker having a 3-million-cubic-foot capacity. Each cubic foot of liquefied natural gas expands to 600 cubic feet of gas, having an energy content of 1000 BTU/cubic foot.

13. According to Figure 5, how many pounds of sulfur oxides are currently being emitted per person per year in the United States?

14. Assume the 2-million-kilowatt Four Corners plant has a heat rate of $10^4$ BTU/kilowatt-hour and burns $1.1 \times 10^4$-BTU-per-pound coal. The coal contains 0.7% sulfur and 21% ash. At peak output, how many pounds of ash and sulfur dioxide will it emit per hour if 4% of the ash and all the sulfur dioxide are released?

15. Assume the Four Corners plant is supplied with coal strip mined from New Mexico land yielding 9 million tons/square mile. (See Table 4.)
   a. How much coal does the plant use in a year if it operates at an average of 80% capacity? (See problem 14.)
   b. How many square miles of land will have to be stripped to supply the plant with coal each year and during its 30-year lifetime?

*It was a universal law: everyone who acts breeds both good and evil. With some it's more good, with others more evil.*

ALEXANDER SOLZHENITSYN*

# The implications of nuclear power

Any discussion of energy shortages and environmental problems leads inevitably to nuclear power. Although nuclear power provided the United States in 1970 with less energy than did the burning of wood, and with only 5 percent of its 1973 supply of electricity, it is potentially a major energy source. (See Table 1.) Some experts predict that over the next several decades nuclear energy will replace fossil fuels as the major producer of electricity. They place their faith in the breeder nuclear reactor, which makes new fuel as it generates electricity. The breeder can be compared to a (physically impossible) coal-burning plant which produces 1.5 pounds of new coal for every pound burned.

**Nuclear and Fossil-fuel Energy.** In some ways, nuclear power plants resemble fossil-fuel plants. Both burn a fuel to release heat which boils water into steam. The steam spins turbines to generate electricity. But nuclear "burning" is very different from the burning of coal or oil. When a fossil fuel burns, carbon or hydrogen atoms combine with oxygen atoms to form carbon

---

* From Solzhenitsyn's book *Cancer Ward* (New York: Farrar, Straus, and Giroux, Inc., 1969).

dioxide $(C + O_2 \rightarrow CO_2)$ or water $(2H_2 + O_2 \rightarrow 2H_2O)$ and release energy. This chemical burning involves only the outer-shell electrons of each atom, and each burned atom releases a comparatively small amount of energy.

**Nuclear Energy and Electric Power Production**

|  | 1960 | 1970 | 1980 | 1990 | 2000 |
|---|---|---|---|---|---|
| Total Electric Generating Capacity (megawatts) | 175,000 | 349,000 | 630,000 | 1,150,000 | 2,000,000 |
| Total Nuclear Generating Capacity (megawatts) | 20 | 5,900 | 132,000 | 508,000 | 1,200,000 |
| Electric Power (kilowatts/person) | 0.97 | 1.71 | 2.73 | 4.42 | 6.98 |

SOURCE: "Nuclear Power 1973–2000," Atomic Energy Commission (Wash-1139), 1972.

**Table 1.** Shown here is a projection of total U.S. electric power capacity and the portion that will be produced by nuclear power plants. Note that the expected growth is ascribed mainly to increases in per-capita consumption, not to a rapidly growing population.

The end product of our present use of nuclear energy is still steam to power a turbine which spins an electric generator. The large pipes shown here carry steam from the reactor to the 1,100,000-kilowatt turbine-generator at left. The plant, operated by Chicago's Commonwealth Edison, takes cooling water from Lake Michigan. *Photo courtesy Westinghouse Electric Corporation.*

By contrast, the "burning" of a nuclear fuel such as uranium-235 (U-235) or plutonium-239 (Pu-239) consists of the splitting, or fissioning, of the individual uranium or plutonium nucleus to form two new elements. Because fission involves the compact, massive, densely charged nucleus, much more energy is released atom-for-atom by fission than by chemical burning. Fissioning 1 pound of U-235 releases about 2.5 million times more energy than does the burning of a pound of coal. This means a million-kilowatt coal plant burning 12 million pounds of coal daily can be replaced by a nuclear plant using only 5 pounds of fuel daily.

In addition to the huge fuel advantage, a nuclear power plant emits no ash, soot, carbon monoxide, sulfur dioxide, or nitrogen oxides. And unlike fossil-fuel plants, nuclear power does not lead to strip mining, acid streams, or oil spills. But like fossil-fuel plants, nuclear power plants create waste heat and therefore thermal pollution. The thermal-pollution problem is more serious with present nuclear power plants because safety considerations require low operating temperatures. This limits their thermal efficiency to 33 percent,[1] compared to a modern coal plant's 40 percent efficiency. A coal plant also exhausts some of its waste heat to the atmosphere via the smokestack, but a nuclear plant dumps all its heat into the cooling water. Overall, a nuclear plant puts much more waste heat into the cooling water than a fossil-fuel plant per unit of electricity produced.

## A Brief History

Although the harnessing of nuclear energy is a scientific and technical achievement, its present prominence is mostly due to an historical accident: the development of the atomic bomb during World War II. As a result of the several billion dollars spent on the Manhattan Project, our understanding and control over nuclear energy increased greatly. Several large plants were built to process nuclear fuels, and a large number of scientists, technicians, and administrators were trained to deal with nuclear technology.

The creation of the bomb faced the nation with the postwar problem of what to do with nuclear energy. The killing of about 200,000 people at Hiroshima and Nagasaki showed its incredible destructive power and the rivalry between the United States and Russia meant that nuclear energy would continue to be developed for weapons. The harnessing of nuclear energy for peaceful purposes seemed very attractive in this context—a modern version of beating swords into plowshares.

**The Atomic Energy Commission.** The Congress created the civilian-controlled Atomic Energy Commission (AEC) in 1946 to develop military and peaceful uses of nuclear energy. The AEC has guided such developments as electric power plants, medical applications of radioactive substances, hydrogen-bomb warheads for guided missiles, and nuclear explosives for canal building and natural-gas stimulation. In peaceful applications, the AEC is both promoter and regulator. It encourages utilities to build power plants and gas companies to use nuclear explosives to free natural gas from its rock. The AEC also determines general safety standards and inspects each individual project for adherence to these standards.

The dual role of promoter and regulator has subjected the AEC to criticism. It has been charged that the two functions are inherently in conflict. This does not mean that the AEC will knowingly be lax in imposing safety standards on individual power plants. Ensuring that no catastrophic accidents occur is consistent with the role of promoter since a bad accident would set back nuclear-power development.

**The Long View.** But the promotional role may discourage the AEC from taking a close look at the long-range dangers of nuclear power. For example, it is generally assumed that any increase in radioactivity in the environment represents an increased threat to health. It is also agreed that no technological system — including a nuclear power plant — can be made 100 percent dependable. There is always the possibility that the system or its operators will behave in an unforeseen way.

An individual or institution predisposed to nuclear energy will evaluate the radiation or accident dangers differently than will a person or institution neutral or hostile to nuclear energy. So even if the technical and scientific facts are not at issue, there would be disputes over what is an acceptable risk and what is a desirable benefit.

Unfortunately, nuclear technology is new and we have not yet accumulated large amounts of adequate and dependable information. Our lack of health and safety statistics and our imprecision in interpreting the statistics that we do have cause us to look closely at each problem that arises. We wonder if the few instances of leaking wastes that have occurred are an isolated, unimportant problem or an indication that we are unable to handle radioactive wastes. If the latter is true, what will happen when fuel reprocessing plants are producing large quantities of waste due to an expanded nuclear power industry? (See Table 2.) The past exposure of uranium miners and the use of radioactive uranium mill tailings as construction material in Grand Junction, Colorado, are also relatively small problems (although not to the miners or to the residents of Grand Junction). But if they are indicative of the way we will handle radioactive materials when the nuclear industry is many times larger, then we are faced with a serious problem.

Some have interpreted present difficulties as meaning that nuclear energy is too dangerous to be used on a large scale; that inevitably a host of small sloppy acts will cause background radiation levels to rise and catastrophic accidents to occur. The critics say that nuclear energy's great power brings with it an almost certain promise of future disaster; they predict that nuclear energy will turn on us in an even more deadly way than autos and fossil fuels.

**Projected Radioactive-Waste Shipments and Waste Storage**

|  | 1980 | 1990 | 2000 |
|---|---|---|---|
| Shipments of High-level Wastes | 23 | 240 | 590 |
| Accumulated Volume of High-level Wastes (ft³) | 3,170 | 74,200 | 319,000 |
| Salt-mine Acreage Used for Storage of High-level Wastes | 9 | 200 | 900 |

SOURCE: "Social Institutions and Nuclear Energy," A. M. Weinberg (*Science*, vol. 177 (7 July 1972), p. 27).

**Table 2.** Each high-level waste shipment is assumed to contain 57.6 cubic feet of waste. A nuclear power plant produces 1 cubic foot of high-level waste for each 76,000,000 kilowatt-hours of electricity produced. Salt-mine storage assumes development of methods of solidifying the wastes.

**A Faustian Bargain.** Others recognize the difficulties nuclear energy will impose, but say that modern society should and must take up that burden. Dr. Alvin Weinberg—former director of Oak Ridge National Laboratory and a strong nuclear-power advocate—compares the coming predicted transition to nuclear energy with man's earlier transition to agriculture.[2] When primitive man moved from a hunting and food-gathering existence to a settled agricultural one, his population grew in step with the increased food agriculture made available. Once this increase occurred, there could be no going back to hunting and food gathering without widespread starvation. Agriculture also made the world a more complicated place. While hunting and food gathering required some skill, agriculture demands both skill and organization. Seed must be stored from year to year, irrigation systems maintained, land surveyed, calendars kept and astronomical observations made so that planting can be done at the proper time and soil fertility maintained. Unlike a hunting society, which merely harvests what nature provides, an agricultural community requires planning, organization, and work at every step of the way.

The result is a more plentiful and dependable supply of food than hunting provides, just as nuclear energy is potentially a larger energy source than fossil fuels. But agriculture has a greater potential for disaster than hunting. Agricultural populations are denser than hunting populations so a bad harvest can cause more suffering than an unsuccessful hunt. Mayan civilization, for example, is believed to have been destroyed by a combination of exhausted soil, dense population, and invasion.[3] Ireland in the 1850s saw its population drop from 8 million to 4 million people due to widespread starvation and migration caused by the potato-crop failure.

So when primitive man shifted from hunting to agriculture he struck a Faustian bargain for all succeeding generations: he obtained an increased food supply but had to pledge himself to eternal care of the land, preservation of seed, the passing on of skills and information from generation to generation, and the surrender of the thrill of hunting and the freedom of wandering. Similarly, Weinberg points out that in return for plentiful energy we will have to remain forever on guard against all manner of nuclear-energy problems. He writes that society was able to adapt to and profit from agriculture and that nuclear energy presents the same kinds of opportunites and challenges.

**Nuclear Power, Railroads, and Police.**  It is interesting to try to predict the changes a growing nuclear-power industry will encourage. The primary effect will be on nuclear power plants, fuel-reprocessing plants, and radioactive-waste storage areas. These installations will have to be made of the most dependable parts, maintained in top condition at all times, and operated by highly skilled and motivated people. To ensure that the parts going into these installations are of top quality, the industrial suppliers to the nuclear industry will have to be as precise and competent as the nuclear industry itself.

Even such seemingly peripheral industries as the railroads will be affected. At present, U.S. railroads suffer 0.3 serious accidents per million car-miles. If this rate persists to the year 2000, and 9500 shipments yearly of high-level and other radioactive wastes are shipped an average of 500 miles, 1.4 serious accidents[4] involving radioactive cargo can be expected yearly. While strong packaging will reduce the danger of radioactive leakage, there will also be strong pressures on the railroads to improve their safety performance. So the nation's most advanced technology will affect one of its oldest technologies.

Police practices will also be drawn into the nuclear complex. Radioactive cargos are very valuable, and if effective security measures are not taken, thefts will occur. The stolen cargo may then be sold on a black market or used to blackmail a city or nation. Atomic bombs, for example, can be made from the plutonium which is a product of breeder reactors and of today's light-water reactors. In fact, several hundred atomic bombs can be made from the plutonium output of one present-day reactor.[5,6] The emerging nuclear industry has before it the disastrous example of the air-transport industry, which a few years ago found itself almost paralyzed by sky-jacking. Only costly security measures solved the problem, which was not foreseen when this advanced technological system was being put together. Sky-jacking also shows that a weakness in a system may not appear for years or decades.

If nuclear energy is to be our major source of power, then not only must all its parts function well, but they must mesh together. This requires a large, competent, and powerful bureaucracy capable of regulating and coordinating electric utilities, fuel-reprocessing plants, railroads, security forces, and manufacturing plants. Such an administrative structure is typical of advanced technological systems. It has often been pointed out that the real miracle of the U.S. moon landing was not any one technical achievement, but the administrative operation that pulled the many individual efforts together. The question is this: What will be the effect on and the costs to society of the nuclear bureaucracy, which must be powerful and pervasive if it is to operate a safe system?

Nuclear energy will affect the general population. Those who work in the nuclear-power industry or in industries that serve it will be most directly affected since their training and discipline will have to be rigorous. But the high degree of precision and dependability required of men and machines by nuclear power will probably affect society as a whole. It is not likely that we will be touched as directly by nuclear energy as we are by today's dominant technology — the auto — but we will be affected.

Nuclear energy will be a remote technology. But we will all be involved in its effects and its mistakes. We will have to make the kinds of political decisions about nuclear energy that we make today about transportation and water-pollution-control bond issues. Thus an understanding of nuclear technology will have to disseminate through all strata of society.

To some observers, the trends in the development of nuclear energy thus far give little hope that the public will eventually become involved in nuclear decisions. Harold P. Green, professor of law at George Washington University, writes:

> Our society has permitted these (nuclear) experts to play God: to assess benefits, to define risks, and to determine what risks the public must assume, cheerfully, just as it pays taxes, in exchange for benefits which the experts think the public should have. What is more, under the carefully nurtured myth that judgements about nuclear safety can be soundly made only by these experts, we have permitted these experts to decide these risk/benefit questions largely behind closed doors and in the esoteric, obfuscatory jargon of their disciplines.*

**Institutionalizing Progress.** The development of nuclear energy can be looked at as an attempt to institutionalize progress; to take over from necessity the mothering of invention. When the historical accident of the atomic bomb presented the opportunity of developing nuclear energy, the United States had an abundance of fossil fuel and was totally unconcerned with environmental problems. Nevertheless, experts were predicting future shortages of fossil fuels and the nuclear-development program was undertaken in part to meet that distant problem.

---

* Harry Foreman, ed., *Nuclear Power and the Public* (Minneapolis: University of Minnesota Press, 1970), p. 136.

To some, the nuclear-energy program seems extraordinarily successful: a distant problem was recognized and decades of research and development done before a need existed. Today with fossil fuels seemingly running short and environmental concerns mounting, nuclear power is about ready to come on the scene. It would seem that we no longer have to trust to the lucky appearance of an Edison or Ford to fulfill our needs. Our increasingly complex society seems to have developed the ability to foresee distant problems and bring its resources to bear to solve those problems.

But another view is possible. Some say that when the government decided to put its resources behind nuclear energy, it guaranteed that nuclear energy would be *the* energy solution because all other possible approaches to the energy problem would be neglected. In order to obtain government funding and to use technological spin-off from government investment in research, universities and private industry concentrated on nuclear energy and ignored such alternatives as solar or geothermal energy or more efficient use of fossil fuels. (See Table 3.) The possibility of doing more with less energy was also neglected because government commitment to nuclear power meant that cheap, abundant energy remained official policy. So the critics say nuclear energy is not a fortunate solution to an inevitable problem, but rather an example of society being bent out of joint to accommodate a new technology. Others say that a growing demand for energy was inevitable whatever the government did and that we are fortunate to have nuclear power available to meet that demand.

## The Nuclear Energy Network

Although most attention is paid to the nuclear power plant itself, it is more realistic to view the plant as one link in a chain. Other links include the uranium mines which produce the ore, the mills which process the ore, the plants which convert the processed ore into enriched fuel, the reprocessing plants which deal with the radioactive wastes produced by the reactors, and the storage areas in which these wastes must then be kept for thousands of years. Tying the whole system together are the railroads, which transport ore, fuel rods, and radioactive wastes between the different facilities.

Uranium Mines, Mills, and Processing Plants.  Until now, at least, the uranium mines, mills, and processing plants have presented workers and the general public with greater dangers than the reactors themselves. Until recently, for example, uranium mines were poorly ventilated. As a result, the mine air contained large concentrations of radon gas—a radioactive substance resulting from the decay of the radium which is found in the uranium ore. As a result of inhaling the radioactive radon gas, the miners developed lung cancer at a rate well above the national

**Federal Funds for Energy Research (millions of dollars)**

| Area | 1973 | 1974 |
|---|---|---|
| Conservation | 32.2 | 65 |
| Nuclear Fission (total) | 406.5 | 530.5 |
| Breeders | 288.8 | 390.3 |
| Safety and Waste Management | 42.4 | 54.8 |
| Fusion | 74.8 | 101.1 |
| Coal | 85.1 | 163.1 |
| Solar | 4.0 | 13.8 |
| Geothermal | 4.0 | 10.8 |

SOURCE: "The Budget of the United States Government" (*Science,* vol. 183 (15 February 1974), p. 635).

**Table 3.** Nuclear breeders command the major share of the federal government's energy-research money. It is only in recent years that anything at all has been spent on conservation, despite the fact that it is estimated that 30% of our energy is wasted.

average. The problem is compounded by the fact that it can take several decades for the disease to occur. So although the mines are now better ventilated and the amount of time miners spend underground is limited, miners and former miners continue to be struck down at a high rate.

The next link in the chain is the uranium mill, which processes the mined ore. The mill produces a sand-like waste product, called tailings, which contains radium but from which the uranium has been removed. Unfortunately, the tailings have proven to be an excellent construction material, and until 1966 they were used in several western communities as a base for roads and homes and as a substitute for sand in masonry mortar. The city of Grand Junction, Colorado (population 30,000), has been hardest hit by these construction practices. From 1951 to 1966, roughly 250,000 tons of tailings[7] were used in the construction of homes, schools, and roads in and around Grand Junction. Just as in the mines, the radium in the tailings decays into radon gas, which then diffuses out of the masonry wall or out from under the floor if the tailings have been used as fill. In addition to the radon gas, the radium emits gamma radiation, which also damages the body.

Because the radon- and gamma-radiation levels are low, no one can say for sure what the effect of prolonged exposure will be. But all agree that everyone would be better off if the radioactive material were removed. This, however, would require the expenditure of $15 million to rebuild or demolish 5000 homes, and neither the AEC, the state of Colorado, or the uranium mills that gave away the tailings is willing to pay the price. They are especially reluctant since the cost will ultimately be much greater than $15 million when other towns affected by the tailings make their claims. At the present time, the inhabitants of Grand Junction are living with the problem while the various levels of government argue over who is at fault.

From the uranium mills, the enriched ore is sent to a plant to be manufactured into fuel rods, which are then used by the reactor to produce its energy. Once the fuel is burned up, the rods are removed from the reactor and replaced with new ones. But the removed rods cannot simply be thrown away. As a result of their year or so in the reactor, they are intensely radioactive. Before they can be shipped to a reprocessing plant, they are stored in a deep pool of water in the reactor for four months. During this time the most active, short-lived radioactive materials decay. The spent rods are then transferred to cooled and armored casks for shipment by rail to a reprocessing plant.

The reprocessing plant, with its 7-foot-thick concrete walls for shielding, treats the fuel rods chemically in order to separate out unburned uranium-235 as well as other radioactive substances useful in medicine or industry or for weapons. The reprocessing plant emits about 100 times more radioactivity[8] than a reactor. The treatment process results in the routine release to the environment of radioactive gases such as krypton-85 formed in the nuclear reactor. With present procedures, the end product of the fuel reprocessing is a highly radioactive, corrosive, boiling hot (due to the nuclear activity) liquid that must be safely stored for thousands of years.

At present, about 42 million gallons of this waste—most of it a result of weapons production—are being stored in concrete-steel tanks in Hanford, Washington, which is the final link in our nuclear system. Small leaks from the tanks occur occasionally, but in 1973 over 100,000 gallons[9] of the hot corrosive liquid ate its way out of a tank and seeped into the ground. The large loss was partly due to improper monitoring of the tank's liquid level—which delayed detection of the leak—and partly due to the AEC's failure to budget money to replace the aging, leak-prone tanks. Work is presently underway to develop ways of solidifying the wastes to make storage easier and safer.

Finally, in addition to the problems of routine release of radiation and accidental leaks, there is the specter of a catastrophic power-plant accident, in which the reactor's fuel and waste products escape to the environment. It was estimated in 1957 that if, due to some unlikely combination of accidents, half of a small reactor's radioactivity escaped and blew toward a city, it would kill 3000 people, cause many more to become ill, and cause $7 billion in damage.[10] The nuclear-power interests—which consist of the electric utilities, nuclear-reactor suppliers such as General Electric and Westinghouse, the AEC, and many independent scientists—say a serious accident is inconceivable due to a multitude of safeguards.

**Insuring Against Disaster.**   Despite their reassuring public utterances, however, the electric power companies insist upon the protection of the Price-Anderson Act. Under this law, the federal government provides

$478 million in accident insurance to electric utilities. The law also limits the liability of the utility to this amount plus whatever insurance the utility can obtain from private insurers. But private insurers refuse to sell more than $82 million of insurance per reactor and the resulting total of $560 million[11] does not come close to covering the damage a bad nuclear accident would cause to the public.

Those critical of the nuclear power industry ask why private insurers are unwilling to insure reactors for greater amounts if a serious accident is so unlikely. They also ask why — if electric utilities are so confident of their plants — they don't operate them without insurance. The utilities unanimously refuse to operate nuclear power plants without the protection of the Price-Anderson Act. It has been argued that it is merely sound business practice for a company to protect itself against even an extremely unlikely occurrence. But it has also been argued that the public is entitled to the same protection.

These arguments are not purely scientific or technical. They involve certain implicit values. The Price-Anderson Act was passed in 1957 by lawmakers who felt it important to encourage the development of nuclear energy. They were therefore willing to shift some of the risk from the electric utilities to the public, who — in theory — will ultimately benefit from the development of nuclear energy. People who believe society has no need for the energy nuclear power can supply or who feel that the risk is greater than the benefit oppose Price-Anderson. But the amount of risk a person is willing to run to get energy or the amount of energy a person thinks is necessary to his or her well-being is not and can not be answered in scientific or technical terms. Some of the risks we do run are listed in Table 4.

**Radiation and Health.** Compared to a coal- or oil-burning plant, the entire nuclear power system (mines, mills, reactors, and so on) releases a minute quantity of pollution per unit of energy produced. But just as nuclear fuel is a much more concentrated source of energy, so its pollutants are a much more concentrated source of danger. It is believed that even small quantities of radioactive material in the environment can cause genetic change and increases in cancer and leukemia.

This is because radioactive substances emit highly energetic, electrically charged and uncharged particles, and electromagnetic waves. As these gamma, alpha, and beta rays travel through a person's body, they give up energy to the cells they strike. In fact, they can be thought of as tiny bullets. If the person receives an intense burst of radiation, a large number of cells will be damaged, causing radiation sickness and possibly death. If the radiation levels are low, the effect is less predictable. Should the cells be damaged rather than killed, they may reproduce abnormally and years or decades later result in cancer. If reproductive cells are damaged, the person's offspring may be born dead, born with some physical defect, or be left with a harmful recessive gene which will affect later generations.

**Some Typical Risks**

| | *Odds Against Per Year* |
|---|---|
| Disability Due to an Auto Accident | 100:1 |
| Cancer Death | 700:1 |
| Auto Death | 4,000:1 |
| Fire Death | 25,000:1 |
| Drowning | 30,000:1 |
| Electrocution | 200,000:1 |

SOURCE: "Radiation Standards, Particularly as Related to Nuclear Power Plants," V. P. Bond (Raleigh, N. Carolina: Address to the Council for the Advancement of Science Writing, 16 November 1970).

**Table 4.** Some typical death risks we take each year are listed here. These would vary with the individual. An electrician would have a greater chance of being electrocuted, and an 18-year-old a greater chance of being killed or injured in an auto accident. The chance of "being killed" by a nuclear reactor is estimated to be much less than 200,000:1. Studies show that people are willing to take a much greater risk voluntarily (due to swimming, smoking, driving, wiring a house) than if it is an involuntary risk such as that imposed by cancer or nuclear power.

So the consequences of releasing radioactive substances to the environment can be quite subtle and long range.

Effects differ depending on whether the radioactive substance is inside or outside the body. For example, we are continually bombarded with so-called background radiation from outer space (cosmic rays) and from radioactive materials in the earth's crust. But the effects are not nearly as serious as if we should receive an equivalent amount of radiation from an ingested radioactive source.

Radium, for example, chemically resembles calcium. Therefore, if it is ingested, the body deposits it in the bones. It then sits there, decaying and bombarding a comparatively small part of the body with radiation. If the amount ingested and deposited is large enough, the result after 10, 20, or 30 years will be bone cancer. So in dealing with radioactive substances, we must not only worry about their activity rate, but also about the way in which they interact with the biological world and the human body.

Nuclear pollutants differ from fossil-fuel pollutants also in their tenacity. If all fossil-fuel burning were stopped today, most of the pollutants will have settled out of the air in a week or two. By comparison, many radioactive substances have half-lives (the time it takes for half of the radioactive material to undergo fission or nuclear decay) of hundreds or thousands of years. This means that once such material gets into the environment it will continue to give off radiation for thousands of years. Therefore even regular, low-level releases of radioactive material represent a possible threat because over a long period of time they will accumulate in the environment. The potential threat of radiation to health is intensified by the fact that the effect on our body is assumed to be cumulative. This means that the possibility of a person getting cancer or suffering genetic damage depends on the total amount of radiation he or she has been exposed to over the years.

At the present time, the amount of radiation emitted directly by existing nuclear power plants, uranium mines, and fuel-processing plants is small compared to natural background radiation and radiation from x-rays and other medical sources (see Table 5). But as Table 1 shows, the amount of nuclear power to be generated in the United States is expected to increase greatly. In evaluating the benefits and risks attached to this nuclear growth, we would like to know how many cases of cancer or instances of birth defects will be associated with the projected environmental radiation. Unfortunately, even approximate predictions cannot be done because the damage caused by low levels of radiation is not known. Any increase in illness caused by the power-plant radiation levels shown in Table 5 could not be detected because of variations due to other causes. Dependable experimental results are also difficult to obtain. Billions of mice would have to be exposed to low levels of radiation for years in order to get significant results. The complexity and long-term nature of the interaction between the human body and radiation make cause-and-effect relations difficult to establish. The situation is comparable to attempts to establish statistical and experimental links between smoking and health, or air pollution and health.

**Radiation Exposure and Radiation Standards**

| | |
|---|---:|
| Expected Effects of Acute Radiation Exposure (whole body) | |
| Half-Exposed Would Die | 450 rem |
| Nausea, Fatigue | 100–200 rem |
| Slight Temporary Blood Change | 25–50 rem |
| No Detectable Clinical Effects | 0–25 rem |
| Radiation Protection Standards | |
| Occupational Exposure | 5000 mrem/yr |
| Individual in Population | 500 mrem/yr |
| Average Sample Population Group | 170 mrem/yr |
| Exposure from Typical Operating Power Reactors | |
| Near Site Boundary | 5 mrem/yr |
| Typical Nonoccupational Exposures | |
| Background from Natural Sources (U.S.) | 80–200 mrem/yr |
| Medical Exposures | 73 mrem/yr |

Source: *Environmental Effects of Producing Electric Power*, Hearings before the Joint Committee on Atomic Energy, U.S. Congress (Washington, D C.: U.S. Government Printing Office, 1970).

**Table 5.** The rem is a unit of radiation dose. The mrem (millirem) is 1/1000th of a rem. The radiation standard for the average population (170 mrem/yr) has been drastically lowered.

The Radiation Standards Debate.   The complexity of the problem is illustrated by the debate that developed in the late 1960s over the effects of environmental radiation. The debate began when Professor Ernest J. Sternglass of the University of Pittsburgh stated that fallout from atmospheric tests of nuclear bombs had caused in some locations a significant number (1 out of 3) of infant deaths.[12] Sternglass reached his conclusions by analyzing fallout patterns and infant death rates in areas he calculated received the fallout.

Although it is known that human fetuses are much more susceptible to radiation damage than the general population, most workers in the radiation-standards field disagreed with Sternglass' conclusions. But in the course of rebutting Sternglass' work, two employees of the Atomic Energy Commission decided that the scientific evidence indicated existing radiation standards were much too high. These standards would in theory allow the population to be exposed to 170 millirems (mrem) of radiation per year due to nuclear power operations. (A millirem is a unit of radiation.) The two AEC employees, John Gofman and Arthur Tamplin, argued that if such radiation levels were reached, the United States would suffer an additional 30,000 cancer deaths yearly.[13]

Gofman and Tamplin agreed with their (numerous) critics that present operations did not come close to such levels. But they said the standards should be lowered to guard against future increases. If such increases were to occur, we would then face the same widespread problems we face now in reducing air-pollution levels.

At first, the Gofman and Tamplin projections were rejected by the AEC and the nuclear-power establishment. They argued that the 170-millirems level would never be reached and that, if reached, nowhere near 30,000 deaths per year would occur. The difference of opinion could not be resolved because the effects of low levels of radiation were and are unknown. However, statistics do exist for cancer cases caused by exposure to higher levels of radiation. Much of this information comes from survivors of the atomic bombing of Hiroshima and Nagasaki and from patients exposed to radiation, such as x-rays, in treatment for a disease. Gofman and Tamplin took these data and extrapolated them linearly to low levels. That is, they assumed that if exposure to $A$ millirems of radiation causes $N$ cases of cancer, exposure to $0.001A$ millirems will cause $0.001N$ cases of cancer. Others in the radiation field interpreted existing data to mean that a threshold exists; that below a certain level, the body repairs radiation damage.[14] If that were true, reducing radiation levels to $0.001A$ millirems might result in $0.0001N$ cancer cases, or even in none at all. Perhaps the uncertainty over how to interpret the various data will be understandable if you recall the difficulty of interpreting auto-accident statistics.

The question is still not definitely settled, but in 1972 a committee decided that the 170-millirems standard was far higher than it had to be and that such levels, if reached, could cause from 3000 to 15,000 extra deaths per year and a 5 percent increase in the nation's ill health. As a result, the permitted radiation levels have been drastically lowered.

Radiation and the Ecosystem. The debate over the danger of radiation continues on other fronts. In part this is because evaluating the dangers of radioactive materials is complicated by the concentrating ability of the natural environment or the body, as already mentioned with regard to radium. A classic example occurred in the 1950s when the United States and Russia were testing nuclear weapons in the atmosphere. The radioactive debris was carried away from the test sites by winds and the debris eventually "fell out" over the land and ocean. Experts had foreseen this and had calculated that the radioactive material would be so dispersed as to be harmless. But they overlooked the grass-cow-child biological chain which acted to concentrate strontium-90 (Sr-90), a radioactive nucleus with a half-life of 28 years which also chemically resembles calcium. Cows eating grass on which strontium-90 had settled would concentrate it in their milk. Children drinking the milk would then incorporate the strontium-90 in their teeth and bones. As a result, small amounts of strontium-90 were concentrated into potentially harmful doses. This is only one of several mechanisms by which radioactive substances can be concentrated in the environment. And although the example cited refers to weapons fallout, the same processes can happen with power-plant emissions.

## Nuclear Technology

We shall now look in more detail at the operation of a nuclear-energy system. We mentioned earlier that a fossil-fuel plant burns coal, oil, or natural gas while a nuclear power plant "burns" U-235. The two burning processes are very different and the quantities of energy released per atom burned differ by a factor of millions. The huge difference occurs because the chemical burning of coal and the nuclear burning of U-235 result from two fundamentally different processes. The combining of carbon and oxygen atoms to form carbon dioxide involves only the atoms' light outer-shell electrons while fission of U-235 involves the massive nucleus. Nuclear fission has nothing to do with the orbital electrons and oxygen plays no role in the process.

We recall that an atom consists of electrons circling a nucleus in orbits which can roughly—very roughly—be compared to planets circling the sun. The electrons are held in their orbits by the attraction between the negatively charged electrons and the positively charged nucleus. In burning, the outer-shell electrons of the several combining atoms rearrange themselves so as to bind the atoms together. This new arrangement of atoms—called a molecule—is in a lower energy state than the uncombined atoms (see Figure 1). The difference between the energy of the separate atoms and that of the molecule is the amount of energy given off in burning.

**Carbon Dioxide**

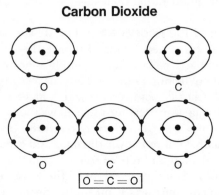

**Figure 1.** Shown here are the oxygen and carbon atoms with the orbital electrons circling the nucleus. The electronic bonding which holds the carbon dioxide molecule together is also shown. The boxed symbols are a shorthand method of showing the molecule. Each line represents a single electronic bond.

**Nuclear Energies.** Fission energy is a result of the splitting of the nucleus. The nucleus consists of the positively charged proton and the uncharged, or neutral, neutron. Both of these fundamental particles are about 1840 times more massive than the electron (see Table 6). The nucleus contains as many protons as there are orbital electrons, which means the atoms are electrically neutral. The number of neutrons in the nucleus is usually equal to or greater than the number of protons. Although the nucleus is the massive, central part of the atom, its physical extent is tiny. The electron orbits are about 10,000 times larger than the diameter of the nucleus (see Figure 2).

This small nuclear size is one factor in producing the tremendous energies. The U-235 nucleus, for example, consists of 92 protons and 143 neutrons crammed into a space about $10^{-13}$ inches in diameter. Over this small distance, the positively charged protons exert tremendous repulsive forces on each other. In stable nuclei such as carbon-12 (6 protons and 6 neutrons), this force is overcome by the very much stronger, short-range, nuclear attractive force which holds the nucleus together. The neutrons act as a sort of dilutant, keeping the protons a bit apart and thereby weakening the electrical repulsion while still exerting the strong nuclear attractive force.

Light nuclei have approximately equal numbers of protons and neutrons. Helium has 2 protons and 2 neutrons, nitrogen 7 protons and 7 neutrons, and oxygen 8 protons and 8 neutrons. But in heavier nuclei, the number of neutrons becomes larger than the number of protons. Physically, the excess neutrons act to counteract the large electric repulsive force between the protons.

### Mass and Charge of the Electron, Proton, and Neutron

|  | *Charge* | *Mass* | *Weight* |
|---|---|---|---|
| Electron | $-1.6 \times 10^{-19}$ coulombs | $9.1091 \times 10^{-31}$ kilograms | $2.01 \times 10^{-30}$ pounds |
| Proton | $+1.6 \times 10^{-19}$ coulombs | $1.67252 \times 10^{-27}$ kilograms | $3.7 \times 10^{-27}$ pounds |
| Neutron | $0$ | $1.67482 \times 10^{-27}$ kilograms | $3.7 \times 10^{-27}$ pounds |

**Table 6.** Note in this table that the neutron is slightly more massive than the proton, but both the neutron and the proton are about 1840 times more massive than the electron.

### The Carbon Nucleus

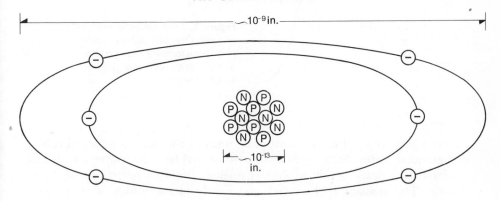

**Figure 2.** The carbon-12 nucleus consists of 6 protons and 6 neutrons. The diagram is out of scale because in reality the diameter of the electronic orbit is 10,000 times the nuclear diameter. If the nucleus were represented by the dot over this "i," the orbits would just barely fit on the page.

But eventually even this dilution fails and the heaviest nuclei tend to be unstable or radioactive. Uranium-235, for example, consists of 92 protons and 143 neutrons. Despite this large neutron dilution, the uranium-235 nucleus is radioactive, emitting helium nuclei, or alpha particles, with a half-life of about $7 \times 10^8$ years. Uranium-238, the heaviest naturally occurring nuclei, also decays by emitting an alpha particle with a half-life of $4.5 \times 10^9$ years. The inherent instability of uranium-235 is the key to controlled nuclear fission. If a slowly moving neutron strikes a uranium-235 nucleus, the probability is high that it will fission into two new nuclei, releasing a large amount of energy.

An analogy is provided by a ball sitting atop a hill. The slightest nudge starts it rolling downhill, transforming the gravitational potential energy into kinetic energy. The energy expended nudging the ball is much smaller than the energy released by the ball (see Figure 3). Analogously, the slowly moving neutron just has to nudge the U-235 nucleus to cause it to fission into two very rapidly moving nuclei plus two or three neutrons. The fission products have a total kinetic energy of about $3 \times 10^{-14}$ BTU, or $2 \times 10^8$ electron volts (ev), which is transferred to other atoms and molecules due to collisions between them. It is this energy which then boils water into steam to power the turbines.

## A Gravitational Analogy

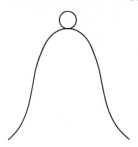

**Figure 3.** The slightest nudge will send the ball rolling downhill, transforming its gravitational potential energy into kinetic energy.

**The Nuclear Firebox.**   In a coal-burning plant, powdered coal is blown into a large box, where it burns. The walls of the box are miles of tubing containing water. Heat from the burning coal boils the water into steam, which then flows to the turbine. A nuclear firebox operates quite differently. The nuclear fuel is packaged neatly in thousands of thin-walled metal tubes. A typical 500-megawatt plant would contain about 20,000 tubes, holding a total of 70 tons of fuel. About one-third of the fuel is replaced each year. Cooling water flows among the tubes, carrying off the heat that is generated and boiling into steam to power the turbines.

Coal can be ground up and burned as it emerges from the ground, but uranium ore must be extensively treated before it can be used in a power plant. This is because uranium ore is a mixture of two isotopes of uranium: it consists of 0.7 percent U-235 and 99.3 percent U-238. The U-235 and U-238 are called isotopes of uranium because they each have 92 protons and 92 electrons. This means that their chemical properties are almost exactly the same. But the U-238 nucleus has three more neutrons than the U-235 nucleus.

While this neutron difference has a tiny effect on chemical properties, it has a great effect on nuclear behavior. The rare U-235 isotope can be fissioned by a slow, or low-energy, neutron, but the abundant U-238 nucleus does not interact with low-energy neutrons. Since the present generation of nuclear reactors use slow neutrons to produce the fission events which generate the energy, it means that the U-238 is useless. For this reason, most modern reactors use enriched uranium ore as a fuel.

The U-235 content is commonly increased to 3 percent from the original 0.7 percent in order to increase the reactor's efficiency. However, some reactors do run on unenriched fuel.

The Chain Reaction.   Once we have the fuel, we are faced with the problem of starting and controlling the nuclear "fire." In a coal plant this is simple. A spark is used to ignite the coal dust and the energy output is raised or lowered by blowing more or less coal dust into the firebox. Controlling the energy level of a nuclear power plant is much more complicated. The total supply of fuel is always present in the reactor core so the energy output cannot be changed by varying the amount of fuel present.

To understand how the nuclear reaction is controlled, it will help if we first look at chemical burning. The match applied to the fuel raises the coal temperature and therefore the atoms' velocity. At the higher speeds, the oxygen and carbon atoms penetrate each others' outer electron shells. At room temperatures, no such penetration takes place. The high-speed penetration made possible by the increased speeds allows the carbon and oxygen atoms to combine to form carbon dioxide and to release energy. Some of this energy is transferred by collisions to other carbon and oxygen atoms, which allows the burning process to continue. Energy not needed to sustain the burning goes to boil water into steam.

### A Gravitational Chain Reaction

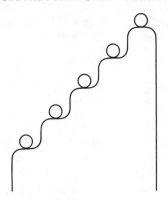

**Figure 4.**   A gentle push starts the top ball rolling, and it, in turn, starts the next ball rolling, and so on down the hill.

This is a chemical chain reaction. The match starts the process going and after that it is then self-sustaining. A gravitational analogy is shown in Figure 4. The top ball is started by a gentle push, which represents the match. As this ball rolls downhill, it starts the next ball moving, which starts still another ball. In this way the hill is swept clean of balls. Some small part of the gravitational energy released goes into maintaining the reaction (knocking the balls free), but most is available in the form of the balls' kinetic energy.

Nuclear reactors and nuclear bombs also depend on a chain reaction. In the nuclear reactor, the "match" is a stray neutron, perhaps emitted by a spontaneously fissioning nucleus. (U-235 has a spontaneous fission half-life of $10^{18}$ years.) When this neutron strikes a U-235 nucleus, it causes it to fission, emitting energy and two or three neutrons. Each of these neutrons can fission new U-235 nuclei, releasing still more neutrons and causing the reaction to build. On the average, U-235 emits 2.5 neutrons per fission. (See Figure 5.)

## A Nuclear Chain Reaction

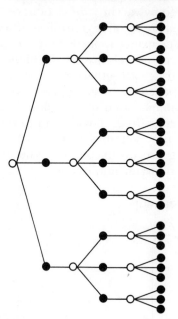

**Figure 5.** The solid dots represent low-energy neutrons and the open dots represent U-235 nuclei. In this schematic diagram we have assumed each fission event yields 3 neutrons. In reality the average is 2.5.

**Controlling the Reaction.** But before the chain reaction can start and be controllable, two complications must be introduced. The neutrons emitted by a fissioning U-235 nucleus are fast neutrons and therefore unlikely to fission another U-235 nucleus. To slow the neutrons, they are allowed to collide with the cooling water, called the moderator. Collisions between the light hydrogen nuclei in the water molecules and the neutrons quickly slow them, at which point they become very likely to fission U-235.

If the moderator (cooling water) is efficient, the reactor has a growing number of thermal neutrons causing a growing number of fission events. Since it takes only 0.0001 seconds to moderate a neutron, an explosive chain reaction can build rapidly. To prevent this, each reactor is equipped with a dozen or so rods made of a neutron-absorbing isotope such as boron-10. When the movable boron rods are fully inserted into the reactor core, they sop up so many neutrons that a chain reaction is impossible. As the rods are withdrawn from the core, more neutrons become available to fission U-235 and the fission rate and the amount of energy the reactor is generating increase. When the reactor reaches the desired power output, the rods are withdrawn no further. In that equilibrium position, one of the 2.5 neutrons emitted during an average fission event goes to cause another fission event. The other 1.5 neutrons either escape the reactor or are absorbed in some nonfission, nuclear-event interaction. So the neutron moderator and the movable control rods allow the chain reaction to be started and controlled.

In addition to 2.5 neutrons, each fission event produces two new isotopes, as shown in Figure 6. The nuclei which result from fission are radioactive. They do not undergo fission but emit several types of radiation as they spontaneously transform from one radioactive isotope to another, eventually becoming stable isotopes. The time this takes depends on the half-life of each of the isotopes in the radioactive decay chain. Some half-lives are listed in Table 7. It is the decay products that make up the dangerous and persistent radioactive wastes mentioned earlier.

## Fission

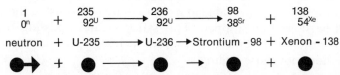

$$\underset{0}{1}n \; + \; \underset{92}{235}U \longrightarrow \underset{92}{236}U \longrightarrow \underset{38}{98}Sr \; + \; \underset{54}{138}Xe$$

neutron + U-235 ⟶ U-236 ⟶ Strontium - 98 + Xenon - 138

**Figure 6.** This schematic diagram represents the neutron-induced fission of U-235. The two resulting new nuclei will almost immediately decay into different isotopes. U-235 can fission into several different pairs of nuclei. (In writing the nuclear isotopes, the upper number is the number of protons and neutrons and the lower number the number of protons. So $^{138}_{54}$Xe has 54 protons and 84 neutrons $(138 - 54 = 84)$.)

**Some Half-Lives**

| Isotope | Half-Life |
|---------|-----------|
| Xenon-133 ($^{133}_{54}$Xe) | 5 days |
| Barium-140 ($^{140}_{56}$Ba) | 13 days |
| Zirconium-95 ($^{95}_{40}$Zr) | 65 days |
| Krypton-85 ($^{85}_{36}$Kr) | 9 years |
| Tritium ($^{3}_{1}$H) | 12 years |
| Strontium-90 ($^{90}_{38}$Sr) | 28 years |
| Cesium-137 ($^{137}_{55}$Cs) | 30 years |
| Plutonium-239 ($^{239}_{94}$Pu) | 24,390 years |
| Iodine-131 ($^{131}_{53}$I) | 8 days |

**Table 7.** Listed above are the half-lives of some radioactive isotopes produced by nuclear reactors.

**Nuclear Reactors.** Let us now look at the hardware which harnesses the nuclear chain reaction to produce electric power. There are two principal commercial reactor types: the pressurized-water reactor (PWR) and the boiling-water reactor (BWR). In the PWR, water under 2000 pounds/square inch of pressure and at a temperature of 600°F circulates through the reactor core, both moderating the neutrons and carrying off the heat released by the chain reaction. This circulating water flows from the core to a heat exchanger, where it gives up heat to water in a physically separate loop. The water in this loop is at a lower pressure and boils into steam to drive the turbine. The advantage of the separate loop is that the cooling-moderating water — which will be somewhat radioactive because it picks up radioactive impurities from the fuel rods — does not flow through the turbine or condenser. (See Figure 7.)

In the BWR, the water that flows through the reactor core as coolant and moderator is also allowed to boil into steam to drive the turbine (see Figure 8). This makes leaks of small amounts of radiation more likely because it is difficult to build an absolutely tight turbine and condenser. But the BWR has a safety advantage over the PWR: if the temperature of a BWR rises, the water in the core will boil more rapidly. This means less water will be available to moderate the neutrons, so the chain reaction will be slowed or stopped. This safety factor is missing from the PWR, where the water in the core is under such high pressure that a temperature rise does not cause boiling.

**Pressurized Water Reactor**

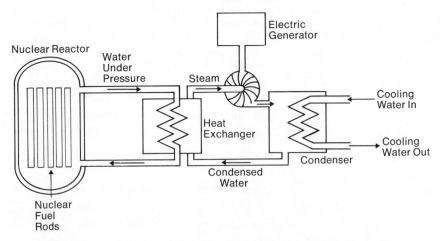

**Figure 7.** This schematic of a pressurized water reactor shows that there are three separate water loops: the pressurized water which moderates the neutrons and carries off heat from the core; the water which picks up heat from the heat exchanger and boils into steam to drive the turbine; and the cooling water from the local lake or river.

## Boiling Water Reactor

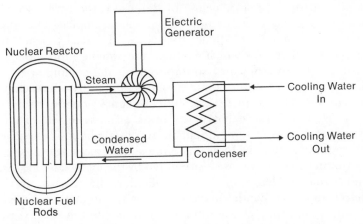

**Figure 8.** This schematic of a boiling-water reactor shows that the water that flows through the reactor core also drives the turbines.

This light-bulb-shaped vessel is the steel shell for a nuclear reactor to be located near Athens, Alabama. The 115-foot-high structure will be encased in 5-foot-thick concrete. The steel vessel and concrete sheath are meant to contain the radioactivity produced by the reactor should a major accident occur. *Photo courtesy Tennessee Valley Authority.*

Safety Measures.   Both the BWR and PWR reactors have a variety of safety measures. The first line of defense is the care with which the reactor's components are manufactured and assembled. The emphasis in the nuclear industry is on "quality assurance." Especially critical is the system of pipes and pumps which circulate the cooling (and moderating) water through the reactor core. So important is the cooling system that a separate, emergency, core cooling system is built into each reactor. If the main system should fail, in theory the emergency cooling system would take over. However, there has never been a full-scale test of an emergency system and in 1971 some doubts were raised about its effectiveness. Work is presently underway to evaluate the system more fully.

Another line of defense is presented by the many temperature, pressure, and radiation detection devices built into the reactor. If these sensors detect abnormal conditions, the reactor is automatically scrammed (shut down) by inserting the boron control rods into the core. If the front line defenses should fail and temperature builds up anyway, there are still three physical barriers guarding against a release of radiation to the environment. First, the radioactive fuel is clad in thin-walled metal tubes. Second, the entire fuel assembly is enclosed in a very strong, primary-metal vessel. Third, if a violent explosion should rip apart the primary vessel, the radioactive material would still be held within a large steel-concrete containment shell. This shell also offers protection against an airplane crashing into the reactor.

This system of defenses has given the nuclear-power industry an excellent reactor safety record. But despite the great safety efforts, possible if unlikely accident scenarios can still be constructed. One such scenario is the "China Syndrome" accident, which postulates a loss of normal and emergency coolant, with perhaps a ton of hot radioactive fuel melting its way out of the reactor and into the ground. The escaped fuel would not reach China, but it could go deep enough to get into the ground water. This might destroy a region's underground water supply and provide a transportation mechanism by which the radioactivity could spread out of the local area.

Breeder Reactors.   The BWR and the PWR are both called nuclear burners because they consume fissionable fuel. If the United States continues to rely on burner reactors, it is estimated that by the year 2000 we will have consumed our cheap, high-grade uranium ore. If the nuclear industry must then depend on expensive, low-grade ore, the power produced might no longer be economically competitive with fossil-fuel power. For this reason, it is assumed by some that burner reactors cannot serve as major power sources much beyond the turn of the century. Some experts challenge the technical, economic, and resource arguments on which this conclusion is based. They say, for example, that if the price of uranium increases, more uranium will be found. However, the federal government has assumed that the burner reactor cannot serve as a long-term source of energy and has intensified its efforts to develop a breeder reactor.

A breeder reactor would have the ability to manufacture fuel as it produces power. For every pound of fuel burned, the breeder could in theory produce 1.5 pounds of new fissionable fuel. The key to this multiplying effect is the excess of neutrons produced by a chain reaction. Each fission reaction produces an average of 2.5 neutrons, but only 1 of these neutrons is needed to sustain the chain reaction. That leaves 1.5 extra neutrons. In present reactors, an average of 1 neutron is wasted when it escapes from the core or is absorbed in an unproductive way. The remaining 0.5 neutron is absorbed[15] by the abundant uranium-238 isotope, which results in the following reaction (Np is neptunium).

$$\underset{92}{238} U + \underset{0}{1} n \rightarrow \underset{92}{239} U \xrightarrow{\text{electron}} \underset{93}{239} Np \xrightarrow{\text{electron}} \underset{94}{239} Pu$$

The resulting plutonium-239 (Pu-239) isotope is very much like U-235. It can be fissioned by a slowly moving neutron to give off about the same amount of energy and neutrons as U-235. However, plutonium-239 is a poor conductor of heat and is subject to severe radiation damage in the reactor, causing the fuel rods to swell. In addition, it is harder to control a plutonium-239 chain reaction than a uranium-235 chain reaction. For all these reasons, the plutonium-239 extracted from reactor waste products is not now reprocessed into fuel for reuse in present-day reactors. Instead, it is being stockpiled for future use in breeder reactors.[16]

Breeder reactors, which are still in the research and development stage, are very different from the burner, or light-water, reactors we have been discussing. A breeder is designed to produce both electric energy and new supplies of fissionable fuel. The breeder will do this by using almost all the excess 1.5 neutrons produced per fissioned nucleus to convert the now-useless uranium-238 into fissionable plutonium-239.

The breeder reactor, as now visualized, will consist of a central core of concentrated plutonium-239 fuel (concentrated uranium-235 could also be used) surrounded by a blanket of uranium-238. The excess neutrons will interact with the surrounding uranium-238 to form the plutonium-239. In 8 to 9 years, depending on specific design, the breeder will double its initial supply of fuel.[17] If it started with a ton of plutonium-239, it will have bred 2 tons of fuel plus made available all the energy released in fissioning the initial ton of fuel.

There are several possible breeder designs, but the U.S. government has invested most of its research money in the sodium-cooled breeder, called the Liquid Metal Fast Breeder Reactor (LMFBR). The sodium coolant circulates through the reactor core. The heat it picks up is transferred to water, which boils into steam to drive a conventional turbine. Sodium is used as a coolant for several reasons. First, it boils at a very high temperature and therefore it does not have to be under pressure, as when water is used as a coolant. Second, it is a very poor moderator of neutrons. This is vital because fast neutrons are needed to efficiently breed uranium-238 into plutonium-239. It is the lack of a moderator that allows a breeder to be three times more efficient than a light-water reactor in turning uranium into plutonium. The breeder is also an efficient electric-power generator. Because it operates at a high temperature, its efficiency is 40 percent compared to the 32 percent achieved by light-water reactors.

But a price must be paid for these efficiencies. Like uranium-235, plutonium-239 is most easily fissioned by a slow neutron. In order to achieve a chain reaction with fast neutrons, the fissionable fuel must be much more concentrated than in a present-day reactor. This makes the breeder more difficult to control. The seriousness of this problem is magnified by the fact that plutonium-239 is much deadlier than other radioactive substances. So it is all the more important that the breeder function perfectly. The breeder's use of large amounts of plutonium-239 also raises the problem of diversion. It would take only 10 pounds of concentrated plutonium fuel to make an atomic bomb,[18] which could be used by the underworld or other unfriendly groups.

But if these problems can be overcome, the world's supply of fissionable uranium would be increased by a factor of 140, since 139 out of each 140 uranium nuclei are uranium-238. As of mid-1974, an intense political, scientific, and economic battle was being fought over the strengths and weaknesses of the breeder. The eventual result of that battle will probably be to make the breeder reactor safer and cleaner, not to stop its development.

**Nuclear Fusion.** The debate over the need for and safety of the breeder reactor is complicated by the prospect of fusion energy. The burner and breeder reactors get their energy by splitting an unstable heavy nucleus into two lighter, more tightly bound nuclei. The energy released is equal to the difference between the final and initial binding energies. In fusion, two light nuclei are combined to form a new heavier nucleus. The new nucleus is more tightly bound than the original nuclei and this results in a net release of energy. Fusion is the sun's and the hydrogen bomb's source of energy.

In one possible fusion reaction, two deuterium nuclei (an isotope of hydrogen) combine to form the helium-3 isotope and release $4.8 \times 10^{-16}$ BTU ($3.2 \times 10^6$ ev) of energy. There is a nearly infinite amount of this type of fusion fuel available in ocean water since 1 out of every 6500 hydrogen atoms is the deuterium isotope. If only 1 percent of the oceans' deuterium were fused, energy equal to 500,000 times that contained in the world's total fossil-fuel supply would be released. But it is not at all certain that fusion power can be tapped. Because a fusion reaction requires very high temperatures, it cannot take place in a material container. One possible solution is the "magnetic bottle," in which strong magnetic fields are used to confine the quickly moving, charged particles. Although progress is being made, no "bottle" has yet been designed which can contain the particles at high enough densities and temperatures for long enough times to extract fusion energy. Most of the recent progress has been made with laser-initiated fusion, which does not require magnetic containment.

It is the possibility of fusion that further complicates the breeder picture. If fusion power is developed, it will probably be a safer, environmentally cleaner and more abundant energy source than breeder energy. Should the government therefore abandon the fission program and invest available talent and resources in fusion? As Table 3 shows, so far most federal funds have gone into the breeder program; fusion research has been maintained at a much lower level.

### Fossil-fuel and Nuclear-fuel Energy Densities.

We wish now to understand quantitatively why U-235 and Pu-239 are such concentrated sources of energy. Throughout the text we have tried to give quantitative and physical pictures of whatever processes were being discussed. That was comparatively easy with water, more difficult with transportation, and much harder with energy. Our word picture of chemical energy is that of atoms coming together to form compounds by the sharing or exchanging of electrons. This rearrangement results in a lower energy state and therefore the release of energy. The release of energy by fission is similarly due to a physical system (the nucleus) attaining a lower energy state, this time by splitting in two.

While it would be possible to build a more complete qualitative model of chemical and nuclear energy, a quantitative treatment is beyond the level of this book. We will instead take for granted the atomic-scale chemical and physical processes that release the energy and see what they mean on a macroscopic scale.

When a carbon atom combines with two atoms of oxygen, carbon dioxide is formed and $6 \times 10^{-22}$ BTU (4 ev) of energy is released. In contrast, when a U-235 nucleus fissions, it yields $3 \times 10^{-14}$ BTU ($2 \times 10^8$ ev). Fission, then, yields 50 million times more energy per atom than does the burning of carbon:

$$\frac{3 \times 10^{-14} \text{ BTU}}{6 \times 10^{-22} \text{ BTU}} = 50 \times 10^6.$$

At first glance it might appear that a pound of U-235 should give off 50 million times more energy than a pound of carbon. However, the U-235 atom is much heavier than the carbon atom. Therefore a pound of carbon contains more atoms than a pound of U-235 and gives off more energy than a straight atom-to-atom comparison would indicate.

As pointed out earlier, almost the entire mass of the atom is due to the protons and neutrons in the nucleus. Since U-235 has 235 protons and neutrons, and carbon has 12 protons and neutrons, to a first approximation U-235 is 19.6 times heavier ($235 \div 12 = 19.6$) than carbon. The actual ratio is slightly different because the weight of the nucleus is not simply the sum of the weights of the individual protons and neutrons. But we shall assume the proton and neutron each have a weight of 1 and that the nuclear weight is the direct sum of the protons and neutrons. The atomic weight of U-235 under this assumption is 235 and of carbon is 12.

The carbon-12 isotope is taken as the standard so its atomic weight is exactly 12. But the other atomic-weight values are not exact multiples of the weight of the protons and neutrons because some of their collective mass is transformed into the binding energy which holds the nucleus together, following Einstein's famous relation between mass and energy: $E = mc^2$. So in all cases the actual weight is less than the sum of the weights of the unbound protons and neutrons. The size of the reduction varies from nucleus to nucleus, depending on how tightly bound the nucleus is.

But let us disregard these binding effects—which are the source of fission energy—and assume that a U-235 atom is exactly 19.6 times heavier than a carbon atom. That means 235 pounds of U-235 contain as many atoms as 12 pounds of carbon, and that 19.6 pounds of U-235 contain as many atoms as 1 pound of carbon. We can generalize this relation to include all the elements. A pound of hydrogen—whose nucleus contains only 1 proton—contains as many atoms as 12 pounds of carbon or 235 pounds of U-235. Similarly, 4 pounds of helium-4—whose nucleus contains 2 protons and 2 neutrons—contain as many atoms as 1 pound of hydrogen, 12 pounds of carbon, and 235 pounds of U-235.

The physical properties of the elements are usually given in metric-system units. So we will momentarily turn to the metric system so that we can develop a comparison of the energy content of coal versus U-235. In the metric system, 1 gram of hydrogen, 4 grams of helium, 12 grams of carbon, and 235 grams of U-235 all contain the same number of atoms. When the atomic weight of an atom is expressed in grams, as, for example, 1 gram of hydrogen, it is called a mole of hydrogen. So 4 grams of helium is a mole of helium, 12 grams of carbon a mole of carbon, and 235 grams of U-235 a mole of U-235. The number of atoms in a mole of a substance is always the same, $6.02 \times 10^{23}$ atoms, which is called Avogadro's number.

To compare the relative energy content of coal (assumed to be pure carbon) and U-235, we note that 12 grams of carbon—1 mole of carbon—contain $6.02 \times 10^{23}$ atoms. If burned completely, carbon yields

$$(6.02 \times 10^{23} \text{ atoms}/12 \text{ gm})(6 \times 10^{-22} \text{ BTU/atom})$$
$$= 3.6 \times 10^2 \text{ BTU}/12 \text{ gm}$$
$$= (3.6 \times 10^2 \text{ BTU}/12 \text{ gm})(454 \text{ gm/lb})$$
$$= 1.4 \times 10^4 \text{ BTU/lb}$$

which is actually the heat content of 1 pound of high-grade anthracite coal. We also know that 235 grams of U-235 contain $6.02 \times 10^{23}$ atoms. Therefore

$$(6.02 \times 10^{23} \text{ atoms}/235 \text{ gm}) (3 \times 10^{-14} \text{ BTU/atom})$$
$$= 1.8 \times 10^{10} \text{ BTU}/235 \text{ gm}$$
$$= (1.8 \times 10^{10} \text{ BTU}/235 \text{ gm}) (454 \text{ gm/lb})$$
$$= 3.5 \times 10^{10} \text{ BTU/lb}.$$

So the ratio of the energy content of a pound of U-235 to a pound of coal is

$$\frac{3.5 \times 10^{10} \text{ BTU/lb}}{1.4 \times 10^{4} \text{ BTU/lb}} = 2.5 \times 10^{6}.$$

Thus U-235 is 2.5 million times more energetic per pound than coal. This means an ounce of U-235 is equivalent to 160,000 pounds of high-grade coal. The same ounce of U-235 is also equal to 384 barrels of crude oil.

Mining the Ore. While the energy advantage of U-235 is huge, we must also look at the amount of ore mined to obtain the U-235. Uranium is not found in a pure, concentrated, ready-to-use state like coal. Within the next 30 years or so, the high-grade uranium deposits we currently use may be exhausted, and we will be dependent on low-grade deposits. A typical low-grade uranium vein may contain no more than 0.006 percent uranium by weight. Such a deposit is the Chattanooga shale bed which underlies parts of Illinois, Indiana, Kentucky, Ohio, and Tennessee. It is 15 feet thick and has a density of about 160 pounds/cubic foot. We wish to calculate the amount of ore that must be removed in comparison with the amount of coal that must be removed to obtain equal quantities of energy. If it turns out that to extract a usable amount of U-235, enormous quantities of ore must be mined and processed, then the economics of nuclear power will be poor and a great deal of land will be disturbed, perhaps needlessly.

Let us assume we are going to extract both the uranium and coal by strip mining. We will compare the amount of land surface that will be disturbed to obtain equal quantities of energy. Since our uranium bed is 15 feet thick, 1 square foot of surface yields 15 cubic feet of ore. This weighs

$$(15 \text{ ft}^3) (160 \text{ lb/ft}^3) = 2.4 \times 10^3 \text{ lb}.$$

The uranium in this 0.006% ore is

$$(6 \times 10^{-5}) (2.4 \times 10^3 \text{ lb}) = 0.14 \text{ lb}.$$

But only 0.7% of uranium is the fissionable U-235 isotope, so the amount of U-235 in this ore is

$$(7 \times 10^{-3}) (0.14 \text{ lb}) = 10^{-3} \text{ lb}.$$

This is equivalent to 2500 pounds of coal since U-235 is 2.5 million times more concentrated than coal.

To compare this with strip-mined coal we assume we are stripping land that yields 10 million tons/square mile of 14,000-BTU-per-pound coal. Doing the calculation shows that we get about 700 pounds of coal for each square foot of surface area disturbed. So to obtain 2500 pounds of coal—which is equivalent in energy to the $10^{-3}$ pounds of U-235—we would have to strip mine about 3.6 times more land ($700 \times 3.6 \approx 2500$).

However, the uranium ore requires extensive refining and concentrating, while the coal can be used as is. Processing the uranium ore requires a large amount of energy, which reduces the energy advantage of the U-235. But if breeder reactors are developed so that the U-238 isotope as well as the U-235 isotope could be used, then the uranium ore would contain 140 times more usable energy. On a surface-area basis, this would yield over 500 times more energy per square foot of land disturbed compared with coal. Probably only the development of the breeder reactor will allow low-grade uranium ores to be mined profitably.

## Conclusion

When looked at in a purely scientific light, nuclear power is a revolutionary innovation. It taps for the first time the enormous, concentrated energy of the atomic nucleus, increasing by about a factor of a million the energy available to man. If fusion energy can be harnessed, it would be the ultimate Promethean achievement, since it is fusion that powers the sun.

But in a technological and social sense, nuclear energy is in many ways more of the same. We have seen in earlier chapters how one technology stands on the foundations laid by preceding ones. The steam engine was an important advance, but it was initially hooked up to machinery developed for waterwheels, windmills, or horses. The railroads made possible a large-scale steel industry, and the steel industry provided the metal needed for trains, tracks, and bridges.

In the same way, nuclear power—at least initially—will merely replace fossil fuels in providing steam for turbines. And without a hundred different industries, ranging from railroads to mining, nuclear power would be impossible. But while, initially, nuclear power may feed off existing industries, as it grows it will begin to affect them. It will inevitably lead to new technologies, greater complexity, greater interdependence, and larger scale problems and risks. Metallurgy will be called on to provide radiation-resistant materials; railroads to provide safe dependable transportation; the instrumentation industry to provide compact ways of detecting radiation; and the medical industry to care for those who will inevitably be injured and stricken with sickness by the new technology.

Nuclear energy, then, like all of our technologies, does more than provide a pure physical service. It becomes part of the context in which we live and it therefore helps shape us. As Jacques Ellul has written in *The Technological Society:*

> But it is requisite that (technological) man have certain precise inner characteristics. An extreme example is the atomic worker or the jet pilot. He must be of calm temperament, and even temper, he must be phlegmatic, he must not have too much initiative, and he must be devoid of egotism. The ideal jet pilot is already along in years (perhaps thirty-five) and has a settled direction in life. He flies his jet in the way a good civil servant goes to his office. Human joys and sorrows are fetters on technical aptitude.

It may seem that the almost infinite amount of energy nuclear fission and fusion could provide differentiate them from fossil-fuel energy. But the steam and internal combustion engines caused immense increases in the energy available to us, and even today, after tremendous use and growth, the United States still has several hundred years of fossil-fuel energy available. So the fact that nuclear energy can ensure that our energy supplies last millenia instead of centuries does not seem a true motivation in our pushing for it. A nation that strip mines, builds parking lots on farmlands, and floods valleys with relatively short-lived reservoirs is not a nation that plans for the coming thousand years.

It has been said that modern civilization is dominated by "know how" to the exclusion of "know why"; that we are always seeking a better, more efficient, more powerful route to carelessly examined ends. Within the internal logic of the machine we have built, nuclear energy makes sense and is perhaps even inevitable. It meshes so well, it grows so logically out of what has gone before. As a result, nuclear technology can probably not be "logically" questioned within the existing social and technological framework. Only if we step beyond the machine to ask the kind of "why" questions which until recently were so neglected can nuclear energy be examined in a balanced way.

## Bibliography

*Source Notes*

1. "Electric Power from Nuclear Fission." Manson Benedict. *Technology Review,* October/November 1971.

2. "Social Institutions and Nuclear Energy." Alvin M. Weinberg. *Science,* vol. 177 (7 July 1972), p. 27.

3. "The Collapse of Classic Maya Civilization." Jeremy A. Sabloff. In *Patient Earth.* John Harte and Robert H. Socolow, eds. New York: Holt, Rinehart, and Winston, 1971.

4. *New Energy Technology.* H. C. Hottel and J. B. Howard. Cambridge, Mass.: MIT Press, 1971.

5. "Bootleg Bombs." John P. Holdren. *Physics Today,* April 1974 (letter to the editor).

6. *Nuclear Energy: Its Physics and Its Social Challenge.* David R. Inglis. Reading, Mass.: Addison-Wesley, 1973.

7. *Use of Uranium Mill Tailings for Construction Purposes.* Hearings before the Subcommittee on Raw Materials of the Joint Committee on Atomic Energy, U.S. Congress. Washington, D.C.: U.S. Government Printing Office, 1971.

8. *New Energy Technology.*

9. "Radiation Spill at Hanford: The Anatomy of an Accident." *Science,* vol. 181 (24 August 1973), p. 728.

10. "The Risk Benefit Calculus in Nuclear Power Licensing." Harold P. Green. In *Nuclear Power and the Public.* Harry Foreman, ed. Minneapolis: University of Minnesota Press, 1970. Page 124.

11. Ibid.

12. "How Many Children?" Michael W. Friedlander and Joseph Klarmann. *Environment,* December 1969.

13. *Environmental Effects of Producing Electric Power.* Hearings before the Joint Committee on Atomic Energy, U.S. Congress. Washington, D.C.: U.S. Government Printing Office, 1970. Pages 1382–1397.

14. Ibid, pp. 1403–1408.

15. "Nuclear Eclectic Power." David J. Rose. *Science,* vol. 184 (19 April 1974), p. 356.

16. Ibid.

17. *New Energy Technology.*

18. Ibid.

*Further Reading*

Hearings before the Joint Congressional Committee on Atomic Energy, U.S. Congress. *Environmental Effects of Producing Electric Power,* vols. 1 and II. Washington, D.C.: U.S. Government Printing Office, 1970.

This immense two-volume work is valuable not only for the testimony and discussion it contains but because it reprints almost every relevant article in the nuclear-safety area.

DAVID RITTENHOUSE INGLIS. *Nuclear Energy: Its Physics and Its Social Challenge.* Reading, Mass.: Addison-Wesley, 1973.

This book presents a very nice survey for the nonscientist of the physical and social aspects of nuclear energy.

SHELDON NOVICK. *The Careless Atom.* Boston: Houghton Mifflin Co., 1969.

This book is a journalistic examination of the safety hazards of nuclear energy.

GLENN T. SEABORG and JUSTIN L. BLOOM. "Fast Breeder Reactors." *Scientific American,* November 1970, pp. 13–21.

This is an informative article on the physics and technology of breeder reactors. The authors are very optimistic about the future safety and utility of breeders.

U.S. ATOMIC ENERGY COMMISSION. *The Safety of Nuclear Power Reactors and Related Facilities* (Wash-1250). Washington, D.C., 1973.
An AEC review of nuclear-reactor safety is contained in this pamphlet.

ALVIN M. WEINBERG. "Social Institutions and Nuclear Energy." *Science,* vol. 177 (7 July 1972), p. 27.
This informative and provocative article is about nuclear breeders. It is here that Weinberg discusses the possible similarities between man's transition to a farming society and the transition to a nuclear-energy society.

## Questions and Problems

1. Sketch a block diagram of the nuclear-power system, showing the relationships between mines, reactors, railroads, and other components.

2. The first large-scale use of nuclear reactors was to power military submarines. What are the major strengths of a nuclear-powered submarine compared to a fossil-fuel-powered submarine?

3. Is it surprising to learn that nuclear power plants are thermally less efficient than fossil-fuel plants? Does it seem that a new technology like nuclear energy should just "naturally" be more efficient than an old one like coal-burning plants? Are there ways in which nuclear power plants are more efficient than fossil-fuel plants?

4. You now know about as much as a lay person could reasonably be expected to learn about nuclear energy. Do you feel you know enough about the area to write letters to your legislators telling them how you would like to see them vote on the Price-Anderson Act, on making a decision about funding the breeder program, and so on? If you don't feel qualified, how do you think these decisions should be made? Should technologies be banned if they are too complex for most citizens? Would we end up banning most technologies?

5. Coal contains many impurities, some of which are radioactive. Assume it is true that a coal-burning plant—because of the radioactive impurities—releases more radiation to the environment than a nuclear plant of the same capacity. Is this an argument for nuclear power? Under what assumptions would it be such an argument? Would the nature of the radioactive isotopes released by the two plant types be a factor?

6. Relatively few of the isotopes found in nature are radioactive. Why should that be?

7. Assume a coal-burning plant is 40% efficient and that one-third of its waste heat is discharged as hot gases out the smokestack with the rest going into cooling water.
   a. If a 33%-efficient nuclear plant discharges all of its waste heat into cooling water, how much more waste heat will be put into the water by the nuclear plant than by the fossil-fuel plant per unit of electric energy generated?

b. Why is it environmentally better to discharge waste heat directly to the atmosphere? Can you conceive of a situation where it will be as bad to discharge heat to the atmosphere as to water?

8. How many atoms of carbon must be burned to produce 10,000 BTU? What would this carbon weigh? How many U-235 nuclei must be fissioned to produce 10,000 BTU? What would the U-235 weigh?

9. Compare the amount of coal a coal-burning plant will use during its 30-year lifetime with the amount of U-235 a nuclear power plant will use during its 30-year lifetime. Assume the plants are both rated at $10^6$ kilowatts, operate on an 83% load factor ($20 \times 10^6$ kilowatt-hours/day), and that the coal plant burns 10,000 BTU/pound of coal and is 40% efficient, and the nuclear plant is 33% efficient.

10. How many atoms of oxygen are needed to completely combine with a pound of carbon to form carbon dioxide? How many pounds of oxygen are needed? (Oxygen has 8 protons and 8 neutrons.)

11. Assume you start out with 10 pounds of strontium-90 (half-life of 28 years). How much will be left after 140 years?

12. Why not use water as a core coolant in fast breeder reactors?

13. How much energy would be yielded by burning 1 pound of carbon-14? Assume it releases the same energy per atom as carbon-12, that is, $6 \times 10^{-22}$ BTU/atom. Is more, less, or the same energy released in the burning of carbon-12? Explain.

14. Assume a fusion reactor consuming deuterium burns up a pound of fuel. Compare the energy output from that pound with the energy produced by a fission reactor consuming a pound of U-235.

15. How much fusion energy could theoretically be extracted from a pound of seawater? Compare this with the fission energy that could be extracted from a pound of Chattanooga shale with breeder reactors. Note that a mole of water is 18 grams. That is, 18 grams of water contain $6.02 \times 10^{23}$ molecules of water. There are two hydrogen atoms per water molecule. Assume 1 out of every 6500 hydrogen atoms is deuterium.

*Conservationists who can say nothing against these depredations but that they are short-sighted or wasteful or ugly . . . have no argument that will find any sizable audience . . . not when the alternative turns out to be as horrendously unthinkable to urban-industrial society as to do without a freeway or enough electric power to keep the picture tube well lit. The despoilers then win every time, because the assumption that nature is "ours" to remake as we see fit . . . already concedes the key line of defense.*

T. ROSZAK*

# 12 Alternatives to a nuclear future

As the last chapter indicates, nuclear energy will not solve all problems. If it is to be used safely and efficiently, nuclear power plants will be large central installations backed by a complex of mines, transportation systems, and waste-processing and disposal facilities. All this will be regulated by a large and powerful bureaucracy. Nuclear-generated energy could eliminate such environmental problems as strip mining, oil spills, and air pollution, but in turn we will be faced with the possibility of a catastrophic nuclear accident or a radiation build-up due to a multitude of small, careless acts.

We considered earlier one alternative to this nuclear future: an expanded use of fossil fuels by tapping oil shale and tar sands, and by converting our plentiful coal supplies into synthetic natural gas and synthetic gasoline. A second alternative is the tapping of what, for want of a better name, can be called "natural" energy sources. This includes hydroelectric and tidal power, geothermal power, direct use of sunlight, use of the ocean's heat, and conversion of manure and garbage into natural gas or oil.

---

\* From Roszak's book *Where the Wasteland Ends* (Garden City, N.Y.: Doubleday, 1973).

**369**

**Advantages and Disadvantages of Natural Sources.** The major appeal of natural sources is environmental cleanliness. When the fuel is sunlight, falling water, or wind, there is no air or water pollution, strip mining, or spilled oil. At a time when the nation is bedevilled with the adverse effects of fossil-fuel energy and fearful of the future effects of nuclear power, this cleanliness is very attractive.

The major environmental disadvantage of natural sources is their impact on the landscape. Because sunlight, wind, and falling water are very dilute energy sources compared to coal, oil, or U-235, they require a large amount of land. A hydroelectric dam and its reservoir may cover a hundred square miles to produce electricity that a coal-burning plant would produce on a few acres. Solar energy can be converted into natural gas or a liquid fuel by growing and processing corn or some other grain, but it takes thousands of acres of corn to equal the energy gained from an acre of strip-mined coal. Similarly, it requires miles of tidal dams and hundreds of windmills to produce as much power as a single fossil-fuel or nuclear power plant.

This dilute energy flow has economic consequences because a large amount of equipment is needed to collect the energy. To heat a home using sunlight requires that the entire roof be covered with solar collectors and that large heat-storage tanks be located in the house. A million-kilowatt solar power plant would cover several square miles of desert with solar collectors. Growing corn or some other crop for conversion into fuel demands not only a huge amount of land but also the machinery to plow, fertilize, and harvest. So although the fuel is free, equipment needed to tap that fuel makes such sources as solar or tidal power expensive.

It is also difficult to store natural energy. Solar cells produce power only when the sun is shining; waterwheels turn only when the river or stream flows; and sailboats move only when the wind is blowing. But fossil fuels are, in effect, stored sunlight. They have been in the ground for millions of years and will keep until wanted. When finally needed, they can be used as quickly as desired, assuming enough mines, wells, pipelines, railroads, and power plants exist. But the rate at which natural sources can be used is limited by their rate of flow. So the tremendous burst of energy production and use characteristic of the present and immediate past would probably have been impossible with natural energy sources.

**Dependability.** In theory, fossil and nuclear-based energy systems are very dependable because they do not depend on such factors as the quantity of sunshine or rainfall. Once a home or office is hooked into the electric power and gas distribution networks, it should get all the energy it demands. By contrast, natural energy systems are inherently undependable. If the sun does not shine for a week, a home using solar-heated water will have to get by on cold water. On a larger scale, the states of Washington and Oregon suffered a severe electric-power shortage in 1973. Those states get most of their power from hydroelectric installations on the Columbia River and its tributaries. Due to light snowfall in the winter of 1972–1973, the Columbia and its tributaries had a greatly reduced flow and therefore could not produce the usual quantity of electricity.

But while Oregon and Washington were suffering a shortage of natural energy, areas that depend completely on fossil fuels were also in trouble. Power blackouts and brownouts due to insufficient power-plant capacity were common. These were accompanied by gasoline, heating oil, and natural gas shortages. So it turned out that the man-made world, like the natural world, was also subject to interruptions and irregularities. Should these problems become the rule, then natural energy sources would lose some of their disadvantage.

If as a nation we attempt to make large-scale use of natural energy, changes in life-style will be required. In many homes it is considered a minor tragedy to be without hot water for a day or two. Such a household would not have a solar hot-water heater unless it was backed up by a fossil-fuel heater, which would make the system expensive. If the family used a lot of hot water for a dishwasher and other appliances, then the amount of hot water a reasonably sized solar heater could produce would be inadequate. But if the family is not panicked by temporary shortages due to cloudy weather, and if water needs are modest, then solar-heated water may be economical and satisfactory. The disadvantage of limited supply may even be offset by the fact that the household is no longer dependent for its energy on some distant utility. At present, if a utility is inefficient or if its fuel supply is cut off, its customers are helpless. In many areas in recent years new housing or factories could not be built because the utilities would not hook the buildings into the gas or electric system due to shortages. A solar energy system might have great appeal since it could provide the same energy independence the auto provided in transportation.

Let us now look at the resource and technological aspects of natural energy sources. Any such discussion must tread on thin ice because so little work has been done on tapping solar, geothermal, tidal, wind, and manure or solid-waste energy. Much of the information that does exist was gathered before increasing environmental and resource concerns created the present context. Nevertheless, it is clear that there is no purely technological barrier to converting sunlight into electricity or gasoline, cattle manure into heating oil, or tides into electricity. The question is whether this energy can be tapped on a sufficient scale and at a high enough efficiency to make the venture successful.

## Solar Energy

Solar energy is considered the most promising of the natural sources because it is incredibly abundant. The United States receives in one-half day as much solar energy as it gets from a year's worth of fossil fuel. It is already the source of all the energy we use: fossil fuels are stored ancient sunshine; food and hydroelectric power are new sunshine; sailboats run on winds generated by solar heating of the atmosphere; and sunshine helps keep our bodies, homes, and buildings warm. Nuclear fuel is synthesized in stars, so it is stellar, if not solar, in origin.

**Solar Power**

| | |
|---|---|
| Sunlight Absorbed as Heat by Land or Water | $81,000 \times 10^{12}$ watts (47%) |
| Sunlight Directly Reflected by Atmosphere or Surface | $52,000 \times 10^{12}$ watts (30%) |
| Sunlight Absorbed by Water Evaporation | $40,000 \times 10^{12}$ watts (23%) |
| Sunlight Generating Winds, Ocean Waves | $370 \times 10^{12}$ watts (0.2%) |
| Sunlight Absorbed in Plant Photosynthesis | $40 \times 10^{12}$ watts (0.02%) |
| Total Solar Radiation Intercepted by the Earth's Surface | $173 \times 10^{15}$ watts (100%) |

**Table 1.** Listed above is the solar power reaching the earth and the way in which it is distributed. A tiny percentage of the $40 \times 10^{12}$ watts that goes into photosynthesis is buried. This stored organic material is converted, over millions of years, into fossil fuels. The rest of the input energy is either directly reflected as short wavelength radiation (30%) or radiated as infrared, or heat, radiation.

But as Table 1 shows, very little of the solar energy reaching the United States is used. Much of it is reflected by the earth's upper atmosphere; and part of the light passing through the atmosphere is scattered in random directions by dust and air molecules. That portion which is absorbed as heat by the earth's surface is reradiated to the atmosphere and space as infrared radiation (see Figure 1). All bodies emit electromagnetic radiation (see Table 2); infrared radiation is given off by objects at temperatures normally occurring on the earth. As an object becomes warmer, it emits energy at a greater rate with the energy concentrated in shorter wavelength radiation. So as the sun's rays warm an object, it emits energy faster. Only a tiny portion of the incoming solar energy is trapped by plants during photosynthesis and most of it is then lost when the plant dies and decays.

Figure 2 lists some of the ways by which solar energy can be tapped. The sunlight reaching the earth can be used to heat water or boil it into steam to power turbines. Devices called photovoltaic cells convert sunlight directly into electricity. Windmills tap the air movements caused by solar heating of the atmosphere, generating electricity or directly doing mechanical work. And dams and water turbines tap the solar energy expended in evaporating water from the oceans and lakes into the atmosphere. Only this last form of solar energy is widely used.

## Solar Radiation

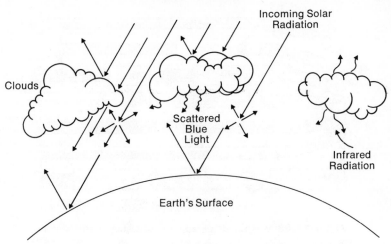

**Figure 1.** The straight arrows represent incoming radiation from the sun. The short-wavelength, or blue, light is preferentially scattered, and it is this scattering that gives the sky its blue color. The curved arrows represent infrared radiation emitted by clouds or the surface. The sum total of reflection, absorption, and infrared radiation acts to keep the earth in overall thermal equilibrium. (Arrow length represents intensity of radiation and not wavelength.)

### The Electromagnetic Spectrum

| Type of Wave | Wavelength Range (ft) |
|---|---|
| Radio | $3 \times 10^5$–$1.5 \times 10^{-1}$ |
| Microwave (radar) | $1.5 \times 10^{-1}$–$3 \times 10^{-3}$ |
| Infrared | $3 \times 10^{-3}$–$2 \times 10^{-6}$ |
| Visible | $2 \times 10^{-6}$–$1 \times 10^{-6}$    $2 \times 10^{-6} \rightarrow$ Red / Orange / Yellow / Green    $1 \times 10^{-6} \rightarrow$ Blue |
| Ultraviolet | $10^{-6}$–$3 \times 10^{-8}$ |
| X-rays | $3 \times 10^{-8}$–$3 \times 10^{-12}$ |

**Table 2.** Listed above are the wavelength ranges of different types of electromagnetic waves. Our eyes are capable of sensing only the narrow wavelength region labeled visible. The sun emits most of its radiation in this narrow band. Electromagnetic waves—whether they are in the visible or radio or x-ray region—all consist of oscillating electric and magnetic fields.

## Solar Taps

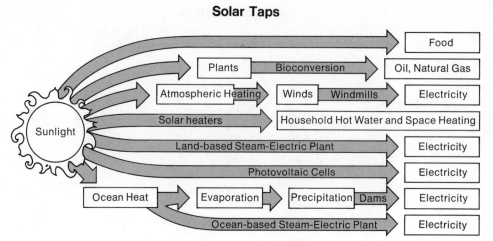

**Figure 2.** Some methods of tapping solar energy are listed here.

**Some Solar Taps.** The most direct method of using solar energy is to use sunlight to heat water for direct use as hot water or for space heating. The simplest water heater is a long black hose coiled in the sun, as shown in Figure 3. The water would be allowed to flow slowly through the hose so that it emerged hot from the exhaust end. It could then be stored in a tank until wanted. A more sophisticated solar heater is shown in Figure 4. It consists of a shallow tray with a black lower surface covered with a

## A Simple Solar Water Heater

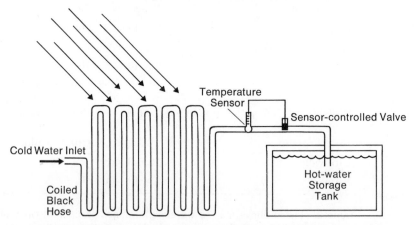

**Figure 3.** Water flows steadily through a coiled black hose. The heated water is then discharged into a storage tank. A temperature sensor at the end of the hose controls a valve opening and thereby the rate of flow through the hose. In weak sunlight the valve would reduce the flow to compensate for the slower heating rate.

glass plate. The short-wavelength sunlight penetrates the glass and water and is absorbed by the black lower surface, which heats the water. Black objects are excellent radiation absorbers and white surfaces are excellent reflectors. But black surfaces are also emitters and some of the absorbed sunlight will be radiated at infrared wavelengths. However, the glass cover will absorb the infrared radiation. The tray-glass combination therefore acts like a greenhouse.

## A Greenhouse-type Hot-water Heater

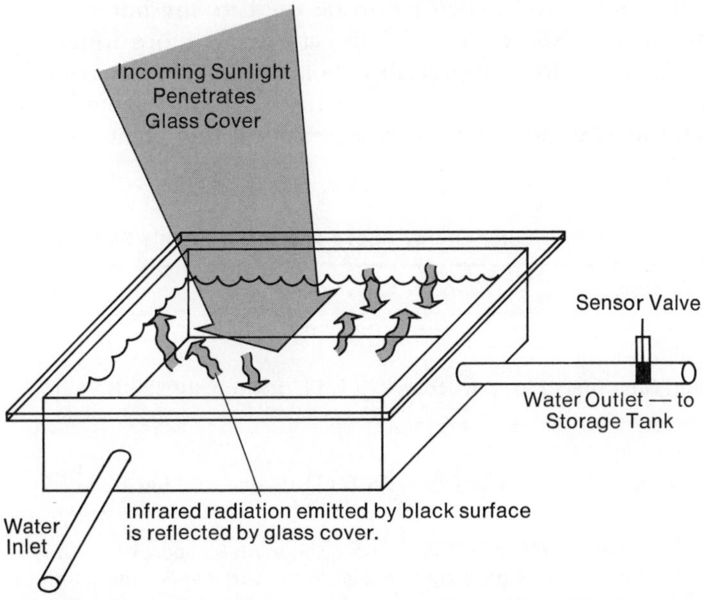

Incoming Sunlight Penetrates Glass Cover

Sensor Valve

Water Outlet — to Storage Tank

Water Inlet

Infrared radiation emitted by black surface is reflected by glass cover.

**Figure 4.** The solar heater above provides a much larger radiation-absorbing surface than the hose. The black lower surface absorbs most of the solar radiation striking it, which raises its temperature and heats the water. The heightened temperature also causes increased emission of infrared radiation. But this radiation is reflected and trapped by the glass cover, which is opaque to infrared radiation and transparent to the incoming sunlight. Thus the tray is more efficient than the hose per unit of surface area since the hose does not trap its infrared radiation.

Solar energy is also used for space heating. Space heating units resemble hot-water heaters but are much larger since they must supply more heat. Unlike hot-water needs – which are more or less constant throughout the year – space-heating needs peak in the winter when incoming solar radiation is lowest. And while a lack of hot water is an inconvenience, a lack of heat on a cold day can be a serious hardship. Therefore a solar heating system must either have a large heat-storage capacity to carry it through a succession of cloudy or cold days or a supplementary fossil-fuel heating system to back up the solar system. Either solution adds to the capital cost and maintenance of the system, and with today's technology solar heating is expensive and rarely used.

**Photovoltaic Cells.** In the above cases, the sun's incoming radiation is trapped as thermal energy. But it is also possible to convert sunlight directly into electricity by means of photovoltaic (photo = light, voltaic = electricity) cells. Single crystal silicon cells capable of converting as much as 15 percent of incoming sunlight into electricity were developed for the U.S. space program.[1] Unfortunately, photovoltaic cells are at present much too expensive to be used in any but very special applications such as space shots. If they are to be more widely used their cost will have to drop appreciably. Solar cells of 10 percent efficiency cost about $250 per watt in the early 1970s.[2] This is about 1000 times higher than the $280 per kilowatt[3] cost of a fossil-fuel plant.

**Solar Energy Above and At the Earth's Surface**

| Location | Power, 24-hour Average | Daily Total Energy |
|---|---|---|
| Above Earth's Atmosphere and Shadow | 130 watts/ft² = 430 BTU/ft²/hr | 10,320 BTU/ft² = 3.12 kw-hr/ft² |
| Average Location in U.S. | 17 watts/ft² = 58 BTU/ft²/hr | 1400 BTU/ft² = 0.42 kw-hr/ft² |

**Table 3.** For a location "above the earth's atmosphere," it is assumed the sun's rays are perpendicular to the surface. For the on-ground location, the surface area is on the ground and its angle during the day relative to the sunlight changes with the sun's height in the sky.

To see the potential of photovoltaic cells and other solar mechanisms, Table 3 lists the energy reaching the earth from the sun. Outside the earth's atmosphere and shadow, sunlight arrives at a rate of 430 BTU/square foot/hour, which is 130 watts/square foot. But atmospheric reflection and 12 hours of night reduce the average energy over the surface of the United States to 1400 BTU/square foot/day. (See Figure 5.) Averaged over a 24-hour period, this is only 17 watts/square foot—down almost an order of magnitude (a factor of 10) from the outer-space value. Assuming 12 hours of sunlight per day, the daytime power intensity is 34 watts/square foot. It will be higher in the summer and lower in the winter. (See Figure 6.)

To see what this power level translates into, let us assume availability of cheap photovoltaic cells capable of converting 10 percent of the incoming sunlight to electricity. One initial novelty use would be to build

## Orientation and Energy

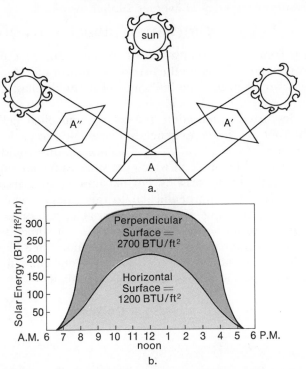

a.

b.

**Figure 5.** a. Area A is flat on the ground and it presents a varying cross section to the sun. Areas A′ and A″ are perpendicular to the sun's rays and present their maximum cross-sectional area to the sun. b. Shown in the graph is the energy absorbed in a typical day by a surface lying flat on the ground (horizontal surface) and by one moved so as to stay perpendicular to the sun's rays throughout the day.

## Solar Position and Seasons

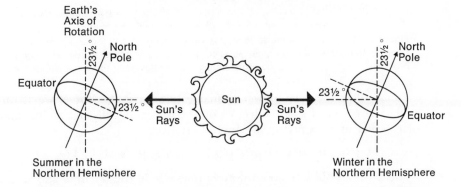

**Figure 6.** The earth is shown at the summer-solstice (left, June 22) and winter-solstice (right, December 22) positions, when the sun is at its maximum and minimum noon-time heights in the sky. The seasons occur (and the sun height changes) because the earth's axis of rotation makes an angle of $23\frac{1}{2}°$ with a line perpendicular to the plane of the sun and earth (the ecliptic).

the cells into a beach blanket. If the blanket were 5 feet by 2 feet, the power output on a day of average sunlight would be

$$P = (5 \text{ ft}) (2 \text{ ft}) (34 \text{ w/ft}^2) (0.1) = 34 \text{ watts}$$

which is enough to power a record player, a fan, or even a small refrigerator. Of course, lying on the blanket would cut off the power so perhaps the cells would instead be built into beach umbrellas, giving shade and electricity.

In a less trivial application, the solar photovoltaic cells could be built into the roof of a home to generate household power. Even assuming the development of cheap and efficient solar cells, this would present numerous problems. The angle at which the sun's rays come in changes during each day and with the seasons. For maximum power absorption, the solar collectors should be perpendicular to the sunlight, which would require an expensive tracking system and movable supports. An inexpensive compromise would be to place the collectors at some angle intermediate between the winter and summer sun direction. (See Figure 7.) Probably the collectors would be placed nearly perpendicular to the winter sun, since it is the period of least and weakest sunlight.

## Solar Collector

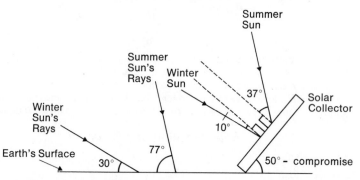

**Figure 7.** In an area of latitude 36.5°, the sun's rays come in at the angles shown on noon of the winter and summer solstice. A solar collector is shown at a "compromise" angle, chosen to be more nearly perpendicular to the weak winter sun.

To calculate the solar power available to an average home, we assume 1000 square feet of solar collectors on the roof and walls and an incoming solar power of 17 watts/square foot. This gives

$$P = (10^3 \text{ ft}^2) (17 \text{ w/ft}^2) (0.1) = 1.7 \times 10^3 \text{ w} = 1.7 \text{ kw}.$$

The power would be about double that rate in the daytime and zero at night, but assume there is a method of storing excess electricity collected during the day for use at night. We saw in an earlier chapter that the average U.S. household in 1970 used 7000 kilowatt-hours per year, which is approximately 20 kilowatt-hours/day. In one day, the rooftop solar collectors would produce

$$\text{energy} = (\text{power})(\text{time}) = (1.7 \text{ kw})(24 \text{ hr}) = 41 \text{ kw-hr}.$$

The extra 21 kilowatt-hours/day can go to meet some of the home's heat demand, which averages $2.5 \times 10^5$ BTU/day ($9 \times 10^7$ BTU/year). The extra heat available per day is

$$\text{heat} = (21 \text{ kw-hr/day})(3.4 \times 10^3 \text{ BTU/kw-hr}) = 7.1 \times 10^4 \text{ BTU/day}.$$

So the solar collectors can supply, on the average, all of the electricity and 28% of the heat needs of the average 1970 household. However, in most areas of the country there will be a seasonal imbalance since total energy needs will be highest in the winter when sunshine is weakest (see Figure 8). Day-to-day fluctuations can be handled by storing electricity in storage batteries, but long-term seasonal imbalances require a large-scale energy-storage mechanism or a supplementary energy supply. All homes could be connected to central electric-power and gas distribution systems

## Solar Energy and the Seasons

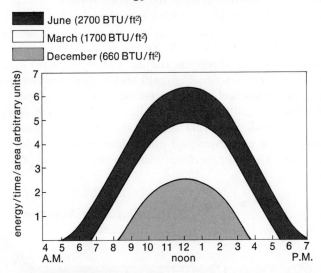

Figure 8. The area under each of the curves is the total solar energy received on an average day in the middle of December, March, and June at 43° latitude. The energy is measured on a horizontal area. If the surface were tilted so as to be kept perpendicular to the sun's rays, the energy received would be higher.

as at present, and at night and during the winter these systems could be tapped for additional energy. Such a procedure would be very expensive, however, because the electric power plants would be tremendously underused. Building and maintaining a huge power-generating-and-distributing system utilized only a small fraction of the time would be uneconomical.

Solar Farms. Predicting whether we will or will not soon develop inexpensive photovoltaic cells is not easy. No physical law states such cells are impossible. But neither is there a law which states they can be developed. The world has been waiting decades for all sorts of developments—such as compact, high-energy batteries or cheap ways to store electric energy on a large scale—that have yet to come. For this reason, investigators have also been looking closely at other methods of using sunlight to produce electricity. Most attention is now paid to use of the sun's rays to boil water into steam to power turbines. Large solar power plants of this type have been proposed for the deserts of Arizona and New Mexico. The plants have been named "solar farms" to emphasize the inexhaustible nature of the fuel and the harvesting that would go on decade after decade.

We shall assume the solar farm receives an average of 20 watts/square foot. The collectors—which in theory are like the glass-covered trays used as hot-water heaters—are assumed to collect solar energy with 90 percent efficiency. To see how large a solar farm is needed to provide the United States with 360,000 megawatts of electric power (1970s total capacity), we assume the collectors absorb the sun's rays with 90 percent efficiency and the heat energy is converted into electricity at 20 percent efficiency. This is a very high figure for solar systems, and it will require sophisticated technology to achieve the required high temperatures.

The solar-energy absorbing surface will be the most crucial component of the solar-farm system. Figure 9 shows one suggested surface. It consists of a stainless-steel base covered with very thin (about $2 \times 10^{-10}$ inches) layers of several different materials. The layers are chosen to create a surface that will selectively absorb energy in the visible region of the electromagnetic spectrum and not radiate energy in the infrared region. In this way, when the surface heats up due to absorption of sunlight, it

**A Thin-film Solar Absorber**

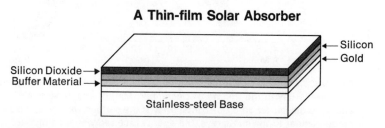

**Figure 9.** The arrangement of thin film layers provides an efficient way to trap the sun's energy as heat. Visible light passes through the silicon dioxide layer but is trapped by the silicon. The silicon temperature rises and it radiates in the infrared range. This infrared energy is reflected off the gold layer and absorbed by the silicon dioxide. The resultant heat is than transferred to a gas or water coolant. The silicon dioxide is also a tough surface layer which protects the absorber.

does not cool by radiating in the infrared. In addition to having these absorption and radiation properties, the surface must also be tough so that it does not degrade at the high temperatures. Neighboring materials must not interact chemically with each other and molecules from one surface must not migrate into another surface. The surfaces must also last at least 30 years to make economic sense.

The surfaces would be manufactured using thin-film technology perfected over the last 10 years for use in the field of miniature electronic circuits. It is estimated that even with this technological "bootlegging" it would still take a decade-long, multibillion-dollar effort to perfect the technology needed for large-scale solar farming.

**Land Needs.** Let us assume a tough, long-lived surface has been developed that is capable of absorbing 90% of the incident solar energy at a temperature high enough to yield a 20% efficiency in converting the solar energy to electricity. If the solar farm is located in an area which receives a 24-hour average of 20 watts/square foot, electric-power output will be

$$P = (20 \text{ w/ft}^2)(0.9)(0.2) = 3.6 \text{ w/ft}^2.$$

The land area needed to provide the nation with 360,000 megawatts of power is

$$\text{area} = \frac{360,000 \text{ megawatts}}{3.6 \text{ w/ft}^2} = \frac{3.6 \times 10^{11} \text{ w}}{3.6 \text{ w/ft}^2} = 10^{11} \text{ ft}^2$$

$$= \frac{10^{11} \text{ ft}^2}{2.8 \times 10^7 \text{ ft}^2/\text{mi}^2} = 3600 \text{ mi}^2$$

which is a plot of land 60 miles by 60 miles.

At this point, no one can guess whether a solar farm can be built for the few hundred dollars per kilowatt of capacity that a fossil-fuel or nuclear plant costs. Our experience is with fossil-fuel boilers, where the energy density is 500 times more concentrated[4] than the flow of sunlight to the earth. The huge scale of the solar plant would require thousands of miles of pipes to circulate the heat-collecting fluid through the solar collectors. The pumping energy required will decrease the system's overall efficiency. The solar plant's cost will be increased by the need for large-scale energy storage to carry it through nights and cloudy weather. As we shall discuss later, if efficient electrolyzers and fuel cells are developed, then hydrogen gas could be used as a storage medium or even as the plant's major output. This would eliminate the need to transmit electric energy from the sunny southwest throughout the nation. An alternative is to store the excess solar energy as heat and use the stored thermal energy at night to generate electricity.[5] A third alternative is to use solar farms in concert with huge hydroelectric projects. Excess electricity generated during the day by the solar farm would pump water from a low to a high reservoir. At night the water would flow down, generating electricity.

When compared with the land needs of fossil-fuel power plants, this 3600 square miles seems huge. A fossil-fuel plant requires only a few hundred acres of land[6] per 1000 megawatts. So 360,000 megawatts would occupy only about 100 square miles. But the fossil-fuel plants reach beyond their borders for fuel, and their air pollutants affect thousands of square miles. Solar energy does not need fuel or spread pollutants of any kind, so the land imbalance is not as large as it seems.

**Solar Energy and the Oceans.** Another suggested approach to solar energy is to use the oceans as heat sources. The world's oceans cover 71 percent of the earth's total area and therefore collect a huge amount of solar energy. But while the ocean's surface is warmed by the sun, its depths remain cold. Circulation between the upper and lower levels is minimal because the density of water increases as temperature decreases. Therefore the warmed surface area is less dense than the underlying water and it remains floating on top. In tropical locations, the surface temperature may be 85°F and the water a few thousand feet below, 40°F. The temperature difference creates the possibility of using the ocean to power a steam engine.

As shown in Figure 10, warm surface water could boil a volatile liquid such as freon into vapor, which would then spin turbines to generate electricity.[7] The vapor would be condensed by cold water from the depths and boiled again into vapor by warm surface water. The electricity could either be shipped to land via underwater power lines or used on the spot to electrolyze water into hydrogen. The hydrogen could be stored in tankers, which would go ashore when full, or could be piped ashore. The ocean surface does not cool at night, or in southern latitudes during the winter, so the ocean plant could produce energy day and night, summer and winter.

There are several possible variations on this basic theme. One design uses ocean water as the working fluid and extracts fresh water as well as energy. In another approach, cold water for the condensers is drawn into a land-based plant from the ocean's depths. After it has cooled the condensers and been warmed in the process, it is discharged to ponds in which fish, shellfish, or seaweed are being raised.[8] Because the deep water in many locations is rich in nutrients that have floated down from above, it is a rich fertilizer. Such an energy system would yield electricity, fresh water, and food.

**The Inherent Inefficiency.** The obstacle to all these plans is the small temperature difference that exists between the ocean surface and the depths. As shown in Table 4, this small difference results in an efficiency of roughly 3 percent, which means an immense amount of water must

## An Ocean-based Solar Power Plant

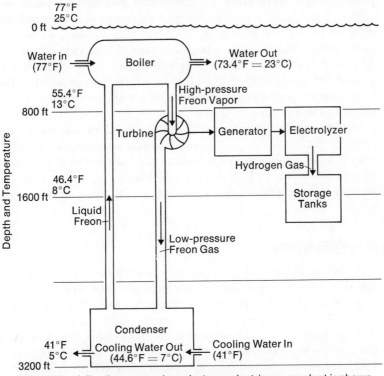

**Figure 10.** A floating, ocean-based, steam-electric power plant is shown here. In an actual design, the boiler, turbine, and condenser would all be within a few hundred feet of the surface, with a long pipe drawing the cold water up from the high-pressure depths.

**Ocean-Based, Solar-Plant Efficiency**

| | |
|---|---|
| Average Boiler Temperature | 20°C |
| Average Condenser Temperature | 10°C |
| Converting to the Kelvin Scale (°K = °C + 273°) | $T_{\text{boiler}} = 293°\text{K}$ |
| | $T_{\text{condenser}} = 283°\text{K}$ |
| Temperature Difference | $T_b - T_c = 10°\text{K}$ |
| Efficiency | $1 - \dfrac{T_c}{T_b} = \dfrac{T_b - T_c}{T_b}$ |
| | $= \dfrac{10°\text{K}}{293°\text{K}}$ |
| | $= 3.4\%$ |

**Table 4.** The 3.4 percent efficiency calculated above assumes no internal energy losses. In reality, frictional and other losses will reduce efficiency below 3 percent.

flow through the power plant to produce significant electric energy. The plant must be very large to handle the amounts of water needed and provide enough surface area for heat exchange at these small temperature differences. By comparison, a fossil-fuel plant is compact because its high boiler temperature allows a large transfer of heat per unit of surface area. The heat transferred, $Q$, is proportional to the temperature difference, $T$, and the area, or $Q \propto (T) (A)$. The higher temperatures also generate higher steam pressures and a more concentrated transfer of energy from steam to the turbines.

Despite the fact that no fuel would be used and no dams required, the tapping of solar ocean power could cause environmental problems. Bringing up large quantities of cold water and nutrients from the depths might disrupt thermal and biological conditions at the surface. Large-scale tapping of the ocean's solar energy might even cause changes in the world's climate.

## A Hydrogen Economy

A different approach to using natural energy sources involves hydrogen gas. The idea is to use the excess electricity produced by the home's solar cells to produce hydrogen gas through electrolysis. In electrolysis, an electric current is passed through water, producing hydrogen and oxygen. The hydrogen gas can be stored until needed and then burned to recover the energy expended in electrolysis. An important component of a solar-hydrogen system would be a more efficient electrolysis unit. Present commercial units are only 60% to 70% efficient, which results in large energy losses. In the laboratory, 85%-efficient systems are achieved,[9] but these systems are not yet commercially available.

Fuel Cells. Another problem is presented by the need to convert the hydrogen gas back into electricity. At present, this can be done economically only by burning the hydrogen in a power plant to produce steam and then generate electricity. However, devices called fuel cells — which can turn hydrogen and oxygen into electricity and water — are under development. It is conceivable that commercially available fuel cells will eventually operate at 55% efficiency,[10] even units small enough to fit in a basement and supply power for a single home or apartment.

To understand the operation of a fuel cell, we must go back to the burning of hydrogen. When hydrogen burns in air, two hydrogen atoms combine with an oxygen atom to form water and release energy:

$$2H_2 + O_2 \rightarrow 2H_2O + \text{energy.}$$

Energy is released because the hydrogen and oxygen electrons are rearranged, achieving a more stable, or lower, energy state.

Exactly the same thing happens in a fuel cell, but the interaction between the oxygen and hydrogen takes place through a wire and an electrolyte (see Figure 11). Hydrogen gas is fed to an anode (positively charged plate), where it gives up an electron. The resulting positively charged hydrogen ion then enters the electrolytic fluid while its electron travels through the wire to the cathode (negatively charged plate). At the cathode, two of the electrons attach themselves to an oxygen atom, which becomes a negatively charged oxygen ion and also enters the electrolytic solution. There it combines with two hydrogen ions to form water. The energy which would be released as heat if hydrogen were burned in air is now available as electrical energy created by the electrons moving through the wire.

## A Fuel Cell

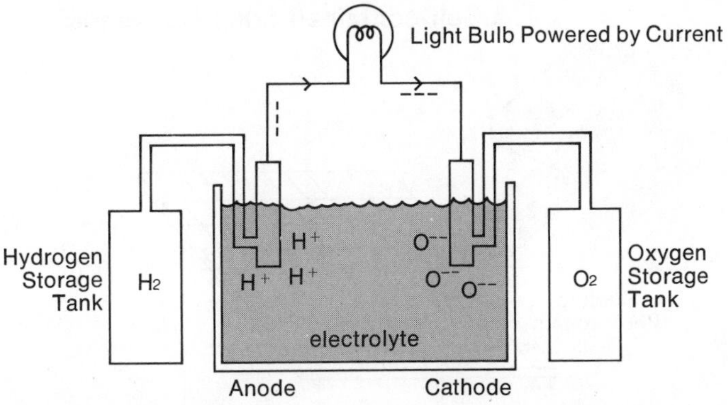

**Figure 11.** Hydrogen atoms at the anode give up their electrons and enter the electrolyte as hydrogen ions ($H^+$). The electrons migrate through the wire (powering the light bulb) and then attach themselves to oxygen atoms, which enter the electrolyte as oxygen ions ($O^{--}$). The hydrogen and oxygen ions combine in the electrolyte to form water.

Since this process is not a heat-into-work process, efficiency is not limited by the second law of thermodynamics. Since fuel cells' only products are energy and water, they are absolutely clean. They are also compact and can be made in a wide variety of sizes.

Much of the research on fuel cells was done in connection with the space program, and they are not yet cheap enough for commercial use. In the early 1970s, fuel cells were estimated to cost $400 per kilowatt of capacity and have a lifetime of 16,000 hours. To be competitive, their cost should drop to $200 per kilowatt and their lifetime double to 32,000 hours.[11]

Building a System.   There are a variety of ways in which efficient and economical solar cells, electrolyzers, and fuel cells could be connected together to form a system. At one extreme, each household could be equipped with rooftop or backyard solar cells, and basement electrolyzers, fuel cells, and hydrogen storage tanks. (See Figure 12). Excess solar energy would be converted into hydrogen gas by the electrolyzer and stored in tanks. The stored hydrogen could be used at night or during cloudy weather to generate electricity via the fuel cell, or burned directly for heat in a gas range or furnace. Such a home would be totally independent of electric and gas utilities; but because there is no back-up energy source, the family would have to practice strict energy budgeting. Such a self-contained system would represent an unlikely reversal of present trends toward central production and distribution of energy but might be attractive in rural areas, where expensive investments in pipelines and power lines are required to serve sparse populations.

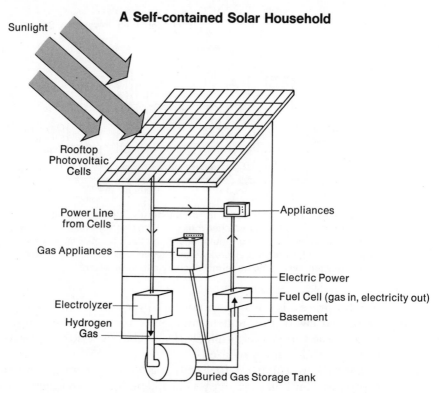

**A Self-contained Solar Household**

Sunlight

Rooftop Photovoltaic Cells

Power Line from Cells

Gas Appliances

Electrolyzer

Hydrogen Gas

Appliances

Electric Power

Fuel Cell (gas in, electricity out)

Basement

Buried Gas Storage Tank

**Figure 12.** Photovoltaic cells send electricity to appliances or to the electrolyzer. The hydrogen gas is stored in the tank until needed by the gas appliances or by the fuel cell to make electricity for night-time or cloudy-day use.

A variation on this system would link each home by gas main to central storage tanks. It would eliminate the need for bulky storage tanks in the home and provide the cushioning effect of interconnection. During the day, some of the electricity produced by the rooftop solar cells would be converted by home electrolyzers into hydrogen. The gas would either be burned in the home for heat or sent out through the gas main to the central storage tanks. At night and during cloudy or very cold periods, gas would be drawn out of the main to be burned for heat or fed to the basement fuel cell to produce electricity. The household gas meter would register a credit when hydrogen was pumped into the line and a debit when withdrawn. Since each home makes its own electricity via solar cells or a fuel cell, connection to a central power station would not be needed. Together the homes are a dispersed power plant. If their energy production is equal to their consumption, then no outside infusions of hydrogen gas would be necessary. If the homes collectively use more energy than they produce, the deficit can be made up by pumping hydrogen gas into the system from an outside source. It might come from southern regions having milder and sunnier weather or from large cental electric power plants which manufacture the gas.

**Nuplexes.** A hydrogen-energy economy is possible even in the absence of solar cells and home electrolyzers. In one version, large nuclear power plants would produce electricity, which is immediately converted into hydrogen for pipeline distribution to home and industry. The home, office, or factory would use some of the gas for heat and some to power fuel cells to produce electricity.

A hydrogen economy has several advantages. It would enable a few large nuclear-power installations to supply much of the nation's energy, which should be safer than having power plants spread throughout the country. Each of the nuplexes (nuclear complex) would have its own fuel and waste-processing plants and perhaps its own waste storage facility. This would minimize the transporting of radioactive materials and the likelihood of accidents or thefts. If the nuplexes used their waste heat to desalinate seawater or to warm nearby cities as part of a total energy system, then additional economic and environmental advantages would accrue.

**Pipelines and Hydrogen.** Such concentration of power capacity is not presently possible because of electric-power transmission losses. But hydrogen gas — like natural gas — can be distributed very cheaply via pipeline. The gas fields of Louisiana, Texas, and Oklahoma provide much of the country with natural gas, but electric energy is almost always produced locally to minimize transportation losses.

Another hydrogen advantage is that it can be distributed through the same 250,000 miles of trunk pipeline now used to distribute natural gas and can be used, with some adjustments, in appliances that now burn natural gas. One can construct a scenario in which hydrogen gradually replaces our seemingly dwindling supplies of natural gas. A minor transportation difficulty occurs because hydrogen is a less concentrated energy source than natural gas. A cubic foot of natural gas at atmospheric pressure yields 1000 BTU, but the same volume of hydrogen gas yields only 325 BTU. This means three times as much hydrogen must be moved through a pipeline per unit of energy. But hydrogen has a low density and viscosity (friction) so that three times as much hydrogen as natural gas can be shipped through a given pipeline. Therefore the energy capacity of a pipeline is the same whether it is carrying hydrogen or natural gas. A 36-inch-diameter pipeline carrying gas at 800-pounds-per-square-inch pressure has an energy capacity of $37 \times 10^9$ BTU/hour.

Hydrogen has advantages over natural gas as a heat source. Because it burns cleanly, furnaces and hot-water heaters using hydrogen need not be vented to the outside. This means the 20 percent or so waste heat that currently goes up a furnace flue with the combustion gases could be used. It also means that rooms in a house could be individually heated by small furnaces instead of by a large central furnace using radiators or hot-air ducts to distribute the heat. Flameless, or catalytic, heaters — which would convert hydrogen gas to heat at a low temperature and without a fire — would be especially useful. The drawbacks to hydrogen are the losses incurred during electrolysis and its explosiveness, which is greater than that of natural gas.

**Whither Hydrogen.** From even this brief description, it is easy to see how difficult it is to predict the scale of future hydrogen use. Factors favoring hydrogen are its compatibility with existing pipelines and appliances, the nation's growing demand for a clean gas, and the decreasing supplies of natural gas. That hydrogen gas can be transported more cheaply than electricity is also on its side.

Future hydrogen use depends on certain things happening and other things not happening. It requires the development of a more efficient electrolyzer and a longer lived, more efficient fuel cell. The manufacture of hydrogen from electricity will require electric-power production on a large scale, which means nuclear energy, or coal plants run on western, strip-mined coal. But if efficient methods are developed to gasify coal, it would be pointless to use the coal to make electricity at 40 percent efficiency to then make hydrogen. If electric-power transmission becomes more efficient — perhaps through development of high-temperature, superconducting materials — then hydrogen would lose a large advantage. So large-scale use of hydrogen probably depends not only on better fuel cells and electrolyzers being developed but also on efficient coal-gasification processes and efficient electric-power-transmission techniques not being developed.

The advent of superconducting (no loss) power-transmission lines[12] might provide a boost for hydrogen gas. Hydrogen condenses to a liquid at 20° above absolute zero (−422.5°F) and is a likely coolant for superconducting transmission lines. Possibly the system would be most economical when both electric power and hydrogen gas were transmitted through it. In this system, some of the central power-plant energy would be used to run electrolyzers with the resulting hydrogen gas – cooled to a liquid – used as a coolant en route and a fuel at the end of the line.

The moral of the preceding flights of technological fancy and of those to come is that all things seem possible because thus far our economic and technological knowledge of these areas is so limited. The situation is complicated by the rapidity with which the resource and environmental pictures are changing.

## Other Energy Sources

Let us now look at other possible energy sources. We have so far considered directly tapping the sun's energy as it impinges on the land or sea. But Table 1 shows that the sun pumps a large amount of energy into evaporation of water ($40,000 \times 10^{12}$ watts, or 23% of the total) and a smaller but still significant quantity into generating winds, waves, and ocean currents ($370 \times 10^{12}$ watts, or 0.2% of the total). As a result of these two energy sinks, water is evaporated into vapor and circulated over the land. There it falls as precipitation and is available as hydroelectric power.

It is estimated there are $3 \times 10^{12}$ watts of hydropower available worldwide.[13] But only the developed nations tap this power on a significant scale. The undeveloped nations do not have the economic or technological base to get at the power. Therefore only about 10% of the world's available hydropower is being used. We saw earlier that in the United States hydropower each year makes an ever smaller contribution to our energy needs even though we are tapping about one-quarter of the available power. If electric-power consumption continues to double, hydropower will soon be relegated to the same energy status as wood.

The solar energy which goes into atmospheric heating has long been tapped on a small scale to power sailboats and windmills, but large-scale use of this energy seems unlikely for several reasons. The $370 \times 10^{12}$ watts of solar power being pumped into the atmosphere is diluted over a vast volume. It is not found in even as concentrated a form as hydropower, which is itself a dilute source compared to oil or coal. Tapping wind power, therefore, will require enormous machinery. One proposal suggests placing 300,000 towers,[14] each 850 feet high, throughout the Great Plains to take advantage of the strong steady winds which blow there. Spaced about 1 to a square mile, the towers would each have 20 propellers with 50-foot diameters (wind turbines) collectively generating 190,000 megawatts, half of the U.S. 1970 total. Even assuming they could be built economically, there would be severe esthetic problems. There is mounting pressure to put electric power grids underground because they mar the landscape. But the power grids are tiny and unobtrusive compared to 85-story towers bearing a score of 50-foot propellers. Undoubtedly, legions of Don Quixotes would appear to fight them.

A third possible energy source is the ocean's tides. Due to the earth's rotation and the pull of the sun and moon on the earth, we experience two high tides and two low tides per day. Even small lakes and the seemingly solid earth rise and fall, but the effect is most noticeable at the ocean shore, where high tides occur every twelve hours and twenty-five minutes. Some of this tidal energy can be tapped if a dam containing turbines is built across a bay or ocean inlet to create a water-level difference between the bay and the ocean (see Figure 13). If the water level is the same on both sides of the dam at high tide, then the ocean side will drop as the tide recedes.

## A Tidal Power Plant

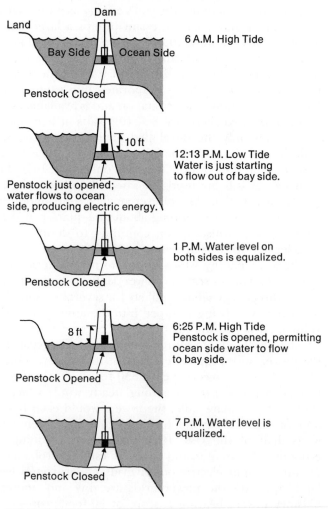

**Figure 13.** The height differences created by the rising and falling of the tides is utilized to produce electricity. Tidal heights vary with geographic location and time of the year. The second, or indirect, tide is smaller than the direct tide.

Although tidal power is clean, dependable, and inexhaustible, it is limited in magnitude and could not supply an appreciable fraction of our energy needs. It is estimated that there are only $0.064 \times 10^{12}$ watts of tappable tidal power, which is 2% of the available hydropower.

As mentioned, tidal power is caused by the uneven gravitational pull of the moon and sun on the earth. To simplify, let us assume it is only the moon's gravitational pull that acts on the earth. The water directly under the moon is attracted most strongly and this creates one high tide. This direct tide is easy to understand. But a second—and more mysterious— tide appears on the diametrically opposite side of the earth (see Figure 14). The water on this side of the earth is attracted less strongly by the moon. In addition, there is an outward force caused by the earth and moon rotating about each other—it is the same outward force experienced when you whirl a rock about your head on a rope or travel round a curve in a car. The result of the weaker moon-earth gravitational pull and the outward force creates the second, or indirect, high tide.

## Tides

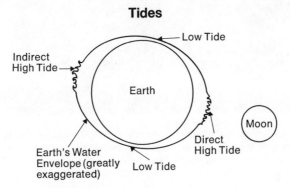

**Figure 14.** The moon's pull and the rotation of the earth and moon around a common center produces two high tides in a 24-hour, 50-minute period.

As the earth rotates on its axis, the position of the high and low tides changes. The high tides can be thought of as racing to stay under the moon. Because the earth makes one complete rotation each 24 hours, every position on earth experiences two high tides and two low tides daily. Actually the period is a bit more than a day because the moon is also circling the earth.

Energy is dissipated due to the rising and falling of tides. As a result of this dissipation, the earth's rate of rotation is slowing, so that the average day becomes 0.001 seconds (1 millisecond) longer each century.[15] Eventually tidal losses will cause the earth to stop rotating completely. The moon has already lost its rotational energy due to tides raised by the earth on the moon and now presents only one face to the earth.

**Geothermal Energy.** The heat leaking out of the earth's interior is another potential energy source. It escapes at a rate of $32 \times 10^{12}$ watts

Pacific Gas and Electric Company of San Francisco uses the geothermal field of the Big Geyser region to generate about 200,000 kilowatts of electricity. *Photo courtesy Pacific Gas and Electric Company.*

over the earth's surface, which is a very dilute 0.005 watts/square foot. On the average, the earth's temperature rises 2°F for every 100 feet you drill below the surface. But in some regions the temperature rises much more steeply and very hot rock or water deposits are found. In the United States most of these geothermal deposits are found in the West, often associated with hot springs.

In several locations, underground thermal deposits are being used to provide steam to drive turbines. Wells drilled one or two miles into the ground are used to bring up hot (up to 700°F) water from underground. At the lower surface pressures, some of this hot, pressurized water flashes into steam. The steam is then separated from the remaining water and fed to turbines to generate electricity. A few geothermal fields produce "dry" steam, which eliminates the need to separate steam from water.

Until recently little attention was paid to developing methods of prospecting for geothermal deposits or of utilizing them once found. Most knowledge of geothermal deposits is a result of surface manifestations such as hot springs. Table 5 lists two estimates of the amount of geothermally

**Estimates of Future Geothermal Power Generation**

| Year | Mw (moderate estimate) | Mw (optimistic estimate) |
|------|------------------------|--------------------------|
| 1972 | 192 | |
| 1975 | 750 | 750 |
| 1980 | 10,500 | 36,000 |
| 1985 | 19,000 | 132,000 |
| 1990 | 35,000 | 242,000 |
| 2000 | 75,000 | 395,000 |

SOURCE: "Assessment of Geothermal Energy Resources," Panel on Geothermal Energy Resources (U.S. Department of the Interior, 1972).

**Table 5.** The moderate estimate of future geothermal electric-power capacity assumes a relatively small-scale research and development program. The optimistic estimate assumes an intensive and successful research and development program.

produced electric power the United States could develop. These estimates are very rough since they depend on a large-scale investment of capital and talent to develop the needed techniques and build the geothermal plants.

**Energy from Waste.** The last potential source of "natural" power we shall look at is solid wastes such as urban garbage, logging debris, and cattle manure. Waste use is attractive because it would help solve the waste and energy problems at the same time. Solid waste such as manure and wastepaper can be used more or less directly by burning the dried material to make steam. There is nothing new about this. Dried buffalo droppings, or buffalo chips, were an important fuel on the Great Plains during the nineteenth century. Even today, some fuel-scarce nations use dried cattle manure as fuel. In this country, some solid waste is incinerated to reduce its volume and in a few cases the heat is even put to use.

Economically it makes more sense to convert the waste to gas or oil than to simply burn it. Three conversion processes are presently under development: hydrogenation, pyrolysis, and bioconversion. In hydrogenation, the organic waste (for example, manure, logging wastes) is "cooked" with steam and carbon monoxide (CO) at about 550°F and under 200 atmospheres of pressure for an hour. Cooking in the steam-carbon monoxide atmosphere reduces (removes the oxygen from) the organic cellulose to yield 2 barrels of 15,000-BTU-per-pound oil per ton of dry waste. Because some of this oil must be used to heat the reaction, the net yield is reduced to 1.25 barrels. The input raw wastes had an energy value of 3000 to 8000 BTU/pound.

In pyrolysis, or destructive distillation, the solid waste is dried, shredded, and then heated in an oxygen-free atmosphere to about 900°F. The oxygen-free heating converts the organic material to natural gas, oil, and burnable char. An average ton of dry waste yields 1 barrel of oil at 10,000 BTU/pound, varying quantities of gas at 400 to 500 BTU/cubic foot, and 160 pounds of a solid fuel called char, as well as 140 pounds of ferrous metals and 120 pounds of glass.[16] Pyrolysis has the economic advantage of not requiring high-pressure cooking. However, marketing the three different fuels is complicated. This is especially true because the low-energy gas is not interchangeable with natural gas. This makes bioconversion an attractive alternate.

In bioconversion, solid organic waste is digested by anaerobic (does not need air, or oxygen) bacteria to produce 10,000 cubic feet of methane gas (1000 BTU/cubic foot) per ton of waste.[17] However, bioconversion is still in a primitive state of development.

Most attention has thus far focused on converting waste into oil or gas, but a neglected and potentially difficult problem is simply getting the waste. Table 6 shows the amount of estimated waste generated in the United States yearly and the portion which could be economically collected for processing. These figures indicate that solid wastes can provide us with only a small portion of our energy needs. It should be emphasized that the numbers are extrapolations from a comparatively small amount of data and are subject to change.

It is also possible that competition from recycling will reduce the amount of waste available for conversion into fuel. For example, a large proportion of urban garbage is waste paper. If current efforts to encourage recycling of waste paper succeed, then the paper will not be available as a fuel. Cattle manure provides another example. As Table 6 shows, it could be an important energy source. But it is also a potentially valuable food source because it is rich in high-protein, one-celled, digestive bacteria from the cattle. In 1973, pilot operations were started in which manure was processed and fed back to the cattle,[18] who are able to extract additional nutrition from it. If this experiment works, the manure produced by the nation's 120 million cattle will not be available as a fuel source.

## Choosing an Energy Future

Our survey of fossil fuels, nuclear energy, and "natural" energy sources shows that there are a large number of ways to meet future energy needs. But each of the choices is hedged by technological, economic, and environmental factors. And at present there is no consensus on the best energy source. The leading contender—nuclear energy—has many problems and numerous critics to keep these problems before the public. Conventional fuels like oil and coal also have environmental problems and expansion of these sources is similarly under attack.

**Solid Waste and Energy, 1971**

| Type of Waste | Total Produced (× 10⁶ tons, dry weight) | Wastes Collectible (× 10⁶ tons, dry weight) |
|---|---|---|
| Manure | 200 | 26.0 |
| Urban Refuse | 129 | 71.0 |
| Logging and Sawmill Wastes | 55 | 5.0 |
| Agriculture Wastes | 390 | 22.6 |
| Industrial Waste | 44 | 5.2 |
| Municipal Sewage Solids | 12 | 1.5 |
| Miscellaneous | 50 | 5.0 |
| Total | 880 | 136.3 |
| Net Oil That Could Be Produced (× 10⁶ bbl) | 1098 | 170 |
| Net Natural Gas That Could Be Produced (× 10⁹ ft³) | 8800 | 1360 |
| 1971 Annual Oil Consumption (× 10⁶ bbl) | 5200 | |
| 1971 Natural Gas Consumption (× 10⁹ ft³) | 23,000 | |

SOURCE: "Fuel from Wastes: A Minor Energy Source" (*Science,* vol. 178 (10 November 1972), p. 599).

**Table 6.** As can be seen, collectible wastes could produce about 3% of our 1971 consumption of oil and about 6% of our consumption of natural gas. These percentages would hold constant if future increases in our demand for energy are matched by increases in our production of waste.

The need to decide on future energy sources is made more urgent by present shortages. In the early 1970s, summer shortages of gasoline and electric power were common. In the winter, heating-oil and natural-gas shortages caused some schools, factories, and other institutions to close. The tight supply situation caused prices to increase, so that it became more expensive to drive a car, heat a home, cook food, and manufacture energy-intensive goods such as plastics and aluminum. The scarcity and increased cost caused a few changes in life-style. Small-car sales boomed; some people kept their homes cooler in winter and wore sweaters around the house; use of advertising and display lighting was curbed in some areas; and so on. The situation could be compared to behavior during a drought, where the population tries to stop leaks and cut down on unnecessary use of water until plentiful supplies are again available.

In a crisis, there are also attempts to place blame. Some segments of industry and government put the responsibility for energy shortages on environmentalists because of their opposition to nuclear and coal power plants, strip mining, offshore oil exploration and development, and construction of new oil refineries and hydroelectric installations. Their opposition, the critics said, had forced energy shortages upon the nation.

The environmentalists responded that very few energy projects had actually been stopped by the early 1970s and that the shortage was actually due to demand increasing more rapidly than supply. The environmentalists pointed out that the environmental movement does not exist in a vacuum. Environmental and citizen groups depend on individuals and foundations for financial support, TV and newspapers for publicity, Congress, state, and local legislative bodies for laws, and government bureaucracies and courts for interpreting and enforcing the laws.

It may indeed be contradictory for environmental groups to oppose power plants and fuel sources while they, their supporters, and society in general continue to use and need energy. But the inconsistency is built into the society and is not created by the environmentalists. Almost all of us want material goods, plentiful energy, clean air and water, and an unscarred landscape. So we urge our legislators to pass laws outlawing environmental damage and we contribute money to environmental groups; but at the same time we remain good customers of our local electric utility, the gas company, and the corner gasoline station.

We are all aware of the inconsistency. The question is, how will it be resolved? That in turn depends on who will do the resolving. The trend over the past several years has been toward greater grass-roots involvement in reaching technological decisions. The trend is most apparent in the case of Ralph Nader and the auto industry, but it has spread through much of industry. Formerly an electric utility would make a power-plant-site decision on a purely economic basis. It would buy the property and obtain almost automatic approval for the plant from the relevant government agencies. Today most electric utilities find power-plant siting a traumatizing business, stretching on for years or even for a decade in a few cases. The same is true for offshore oil wells, power grids, and oil refineries.

As a result, the energy industry and the relevant government agencies have become much more sophisticated in their handling of potentially controversial projects. Some are careful to adhere to the letter and spirit of the various environmental laws. Others attempt to bring citizens into the planning process early so as to anticipate areas of conflict before the company or agency is committed to a particular site or method.[19] Still others use publicity to dramatize the need for electricity or oil or whatever, trying to turn public opinion against the people who oppose the various projects.

The energy shortages especially have given a powerful weapon to those who think grass-roots participation in technology is unworkable. It is argued that the delays and uncertainties surrounding energy projects are crippling. If the country is to continue to grow and prosper, then, it is claimed, decisions must be made quickly. In a few cases, Congress has responded to this argument and resolved environmental objections by fiat. It removed the Trans-Alaska Pipeline in 1973 from environmental litigation by passing a special law. It is possible that objections to the breeder reactor will eventually be resolved in the same way.

If the laws or public opinion in the nation change so that environmental and citizen groups can no longer win legal and legislative victories, then our future energy course is reasonably clear. We can expect nuclear power to supply an increasing amount of electric-power needs; the Atlantic coast will be extensively explored for the oil believed to be there; and western coal will be strip mined to provide electricity for the Pacific, southwestern, and north central states, and synthetic natural gas for pipeline transmission throughout the nation. All of this will be done as cleanly as possible, if only to avoid an environmental backlash. But the scale of our energy needs and the fact that we will have to use offshore oil and strip-mined coal mean that it will take greater efforts to keep us as clean — or dirty — as we are now. Environmental precautions will have to increase faster than the scale of energy use if any progress is to be made toward improving the environment.

If, on the other hand, environmental concerns remain strong, then a very different and much less predictable energy future is likely. Large-scale strip mining, nuclear power, and offshore oil — which fit in so well with present energy systems and technological know how — would be less attractive in an environmentally and safety-conscious future. We would instead expect increased emphasis on reducing energy demand by more efficient practices and possibly by life-style changes. The pattern of increasing consumption which has thus far characterized America and much of the western world might be replaced by a leaner, more austere style.

If citizens do have a strong voice in deciding the form future energy technology takes, then such factors as consumer appeal and simple intelligibility of proposed systems may become important. The fact that hydrogen can be used with flameless heaters to provide warmth in individual rooms, that it burns cleanly, and that it can be used with a home power plant (fuel cell) to provide electricity might convince a large number of people of the desirability of a hydrogen economy.

Land-based or sea-based solar energy may also have public appeal. The technology is comparatively easy to understand and the environmental and safety advantages are obvious. It could be that from the standpoint of cost, solar energy would be two or three times more expensive than nuclear energy. But if the solar energy appeals to — or is at least acceptable to—a large number of people, then cost may not be the most important factor. If the cheap approaches are politically and socially unacceptable, cost may become a secondary factor.

The importance of social acceptability of an energy source can be seen by looking at nuclear energy. Nuclear proponents often and justifiably complain that much of the opposition to nuclear energy comes from hysterical uninformed people who will not or can not understand the inherent safety of reactors. It is also true—although not usually mentioned by the nuclear people—that much of the support for reactors comes from other uninformed people who put great trust in advanced technological systems and their makers.

If most of the population falls into one of these two categories, then a large part of society is cut off from understanding our most likely, future energy technology. We have seen in the cases of water, transportation, and present energy systems that ignorance of even an efficient, well-run system can result in exorbitant demands and abuses. Demand may increase so much that we overwhelm the system. Or we unthinkingly destroy watersheds, develop our land in ways that produce highway congestion, and consume electricity, natural gas, and gasoline as if they came out of thin air.

Will we similarly strain and abuse nuclear power out of ignorance? We mentioned that nuclear safety will require great competence and attention to detail throughout the nuclear system. Can that be maintained in the face of public ignorance or indifference? Might not pressure develop to cut costs by reducing safety measures, just as we now neglect the purity of our water systems and scrimp on sewage treatment? And if a serious nuclear accident occurs, will public ignorance result in a widespread hysterical reaction? Might not the same people who put blind trust in nuclear technology and technologists be transformed from uninformed proponents to uninformed opponents?

We are now unconnected from many of the systems which supply us with water, energy, and even food. Few are in any way involved with our physical systems. A small percentage work in slaughter houses, coal mines, oil fields, and the like. Out of ignorance and alienation come abuses and environmental problems. The current energy difficulties give us a chance to rectify the problem in at least this one area.

## Bibliography

*Source Notes*

1. "Solar Energy as a National Energy Resource." NSF/NASA Solar Energy Panel. Washington, D.C.: National Science Foundation (NSF/RA/N-73-001), 1972.

2. *New Energy Technology.* H. C. Hottel and J. B. Howard. Cambridge, Mass.: MIT Press, 1971.

3. "Hydrogen: Its Future Role in the Nation's Energy Economy." W. E. Winsche; K. C. Hoffman; F J. Salzano. *Science,* vol. 180 (29 June 1973), p. 1326.

4. *New Energy Technology.*

5. "Physics Looks at Solar Energy." Aden Baker Meinel and Marjorie Pettit Meinel. *Physics Today,* February 1972.

6. *The 1970 National Power Survey.* Federal Power Commission. Washington, D.C.: U.S. Government Printing Office, 1971.

7. "Solar Sea Power." Clarence Zener. *Physics Today,* January 1973.

8. "Power, Fresh Water, and Food from Cold, Deep Sea Water." Donald F. Othmer and Oswald A. Roels. *Science,* vol. 182 (12 October 1973), p. 121.

9. "The Hydrogen Economy." Derek P. Gregory. *Scientific American,* January 1973.

10. "Fuel Cells: Dispersed Generation of Electricity." *Science,* vol. 178 (22 December 1972), p. 1273.

11. Ibid.

12. "Superconductors for Power Transmission." Donald P. Snowden. *Scientific American,* April 1972.

13. "Energy Resources." M. King Hubbert. In *Resources and Man.* Committee on Resources and Man. San Francisco: W. H. Freeman, 1969.

14. "Windmills." Julian McCaull. *Environment,* January/February 1973.

15. *Survey of the Universe.* D. H. Menzel; F L. Whipple; G. DeVaucouleurs. Englewood Cliffs, N.J.: Prentice-Hall, 1970.

16. "Fuel from Wastes: A Minor Energy Source." *Science,* vol. 178 (10 November 1972), p. 599.

17. Ibid.

18. "Beef Cattle Given a New Feed Derived from Manure." *New York Times,* 9 September 1973, p. 1.

19. *Engineering for Resolution of the Energy-Environment Dilemma.* National Academy of Engineering. Washington, D.C., 1972.

## Further Reading

FARRINGTON DANIELS. *Direct Use of the Sun's Energy.* New Haven, Conn.: Yale University Press, 1954.
The field of solar-energy utilization changes so slowly that this book is still quite useful even though it was first published in 1954.

PETER GOLDREICH. "Tides and the Earth-Moon System." *Scientific American,* April 1972, p. 43.

This article is about the physical nature of tides.

DEREK P. GREGORY. "The Hydrogen Economy." *Scientific American,* January 1973, p. 13.

A description of an energy system centered around hydrogen is presented in this article.

H. C. HOTTEL and J. B. HOWARD. *New Energy Technology.* Cambridge, Mass.: MIT Press, 1971.

This book is an excellent survey of the technology and economics of possible future energy sources.

M. KING HUBBERT. "The Energy Resources of the Earth." *Scientific American,* September 1971, p. 60.

A concise survey of the earth's fossil, nuclear, and natural energy resources is presented in this article.

JULIAN MCCAULL. "Windmills." *Environment,* January/February 1973, p. 6.

McCaull gives here a survey of the use of windmills to produce energy.

ADEN BAKER MEINEL and MARJORIE PETTIT MEINEL. "Physics Looks at Solar Energy." *Physics Today,* February 1972, p. 44.

In this article the authors describe a solar farm.

DONALD F. OTHMER and OSWALD A. ROELS. "Power, Fresh Water, and Food from Cold, Deep Sea Water." *Science,* 12 October 1973, p. 121.

The contents of this article are exactly as the title states.

CLARENCE ZENER. "Solar Sea Power." *Physics Today,* January 1973, p. 48.

Zener describes here an ocean-based power plant which turns the ocean's thermal energy into electricity.

## Questions and Problems

1. The text speculates that nuclear energy is likely to be a mysterious, distant source in comparison with solar or manure-generated energy. Are such considerations relevant? Does it matter whether or not the public understands a technological system, so long as it operates safely and cleanly?

2. Would you classify geothermal energy with natural sources like solar or tidal power, or would you put it with fossil or nuclear power? Explain.

3. It was mentioned in connection with converting solid wastes into energy that cattle manure is rich in protein and may become widely used as a feed. Assuming that meat from cattle raised on a partial diet of processed, sanitized manure is as tasty and nutritious as meat from cattle raised on a total grain diet, can social and emotional objections be raised to the procedure? Does it create, perhaps, a spaceship mentality which will make people feel trapped and claustrophobic? Or will it make us more aware of the many ways in which we can recycle and reuse and thus create a better, richer life?

4. Table 3 shows that, above the atmosphere, solar energy pours in at 430 BTU/square foot/hour. Confirm that this is 130 watts/square foot.

5. It has been suggested that a space satellite be placed in synchronous orbit out of the earth's shadow and atmosphere. The synchronous orbit means that the satellite would remain fixed above the same position on earth. The satellite would have a large photovoltaic collecting surface and the electricity collected (130 watts/square foot) would be converted into microwave radiation and beamed to an earth station. There it would be converted back into electricity for transmission throughout the United States.
   a. What are the advantages and disadvantages of such a system?
   b. Assume that the electricity can be collected, beamed to earth, and converted back into electric energy with 10% efficiency. How large would the solar-collecting surface have to be to generate 400,000 megawatts of electricity on the ground? Assume the satellite orientation is controlled so as to keep the surface perpendicular to the sun's rays at all times.

6. The text states that 1000 square feet of solar collectors can generate all of the electricity and 28% of the heat for a home using an average (for 1970) amount of energy. Calculate how many square feet of solar collectors are needed to completely satisfy the home's energy demands using the assumptions in the text.

7. Assume an all-electric home uses 36,500 kilowatt-hours of electricity per year. 40% of its electricity will be used during the daytime, when the solar-cell-generated electricity can be used directly; 60% will be used at night and must be produced by 50%-efficient fuel cells burning hydrogen gas made by 80%-efficient electrolyzers. If the home is in a region receiving 20 watts/square foot (24-hour average), how much area must be devoted to 10%-efficient solar cells?

8. The text discusses the possibility of homes having rooftop photovoltaic cells, an electrolyzer, a fuel cell, and in-house or central gas storage.
   a. Assume the electrolyzer and fuel cell are 100% efficient. Does it matter in terms of energy use if the household hot water, space heating, and cooking appliances use electricity or hydrogen, assuming the various appliances have the same efficiency?
   b. What is the most efficient arrangement (hydrogen or electric appliances) when (i) the electrolyzer is 100% efficient and the fuel cell 70% efficient? (ii) the fuel cell is 100% efficient and the electrolyzer 70% efficient? (iii) both are 70% efficient? Explain.

9. The text states that fixed-angle solar collectors would be placed so as to be nearly perpendicular to the winter sun. This way the summer and winter solar energy collected would be nearly equal. Would this be the optimum angle for all possible situations or would it be influenced by such things as when the peak load occurred, the existence of a fossil-fuel back-up system, the existence of a long-term method of storing the energy, and the like? Discuss qualitatively the influence these and other factors would have.

10. At 40° latitude, the winter-solstice sun makes an angle of 26.5° with the horizon and a summer-solstice angle of 73.5° with the horizon. The house shown in Figure 15 has an overhang on the southern exposure side to make use of the sun's energy most effectively. Explain the reasoning behind the overhang.

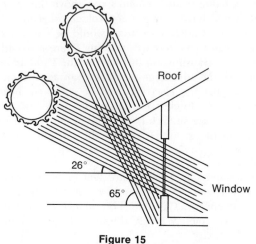

**Figure 15**

11. Another home is equipped with white venetian blinds. To minimize heating and cooling costs, when should the blinds be open and when should they be closed?

12. Figure 16 is a schematic diagram of the sun's rays hitting the earth at the winter solstice. The horizon and zenith (point directly above the observer's head) are drawn for 37° latitude. For convenience, all lines have been moved to the center of the earth. Use the figure to calculate the angle the noon sun makes with the horizon at the winter solstice (December 22). Redraw the figure for the summer solstice (June 22) and do the same calculation.

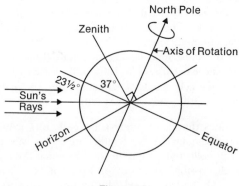

**Figure 16**

13. The incident solar power of 17 watts/square foot used in the text is for a surface flat on the ground. Actually, solar collectors would be tilted nearly

perpendicular to the sun's rays to increase their efficiency. A surface perpendicular to the sun would collect — let's say — 20 watts/square foo. Does this mean the land needed for solar collectors would be reduced? Explain with the aid of a diagram. Would the solar collector area itself be changed?

14. Figure 17 shows schematic diagrams of two possible energy-storage mechanisms to be used with solar farms to carry them through the nights and cloudy days.
    a. Which system would require the largest turbine-generator system?
    b. Assume the electrolyzer and the fuel cell in Figure 17b are both 80% efficient and the heat stored in the thermal storage device in Figure 17a can be converted into electricity with the same efficiency as heat going directly from the collectors to the turbine. Under these assumptions, will the area of solar collectors needed differ for the two storage systems? If so, by what percent? Assume 30% of the energy is generated at night or in cloudy periods.

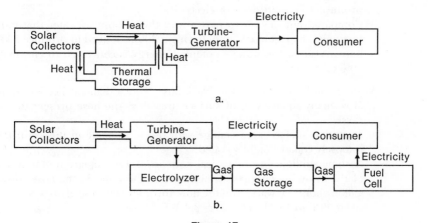

**Figure 17**

15. The area around Lake Mead (Hoover Dam) is a good site for solar farms because of its semidesert climate. It has been suggested that excess electricity generated during the day by a solar farm could be used to pump water up into Lake Mead with the energy recovered at night when the solar farm is not working. Lake Mead contains 30 million acre-feet of water with a head, or height difference, of 600 feet.
    a. Assume no appreciable change in head occurs when 10% of Lake Mead's water is let out, and calculate how many kilowatt-hours of electricity this would produce at 90% efficiency.
    b. U.S. energy consumption in 1970 was $4 \times 10^9$ kilowatt-hours/day. If 30% of this energy was used at night, could Lake Mead store enough electricity to get the nation through the night?

16. Figure 18 shows a large dammed-off bay in an arid region where evaporation is 10 feet per year. This evaporation has created a height difference of 40

feet, and now water is allowed to flow into the bay, generating electricity and maintaining the height difference at 40 feet. At what rate can power be produced if the bay is assumed to have an area of 400 square miles?

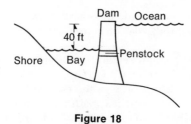

**Figure 18**

17. The ocean-based solar plant illustrated in Figure 10 has an ideal efficiency of 3.4%. Seawater enters the boiler at 77°F and leaves at 73.4°F. Assume a heat capacity of 1 BTU/pound/°F and an actual efficiency of 3%.
    a. Calculate how many pounds of water must flow through the "boiler" to produce 1 kilowatt-hour of electricity.
    b. Compare your answer to part a with the amount of water that must flow through a hydroelectric dam having a 300-foot head to produce 1 kilowatt-hour. Assume the water's potential energy is converted to electricity with 90% efficiency.

18. Assume you have 1200 feet of black hose (1-inch diameter) coiled in the sun.
    a. How many square feet of surface area does the hose present to the sun's rays?
    b. Does that surface area change with the sun's angle in the sky if the hose is loosely coiled? Tightly coiled?
    c. Assume sunlight in one typical hour is 50 watts/square foot and that 40% of the incoming energy is transferred to the water in the hose. How many gallons/hour of water should flow through the hose if it is to be heated from 50°F to 140°F? (1 watt = 3.4 BTU/hour.)

19. The text states that the U.S. land area in half a day receives about as much solar energy as we get in a year from fossil fuels. Check this statement assuming that 1970 energy consumption was $68 \times 10^{15}$ BTU and average solar radiation over the United States is 17 watts/square foot (a 24-hour average). U.S. area is 3.6 million square miles.

20. What color would the sky have if dust and air molecules did not scatter the incoming sunlight? (See Figure 1.) Why is the setting sun generally redder than the noon sun?

21. The moon takes 29.5 days to make a complete orbit of the earth. From this, calculate the time between two high tides.

22. Figure 14 shows the earth's water envelope on a greatly exaggerated scale. Assume the oceans are 2 miles deep and the earth has a 4000-mile radius.
    a. Calculate how thick a line should be used to represent the water envelope if the earth is represented by a circle two inches in diameter.
    b. How large would a 10-foot tide be on this scale?

23. The earth's daily rotational period is increasing at a rate of 0.001 seconds/ century. How long will it take for the day to lengthen from 24 hours to 25 hours?

24. Assume a geothermal deposit is estimated to be $4 \times 10^{15}$ BTU. A company intends to convert that energy to electricity at 25% efficiency. If the deposit is to last 50 years, what will its power output be if it operates continuously?

25. The text states that a 36-inch-diameter gas pipeline can carry $37 \times 10^9$ BTU/ hour of natural gas (1000 BTU/cubic foot).
    a. How many cubic feet of natural gas would it move per hour?
    b. How many 100-ton-capacity railroad cars carrying 10,000-BTU-per-pound coal does the pipeline replace?

# Epilogue

On one level, this text is meant to describe the physical functioning of water, transportation, and energy systems. It is believed that unless there is wide understanding of our various life support systems, our resources and environment will be strained and abused. Unless we understand our physical economy, we will demand too much and eventually bankrupt the earth.

But the text also intends to raise fundamental questions concerning technology. The historical surveys of our technology show the immense distance we have come, in terms of technological capability, over the past several centuries. But while the technological advances have solved some old problems, they have created serious new problems. This compels us to ask what we can reasonably expect from future technological developments, such as breeder reactors and fusion, now in the pipeline. Historical perspective on the "progress" we have already achieved raises questions about what we mean by progress.

Related to the question of progress—and raised repeatedly in this text in our discussions of various technological cycles which tend toward an increasingly man-made world—are the dynamics of our technology. Is the evolution of technology controlled by man or is it evolving in accord with some internal dynamic? Is the increasingly man-made character of the western world due to a conscious choice on our part or a result of technological evolution which functions more or less independent of human needs and motivation?

Closely tied to this question is the effect of technology on human behavior. Ideally, this text should be accompanied by a viewing of Charlie Chaplin's *Modern Times,* in which the Little Tramp is mauled and twisted by the factory equipment he is supposedly running. But at the least, the text's treatment of water systems, highways, jetports, and power systems should raise questions about their effect on us.

The difficulty is to somehow stand outside ourselves and our system and ask how our various technologies have shaped, or misshaped, us. If, indeed, technology is evolving in some inexorable way—independent of human well-being and health—it must be because we are somehow in technology's thrall.

But these are open questions and hopefully the text does not even pretend to provide answers but only information and methods that may be useful in pursuing the questions raised. Clearly, if this is a society of individuals with individual values, very different answers may be obtained by different people using the same methods and data.

# Appendix A

Many of the situations we will investigate involve large numbers. There are over 200,000,000 people and 100,000,000 motor vehicles in the United States. We use about 800,000,000 gallons of petroleum each day. Writing and manipulating such large numbers are time consuming activities which can lead to errors. To avoid these problems, we shall write numbers in terms of the power of ten notation, called by some "scientific notation."

In this notation, the number 10,000 is written as $10^4$; $10^4$ means 10 raised to the fourth power. That is, $10^4 = 10 \times 10 \times 10 \times 10 = 10,000$. All numbers can be written in this notation, as is shown below.

$$1 = 10^0 = \text{one}$$
$$10 = 10^1 = \text{ten}$$
$$100 = 10^2 = \text{one hundred}$$
$$1000 = 10^3 = \text{one thousand}$$
$$10,000 = 10^4 = \text{ten thousand}$$
$$100,000 = 10^5 = \text{one-hundred thousand}$$
$$1,000,000 = 10^6 = \text{one million}$$
$$1,000,000,000 = 10^9 = \text{one billion}$$
$$1,000,000,000,000 = 10^{12} = \text{one trillion}$$
$$1,000,000,000,000,000 = 10^{15} = \text{one quadrillion}$$

To express the number 1500 we write

$$1500 = 1.5 \times 10^3.$$

Clearly this is correct since

$$1.5 \times 10^3 = 1.5 \times 10 \times 10 \times 10 = 1500.$$

Power of ten notation allows very quick multiplication. To multiply 1000 by 100,000 we write

$$(1000)(100,000) = (10^3)(10^5) = 10^8$$

since in multiplication the exponents of 10 (3 and 5) are added. To verify this we can write

$$(10^3)(10^5) = (10 \times 10 \times 10)(10 \times 10 \times 10 \times 10 \times 10)$$
$$= 100,000,000 = 10^8.$$

To multiply 8000 by 140,000 we write

$$(8000)(140,000) = (8 \times 10^3)(1.4 \times 10^5) = (8)(1.4)(10^3)(10^5)$$
$$= 11.2 \times 10^8 = 1.12 \times 10^9.$$

We can rearrange the order of appearance of the numbers in the preceding operation because multiplication is commutative. That is,

$$8 \times 3 \times 7 = 3 \times 7 \times 8 = 7 \times 3 \times 8$$

and so on. Note that if we wish to add 8000 and 140,000, it is usually simpler not to use power of ten notation:

$$8000 + 140,000 = 148,000.$$

To divide 10,000 into 200,000 we write

$$\frac{200,000}{10,000} = \frac{2 \times 10^5}{10^4} = 2 \times 10 = 20.$$

Similarly, to divide 140,000 by 8000,

$$\frac{140,000}{8000} = \frac{1.4 \times 10^5}{8 \times 10^3} = \frac{1.4 \times 10^2}{8} = \frac{140}{8} = 17.5.$$

Notice that in division, the powers of 10 are subtracted:

$$\frac{10^8}{10^3} = 10^{(8-3)} = 10^5$$

just as in multiplication the powers of 10 are added.

Numbers less than one can also be expressed, as shown in the following table. However, we shall not make much use of this in the text.

$$1 = 10^0 = \text{one}$$
$$0.1 = 10^{-1} = \text{one tenth}$$
$$0.01 = 10^{-2} = \text{one hundredth}$$
$$0.001 = 10^{-3} = \text{one thousandth}$$
$$0.000001 = 10^{-6} = \text{one millionth}$$

Negative exponents are manipulated in the same way as positive exponents. To multiply 0.001 by 0.01 we write

$$(0.001)(0.01) = (10^{-3})(10^{-2}) = 10^{-5}.$$

To multiply 0.00015 by 600 we write

$$(0.00015)(600) = (1.5 \times 10^{-4})(6 \times 10^2) = (1.5)(6)(10^{-4})(10^2)$$
$$= 9 \times 10^{-2} = 0.09.$$

**Appendix B**

Although we shall use only the British system of units, we shall often have to convert from one unit to another within that system. Such conversion is straightforward, assuming both units refer to the same physical dimension. That is, we can convert from feet to inches but not from feet to pounds. To convert between two units it is only necessary to know the relation between the units. For example, assume we wish to convert 30 inches (in.) to feet (ft). We know that

$$12 \text{ in.} = 1 \text{ ft.}$$

If we divide both sides of this equation by 12 inches, we get

$$\frac{12 \text{ in.}}{12 \text{ in.}} = \frac{1 \text{ ft}}{12 \text{ in.}}$$

$$1 = \frac{1 \text{ ft}}{12 \text{ in.}}$$

Since we can multiply any number by 1 without changing its value, we can proceed with the conversion:

$$30 \text{ in.} = (30 \text{ in.})(1) = (30 \text{ in.})\left(\frac{1 \text{ ft}}{12 \text{ in.}}\right) = 2.5 \text{ ft.}$$

The conversion factor of (1 ft/12 in.) is equal to one and can therefore be multiplied times the quantity we wish to convert. We could have multiplied by (12 in./1 ft), which is also equal to one. But we want to convert from inches to feet, which requires that the inch unit be in the denominator. If we were converting from feet to inches, then (12 in./1 ft) would be the proper conversion factor.

To find the number of seconds in a day we write the following steps.

(1)     $1 \text{ day} = 24 \text{ hr}$

$1 = (24 \text{ hr/day})$

$1 \text{ day} = (1 \text{ day})(1) = (1 \text{ day})\left(\frac{24 \text{ hr}}{\text{day}}\right) = 24 \text{ hr}$

(2)     $1 \text{ hr} = 60 \text{ min}$

$1 = (60 \text{ min/hr})$

$24 \text{ hr} = (24 \text{ hr})(1) = (24 \text{ hr})(60 \text{ min/hr}) = 1440 \text{ min}$

(3)     $1 \text{ min} = 60 \text{ sec}$

$1 = (60 \text{ sec/min})$

$1440 \text{ min} = (1440 \text{ min})(1) = (1440 \text{ min})(60 \text{ sec/min}) = 86{,}400 \text{ sec}$

This conversion is unduly drawn out. Most of us would almost immediately multiply $(24 \times 60 \times 60)$. But the step-by-step approach shown above is useful in complicated situations where we are converting between units of area (for example, square feet, square miles, acre) or speed (for example, miles/hour, feet/second).

There are two ways to convert 72 square inches to square feet. If you happen to know that

$$144 \text{ in.}^2 = 1 \text{ ft}^2$$

then

$$1 = \frac{1 \text{ ft}^2}{144 \text{ in.}^2}$$

$$72 \text{ in.}^2 = (72 \text{ in.}^2)(1) = (72 \text{ in.}^2)(1 \text{ ft}^2/144 \text{ in.}^2) = \tfrac{1}{2} \text{ ft}^2.$$

If you do not know the relation between square inches and square feet, it turns into a two-step problem. Assume you do know that

$$12 \text{ in.} = 1 \text{ ft}$$
$$1 = (1 \text{ ft}/12 \text{ in.})$$

We apply the (1 ft/12 in.) conversion factor twice.

$$72 \text{ in.}^2 = (72 \text{ in.}^2)(1) = (72 \text{ in.}^2)(1 \text{ ft}/12 \text{ in.}) = 6 \text{ in.-ft}$$
$$(6 \text{ in.-ft})(1) = (6 \text{ in.-ft})(1 \text{ ft}/12 \text{ in.}) = \tfrac{1}{2} \text{ ft}^2$$

Converting 60 miles/hour to feet/second is a little more complicated.

(1) $$60 \text{ min} = 1 \text{ hr}$$
$$1 = (1 \text{ hr}/60 \text{ min})$$
$$(60 \text{ mi/hr})(1) = (60 \text{ mi/hr})(1 \text{ hr}/60 \text{ min}) = 1 \text{ mi/min}$$

(2) $$60 \text{ sec} = 1 \text{ min}$$
$$1 = (1 \text{ min}/60 \text{ sec})$$
$$(1 \text{ mi/min})(1) = (1 \text{ mi/min})(1 \text{ min}/60 \text{ sec}) = \tfrac{1}{60} \text{ mi/sec}$$

(3) $$1 \text{ mi} = 5280 \text{ ft}$$
$$1 = 5280 \text{ ft/mi}$$
$$(\tfrac{1}{60} \text{ mi/sec})(1) = (\tfrac{1}{60} \text{ mi/sec})(5280 \text{ ft/mi}) = 88 \text{ ft/sec}$$

Again the conversion could have been done much more quickly, but it is useful to at least once see every step written.

# Appendix C

### Length

1 mile = 1.6 kilometers = 5280 feet $\approx 5.3 \times 10^3$ feet
1 meter = 39.37 inches $\approx$ 40 inches

### Area

1 square mile = 640 acres = 27,878,400 square feet $\approx 2.8 \times 10^7$ square feet
1 acre = 43,560 square feet $\approx 4.4 \times 10^4$ square feet
1 square foot = 144 square inches
1 square meter = 10.76 square feet $\approx$ 10.8 square feet

### Volume

1 acre-foot = 43,560 cubic feet $\approx 4.4 \times 10^4$ cubic feet
1 acre-foot = 325,900 gallons $\approx 3.3 \times 10^5$ gallons
1 cubic foot = 7.48 gallons $\approx$ 7.5 gallons

### Density of Water

62.45 pounds/cubic foot $\approx$ 62.5 pounds/cubic foot

### Speed

1 mile/hour = 1.467 feet/second $\approx$ 1.5 feet/second
1 mile/hour = 1.609 kilometers/hour $\approx$ 1.6 kilometers/hour
1 foot/second = 0.6818 miles/hour $\approx$ 0.7 miles/hour

### Time

1 year = 365 days = 8760 hours $\approx 8.8 \times 10^3$ hours
1 year = 31,536,000 seconds $\approx 3.2 \times 10^7$ seconds
1 day = 24 hours = 86,400 seconds $\approx 8.6 \times 10^4$ seconds
1 hour = 3600 seconds

### Energy

1 BTU = 777.9 foot-pounds $\approx$ 778 foot-pounds
1 BTU = $6.585 \times 10^{21}$ electron volts $\approx 6.6 \times 10^{21}$ electron volts
1 kilowatt-hour = 3413 BTU $\approx$ 3400 BTU
1 kilowatt-hour = 2,655,000 foot-pounds $\approx 2.7 \times 10^6$ foot-pounds
1 foot-pound = $8.464 \times 10^{18}$ electron volts $\approx 8.5 \times 10^{18}$ electron volts
1 kilocalorie = 3.968 BTU $\approx$ 4 BTU

### Power

1 horsepower = 550 foot-pounds/second
1 kilowatt = 737 foot-pounds/second = 1.341 horsepower $\approx$ 1.3 horsepower
1 watt = 0.737 foot-pounds/second

## Chapter 2

**Selected Answers**

4. Water use drops at night, increasing water pressure. Those few faucets which are opened will therefore flow at a greater rate.

5. An earthquake might break the water mains, cutting off the flow to the hydrants.

6. As low as possible, since a reservoir can only collect runoff from the land above it.

8. a. It is another example of the fact that our society and its support systems evolve together. None could stand without the others. b. Water and electricity cannot be hoarded, while meat, canned goods, and fuel can be. So while conservation is likely to occur during water and electric power shortages, scarcity of other items is likely to achieve the reverse effect.

9. If a three-lane highway has a two-lane bottleneck in it at some point, its traffic-carrying capacity is that of a two-lane highway. The narrowest part of the road determines its capacity. The same situation holds for an aqueduct. Water in the wide part of the aqueduct will move more slowly towards the constriction. Its speed will increase to the 5-feet-per-second maximum in the constriction and then drop below 5 feet/second past the constriction.

10. The deep reservoir will use less land. In addition, since evaporation is proportional to surface area, the deep water will lose less water to evaporation.

13. A nonpsychological reason is provided by economics. Modern plumbing is expensive, which discourages installation of two toilets in the same room. The darkness and isolation of the typical outdoor privy provides a reason why users desired company more than privacy. The fact that most of us consider such a practice a bit bizarre indicates the extent to which technological changes can influence social behavior.

15. Lakes receive most of their water from runoff draining into them from the land above, not from direct rainfall.

16. One can only speculate, but clearly we must spend time earning money so that we can afford the systems which provide us with running water, gas, electricity, and so on. Some argue that lack of exercise resulting from labor-saving devices causes health problems, which are yet another cost.

17. The depth of water accumulated in pan a would be equal to the rainfall. All could be used, however, if they were calibrated. Pan c, once calibrated, would be most useful in a light rainfall since it would collect a greater depth of water than the actual rainfall.

18. The water would accumulate to a depth of 16.9 inches.

19. The mountain snow fields can be viewed as reservoirs, storing the water in a solid form on the land. Whether the snow fields reduce the need for storage reservoirs depends on when the snow melts and on the pattern of water use. If the mountains are high enough so that the snow fields persist into the heavy water-using periods of the summer, then they will reduce the need for storage reservoirs. But if the snow melts in the early spring before heavy water use begins, there will be little effect on reservoir needs.

20. From 1950 to 1970, rural domestic water use decreased about 6%, indicating a declining rural population. At the same time, irrigation water use increased by 20%, indicating that additional farmland was put under cultivation, or existing land more intensively cultivated.

## Chapter 3

1. a. 4700 people/square mile; 7.3 people/acre   b. 50 million cubic feet; by a factor of 6.2
2. a. 31 feet   b. It would gain 700 million gallons yearly.
4. No. They will be short by 8000 cubic feet/acre/year.
7. 10.6 feet   8. 7.6 feet   9. a. $\frac{1}{2}$ inch/hour   b. $\frac{1}{8}$ inch/hour
10. 25 feet wide   11. a. 8000 gallons/person/day   b. 1 billion people
12. a. 8 percent   b. 64 percent
13. a. 6.2 gallons/person/day, which is sufficient for cooking and drinking.
15. 130 square miles
16. a. 200 billion gallons   b. 1.7 feet   d. 215 square feet
17. a. 85 million people   b. 100 feet   18. 7.8 years
19. 590 billion gallons   20. 5 percent   21. 8800 freight cars/day
22. $2.6 million/day; $960 million/year   25. 4 feet
28. 0.05 percent; the year 3536

## Chapter 4

5. a. 5600 deaths   b. 9000 deaths; $480 million
6. a. 4000-1   b. 4000-1   c. 260-1
7. a. 9 billion vehicle-miles   b. 3900 miles
9. a. $1.90   b. $0.13
13. In the 10th year, annual savings would equal annual costs. In the 11th year and thereafter, savings would exceed costs by $5 million.
14. a. rear impact   b. roll over   15. ejection
16. Some cars occasionally carry seven or more passengers.
17. a. population per age-group

## Chapter 5

1. a. increase   b. positive   2. 2.9 feet
4. They will have a smaller crush constant and will therefore be more crushed.
5. b. 5800 feet   6. a. 250 feet/second   b. 3125 feet
7. a. 50 feet/second   b. 240 feet   8. a. 140 slugs   b. 560 pounds
9. a. 1 foot   b. 160 feet/second$^2$   c. 640 pounds
10. a. 540 feet/second$^2$   b. 2700 pounds
11. a. 160 pounds/square foot   b. 480 pounds/square foot
12. a. 2200 pounds   b. 31 pounds/square inch
13. a. 670 feet/second$^2$   b. 3350 pounds
14. 121 feet, or a 12-story building   15. 0.036 seconds
16. The seat belt would exert a greater pressure.

## Chapter 7

3. 900,000 trips in 1953; 1,700,000 trips in 1965
4. $2040   10. $0.006/gallon by truck; $0.001 by pipeline
12. four standard car lengths, or 80 feet   14. 1.5 seconds   15. 960 feet

16. a. 109 feet     b. 32 feet
    c. They will collide. When struck, the lead car will be going 8 feet/second and will be 192 feet from the spot where its brakes were first applied. The second car will be going 48 feet/second.
21. 19,440 people/hour     22. 1.5 passageways, or 18 feet
23. e. 15,940 vehicles/hour assuming a front-bumper-to-front-bumper spacing of 20 feet
24. b. eight     26. a. 10,006 feet   b. 7420 feet
27. a. 108 feet/second (74 miles/hour)   b. four seconds
28. a. 210 miles   b. 25 miles   c. about 12 miles
29. 5.8 billion gallons     30. a. 5.3%   b. 1.3%
31. a. no     32. 16 feet

## Chapter 8

4. 8 people     5. 500 kilocalories     6. $9.4 \times 10^5$ foot-pounds
7. 10°F     8. 64°F
9. a. 32 kilowatt-hours   b. 27 pounds
11. 27 kilowatts, 37 horsepower     12. 22 feet/second     14. 45,000 kilowatts
15. 470 pounds/second (the heat rate is 8500 BTU/kilowatt-hour)
16. 22,000 pounds/second
17. a. 0.7 kilowatt-hours   b. 68 cubic feet
18. a. $1.4 \times 10^{12}$ kilowatt-hours   b. $150 \times 10^6$ kilowatts
20. a. $4.7 \times 10^4$ pounds/second; $5.5 \times 10^3$ gallons/second; $1.7 \times 10^8$ pounds/hour; $2 \times 10^7$ gallons/hour   b. $9.4 \times 10^6$ feet/pound/second; $3.4 \times 10^{10}$ feet/foot-pound/hour
21. a. 25,000 pounds/second   b. 670 pounds/second

## Chapter 9

8. a. 630 million tons   b. 126 square miles
9. a. 15 million barrels per day   b. 10 pipelines
10. industry: $27.8 \times 10^{15}$ BTU; commercial/residential: $24.7 \times 10^{15}$ BTU
11. 1100 pounds per year     12. about ten times as much to run it as to build it
14. 120 ton-miles/gallon
19. a. continuous burning: $240,000; intermittent: $72,000
    b. continuous burning: $50,000; intermittent: $21,000 (pro-rated)
20. 66 BTU/hour/square foot     21. 13 million BTU     22. 6.3 million BTU

## Chapter 10

1. $3.8 \times 10^{15}$ miles     2. 1200 trillion cubic feet
3. a. 114 cars   b. 13.4 million cars   c. 4.1 miles less per day
   d. by 2.3 miles/gallon to 14.3 miles/gallon
4. a. 5.9 cubic feet/barrel   c. 4.8 days
5. 16 days     6. 0.04 percent     7. a. $5.9 \times 10^5$ cubic feet, or $10^5$ barrels
8. a. $1.1 \times 10^6$ barrels/day   b. 18 feet/second
9. 80 percent     10. 270 ton-miles/gallon

11. $4.6 \times 10^6$ BTU per ton of oil shale and $20 \times 10^6$ BTU per ton of coal
12. oil tanker: $11 \times 10^{12}$ BTU; liquefied-natural-gas tanker: $1.8 \times 10^{12}$ BTU
13. 360 pounds/person/year, or almost 1 pound/person/day, in 1976, assuming a population of 210 million
14. 15,000 pounds of ash per hour; 31,000 pounds of sulfur dioxide per hour
15. a. $6.5 \times 10^6$ tons/year   b. 0.72 square miles/year; 22 square miles over 30 years

## Chapter 11

2. small quantities of fuel; no need for combustion oxygen
7. The nuclear plant will dump about twice as much waste heat in the cooling water.
8. a. $1.6 \times 10^{25}$ atoms; 0.7 pounds   b. $3.3 \times 10^{17}$ atoms; $2.9 \times 10^{-7}$ pounds
9. coal plant: $1.9 \times 10^{11}$ pounds; nuclear plant: 63,000 pounds of U-235
10. $4.6 \times 10^{25}$ atoms, or 2.7 pounds of oxygen
11. 0.156 pounds      13. 11,700 BTU; less
14. $3.3 \times 10^{10}$ BTU/pound of deuterium; almost the same as U-235
15. The $4.6 \times 10^{21}$ atoms of deuterium would yield $1.1 \times 10^6$ BTU.

## Chapter 12

5. b. 1100 square miles      6. 2300 square feet      7. 4200 square feet
8. a. no   b. i. hydrogen ii. both the same iii. hydrogen
12. Winter angle is 29.5°. Summer angle is 76.5°.
14. a. schematic a   b. Schematic b will require 17 percent more solar collector area.
15. a. $1.6 \times 10^9$ kilowatt-hours   b. yes
16. 12,000 kilowatts      17. a. 30,000 pounds   b. 10,000 pounds
18. a. 100 square feet   c. 22 gallons/hour      21. 12 hours and 25 minutes
22. a. $5 \times 10^{-4}$ inches   b. $5 \times 10^{-7}$ inches
23. $3.6 \times 10^6$ centuries      24. $2.7 \times 10^6$ kilowatts

# Index